LIGHT IN THE DARK ROOM

LIGHT IN THE DARK ROOM
Photography and Loss

Jay Prosser

University of Minnesota Press – Minneapolis – London

An earlier form of chapter 5 appeared as "A Palinode on Photography and the Transsexual Real," *a/b: Autobiography Studies* 14 (1999): 71–92.

Poetry by Gordon Parks, from *Moments without Proper Names*, is reprinted with permission.

Excerpts of unpublished writings and letters by Elizabeth Bishop are reproduced with permission of Special Collections at Vassar College Libraries and the Houghton Library at Harvard University.

Published by the University of Minnesota Press
111 Third Avenue South, Suite 290
Minneapolis, MN 55401-2520
http://www.upress.umn.edu

Library of Congress Cataloging-in-Publication Data

Prosser, Jay.
    Light in the dark room : photography and loss / Jay Prosser.
        p.   cm.
    Includes bibliographical references and index.
    ISBN 0-8166-4483-7 (hc : alk. paper) — ISBN 0-8166-4484-5 (pb : alk. paper)
    1. Photography—Philosophy.   2. Loss (Psychology).   I. Title.
    TR183.P76 2004
    770'.1—dc22
                                                                    2004015600

Printed in the United States of America on acid-free paper

The University of Minnesota is an equal-opportunity educator and employer.

12 11 10 09 08 07 06 05   10 9 8 7 6 5 4 3 2 1

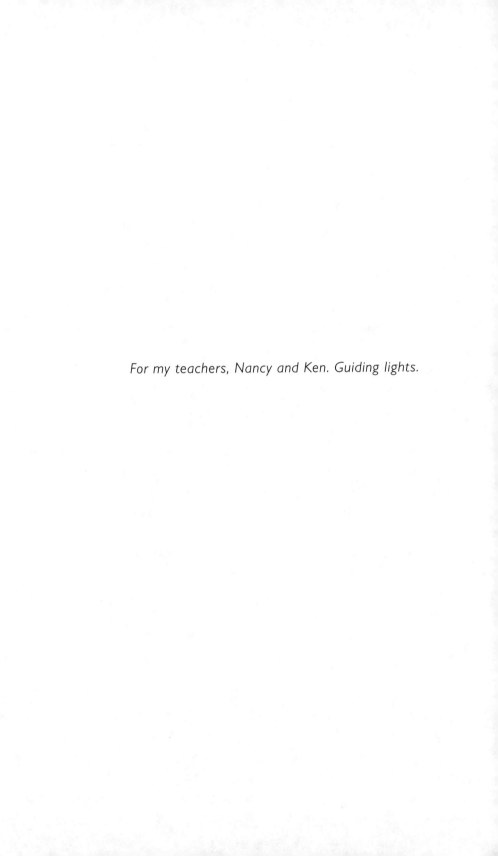

For my teachers, Nancy and Ken. Guiding lights.

It is as if someone were to point out the way
to one who had got lost,
or to bring an oil-lamp into a dark place,
so that those with eyes could see what was there.

—*The Long Discourses of the Buddha*

CONTENTS

ACKNOWLEDGMENTS

I THANK THE UNIVERSITIES IN THE UNITED KINGDOM that have allowed me a forum for this work. My own has been considerate in allocating leave and support. Mick Gidley here has been caring and encouraging throughout. Vassar College Special Collections, especially Dean Rogers, smoothed my research on Elizabeth Bishop. And I thank the authors, artists, and collections for granting permission to reproduce their work here.

I'm particularly indebted to my contacts in Brazil: To SENAPULLI, the Brazilian National Seminar of Professors in English, for inviting me there in the first place and for taking me back. To the Universidade Federal de Santa Catarina for my deep week with colleagues and students. And to my friends Maria Lúcia Milléo Martins, Gláucia Renate Gonçalves, and Dilvo Ristoff for the generosity of their work, their friendship, and for helping me round Brazil.

The British Academy funded me in my initial research trip on Brazil, and the Arts and Humanities Research Board helped me complete. To Laura Marcus and Jane Gallop, the readers for that grant, and to the readers for this manuscript, I am grateful for their open, moving response and their wisdom. The enthusiasm, commitment, and kind like-mindedness of Andrea Kleinhuber, my editor at the University of Minnesota Press, have been a buoy. Margaretta Jolly read much of this writing with patience and untrammeled generosity. My family, especially my mother, held me in their love and belief.

But the dedication of this book is for Nancy K. Miller and Ken Bails, because their conversation really does have the power to turn me about.

LIGHT IN THE DARK ROOM

W̲E TREAT PHOTOGRAPHS as if they had a kind of presence. Photography is the commonest way for us to record our own and our loved ones' lives. And we arrange photographs in our rooms of our beloved, often because they cannot be with us there—often (and eventually) because they are dead. Photography is the medium in which we unconsciously encounter the dead. Yet herein lies photography's hidden truth. Photographs are not signs of presence but evidence of absence. Or rather the presence of a photograph indicates its subject's absence. Photographs contain a realization of loss. This book on photography enters into that loss.

Photographs contain a realization of loss in the fundamental sense that every photograph represents a past real moment that actually happened but is no longer. It is a myth that photographs bring back memories. Photographs show not the presence of the past but the pastness of the present. They show the irreversible passing of time. Our most lyrical writers on photography have understood the tense of photography. Walter Benjamin: in "the cult of remembrance of loved ones, absent or dead," "the aura emanates from early photography in the fleeting expression of a human face."[1] Susan Sontag: "Photography is a message from time past," "a trace, something directly stenciled off the real, like a footprint or a death mask."[2] Roland Barthes: "what I see . . . has been here, and yet immediately separated; it has been absolutely, irrefutably present, and yet already deferred."[3] For all, photography is a melancholic object. Not an aide-mémoire, a form

1

for preserving memory, it is a memento mori. Photography is not only a reminder of our loved ones' death, it tells our impending own. It is evidence of the fact of death itself. Photography's commentators have been less concerned to convey the significance of the realization of loss in photography. There are two senses to photography's realization. Photography makes real the loss. But then it makes possible the apprehension of this loss. This is my recovery. As offering insight into the inexorable loss that *is* life, photography captures a reality that we would otherwise not see, that we would choose *not* to see. It holds out the promise of a kind of enlightenment. It is this that makes me enter the dark room of photography.

The earliest responses to photography understood this mystical quality. Some of the first photographs were shown in magic shows; its innovation was thought to make visible the invisible.[4] To some eyes so apparently miraculous was the new medium, so unprecedented its realism, that something of the divine seemed to inhabit photography. Only God had previously had, only God *should* have, that kind of reproductive power. Photography's emergence was coincident with a decline in religious belief. Along with the development of other forms of technological reproduction, the invention of photography was both enabled by, and contributed to, the death of God. But perhaps something of the faith in the divine as ultimate reality and elucidating force transferred from God to photography. Certainly the first names for photography suggest the marveling in a form of creation almost beyond human capacity, that required limited human intervention: *heliographs*, or "sun-drawings." It was as if light alone produced the image. The name eventually chosen, *photography*, means "light-writing."[5]

As a modern technological form photography emerged in the middle of the nineteenth century when the discovery of a certain combination of chemicals made possible the fixing of images first on metal, then on glass, and finally in the form in which it has been predominantly practiced, on celluloid film printable on paper. But photography has a much longer history prior to its chemical invention. The Han Dynasty Chinese (from 200 BCE), who were possibly the first to use spectacles and lenses, were among the most advanced in optical technology in the world.[6] The Chinese Lantern contains in embryo the Magic Lantern. The thin paper shade of the Chinese lamp serves to catch in a play of light and shadow the movements and objects around it, what would later be more firmly outlined and the shades distinguished by the slide projector, or Magic Lantern. The effects of light in a dark room become evident in any country that is hot enough one needs to shut out the light to keep out the sun. Plato might have dismissed the shadows on the wall of his cave. But his most famous student,

Aristotle, succumbed to the magic that happens when you sit inside a darkened room and allow a bright light to bring in a piece of the world outside. Aristotle, in effect, knew all about the camera obscura. The camera obscura, literally a "dark room," was the earliest form of a camera. It consisted of a darkened space in which a hole or window cut into one wall projected onto the opposite inside wall the scene outside the room. Initially because light reflects objects, the scene appeared in the image in inverted form. Later a mirror was added to the "lens" of the window and the dark room; and this combination, lens, mirror, and dark room, remains the basis of every photographic mechanism today. The "room" of the camera may have shrunk, the camera become progressively more box-like and eventually handheld. But the camera retains, in its name, a reference to that magical space one originally occupied: the dark room where one went to receive an illuminated version of reality.

Photography's powers of realization have been more determining of the history of representation than we think. For centuries artists used the camera obscura as an aid to achieving greater realism in their drawings and paintings. In the nineteenth century the camera obscura was propagated into the camera lucida, which introduced a prism into the design, thereby refracting the reflected light onto a drawing surface and allowing for even greater realism. The artist David Hockney has presented evidence that suggests camera obscuras were in use at least since the Renaissance and that the camera may even have spurred the massive advances toward the attainment of realism and accurate perspective that *was* the Renaissance.[7] So dominant became the kind of naturalism that could only have been achieved by the lens-mirror combination that soon all painting aspired to photographic reproductive realism. Reproductive realism remained the aspiration of most painting until the second half of the nineteenth century. At this point painting, in the form of modern art, turned back to an impressionistic rendering of the world, now deliberately naïve and mediated. Photography could again have been pivotal. For if painting had so long aspired to *be* photography, how was it going to survive the advent of a mere machine that far exceeded the artist's capacity for realism? Amid prophecies of its obsolescence, painting would have to distinguish itself radically from photography. And it did. We are still dealing with the repercussions of the antirealistic turn in representation. One is that modernist and postmodernist photography is most typified by photographs that turn against, or complicate, photographic realism. Modernist and postmodernist photography is photography that aspires now to the condition of painting. Like digital photography and the manufacture of photographic images on computers that looks set to supersede film/paper as the means of photo-graphic development, artistic modernist and postmodernist photography has changed forever the notion of photographic realism.

The changes in photography have tallied with changes in our models of realism in representation generally. We have traveled from a notion of reality as reproducible (the naïve or credulous realism ushered in by the Renaissance); to a notion of reality as hidden or subjective (the first half of the antirealistic turn in modernism); to a notion of reality as impossible or invented, or more radically as an effect of representation (the second half of antirealism in postmodernism). We are confronted now with a notion of reality as lost, with an apprehension of reality as consisting in that which can only be lost. The history of representation in modernity can be told through the story of how reality became lost. The model of representation we now face is one that began to be sketched at the turn of the twentieth century, when in part the shock of modernity and its technologies de-manded a new description of relations between word and thing, world and image. The terms for the model emerged from structuralist linguistics, but they soon spread to describe every operation of representation in the human sciences, including those in the visual arts. The model now rendered the re-lation between representation and reality as between *sign* and *referent*. The *sign* was further split into two parts, *signifier* and *signified*, the marks on the page and the meaning they connote respectively. And in poststructuralism and postmodernism there was a growing sense of a gap between signifier and signified, resulting in questions about whether representation can ever close on meaning, about how exactly representation touches reality. An in-creasing concern with the terms of signification meant a demotion in status of the referent. The referent was sidelined, deferred. The referent, which carried the weight of vestigial reality, went almost out of the picture.

This "almost" is important though. It is within modernity's creeping sense of reality as lost, leading to late postmodernity's yearning for a lost reality, that I read photography in this book. Photography has poignancy now as a realization of reality as lost. The photographic instant that actually happened but is now over coincides in elegiac timing with our apprehension of reality. In his history of the representation of reality in modernity, the art historian and theorist Hal Foster has introduced a term for describing our contemporary relation to reality, "traumatic realism." With the crisis in representation that was modernity, the "symbolic order in crisis," reality in the form of the referent split off from the sign and can now only return—as the repressed can only return in trauma—as the real.[8] Traumatic real-ism can also be rendered Lacanian realism. I want to go back to Foster's source to emphasize the key role photography plays in the emergence of an apprehension of reality as lost. Lacan's *real* is particularly useful for understanding how this model of reality is historically apposite. Lacan took up *real* as a noun and made it a fundamental psychoanalytic category in 1953[9]—precisely the moment when structuralism and the terms of signification began to infuse academic disciplines and therefore theories of representation. The real emerged in Lacan when we began to lose the referent in theory. This was also the moment that crystallized, in different ways, the work of the authors whose photographs I examine in this book. They come from different sides of the representational divide. A semiotician and structuralist critic who spent his career debunking reality and analyzing signs writes in his relation to photographs about the worst loss from his life. Following him a structuralist anthropologist who uncovered in his subjects the signs of culture looks back at his old photographs and finds in them a reality he couldn't represent in his anthropological writing. A documentary photographer, who worked to photograph his culture as thoroughly as an anthropologist, recovers in his photographs a loss from his own life he couldn't document. And a poet who prized above all the factuality of her poetry encounters, in the process of collecting photographs, the inevitable detractions of realism. From different points along the continuum of representation the four meet in a realization that photography can reveal a real that previously escaped them and that remains, in echo of the mystical conception of photography, elusive of their lived reality.

In Lacan the real is not reality. It is that which escapes reality. The real only becomes apparent to us in "the return, the coming-back" of trauma.[10] Yet in the return of the real we realize we missed reality in the first place and are doomed to remain remiss of it. We meet the real in "an essential encounter—an appointment to which we are always called with a real that eludes us" (53). The real returns as if by chance or accident, what Lacan calls, using the Aristotelian term, *tyche;* but because it returns as a result of trauma there is something inexorable in the return of the real. "What is repeated in fact is always something that occurs—the expression tells us quite a lot about its relation to the *tuché—as if by chance*" (54). Lacan's realism is illustrated through vision, or more accurately the gaze, since he makes a distinction between gaze and vision where gaze returns the real overlooked by the more credulous and conscious vision of reality ("I see" as equivalent to "I know"). The gaze founders this post-Renaissance model with the real. Modernist poet Paul Valéry's statement for self-consciousness, "*I saw myself seeing myself*" (80), captures the traumatic doubling of the gaze, when our vision seems to turn back on ourselves, reflected and refracted, and we catch ourselves unawares. "What isolates this apprehension of thought by itself is a sort of doubt, which has been called methodological doubt" (80), and in this moment self-realization is uncovered as "illusion" (83). Lacan's anecdotal sardine can has the same effect of derealization. The sardine can, which floats on the sea, refracts back his sight of it as a gaze at him. Glinting in the lens of the sun and the mirror of the water, it seems to be looking right at him, giving him the feeling of being, in the old sense, unreal, out of the picture.

Photography with its reflective and refractive dynamics belongs in the realm of the gaze. To encounter the real in Lacan is "tirer" (67), which means "to draw" as in to draw lots (chance) and to draw curtains (revelation), but also "to shoot" as in to shoot a photograph. "I am *photo-graphed*" (106), Lacan writes, of this moment when the gaze of the sardine can hits him. When we are photographed, especially when we see ourselves in a

Hans Holbein the Younger, *Jean de Dinteville and Georges de Selve ("The Ambassadors")* (1533). Copyright National Gallery, London. Reproduced with permission.

photograph, we are at our most real. We are most ourselves and yet simultaneously we see our annihilation as subjects. The conundrum is one of time inextricable from representation. If that is me in the photograph, what is the status of my existence *here and now*? In its re-presentation of a moment that is over, the photograph foretells our own future nonexistence. This is why Lacan writes "photo-graphed" in its "fragmented form" as he often says he does (106), in order to indicate the splitting between reality and representation, between the light and the writing. Lacan's visualist explanations of the real come best in the death's-head in Holbein's *The Ambassadors*. The Renaissance work is not only as precise as a photograph, in its acute realism and in the fall of light and shadow on the optical instruments (sundials, astronomical equipment, celestial and terrestrial globes showing the new Americas—possibly a telescope) which give us the exact time and place of the scene. The painting, whose science is its mystery, is also thought one of the most likely to have used a camera obscura to have done so, or that the artist worked inside the room/camera, with a sheet of glass, a single candle, and the necessary darkness.[11] The clue may be the distorted skull at the bottom of the painting. The skull can be seen in perspective only with the help of a lens to correct the distortion and a mirror to project the image anew. With the naked eye the skull can be recognized only if we approach the picture from such an angle that we can no longer see Holbein's human subjects or the technology for mastering reality behind them. Lacan writes that the most real thing in the picture is the distorted skull, which is "an anamorphic ghost," since "Holbein makes visible for us something that is simply the subject as annihilated—annihilated that is, strictly speaking, the imaged embodiment of the *minus-phi (gk) of castration*" (89). He "reflects our own nothingness, in the figure of the death's head" (92). Holbein's skull is the most famous example of anamorphosis in art, the technique in which a distorted image can be changed back to reveal its correct (realistic) projection. Photography too, with its mirrors and lenses, works according to anamorphic optics, to reveal the excessively real, the reality that escapes straight-on representation. Such anamorphic optics, Lacan writes, "allow vision to escape. They are within the grasp of the blind" (92); "How we try to apprehend that which seems to elude us" (93).

Photography's realizations in an age that has repressed the referent can only be unconscious. "The camera introduces us to unconscious optics as does psychoanalysis to unconscious impulses," wrote Benjamin, himself fleeing modernity and with concern at its technological reproductions.[12] Jacqueline Rose remarks that references to the camera and optics in psychoanalysis outnumber those to psychoanalysis in visual theory.[13] Freud himself compared the unconscious to a camera, at the beginnings of psychoanalysis and not far along in the history of photography. In *The Interpretation of Dreams* Freud writes: "we should picture the instrument which carries our mental functioning as resembling a compound microscope or photographic apparatus," that is as enlarging and imprinting.[14] And Freud later described trauma as a photograph. The child receives impressions like "a photographic exposure which can be developed after any interval of time and transformed into a picture."[15] In both uses the loss of the real, its inscriptive force and yet its unrealizability, is the basis for the analogy between unconscious realization and photography. What cannot be realized in reality can only be unconsciously realized later in trauma: photo-graphed. It is to Freud's concept of realization in trauma that Lacan makes reference when he elaborates his return of the real, to an episode in *The Interpretation of Dreams*. A man falls asleep next to a room in which his dead child's body is surrounded by candles and is being kept watch over by an old man—inadequately, for he has fallen asleep. The bereaved father dreams his child comes to his bedside and *"whispered to him reproachfully: Father, don't you see I'm burning?"*[16] He awakens to find one of the candles has overturned, started a fire, and already burned part of his dead child's body. For Lacan what returns in the dream is "the missed reality that causes the death of the child," a real which, since the child is dead, is "too late now" (58). The gap between dream and reality "constitutes awakening" (57), but since one cannot recover the dead (or can one? Photography raises this question about raising the dead) it is an awakening to loss. Photography is "a firebrand" (59) in a dark room, a dream of light that is always "too early or too late" (69). In their photographs in this book my authors chase referential ghosts: dead loved mothers; lovers who resurrect dead mothers; the subjects who've made their careers; the subjects left out of their careers; and ultimately a self they hadn't realized.

For photographs may be the closest we get to another's autobiography. The photographic collections we leave when we die are approximations of the life story that remains typically unwritten. And because in our life we view them through our eye and our I, photographs that have significance for us are often autobiographical, although often they are those in which this is not conscious to us. Photography's approximation of autobiography remains true even with the appearance of home movies and video cameras. The predominance of photography as a form for recording our lives may be due not simply to its lesser expense and greater ease of use. With their frozen disjointed moments, photographs are closer to the life as it is lived. Unlike the moving image of film, snapshots don't require the joining up of instants into a narrative, and especially not the explanatory voice-over making sense of the life. In those autobiographies that are written and published, photographs are increasingly used as shutes into something missing, pointers to a loss that can't be recovered in the text. In Hélène Cixous's autobiographical reflections, indicatively titled in the French *Photos de Racine* ("Rootprints"), photographs of two sets of Jewish grandparents, in pre-Weimar Germany and pre-independence Algeria, initiate the autobiography as an "album of abandonment," its author's "genealogy of graves."[17] Writing an account of his parents' marriage, Michael Ondaatje can find only one photograph of them together. Recognizing it as "the photograph I have been waiting for all my life," he publishes it as, contrary to the sense of his memoir and his memory, "the evidence I wanted that they were absolutely perfect for each other."[18] And in Gabriel Josipovici's memoir of his mother written after her death, photographs carry a referent that has been forgotten or was never actually known. "I find many of them baffling, try as I will, [to] recall," he writes as he pores over images of his mother in Egypt.[19] Even photographs that do not actually appear in autobiographies or appear only marginally as traces in the text, as in Tim Lott's attempt to make sense of his mother's suicide, only on the inside cover, exemplify photography in autobiography as loss. Lott senses in photographs of his family's life something essential out of reach of his understanding. "It is as if a sudden flashlight had been held up to illuminate my past and then switched off, leaving only an engram, a faint memory trace."[20] The engram or *graphe:* like the dream of fire that comes after the burning, the photograph seared inside autobiography elucidates not memory's presence but memory's loss, the inevitable fading of lives in our lives.

The flickering of presence and absence in the convergence of photography and autobiography, their both wavering between memory and loss, has attracted recent critics. Timothy Dow Adams pithily emphasizes the *graphe* in both photography and autobiography in order to read photographs in writing even when they are not referred to (as ghosts for example in Maxine Hong Kingston's *Woman Warrior: Memoirs of a Girlhood among Ghosts*).[21] Linda Haverty Rugg's work is more focused on the literal incidence of photography in autobiography. She finds in photography and autobiography a "referential paradox" that speaks to our confusions about reality: "A simultaneous belief in linguistic and photographic referentiality and suspicion of linguistic and photographic referentiality offer the only solution to the conundrum of the age."[22] Both critics have in common the claim that photography and autobiography are similarly representational and reality, are at once referential and signifying. But incarnating a moment that was actually there and that in all but the photograph has gone, does not photography exceed autobiography's ties to the real? Hence Lacan's choice of it as a conductor for the traumatic return of the real. Photography preserves autobiography's lost referent. Even Paul de Man, poststructuralist critic of autobiography's claims to referentiality, finds in photography an ineluctable reference that remains unconscious to him. "But are we so certain," he asks in the very sentence in which he defers the referent in autobiography, "that autobiography depends on reference, as a photograph depends on its subject?"[23] Photography embodies the vestigial reference displaced from autobiography.

Thus other recent critics who move between photography and autobiography more allusively—and who write autobiographically and with more of the snapshot moments of enlightenment of photography—are more my guiding lights in this book. Of parents and a reflecting, unreconciled child in Nancy K. Miller's *Bequest and Betrayal: Memoirs of a Parent's Death*; of incomplete and recurrent mourning in Marianne Hirsch's *Family Frames: Photography, Narrative and Postmemory*; and of families that don't reveal the silences that found them in Annette Kuhn's *Family Secrets: Acts of Memory and Imagination*—photographs are interesting in their books for embodying the intimate affects of what might otherwise escape even these perspicacious autobiography critics' conscious representation.[24] The photographs often interrupt the flow of narrative, which in all cases is a work of mourning, with traumatic realization. Such critical works are about trauma of various kinds for, true to contemporary Lacanian realism, this is how realism is now most encountered in memoirs: in real people's (and real critics') traumatic experiences.

I call this way in which photography can interrupt the narrative and return the extreme moments of autobiography *ph/autography*, which is a new description of what proves to be a not-so-new combination: all of the texts I look at here are between autobiography and photography. From an essay on photography that becomes its author's most autobiographical work, to a photographic memoir, to an autobiographical account of a photographical assignment, to an autobiographically framed album of photographs and recollections, *Light in the Dark Room* catches the lens of photography and the mirror of autobiography in interplay. My term *ph/autography*, intended to suggest how photography when we really engage it inevitably becomes autobiographical, draws on the coinage of one writer for the photographical self-portrait, the "phauto"—although as his unslashed neologism indicates, for Philippe Lejeune the currents between autobiography and photography are more free-flowing. Lejeune is in fact an autobiography critic, but he realizes something he had overlooked about autobiography, realizes loss, when he is writing about another writer writing about photography, who ultimately made his relationship to photography autobiographical—and whose ultimate relationship was an insurpassably autobiographical one with photography. Lejeune finds that he and Roland Barthes meet in discovering the referent of the actual past in the manifest presence of the visual image: "The self-portrait is the only pictorial genre that has given me the poignant feeling, which Barthes describes so well with regard to photography in *La Chambre claire (Camera Lucida)*, of having before my eyes not an image of the past, but an impression directly inscribed by it."[25]

But it is Barthes's autobiography written before *Camera Lucida*, which contained photographs and compelled the need to return and do something more autobiographical than in the autobiography in *Camera Lucida*, that prompts Lejeune to realize what he may have overlooked in writing about autobiography. In particular Barthes's autobiography prompts him to realize the loss of reference, especially in the arena of self-representation, Lejeune's home ground. Lejeune had argued that autobiography holds together as a genre because of a "referential pact" (22) between author and reader: the reader agrees to read the author, narrator, and protagonist as identical and all of these as referencing an actual person. Acknowledging that Barthes's autobiography *Roland Barthes by Roland Barthes* exerts a kind of fascination over him, Lejeune finds it "anti-*Pact* par excellence," for it "proposes a dizzying game of lucidity around all the presuppositions of autobiographical discourse—so dizzying that it ends up giving the reader the illusion that it is not doing what it is nevertheless doing. 'In the field of the subject, there is no referent'" (131–32). Barthes's autobiography is at once referential (it is his manifest autobiography) and yet declares the impossibility of reference. It propels Lejeune to realize that his referential pact had been based on a fetishized presence. But he goes on nevertheless, as Barthes does with photography, believing he finds in autobiography a direct impression of the past. He responds to Barthes: "We indeed *know* all this; we are not so dumb, but, once the precaution has been taken, we go on as if we did not know it" (132). In fact what Lejeune had cited from Barthes's autobiography turns into a statement about the nonexistence of the referent what had been Barthes's self-directed question indicating the costs of the loss of the referent. What Barthes had actually written in full was, "Do I not know that, *in the field of the subject, there is no referent?*"[26]

A statement about no reference at all would mean no autobiography—and no photography; and Barthes in *Roland Barthes by Roland Barthes,* and even more in *Camera Lucida,* clearly doesn't buy this. As J. Gratton recognizes in discussion of the misquotation that generally takes place of this of Barthes's thought, "Barthes's assertion turns out to be set in a question whose status is rhetorical: not only self-directed, but requiring no answer as such. Doubly rhetorical, in fact, in that it seems to amount to an effort of self-persuasion, as if Barthes had to remind himself of what he knew; as if somewhere along the line there were a *vouloir* at odds with this *savoir,* a resistance to the authoritative thrust of such an assertion (of assertion in general?)."[27] Barthes's desire for the referent ("vouloir") in the face of his knowledge of the loss of the referent ("savoir") is conveyed best in *Roland Barthes by Roland Barthes* in the photographs that appear in the margins of this autobiography. The photographs pick up and embody the referent of the subject Roland Barthes that is lost in the more mediated, signifying writing of *Roland Barthes by Roland Barthes.* The photographs, as Paul John Eakin has written, are "like the return of the repressed"—and thus he uses Barthes's trajectory to "reopen the file on reference in autobiography."[28] In Lejeune's reading of Barthes, and in the unfurling of Barthes's biography as a writer, photography propels realization into loss.

Lejeune's realization of the loss of the referent—his encounter with the real, then—comes in the form of what is termed a *palinode.* My access to the significance of photography is in all authors provided by a text that constitutes a palinode. In each case the turn to photography as a form for realizing loss is in truth a *re*turn to photography, and a retraction or recantation (homonym for the palinode as a "singing back or again") of a prior position on photography. These palinodes are remarkable texts in the lives of their writers. In the palinode, in which one reads oneself, one's ode or the first statement that had made one's life, writers are at their most autobiographical. Part of the work of focusing on photography in its representation in the palinode is to propose the palinode as a newly described autobiographical mode for how we might reflect on the losses and oversights inevitable in the progression of our work, as photography is a form for realizing the losses inevitable in our life. The palinodes in this book trace a retreat from models of realism that turn on either significa-tion or reference—reality as produced versus reality as reproduced—to meet in a Lacanian model of the real as lost. They do so progressively, for my chapters work, in order, through two structuralist critics who built their professions in skepticism about reality, finding reality in the code or sign; to the documentary photographer and then realistic poet who on the contrary held as their goal (and had faith in) realism. The palinodes of all are texts that cast shadows on their previous visions. They also comprise their authors' most underread, misread—or in the case of one author unpublished and what proved to be unpublishable—texts. But bringing the blindnesses in the palinode to light can be elucidating for us. The palinode is literally the ode in reverse (*palin* means "back" or "again") and it like photography works by reversal and refraction. It brings to view what one could not see before, throws light where one was previously in the dark. Lejeune's realization about what he had overlooked in autobiography is hooked graphically in his writing as he looks back on a diagram that he had designed to demonstrate the referential pact in autobiography. In his diagram there were two blacked-out squares, and in these Lejeune realizes that he had attributed to autobiography a blinkered vision he now sees belongs to himself: the blind spots were his own. "There are two 'blind' squares, corresponding to the cases 'excluded by definition.' It is undoubtedly I who was blind" (134). If he previously saw the "image of the real," now what returns, as in the Lacanian gaze reflected by those dark spaces, is "the effect of the real" (22).

As uncovering oversight—and realizing that only the oversight or first losses made possible a true insight—the palinode in its emergence and history is caught up with the dynamics of seeing and blindness, light and darkness. The origins of the form lie in the *palinoidia* that Stesichorus of Himera sings to Helen in reparation for his insults to her, which had caused him to be struck blind. After his palinode his sight is restored.[29] Stesichorus's palinode is known to us for its citation in Plato's *Phaedrus,* where it is used to preface Socrates' renunciation of a denunciation of love he had just made. Socrates enacts the revelation achieved by his reversal in a visual scene. Covered by a cloak in his ode, he removes it in his palinode. He literally recovers the light as he figuratively discovers his insight.[30] In the genealogy of the palinode the enlightenment its author attains often comes at the end of the life and contains what the life, and the works written in it, left out. In his *Retractions* Saint Augustine looks back in his old age at his massive religious oeuvre to find it lacking the spiritual light he had always sought but that he believed he had only recently approximated.[31] Augustine's palinode may in turn have influenced Chaucer, who wrote, apocryphally on his deathbed, the "retracciouns" in which he regrets the "unkonnynge" concern with "worldly vanitees" that make up the romance and satire of his *Canterbury Tales.*[32] Nietzsche wrote "Attempt at a Self-Criticism" in recoiling reconsideration of his first book, *The Birth of Tragedy,* two years before his fatal collapse into madness.[33] In palinodes the enlightenment is often coincident with trauma, our greatest insight ensuing from our greatest loss. As heir to Socratic irony and perhaps master of the palinode in modern philosophy, Kierkegaard, puts the paradox, the sympathetic reader of the palinode "can understand that the understanding is a revocation—the understanding with him as the sole reader is indeed the revocation of the book. He can understand that to write a book that does not demand to be as important for anyone is still not the same as letting it be unwritten."[34] The key to revision—and there's something godly and realistic in it—is repetition: "If God himself had not willed repetition, the world would never have come into existence. . . . Repetition is reality, and it is the seriousness of life."[35] As we might gloss Kierkegaard's life of retractions, better to have realized loss than never to have realized at all. The light only looks bright in darkness.

I begin in chapter 1 with the seminal essay on photography as loss, Roland Barthes's *Camera Lucida*. Barthes gets real on photography when he declares he is writing a palinode. "Camera lucida" is literally the light room, but Barthes's thoughts on photography actually take shape in the dark room of his incomplete mourning for his mother. The loss of his mother propels him to see the real of photography and to retreat on his previous, structuralist skepticism toward photographic realism. Looking with Barthes at the autobiographical loss of his dead mother, I also revisit the extraordinary circumstances of Barthes's death which followed so soon after hers. The double loss frozen by *Camera Lucida* proves ultimately unrepresentable, except in photography—an original loss before speech that we are born into.

Chapter 2 reads the photographic memoir of the structuralist anthropologist who provided Barthes's initial terms for thinking about photography. Like Barthes, Claude Lévi-Strauss in his career rejected a documentary approach to cultural reality, and with it photography. Photography had a foundational role in anthropology. Lévi-Strauss worked hard against this to find the signs and symbols of complex cultures in what had been denigrated as given and simple referents. But what loss is incurred in the focus on the sign? In his last published book, his autobiographical collection of his old photographs, Lévi-Strauss returns to the outset of his career in Brazil in order to realize what is changing at its end. His wonderful, overlooked photographs tie loss to advances in global technology and want us to see something now. His need, finally, to fall back on photography in order to warn of impending and massive planetary perdition is both enabled by the latest technology and returns to a more magical, and in his inverting, appreciative terms, primitive, relationship to photography.

Chapter 3 takes up the legacy of the realistic tradition of documentary photography. It was this that generated the field of visual anthropology, to which photography in anthropology now belongs. The documentary photographer Gordon Parks has worked most successfully as a participant observer to produce what amounts to a visual anthropology of African American lives. But what is exacted in return, what are the costs of a life of documentation? Who gets to represent reality, and how? Parks worked for *Life* magazine, where we see the (U.S.) nationalization of documentary realism. I tell the story of how, at *Life*, Parks's photographs redeemed a life; but I also look at the worst instance resulting from the encounter of the *tirer:* the horrible realness involved in the "taking" of life in the act of photographing. Parks in his photographs of a Brazilian boy initially thought he was bringing light, in his words, to a dark underworld. But his return a decade later to reconsider his assignment, and his second journey to the slums of the Rio de Janeiro shantytown called "Catacumba" ("tomb"), recall more than one ghost that he had sought to use his photography to dispel.

The poet Elizabeth Bishop saw Parks's assignment in *Life* magazine while she was living in Brazil. In her poetry concerned to convey the reality of places, she was persuaded to edit a book collection of photographs for *Life*'s World Library series about this country she loved and in which she had made her home. But the realism of this largely overlooked photographic edition turns out to be thwarted by political causes that entailed the suicide of Bishop's lover, the partner for whom she had settled in (and fallen in love with) Brazil. The political circumstances resulted in Bishop's deepest regret for this book. Chapter 4 recovers Bishop's original drafts and correspondence for her collection and discovers how her profound sense that she had failed to capture reality catalyzed her plans for another book about Brazil, one that would contain her own photographs and would be more autobiographical. I focus—and this marks their first encounter with criticism—on Bishop's lyrical photographs, which are as precise in their detail as her poetry and equal to if not surpassing the observant eye of her recently published paintings. I try to recover as much as possible this book Bishop said would have been about loss, all the while aware that Bishop found her losses so insuperable she did not publish the work. This may be the palinode taken to its most extreme, elusive mode.

Chapter 5 provides an instance of a palinode in the making—my own. I return to an earlier use I made of photography as referential. Contrary to the claim of my preceding book that photographs show the sex change of transsexuals, I now realize what I had left out of this manifesto about transsexual autobiography: precisely the fact that transsexual narratives can't be realized, can't be closed. My misapprehension of photography turned on a misreading of *Camera Lucida*, or more precisely a failure to take in what Barthes leaves out—a photograph of his mother that Barthes couldn't show. I, too, now touch on inevitably lost parts: photographs cut from my own and another transsexual's book, a cut footnote about photographs, and ultimately for me a sense of lost body parts. Circling back to Barthes and chapter 1, I show how reading others' losses (Bishop cites Lévi-Strauss as well as Parks) can spur our own realizations. *Light in the Dark Room* stemmed from looking, in photography, at my own autobiographical losses. This chapter was first presented in Brazil.

Why Brazil? Lévi-Strauss's photographic memoir is called *Saudades do Brasil*, and the term *saudades* appears in two other works here and runs as the spirit of them all. *Saudades* is as intrinsic to Brazil as it is to the conception of photography in this book. It is a word that Brazilians are proud of as having significance to their country. I avoid direct translation; Bishop writes there's always loss incurred in translation. But at the outset, *saudades* is best glossed as a realization of loss. My choice of these writers is considered: in reverse order, a Canadian-born (and ultimately U.S.-settled) American; an African American; a European American*ist*, all of whom moved between Brazil and the United States; and, key start, a Frenchman who, in his book on photography, sees at the end of his life the United States as the worst example for the way in which reality is subsumed into signs, in which photography is made yet another readable text. My writing about realizing loss in photography in these particular authors moves toward a larger question about where exactly we are locating reality in an age dominated by global technologies: what's left of the real in our lives when our ultimate realities seem taken by technology, with its attendant progress, acquisition, development, gain—corporate, national, and individual? The United States and Brazil are not the confines for my concerns about the losses incurred in modernity's technologization; but as the United States is the greatest source and purveyor of global technologies, and as Brazil shows some of their more obvious effects, the relations between these two countries form an apt and animated backdrop for reading loss in photography. In brief and to foreshadow: I suggest in the focus on Brazil that Brazil may (yet) contain an instance of the real lost from the dominance of the U.S. symbolic. I end, then, in my epilogue with a few autobiographical snapshots going back to my own recent trips to Brazil and my own *saudades* or realizations of losses there. Like my authors here I go with the I and the eye—in a form that, like photography, doesn't master reality but lets it go. As well as chasing some of the referents of their photographs—mostly, of course, lost—I tell how, in the Amazon on the Rio Negro, there's a particular quality of light that made me want to take, and then give, up photographs . . . and to live with the realism and illumination (attention to presence, acceptance of absence) given us by photographs.

CHAPTER 1

ROLAND BARTHES'S LOSS

PALINODIC DEATH

Has there been a critic whose loss has been less worked through than that of Roland Barthes? It is not that we haven't mourned Barthes. Since his death in 1980 there have been some ten book-length studies, a biography and a wealth of critical essays, and much of this material is characterized by an incredible sense of loss. To take the most recent collection as an example, Colin MacCabe describes Jean-Michel Rabaté's *Writing the Image after Roland Barthes* as "a kind of memorial" for Barthes—and this is seventeen years after Barthes's death. Another contributor, Daniel Ferrer, states therein that "Barthes cannot be safely distanced, he is still relevant to us; the mourning period is not over, and I do not see any sign that it is coming to an end."[1] The notion that our "mourning" for Barthes might be "interminable" and "collective" is first suggested—and these words first linked—in an essay that Derrida wrote six months after Barthes's death.[2] This essay functions as a kind of anti-eulogy for Barthes, since Derrida refrains from the gesture of the obituary or funereal ode that would sum up and therefore summarily dismiss Barthes. He refuses to "pay homage . . . [to] the author who has passed away (whose tastes, curiosities, and project should, it seems, no longer surprise us)" (51). Instead Derrida incorporates Barthes as a ghost. He sketches the ghost as the return of the dead, the return of the dead in and as the living—"Neither life nor death, it is the haunting of the one by the other. . . . Ghosts: the concept of the other

19

in the same . . . the dead other alive in me . . . a relationship of haunting which is perhaps constitutive of all logics" (41–42). The incorporation is extraordinary for it results in a kind of palinode for Derrida, as Derrida speaks subjectively and fragmentedly (dare one say sentimentally?) of what Barthes meant "for me" (35). He praises Barthes for pointing to the possibility of a "something else" beyond all language (46) and describes this almost wistfully as a "love" that "shatters" "all discourses . . . all theoretical systems" (48). *After* Roland Barthes here means Derrida speaking *in the style of* Barthes. After Barthes we are anything but *over* him. Indeed, that Barthes may be more influential now in his death than he was in his life is suggested by the sheer numerousness of these posthumous citings and by their emphasis on his loss. The criticism has become a kind of palinodic tomb for Barthes: a space not for burying him or for keeping him alive but for returning him interminably as dead—the dead in our life.

Of Barthes's texts it is especially *Camera Lucida* that holds our melancholia. It has become the epitaph on Barthes's tomb, or rather the stone we repeatedly roll back to keep Barthes's tomb open. *Camera Lucida's* threnodic status can be explained in part by the fact that this was Barthes's last text and hence represents his most complete last word. Moreover its subject matter is death and loss, since Barthes finds in photography "that rather terrible thing which is there in every photograph: the return of the dead," as he turns to write on photography while he was in interminable mourning following the death of his mother.[3] And in the precise timing of its publication *Camera Lucida* seemed to coincide these losses—to coincide Barthes's loss of his mother with our loss of him. *Camera Lucida* was published as *La chambre claire: Note sur la phtographie* in France on January 28, 1980. Barthes was knocked down by a laundry van on February 25, 1980 and died on March 26, 1980. The English translation was published posthumously then, in 1982. As Tzvetan Todorov notes in *his* elegy for Barthes, *Camera Lucida* marks a "disturbing coincidence between the accidental (surely the right word here) and the essential."[4] Barthes's essay on photography was sparked by the *tuché*—the accident that returns the real—of Barthes's mother's death; and it collided with or elided into the *tuché* of his own death. Derrida has noted the incarnate place this book has in our interminable mourning for Barthes, and in doing so he uses a figure that suggests the elision of these double losses into a single, redoubled loss: *Camera Lucida* is a book "whose time and tempo accompanied his death as no other book, I believe, has ever kept vigil over its author" (36). The figure puts the book in our mourning for Barthes in the same place that Barthes occupied as he kept watch over his dying mother. It is as if whatever Barthes were mourning—or failing to mourn—in *her* has come to be embodied in our mourning (failing to mourn) *him*.

The more interminable our mourning for Barthes, the more *Camera Lucida* and its conception of photography as autobiographical and inextricable from loss have come into our present tense. Early critics did not know what to make of the autobiographical rawness and the notion of photography as real that characterize *Camera Lucida*. These features seemed to turn their back on the suspicion toward subjecthood and the referent for which we had canonized Barthes. Writing in 1982 for an introductory study of Barthes as a theorist, a critic of cultural mythologies from literary historian to semiologist to structuralist and poststructuralist, Jonathan Culler is obviously exasperated at *Camera Lucida*'s upset of his neat trajectory for Barthes. "How did Roland Barthes, the critic of bourgeois myth, reach this point?" For Culler, Barthes had already lost it in *Camera Lucida,* and he begins his work of mourning before Barthes's death. "Defying all the most convincing work on meaning, he affirms the powerful myth, he taught us to resist." Culler rues "this strangest moment, when what has been denigrated returns."[5] Later critics in contrast saw *Camera Lucida* as presaging new times. Elaine Hoft-March, writing in the nineties and taking specific issue with Culler's reading of Barthes as recidivist (falling back), suggests that *Camera Lucida* heralds a new feminine discourse, an imaginary relation to the mother that "upends certain gender-codified meanings, a subversion enabling him to indicate a new theoretical direction rather than to exhibit critical resignation."[6] And in 1981 even before the English translation of *La chambre claire* had been made, J. Gerald Kennedy predicted that the text would one day be recognized as heraldic. What is interesting about Kennedy's observation is the notion that *Camera Lucida* would be seen as precursory only retrospectively—that it would have to wait its time not only in order to come into but in order to be noted as ahead of its time: "As we begin to assess the impact of Barthes's work on modern critical thought, it seems unlikely that *La chambre claire* will figure as a major work. Insofar as his career has provided an accurate barometer of French intellectual trends, the book may some day mark a general turn away from structuralist and post-structuralist abstraction toward a more pragmatic and humane discourse."[7]

That that time has now come is suggested by the books enmeshing photography and autobiography cited in my introduction. So many of them see *Camera Lucida* as initiating but recognize that what it is initiating of is loss, the irrevocable moment. We have come into sympathy with *Camera Lucida* and with its notion of photography as autobiographical loss. Two of the most recent contributions to Barthes studies are focused on photography. Rabaté's collection treats the photograph as an open memorial for Barthes. Nancy Shawcross's book, the first monograph devoted to Barthes on photography—while the body of her work sees Barthes in *Camera Lucida* as disconsolate with postmodernism and reverting to modernism—in her last few sentences rightly suggests that *Camera Lucida* needs to be read in two directions at once, backwards and forwards. "Barthes's essay can be viewed as the voice of either the past or the future. Or he may be read with the duality of impulse that has marked his writings from the beginning."[8] Critics have always agreed that *Camera Lucida* marks a turn in Barthes's writings, might have disagreed about what this turn represents; but what is indisputable is that the turn was not fully exercised. Is *Camera Lucida* the beginning of Barthes's career as a novelist? The fact that Barthes was planning a novel is well known. Is it in fact this novel? Or is it rather the book Barthes says within *Camera Lucida* he was planning to write about his mother? Crucially, there is something unfulfilled, something unrealized in *Camera Lucida;* yet Barthes's swan song is all the more powerfully real because of that. Barthes's death froze realization. If we have a conception of photography as loss in autobiography and in the palinode, if this form is seminal then, it is because *Camera Lucida*, this ph/autographic palinode, photographed loss: made it real and insuperable. And this loss of Barthes—that is, our loss of him and his loss in photography—is absolutely intricated with the marvelous temporal dynamics of the palinode.

PALINODIC LIFE

Barthes is clearly not interested in writing a history of photography. But his title, *La chambre claire,* French for a camera lucida, and his cover illustration of a man using a camera lucida to portray a woman, make the anamorphic, palinodic dynamics of this earliest form of the camera immediately relevant to his text. The palinode within his text is explicit and structuring. The book is divided into two equal parts of a total of forty-eight chapters—or "notes," to use the French term from *La chambre claire*'s subtitle for Barthes's numbered fragments that, with its musical meaning also, is more appropriate than the English translation of the visual and deliberate-sounding "reflections"; for we are here in the realm of the gaze, not of vision.[9] The palinode appears exactly halfway through the book. It is promised at the end of chapter 24, entitled "Palinode" and the shortest chapter: "I would have to descend deeper into myself to find the evidence of Photography, that thing which is seen by anyone looking at a photograph and which distinguished it in his eyes from any other image. I would have to make my recantation, my palinode" (*Camera* 60). The photographs, chapter 24 acknowledges, have been "public ones, up to now" (60). Barthes's quest through photography has been accordingly "ontological" (3), an attempt to "learn at all costs what Photography was 'in itself'" (3)—a largely theoretical endeavor in mastery and knowledge of this form in keeping with the phenomenological approach suggested by the book's dedication to Sartre. But, following startlingly the discussion of the "'light' (good) desire of eroticism" in a Mapplethorpe photograph (59), the chapter promising the palinode confesses that Barthes has not yet found the essence of photography: "I had perhaps learned how my desire worked, but I had not discovered the nature (the *eidos*) of Photography" (60). Now, as Barthes descends deeper into himself to make his recantation, he immerses photography in autobiography—to produce ph/autography. As part 2 begins we know immediately we're in a different realm, a private underworld of profound sadness: "Now, one November evening shortly after my mother's death, I was going through some photographs. I had no hope of 'finding' her" (63).

This second half of *Camera Lucida,* the palinode, is a work of failed personal mourning for Barthes's mother. It is important to be precise here. *Camera Lucida* is not a work of mourning, or even of something in between melancholia and mourning, as it has been albeit intuitively read.[10] Rather it is a classical case of melancholia, corresponding to Freud's conception of melancholia as inarticulable and frozen in his famous distinction of melancholia from mourning. Even from the first part, which takes "Emotion as Departure" (viii), *Camera Lucida* is freighted with sadness and loss. The shock of grief, violence and bodily pain characterizing several of the photographs here punches through the attempt to circumscribe photographic form. Perhaps the most telling image of the autobiographical generational loss that is to follow shows a mother in Nicaragua carrying sheets around a covered corpse (her child?) (24). In the second part death acquires its referent, or rather the reason for its unnameability, its veiling or covering in the first place (that is, in the ode). The first photograph, appearing in the French edition only, of the curtains drawn almost closed performs this function of hiding and suggesting future revelation. Barthes does finally find his mother's essence, in the famous "Winter Garden Photograph," which, he writes, "achieved for me, utopically, *the impossible science of unique being*" (71). But in front of this photograph he cannot move forward in his mourning: "I suffer, motionless. Cruel, sterile deficiency: I cannot *transform* my grief, I cannot let my gaze drift; no culture will help me utter this suffering which I experience entirely on the level of the image's finitude (this is why, despite its codes, I cannot *read* a photograph): the Photograph—my Photograph—is without culture: when it is painful, nothing in it can transform grief into mourning" (90). The Winter Garden Photograph stops language, like melancholia: "The horror is this: nothing to say about the death of one whom I love most, nothing to say about her photograph. . . . I have no other recourse than this *irony:* to speak of the 'nothing to say'" (93).

This is why the Winter Garden Photograph is not reproduced within *Camera Lucida.* Instead we have Barthes's explanation of the reason that he cannot include the photograph, itself in parenthesis as if it hardly bears speaking in the primary voice of this *Note sur la photographie,* this essay on photography. Of parenthesis elsewhere in Barthes Derrida says that it "does not enclose an incidental or secondary thought but "lowers the voice—as an *aside*—out of a sense of modesty" (40). "(I cannot reproduce the Winter Garden Photograph. It exists only for me. For you, it would be nothing but an indifferent picture, one of the thousand manifestations of the 'ordinary'; it cannot in any way constitute the visible object of a science; it cannot establish an objectivity, in the positive sense of the term; at most it would interest your *studium*: period, clothes, photogeny but in it, for you, no wound)" (73). Melancholy, Freud writes, "behaves like an open wound.[11] The Winter Garden Photograph is Barthes's wound; its absence is evidence of his melancholia. It is the "petit trou" (*La chambre* 49), the little hole in the text in which Barthes's trauma lies *un*buried: sunken, profound, but uncovered. As Eakin notes, the Winter Garden Photograph is "truly . . . the most memorable photograph in the book"—and it is surely memorable because of its absence—and that it is "in order to illustrate what he has shown and what he cannot show [that] Barthes deliberately omits the 'Winter Garden Photograph.'"[12] If Barthes's absent photograph evidences that he cannot speak, show, or work through his loss, his ph/autographical palinode is compelled by this melancholia; he must move back *because* he cannot move forward in his mourning for his mother. The whole book takes its organization from this palinodic retreat/descent. As Ralph Sarkonak has noticed, *Camera Lucida* with its 48 chapters, its 24 photographs (at least those in the text, excepting the prefacing, curtaining one in the French edition then), and 12 bibliographic items has a rigid numerical—we might almost say numerological—structure. Each number is half of the previous number. The total of all numbers is 84, which Sarkonak guesses to be the age at which Barthes's mother died. He turns out to be right. Barthes's biographer, Louis-Jean Calvet, has since independently cited this figure as the age at which Henriette Binger Barthes died.[13]

The palinodic structure contains, or barely contains, *what* Barthes is failing to mourn in his mother.

The palinodic turn in the essay produces a notion of photography as itself a kind of melancholy. Like Sontag and Benjamin, Barthes speaks of the melancholy of photography yet adds to this his loss of his mother—the autobiographical to the photographical. *Camera Lucida* knows early on that "Death is the *eidos* of Photography" (15)—"the Photograph always carries its referent with itself . . . like the dead man and the corpse" (5–6); but the beginning of the palinode acknowledges that he had not made this desire or death—or this desire *for* death—his own. In the Winter Garden Photograph Barthes discovers not only the essence of his mother but the essence of photography. It is this photograph that impels him into writing the book about photography in the first place, that draws him in that Lacanian sense—"me tirait vers la Photographie" (*La chambre* 114). The Winter Garden Photograph is not part of the *studium*, to bring forward the structuring Latinate terms of *Camera Lucida*. *Studium* is that which can be studied or articulated about photography. *Studium* is always coded. It moves forward—it moves the subject forward—into language. The Winter Garden Photograph in which Barthes realizes the essence of photography is, to use the term *Camera Lucida* counterpoints to *studium,* the *punctum*. Initially the *punctum* is the poignant partial detail that ruptures or punctures the *studium*. Appearing "by chance" (42), not the intended material that the photographer would have us see but the involuntary, the nondeliberate, the *punctum* is described as a "lightning-like" flash (45), a "fulguration" (49) that comes to revelation deferred: "[D]espite its clarity, the *punctum* should be revealed only after the fact" (53). Identified through its essence of the *punctum* that it is Barthes's purpose to pursue, photography, like Barthes, doesn't move forward but remains frozen. Unlike cinema, it presents a moment of intense immobility, and it is this temporal immobilization that renders photography melancholic: "It is *without future* (this is its pathos, its melancholy)" (90). The *punctum* is also unspeakable. "What I can name cannot really prick me. The incapacity to name is a good symptom of disturbance" (51). Not surprisingly then, Barthes introduces the *punctum* through and as a shard of Lacan's real: "it is the absolute Particular, the sovereign Contingency, matte and somehow stupid, the *This* (this photograph and not Photography), in short, what Lacan calls the *Tuché,* the occasion, the Encounter, the Real, in its indefatigable expression" (4). *Punctum* in photography carries the gaze that ruptures our vision, an undrifting gaze (before the Winter Garden Photograph, the photographic *punctum* of the book, Barthes "cannot let [his] gaze drift"). It is what we do not consciously notice about the photograph. It is the "blind field" (57) that we can only "see" when we "shut [our] eyes" having looked at the photograph (55). *Punctum* is derived from the Latin "to prick" ("this wound, this prick" [26]), in echo of *trauma* from the Greek for "wound." In sum, the *punctum* is the photographic incarnation of Barthes's melancholia. It is loss that won't be healed.

Barthes's terms for photography, *punctum* and *studium*, guide us how to read the palinode in relation to the ode. The palinodic organization has challenged critics. The ode/palinode structure is less than a "scission en deux parties dissymétriques et inajustables" a splitting into two parts asymmetrical and irreconcilable, as Chantal Thomas has suggested.[14] And it is more than a "signal that Barthes wants the reader to *glisser* [slide] between the two parts . . . while simultaneously approaching part two as a clean slate on which to begin his inquiry into photography," as Shawcross has conversely proposed (75). The palinode is between these two models. It chiastically reverses the ode so that we do transition across the two parts but to note how the second part retreats on (descends from) the first. The second part is best understood as the *punctum* to the first part's *studium* that has stayed largely in the realm of that which can be studied or spoken about the photograph. The palinode punctures through the study of the ode with the poignant autobiographical detail—the unspeakable that moves us about Barthes's essay *Camera Lucida*. And as *Camera Lucida* descends deeper into Barthes's subjectivity and his grief, it punctures and reverses conventional discourse on photography as a whole. It is the *punctum* in writing on photography. Barthes departs from the *savoir* of photography, a mastery or knowledge of the form, into his *vouloir,* a desire to point toward that which moves him subjectively about photography and whose eventual *eidos* is death. Barthes is not interested in writing *about* photography. This he calls "scientia" (7). He dismisses most other writing about photography about and like the *studium* as an education into "savoir" (*La chambre* 51). "What did I care about the rules of composition of the photographic landscape, or, at the other end, about the Photograph as a family rite?" (7). "The photograph touches me if I withdraw it from its usual blah-blah" (55). "I wanted to explore [photography] not as question (a theme) but as a wound" (21).

In pursuing this *punctum* or wound *Camera Lucida* not only contains a palinode, it becomes a startling palinode of Barthes's previous work, particularly his work on photography. As Shawcross has neatly documented, Barthes's work on photography underwent shifts. She notes four, and I suggest the following as turning points. In the fifties at the beginning of his career Barthes was the mythologist analyzing the mythology or ideology of the photograph in contexts such as, in his *Mythologies,* Edward Steichen's anthropological exhibition, "The Family of Man." In the sixties as a semiologist and structuralist he read the "rhetoric of the image"—the title he gave to an essay that is exemplary in treating photography as a linguistic-like structure that can be broken down into "signifieds" and "signifiers." As a poststructuralist in the seventies Barthes placed photographs at the beginning of his autobiography, *Roland Barthes by Roland Barthes,* now crucially in excess of the writing, in the margins of the unraveling linguistic structures. Much of this work is *studium.*[15] In his mythologist and structuralist phases for example, Barthes was writing about photography precisely as a cultural "family rite" (on Steichen) or about its "rules of composition" ("Rhetoric of the Image"). Shawcross suggests that what Barthes produces in *Camera Lucida* is a difficult "third form" that resists classification, a text between fiction, autobiography, and essay—although one that reverts to modernist and even nineteenth-century mythologies of photography (68 and passim). Yet while Barthes's thinking on photography underwent shifts and these seem to correspond to the phases recognized as marking Barthes's career—typically from mythologist to structuralist (to semiotician) to poststructuralist; or structuralist to poststructuralist to something in excess (Kennedy), or in reversion (Shawcross, Culler)—photography serves not simply to indicate those shifts but more interestingly, ab initio, to resist them. Photography is the form that has something in it already and evident in Barthes all along to enable and propel the palinode: the return to something in excess of the writing.

In "The Photographic Message," an essay published in 1961 from the same structuralist era as "The Rhetoric of the Image," Barthes identifies most clearly what is distinct about photography. The essay is a self-declared "structuralist analysis," but it is important for showing how photography resists structuralist analysis—for suggesting, as odes do when read retroactively through the palinode, an existent tension.[16] Photography for Barthes is a "structural paradox" (19). On the one hand like any other text analyzed by structuralists, photography works according to various "connotation procedures" (20), the text/captions, photographic composition, and layout in publication that seek to "connote" the photographic message: the "blah-blah" that here Barthes *is* interested in reading. On the other hand photography "transmit[s] . . . literal reality," is a "perfect *analogon*" of the thing represented and hence "*it is a message without a code*"

(20). Connotation is countered by denotation, and it is denotation that exclusively constitutes photography, for connotation, Barthes acknowledges, is "not strictly part of the photographic structure" (20). A paradox, photography already contravenes the notion of reality as produced by codes that was the structuralist *doxa* or opinion. This structuralist orthodoxy Barthes had represented in, say, an essay from the same decade as "The Photographic Message" entitled "The Reality Effect," in which "the *referential illusion*" is said to characterize verisimilitude in the literature of modernity—interestingly from around the beginnings of photography: Flaubert's *Madame Bovary* is Barthes's example.[17] Or again the approach to reality as produced is evident even in the later structuralist-transitioning-to-poststructuralist *S/Z*, where the "referential code" similarly shows how reality is coded in Balzac's *Sarrasine*.[18] These ideas are in line with Lejeune's "image of the real," not his "effect of the real."[19] And it is surely to "The Photographic Message" that Barthes refers back when he writes in *Camera Lucida* that he did not try to escape from the "photographic paradox" (20), that he was already a realist when he asserted that the photograph was an image without a code.

And yet—and here's the real structural paradox of photography, the paradox *for* structuralism in the real that *is* photography—Barthes in "The Photographic Message" recognizes that we cannot isolate the pure denotative state that is the *eidos* of photography. Denotation moves necessarily into connotation, the message into the code; reality can only be accessed through representation, and for Barthes as a structuralist critic representation is understood through language. "From this point of view, the image—grasped immediately by an inner language itself—in actual fact has no denoted state, is immersed for its very social existence in at least an initial layer of connotation, that of the categories of language" (*Image* 28–29). *Connotation* in "The Photographic Message" corresponds to *studium* in *Camera Lucida*: "connotation is present in *studium*" (*Camera* 26), and both are derived from "culture" (*Image* 22; *Camera* 28). *Denotation,* which points to the thing itself, will become the much more traumatic, wounding, but similarly "deictic" (pointing) *punctum* (*Camera* 5). In other words "The Photographic Message" shows that Barthes already knows the *eidos* of photography but can't—a paradox for him as a structuralist as well as in photography—stay with or articulate it. Toward the end of the essay, however, he foretells in an eerie prophecy what might happen to enable him to grasp and write the real that is distinct about photography:

These few remarks sketch a kind of differential table of photographic con-
notations, showing, if nothing else, that connotation extends a long way.
Is this to say that a pure denotation, a *this-side-of language,* is impossible?
If such a denotation exists, it is perhaps not at the level of what ordinary
language calls the insignificant, the neutral, the objective, but on the contrary at the level of absolutely traumatic images. The trauma is a suspension of language, a blocking of meaning. (*Image* 30)

This is what happens in *Camera Lucida* then. It is the trauma of losing his
mother that suspends the connotation procedures of photography, levers up
the structural codes, and sparks his return forty years later to seize photography through one particular photograph as the *this-side-of language* that
it is. And *photography* in the process becomes *Photography*: capitalized and
iconized, a talismanic gate or *trou* ("hole") through which Barthes falls to
the underworld of Lacan's similarly capitalized Real; "je tombai," "I fell," is
the first verb for Barthes in *La chambre claire* and it describes his first relation to photography (13). The earlier essay, which comes close to the distinctness of photography, shows that the paradox of photography already
laid bare a tension between representation and reality; for photography is
a reality that does not signify. This *paradox of* photography becomes in
Camera Lucida a *palinode in* photography—in fulfillment of this prophecy
of how to return to a moment before.

In fulfillment of this prophecy Barthes's last work on photography
becomes a palinode of his entire career, or at least the critical part that
had made up the bulk of it: the criticism. Barthes, our cultural critic par
excellence, decoder of languages, and then playful unthreader of systems,
in the wake of his mother's loss writing about photography in *Camera
Lucida,* a text doubly in extremis, looks back and questions the discourses
that had made up his career. His draw to photography *(tirer)* opens up the
confusion—indeed he is drawn to photography surely *because* it opens up
confusion, is a paradoxical mode as he inferred before. This is a point made
early on in *Camera Lucida*:

> Then I decided that this disorder and this dilemma, revealed by my de-
> sire to write on Photography, corresponded to a discomfort I had always
> suffered from: the uneasiness of being a subject torn between two lan-
> guages, one expressive, the other critical; and at the heart of this critical
> language, between several discourses, those of sociology, of semiology,
> and of psychoanalysis—but that, by ultimate dissatisfaction with all of
> them, I was bearing witness to the only sure thing that was in me (how-
> ever naïve it might be): a desperate resistance to any reductive system. (8)

As we descend into the palinode of *Camera Lucida* we move inexorably away from the languages of criticism, sociology, semiology, and even psychoanalysis, into the expressive, the autobiographical—from a critique of the highly linguistic, to the pointing at the ineffable. This doubt in the languages that had made up Barthes's career had already been hinted at, but in the characteristic Barthesian distancing third person in the antecedent (by two books) autobiography, *Roland Barthes by Roland Barthes*: "what if all his life *he had chosen the wrong language?*" (*Roland Barthes* 115). In this ambivalence, in this doubt, the autobiography hews the pathway for the ph/autographical palinode. As I said in my introduction Eakin notes that the photographs in *Roland Barthes by Roland Barthes* are the return of the repressed in the autobiography, are the most autobiographical thing about that autobiography. The photographs cohere the body into identity—Roland Barthes—even in the playful, split, evacuating subject of that poststructuralist autobiographical writing. It is notable that in *Camera Lucida* Barthes has resolved the split subject and writes wholly and integratingly in the first person—as if the ph/autographical palinode were the more autobiographical book, which, in its revelation of a profound self, it is. But in the prevenient autobiography we realize that Barthes had always made turns in on himself, had constantly suffered doubts about the loss of the expressive from the critical, the real from its code. Critics have recognized that, if he had not always had a strictly palinodic way of working, Barthes's work operates through shifts, whether these are seen as two "ecstasies," three "subjects," or three "paradoxes."[20] These shifts may be correlated to those in theory, but they move off its edge to something ethical or moral as Kennedy suggests—a Kierkegaardian trajectory from aesthetics to ethics eventually to the spiritual, in its increasing concern with pursuing an elusive, transcendent real over analysis of form or structure and in its apprehension of where this real lies. Barthes more than any other is a theorist whose trajectory has kept pace with, indeed set but also repeatedly revoked the times. In a chart entitled "Phases" in *Roland Barthes by Roland Barthes,* Barthes describes how "each phase" in his writing life, here given as "social mythology," "semiology," "textuality," and "morality," is "reactive" (145). And what he reacts to is the *"doxa,"* which he defines as "popular opinion" (71). In other words he makes these turns out of his theoretical phases, these *para-doxa*—which he had been crucial in helping render dominant—just as the rest of us were getting into them. And consummately at the moment when the referent was being deferred in theory, when Derrida and de Man were being read (and Jane Gallop's date of "around 1981" for the point at which feminism encountered theory in the academy might serve as a useful watershed for the general arrival of theory in the U.S./U.K. academy),[21] Barthes went out of theory, not only in these books with autobiography and then ph/autography but crucially, coincidentally, with his death. No wonder our sense of *interruptus,* of some unspeakable loss frozen and photographed in *Camera Lucida.* Our entry into theory coincides with Barthes's final exit.

Barthes's oeuvre thus represents a project of "perpetual self-correction," as Sontag writes in her introduction to the *Barthes Reader,* which has the advantage of being able to look back and select from all of his writings.[22] In the autobiography Barthes writes that his "foible" is to produce serial "introductions," "postponing the 'real' book til later" (*Roland Barthes* 173). This foible, the nonrealization of the "perfect Book" (173)—which we will see carried to fulfillment in our poet in a later chapter when she doesn't produce the book and this is what is so perfect about it—Barthes calls "prolepsis" (173). But prolepsis only results in *analepsis,* which is the need to go back and restore that constitutes the palinode. Analepsis is less the opposite of the predictive prolepsis than its retrodictive inevitability. The putting-off-till-later requires the return of what was left unfinished; and the deferral, which always, Barthes suggests, has reality in its sights—is always a deferral *of* reality (which then returns as the real)—sets up the conditions for a return: "But the dilatory, denial of reality (of the realizable), is no less alive for all that: these projects live, they are never abandoned; suspended, they can return to life at any moment" (173). Yet the return to life is never a nostalgic recovery of what was there, the return, say, of the dead into life. It is instead the discovery of a new place or text that includes recognition of the loss, of the oversight—of the dead as interminably lost, living *as dead.* Barthes's language suggests that such recognition involves a kind of spiritual pilgrimage and is perhaps the enlightenment that comes at the end of an initiate's journey: "Yet for him, it is not a question of recovering a pre-meaning, an origin of the world, of life, of facts, anterior to meaning, but rather to imagine a post-meaning: one must traverse, as though the length of an initiatic way, the whole meaning in order to be able to extenuate it, to exempt it" (87). Barthes's image of history—and his favored image (via Vico)—of the spiral encapsulates this palinodic reversal that yet creates something new in return: "history proceeds in a spiral, and things of the past return, but obviously not in the same place; thus there are states, values, behavior, 'writings' of the past that may return, but in a very modern place."[23] And what he seeks in the return is always the real—the exemption from meaning. In the autobiography Barthes writes that his project has always been one of return and that from his first book, *Writing Degree*

Zero, he has been seeking the same thing, a place or a moment—moment frozen as place—that does not signify, a utopia before or outside cultural connotation. Of his first book he writes, looking back on himself in the third person in the autobiography, "Evidently he dreams of a world which would be *exempt from meaning.* . . . This began with *Writing Degree Zero,* in which is imagined 'the absence of every sign'" (*Roland Barthes* 87).

But why this palinodic way of working, this *tirer* into anamorphic inversions culminating in *Camera Lucida*—this desire for the "zero degree" that pulls him back? There must have been a sense of irrevocable loss motivating such returns, such compelled attempts to recover the real. Critics have posed this almost as a psychological question, and this seems right, to wonder about—to *worry* about—the psychic implications of such a self-retracting (undermining?) mode. Antoine Compagnon asks "what he was running after, why he had to give up any position he had just conquered, as though the best, or only defense were to run away, radicalize and overturn his views on the spot."[24] Or back to Culler's bewilderment: "he tries to uproot his seedlings as they sprout."[25] And Stephen Ungar, in relation specifically to the palinode in *Camera Lucida* and in response to the question of why not simply *begin* with part 2, why does Barthes invoke terms and tones he later rejects, identifies that the palinode allows for a kind of self-analysis, a critical focus on the self.[26] Barthes had a term in his autobiography for this pulling the rug from under his own feet, "self-criticism"—like Nietzsche and as in Lejeune's palinode and possibly where Lejeune (in his fascination for Barthes's self-ambivalence) got it from. Self-criticism, turning to criticize and correct the self, is the palinode in generic form: not in relation to a specific text but a way of working, a methodology. But as for Lejeune "self-criticism . . . is an impossible undertaking,"[27] Barthes also writes in his definition that "nothing is more a matter of the image-system, of the imaginary than (self-) criticism" (*Roland Barthes* 120). Although *Roland Barthes by Roland Barthes* would seem to be a classic piece of self-criticism as Barthes writes of himself in the third person and "it is a *recessive* book (which falls back, but which may also gain perspective thereby)" (119), Barthes writes here under the heading "Le livre du Moi—The book of the Self"—that what disappears in self-criticism is the self so that one is left in self-analysis with an ungraspable real. Thus Lejeune's description, in his discussion of self-criticism, of *Roland Barthes by Roland Barthes* as Barthes's most *un*autobiographical book is absolutely correct. The zero degree, a world exempt from meaning, proves unoccupiable. In a fragment in *Roland Barthes by Roland Barthes* entitled "La coincidence," which is where he asks himself that famous, often-truncated question of the autobiography, "Do I not know that *in the field of the subject, there is no referent?*" (56), Barthes wonders about how one represents, how one joins with a past self. He makes an analogy between self-criticism in writing—"When I pretend to write on what I have written in the past" (56)—and listening to himself playing music. In the moment of analysis of the self, the mediation—of self, of the gap between past and present—disappears. Self-realization, grasping of the past self, elides or rather *coincides* (the title of the fragment) the self into the thing itself. The self becomes referent—and then real. Self-criticism in Barthes's analogy disappears or voids the self. When he listens to a recording of himself playing Bach or Schumann, "very soon I no longer hear myself; what I hear is, however pretentious it may seem to say so, the *Dasein* of Bach and of Schumann, the pure materiality of their music; because it is my utterance, the predicate loses all pertinence" (55–56). What is said about Bach or Schumann (the predicate, the playing) loosens its hold (its pertinence), and as in writing on the self "there occurs . . . a movement of abolition," an abolition that is "a simple idea: simple as the idea of suicide" (56).

Barthes's first book had begun his career with this quest for how to free representation, in this case literature, from the weight of forms: how to recover from the clichéd language, the technical reflexes, automatic reflections, and literary self-consciousness that Barthes noted had burdened literature over the course of history into Literature. And he uses the very same term there, repeated in his musical analogy years later in his autobiography, for the abolition of mediation. Such abolition can be achieved but only at the risk of suicide, silence. He seeks "this precarious moment of History in which literary language persists only the better to sing the necessity of its death. . . . This art has the very structure of suicide."[28] If in retrospect we can see that Barthes's work had always quested this suicidal, self-abolishing art, it is in his return to photography that he finally finds it—the abolition of language, of code, of mediation: a message without a code in the representation of death. But in an uncanny, preternatural sense, is it not also possible that with his last work, *Camera Lucida*—in writing about photography after his mother's death—Barthes's *life* took the structure of a suicide? Did his life not turn in on itself after the writing? After his mother's death, in his melancholia—which is after all *depression*—Barthes writes in *Camera Lucida* that he has nothing to live for except his writing. "Once she was dead I no longer had any reason to attune myself to the progress of the superior Life Force . . . (unless, utopically, by writing, whose project henceforth would become the unique goal of my life)" (72). This near evacuation of a desire to live and write is quite different from the last lines of the prevenient autobiography, where a persistent and tenacious desire is expressed as motivating and making possible writing: "And afterward? What to write now? Can you still write anything? One writes with one's desire, and I am not through desiring" (*Roland Barthes* 188). But if you've discovered in photography a form that abolishes (finally) mediation and language—an art that realizes the structure of suicide, accessed through death, with desire left behind—what is left of life? Barthes goes on in *Camera Lucida,* eerily, presciently to speak of his own death: "From now on I could do no more than await my total, undialectical death" (72). Barthes's biographer, Calvet, who has said that, after Barthes's childhood illness, depression "was to be his most typical mood" (39), asks of Barthes's death: "The question still remains: was this a form of suicide?"(252). For not only did Barthes not actually die from the road injuries of his accident. The forensic surgeon's report concluded that the actual cause of death was pulmonary complications from the TB that Barthes had endured since a child; Calvet writes: "It was as if, thirty-five years later, Saint-Hilaire-du-Touvet and Leysin [the sanatoria where Barthes had spent his youth] had finally taken their revenge on the body that had escaped them" (253)—what was put off "til later" returns. Calvet also suggests that Barthes had some unconscious pull toward death: a death wish. He notes that at first Barthes's condition gave doctors and friends no cause for concern. Barthes could speak after his accident and was sufficiently well to be unhappy in his environment, complaining about being stuck in hospital and interrupted by unwanted visits that intruded on this introspective self. Yet while he seemed well enough, something in Barthes would not recover: "his body was not responding to treatment: it was as if his body could not get going again" (251). Calvet interviewed friends who wonder whether Barthes had lost the desire to live, particularly after his mother's death, and who suggest that there was a sense of something willed—something willful—in Barthes's death: "Some visitors felt that the doctors were annoyed by his resistance or refusal to get better" (252).

And of the accident itself it was in some respects peculiarly nonaccidental, more in line with the "coincidence" not only of which Todorov speaks, but of which Barthes writes in *Roland Barthes by Roland Barthes* in which the mediating watchfulness of the self is abolished into the real. Apparently Barthes was looking *right in the direction of the van* that ran him over. "Were his thoughts elsewhere?" Calvet asks (249). A gaze without seeing. This was a child's death, Todorov notes, not unkindly. Or a depressive's, a melancholic's. James Beighton, in MA work, has simply but persuasively correlated Barthes's inattention at his accident and what he calls "Le texte symptomal" from Barthes's later writings—their undeniable tonal fatigue—to the *Diagnostic and Statistical Manual of Mental Disorders*'s diagnostic criteria for depression and to recent studies of depression that have stressed its inarticulability, its unrepresentability.[29] Beighton suggests that there were many signs that Barthes was suffering from depression at the end of his life after his mother's death. And Julia Kristeva, who after speaking with him around this time found Barthes depressed, writes that, whatever difference she may find as a post-Freudian between depression and melancholia, "Freudian theory detects everywhere the same *impossible mourning for the maternal object.*" The depressive/melancholic suffers from the loss of signification or meaning—"symbolic abdication," which leaves the sufferer in the realm of the real. After speechlessness, there is only death: "Melancholia then ends up in asymbolia, in loss of meaning: if I am no longer capable of translating or metaphorizing, I become silent and die."[30] Along with *Camera Lucida* Barthes's journals written after his mother's death, "Deliberation" and "Soirées de Paris," the latter published posthumously (and it's so painful one wonders about the rightness of this), are overwhelming in their sense of desolation—and all of it hinged onto Barthes's mother's death. "Soirées de Paris," beginning with an epigraph from Schopenhauer's suicide note, feels like *Barthes*'s suicide note: "I have a melancholy life, that finally, I'm bored to death by it."[31] Literally. It is as if art really did achieve the structure of a suicide: as if *that* Photograph really did take Barthes's soul.

As Barthes approximates more closely the palinode throughout his career and finally produces it after his mother's death in *Camera Lucida,* what constitutes the "zero degree" and the recognition of it, its realization, becomes enmeshed in the Orpheus myth. Following Maurice Blanchot and the modernist movement, for whom the Orpheus myth is installing of modernism, a symbol for looking back beyond custom in the attempt to revive an art that had died, Barthes had long been fascinated by the Orpheus myth—by his look back. Blanchot had written that in looking back "Orpheus had done no more than obey the profound necessity of art"; Orpheus chooses inspiration, carelessness, and desire over laws and the familiar and thus, to draw out the title of Blanchot's essay, "Writing begins with Orpheus' gaze"; "everything depends on the decision to look back."[32] In *Writing Degree Zero* Barthes uses the Orpheus myth to capture—both murderous and suicidal—the task of the modern writer who must ignore all the conventions and laws of literature in order to recover a pure language or form from Literature. The writer must recover writing without discourse, the *vouloir* without *savoir.* The modern writer confronts the

"Orphean problematics of modern Form" (67). If "This art has the very structure of suicide," it is because "This language [of the writer: which "is not so much a fund to be drawn as an extreme limit" (16)] is like Orpheus who can save what he loves only by renouncing it, and who, just the same, cannot resist glancing round a little; it is a Literature brought to the gates of the Promised Land: a world without Literature, but one to which writers would nevertheless have to bear witness" (81–82). In order to retrieve, to *reprieve* what they love, writers must cede Literature—but nevertheless use literature to do so. The Orpheus myth appears again in *Roland Barthes by Roland Barthes*, in a fragment titled "Recession," to show that "blind spot" in representing the self—"only in the fashion of Orpheus: without ever turning around, without ever looking" (152–53). The myth reappears in the essay "Literature and Signification," to express the irrevocability of, now, reality: "One could say that literature is Orpheus returning from the underworld; as long as literature walks ahead, aware that it is leading someone, the reality behind it which it is gradually leading out of the untamed—that reality breathes, walks, lives, heads toward the light of a meaning; but once literature turns round to look at what it loves, all that is left is a named meaning, which is a dead meaning."[33] And the Orpheus myth is cited in *A Lover's Discourse*, with Barthes showing some self-consciousness about how much *he* is turning to look back at the Orpheus myth: "I cannot *write myself.*" To use the word "'suffering' expresses no suffering," and hence "Someone would have to teach me that one cannot write without burying 'sincerity' (always the Orpheus myth: not to turn back").[34] But it is above all in *Camera Lucida* that Barthes not only cites the Orpheus myth, in relation to the photographer whose insight ("la voyance" [*La chambre* 80], which Richard Howard, Barthes's translator, renders as "second sight" [*Camera* 47]), consists not in "seeing" but in giving the sense to the photograph of pure accidental presence, the detail (the *punctum*) that will gaze back at Barthes: "above all, imitating Orpheus, he must not turn back to look at what he is leading—what he is giving to me!" (47). Beryl Schlossman glosses this as "the moment when the referent slips away forever. The myth of Orpheus captures this moment in the fateful turn, the moment when Orpheus turns to look at Eurydice."[35] In *Camera Lucida* Barthes *enacts* the Orpheus myth, because he *does* look back, finally, fatally, fails the injunction to look forward, to progress. Orpheus is, of course, a myth about melancholia—about unsuccessful, refused mourning. Orpheus, whose love is "too much" to "endure [his] grief" in Ovid's version of this myth, loses his recently married wife to death. Contravening all the rules of nature and culture, transforming his life into as near death as possible in order to recover her from the dead, he descends to the underworld to plead for her return ("I would have to descend deeper into myself"). His song is so moving that the gods agree—but then Orpheus transgresses their condition not to look back at Eurydice and the outcome is her second, eternal death followed soon by his own: "Eurydice slipped into the depths. Orpheus stretched out his arms, straining to clasp her and be clasped; but the hapless man touched nothing but yielding air, Eurydice dying now a second time."[36] After her death Orpheus himself meets a violent death, ripped apart by women who desire him but whom he cannot love (for Ovid and for some other renderers Orpheus was the first homosexual as well as consummate poet).[37] The price of their reunion is death. But why look back—a question that surely is what fascinates about the myth—if not in order to look upon death itself, or because the love is so extreme it overrides the injunction, can't abide the gods' law? That previous Barthes critics have noted Barthes's use of the Orpheus myth without collating either Barthes's citations of it or each others' suggests, strangely and at odds with Barthes, the injunction not to look back has been heeded.[38] But the palinode says one must look back. In this the Orpheus myth is the *mythos*, the mythic motif we might say, of the palinode.

Who or what is the Eurydice that vanishes in the moment of Barthes's looking, of really looking? In the Orpheus myth she is death. But she is also the object of an extreme love that is a refusal of mourning. Blanchot writes that Orpheus looks round at Eurydice not because he wishes to see her live but because he wishes to see her dead—to love her in the fullness of death, we might say then. For Barthes, Eurydice is equivalent to the zero degree that his art has always quested. Hence he looks back to, invokes and constantly revokes, both myth (Orpheus) and what is in fact a term of temperature measure (the zero degree comes from the Celsius scale) together. Initially, what Barthes means by the *zero degree* is no meaning, or exemption from meaning. But the zero degree comes to acquire its meaning or its object. First, what is zero degree but death, and if art quests zero degree no wonder it has the structure of a suicide. Emptiness, the void. But in *Camera Lucida*, via an expressed extreme love, the zero degree/Eurydice becomes finally incarnated in Barthes's mother after her death. Deferred from the first book to the last ("à l'origine de l'oeuvre, la nostalgie du réel"),[39] the zero degree comes to rest in an extreme love for a dead mother. In *Camera Lucida* Barthes finds that, although it comes closest of all forms of representation, in photography his "body never finds its zero degree, no one can give it to me (perhaps only my mother? For it is not indifference which erases the weight of the image . . . but love, extreme love)" (12). Behind the palinodic retraction of *Camera Lucida,* then, the ultimate referent of the look back that is this book is an extreme—extreme to a degree that has not been seen before (for indeed how can one see "zero"? how to circumscribe the extreme?)—love for Barthes's mother. What is the most extreme love but a love almost outside of love, in the excess, in the "almost"—that begins what we think of as love? Barthes's interest in the Orpheus myth culminates in transgressing the interdiction of what one loves—not to look back in love—and this takes him into the verges of another myth, of generational transgressions: the Oedipus myth.

PALINODIC LOVE

Like Orpheus with Eurydice, Barthes loses his mother twice over. That there are two palinodes in *Camera Lucida* has been suggested by criticism (Sarkonak), but not that their ultimate referent is love for the mother, a love that is itself palinodic, a desire to go back (transgressing narrative rules) in all kinds of ways. The first palinode, in the ode part of *Camera Lucida,* moves Barthes from the *studium* to the *punctum* as the accidental detail that makes its way into the photograph. This is how the *punctum* is originally defined. The photograph "is never distinguished from its referent (from what it represents)" (5); "the referent adheres" (6); "every photograph is somehow co-natural with its referent" (76); "I call the 'photographic referent' not the *optionally* real thing to which an image or a sign refers but the *necessarily* real thing" (76); "it is Reference, which is the founding order of photography" (77). This is one of the most reiterated tenets of *Camera Lucida,* and it puts into retraction ("reacts to") Barthes's previous work on the sign and his emphasis on attending to the codes of photography. Yet while it may be reference that is the *founding* order of photography, the final order of photography becomes the real. The second, far more powerful palinode is the *loss* of this referent, as the *punctum* is recast from detail or object to time. Reflected in the titles of the two chapters from part 1 and part 2 respectively, "*Punctum*: Partial Feature" (chapter 7) and "Time as *Punctum*" (chapter 8), this recasting entails a recognition of the pastness of the referent in the photograph, as Barthes looks back, looks back in an Orphean move, to realize that what the photograph represents is a lost referent. Photography's reference is in the past tense: "I can never deny that *the thing has been there.* There is a superimposition here: of reality and the past" (76). "Ça-a-été," "interfuit" (*La chambre* 120, 121): photography's past is aorist, an ontology that certainly occurred but that is irrevocably over, "the Intractable" (77). Photography itself then becomes not only melancholic but palinodic, for it gives us the thing only to retract or lose it, only to present it as already lost. Photography is marked by "a strictly revulsive movement which reverses the course of the thing" and which Barthes calls "the photographic ecstasy" (119)—madness or love; madness *in* love. It is this pastness of the referent, the repeal of presence, that makes photography so fatal, so inextricably tied to death.

Barthes says that photography's desire is "fantasmatic, driving from a kind of second sight [here is *"voyance"*] which seems to bear me forward to a utopian time, or to carry me back to somewhere in myself: a double movement which Baudelaire celebrates in *Invitation au voyage* and *La Vie intérieure.* . . . it is as if *I were certain* of having been there or of going there" (40). Where is this place one is certain of having been and of going there if not a place from before birth and after death? Barthes immediately connects this certain retrospective and prospective space to the Freudian maternal body, which Freud says is the only place we can be sure we have already been there and to which we retain the desire to return.[40] Barthes writes that there is "nothing Proustian in a photograph" (82), by which he means that photography does not recall the past, cannot return memory: it is not "an aid to memory" but a "counter-memory" then;[41] or even stronger, not an aide-mémoire but a memento mori. Photography "does not take a nostalgic path out of memory" (85). Even for Proust there is nothing really "Proustian" in a photograph. The narrator of *Remembrance of Things Past* does not console himself with a photograph of his grandmother after her death. And at Albertine's death the photograph forms an analogy for, at first, the horrible livedness of her death, its refusal to move from living death to a memory he can mourn. "Things past" are instead sparked famously in Proust's opus by the smell, the scent, the taste of a madeleine with a cup of tea; photography is almost too real for the psychological world of Proustian memory. For Barthes photography is a horrific haunting, the incarnation of the dead, not a carrying across *(metaphor)* to life. "In Photography, the presence of the thing (at a certain past moment) is never metaphoric. . . . if the photograph then becomes horrible, it is because it certifies, so to speak, that the corpse is alive, as *corpse*: it is the living image of the dead" (78–79). This is why photography can become invested with Barthes's melancholy ("the melancholy of Photography itself" [79]). The form itself makes irrevocable loss. Photography instead "has something to do with resurrection"; it is not memory but "reality in a past state"—the presence of death—and hence our astonishment at photography is "religious" (82).

Barthes's palinodic retraction of the *punctum* as pure presence is impelled by his palinodic approach to the Winter Garden Photograph, by finding then losing his mother's presence, and by the palinodic reference that *is* this photograph. Going through photographs of her that November evening, with a light in a dark room, "alone in the apartment where she had died, looking at these pictures of my mother, one by one, under the lamp, gradually moving back in time with her, looking for the truth of the face I had loved" (67), Barthes, in the evocative French, "remonte." Variously translated by Howard into the English as "moving back," "worked back," and "traversing" (71), the verb *remonter*, used in *La chambre claire* in two closely spaced chapters four times (106, 111), is a double movement. It is "to go back" (in time), to "date back," "to descend," "to have again"; but also simultaneously but inversely "to go towards," "to get on one's feet again," "to wind up" (a clock)—or "to set upright" (an oil lamp for instance). *Remontant* is the dynamic of the palinode, of Barthes's approach to the photograph, and of the subject of the photograph. Looking for the image that will return her to him, Barthes moves back in time with his mother, starting with the most recent images taken in the summer before her death. The Winter Garden Photograph shows her as a child of five in a conservatory, a "winter garden." The photograph is not of his mother but his "mother-as-child" (71), or again in the more evocative French, "mère enfant" (*La chambre* 128 and passim). The French elides or coincides the generational differences, slips over the *relative* (metaphoric) conjunction *as*—and puts the mother in the place of the child. The child (Barthes) finding his mother in the child is of course a palin*dromic* dynamic (a reversal in the second set of terms of the order in the first: child; mother; child). But this is not a word game. *Palin-* represents the truth of their final relationship for Barthes, the ultimate reality. "This movement of the Photograph (of the order of photographs) I have experienced in reality" (71). At the end of her life, *their* life, during her illness Barthes nursed her: "she had become my little girl, uniting for me with that essential child she was in her first photograph. . . . I who had not procreated, I had, in her very illness, engendered my mother" (72).

The scene of the photograph is itself caught up in the recursiveness of time and relationship. It is in its representation of closeness a foretelling of a separation that has yet to happen—but that of course has happened by the time Barthes comes upon the photograph. Again these inversions are best in the original. The photograph shows Barthes's mother alongside her slightly older brother: "Le frère et la soeur, unis entre eux, je le savais, par la désunion des parents, qui devaient divorcer peu de temps après, avaient posé côte à côte, seuls" (106). The palindromic juxtapositions, the balancing of this sentence, are startling in Barthes's language. The children are "unis entre eux . . . par la désunion des parents": "*united* by the *disunion* of their parents"—with Barthes's knowledge ("je le savais") separating, yet the copula of, the inverting phrases. The children "avaient posé côte à côte, seuls": "had posed *side by side alone*," again impelled togetherness making them alone, or rather surely their aloneness forcing them together. And finally the double movement of time: the parents "qui devaient divorcer," "who were to"—imperfect indicative but with the sense of something futural about the verb *devoir*—"to be fated," "to be about to," "divorce." The description of the scene of the photograph, packed into this one sentence, is a tight weave of the chiastic inversions (the back and forth and up and down, the proximity and separation) that also describe the relationship of Barthes to his mother in the body of *Camera Lucida*. One final point before we leave the scene of the Winter Garden Photograph, on the idea of the winter garden: what could be more an inversion of time and more unnatural, more against the laws of nature and generation, than a garden (with palms) in winter? It was the house, Barthes writes settling on it to represent his mother's death, where his mother was born.

How we get from *this* photograph to Barthes's relationship with his mother is through *other* photographs that *remontent*. Other readers have recently noted (with the attention to Barthes on photography) the remarkable generational slips that are made in relation to other photographs in *Camera Lucida*. In these they find the absent Winter Garden Photograph, metaphorized or indicated if not deictically revealed. Most notably there is a photograph by Nadar that appears in the midst of note 28 as Barthes describes and discusses the Winter Garden Photograph and makes his move back in time with his mother. This photograph, under which Barthes cites Nadar as "the world's greatest photographer" (68), shows an old woman, grey, probably sick, with dark rings under her eyes, but still striking. It is the photograph that could most be "allegorically in Nadar's beautiful and sensual portrait of a woman with dark eyes and luminous white hair," as Schlossman puts it, Barthes's aging and sick mother absent in the absent Winter Garden Photograph.[42] In the edition of Nadar's works from which Barthes takes the image this photograph is listed as Nadar's *mother*, but it is catalogued in the Bibliothèque Nationale in Paris as Nadar's *wife*. In his caption Barthes keeps open the ambiguity of the photograph, and in so doing, Daniel Grojnowski writes in his research on the provenance of the photograph, expresses the desire of a child, "un désir d'enfant."[43] Barthes's caption reads: "Nadar: The Artist's Mother (or Wife)" (68). If the slip consciously adheres to the confusion surrounding the referent of Nadar's photograph, nevertheless it is crucially significant to the generational slips in the unconscious logic of the narrative of *Camera Lucida*. Like *mère*

*« Quel est, à votre avis,
le plus grand photographe du monde?
— Nadar. »*

"Who do you think is the world's greatest photographer?—Nadar." "Nadar: The Artist's Mother (or Wife)," from Roland Barthes, *Camera Lucida*.

enfant, the parenthesis in Barthes's caption (and Derrida's remarks that Barthes's parentheses do "not enclose an incidental or secondary thought" but rather "[lower] the voice" "out of a sense of modesty" could not be more pertinent—as if the parenthesis marks off the crucial but unspeakable thought), runs the relationship backward to skip a generation—but here not to skip two generations so that his mother becomes his child, the reflection of his reality, but a single generation so that the artist's mother *could be* his wife (the projection of his fantasy?). Family palindromes. Diana Knight believes, compellingly but ultimately falling short of the mood of *Camera Lucida* (for it makes the book seem too contrived, too conscious), that "the Winter Garden photo is simply an invention" and is instead a "transposition of the 'real' photo ('The Stock')."[44] "The Stock," which is the only photograph appearing in *Camera Lucida* to come from the author's private collection, shows an old man with a girl and boy who although slightly younger than the five and eight of Barthes's winter garden subjects nevertheless seem to share their same age differential, and the little girl has the same "brightness of . . . eyes," the same "physical luminosity" (66) Barthes attributes to his mother elsewhere in *Camera Lucida.* "The Stock" appears in a note entitled "Lineage" (103) where *another* generational mistake/uncertainty occurs: "Sometimes I am mistaken, or at least I hesitate: a medallion represents a young woman and her child: surely that is my mother and myself? But no, it is *her* mother and her son (my uncle)" (103). Knight notes "another confusion of generations" (140) in Barthes's comments on a photograph by Van der Zee, again parenthetical: "the sister (or daughter)" (*Camera* 43).

Knight takes these generational slips back to Barthes's homosexuality and her sense that what he sees in the Winter Garden Photograph, and hence in his mother, is acceptance of his homosexuality, "the example of this mother's goodness" (141). I'd insist we take them further back, back to the "love, extreme love," the zero degree of meaning that Barthes suggests only his mother can offer him—did give him. It is love for the mother that is extreme. Obviously this love is extreme in the face of her death. Barthes speaks of resurrection of his mother twice, and clearly his investment is to *remonter* (to raise again but also himself to go towards) his dead mother. His is an insufferable grief: "why is that I am alive *here and now?*" (84). In other words, after the death of my mother how can I still be alive? But *remonter* expresses a desire that was even shaping of their life. He dreams about her (he only dreams about her), but it is never quite her. Instead, "love's dreadful regime" is the "almost" (66): "Le presque" (*La chambre*

104). The almost, a proximity that is too much but not quite enough, a desire for equivalence or conjunction or identity that is held apart by just a gap (the curtains)—a just: might this not also describe an impossible, overwhelming love between generations that, in its most representable but literal form, is named incest? One wants the parenthesis here to express a love that slips through language. Homosexuality is conventionally the unspeakable love, but what's more primordial and unspeakable? Barthes writes that he and his mother had no need for language: "in a sense I never 'spoke' to her, never 'discoursed' in her presence, for her; we supposed, without saying anything of the kind to each other, that the frivolous insignificance of language, the suspension of images, must be the very space of love, its music" (72); and, "she never made a single 'observation'" (69). The suspension of images as the space of love has a double meaning. The images are suspended in their freezing of time and history, but suspended also in the sense of their absence—as in the absence of the Winter Garden Photograph. The last complete piece of writing that Barthes produced, a talk on Stendhal that he was due to give in Milan and that was found lying on his desk after his death (he never gave it), was entitled "On échoue toujours de parler ce qu'on aime": "one always fails in speaking of what one loves."[45] In *A Lover's Discourse,* the book that Barthes wrote just before moving to *Camera Lucida,* in spite of the book's title and its articulacy and the embrace of its articulacy (*A Lover's Discourse* is Barthes's most popular work, the one through which he entered popular discourse), love is also above all inexpressible. In a fragment entitled "Inexpressible Love," which is where the Orphic injunction in *A Lover's Discourse* not to turn back appears, Barthes confronts the impossibility of putting love into language: "On the one hand, this is saying nothing; on the other it is saying too much: impossible to *adjust.* . . . Love has of course a complicity with my language (which maintains it), but it cannot be *lodged* in my writing" (98). And yet at the end of this fragment, to know this loss, to see that the real cannot be lodged, is suspended as absence, is to make writing possible: "to know that writing compensates for nothing, sublimates nothing, that it is precisely *there where you are not*—this is the beginning of writing" (100). Barthes makes the same point a theoretical one in his "Inaugural Lecture" to the Collège de France. In a talk that infamously calls language "quite simply fascist," Barthes writes of the impossible double bind between representation and the real: "literature is categorically realist, in that it never has anything but the real as the object of desire," not because it can realize desire but because it can't: "From our ancient times to the efforts of our avant-garde, literature has been concerned to represent something. What?

I will put it crudely: the real. The real is not representable, and it is because men ceaselessly try to represent it by words that there is a history of literature."[46] As Blanchot writes, it was because Orpheus lost Eurydice that he sang; return, representation issues from loss.

What is the love that is inexpressible, that is not simply representable as unspeakable—for this would be the homosexuality that Barthes "spoke" in coded form elsewhere (in *Roland Barthes by Roland Barthes*, the goddess H.)—but that has no need for language, that ultimately may be this absence of or antecedence to language? Is it not a love that a child has for its mother, not so much a "pre-Oedipal love" (I don't want to psychoanalyze: Barthes insists he has lost not "the mother" but *his* mother [75]; hence the shortfall—or overstep—of Elaine Hoft-March's neatly packaged Oedipal reading), as an exclusive, perfect original love, a love that, if we are fortunate, we are born into and that no other love can replace? Here is where *Camera Lucida is* Proustian. For Proust's narrator, the consuming love for his mother with which *Remembrance of Things Past* begins, so that he must kiss her goodnight at the risk of banishment from her, means that from then on "reality will take shape in the memory alone." No love can give him "that untroubled peace" and that past original love must be the paragon—of his love for Albertine, and even for his grandmother, since Proust transposes his own real dead mother to his fictional dead grandmother.[47] All Proust's remembrance comes from this. Barthes acknowledges mother-love as his connection to Proust since in another late essay, which suggests Proust as his guide for whatever Barthes was going to go on to write—Proust, he says, was "seeking a form which will accommodate suffering (he has just experienced it in an absolute form through his mother's death)"—Barthes writes that "it is at the painful price of this inversion [of the irreplaceable mother's kiss] that Proust's *Search* . . . , night after night, will be written."[48] As Kennedy writes of Barthes's "nothing to say" at his mother's death, "There was nothing to say because there was so much that wanted saying."[49] This is the referent of the palinode.

Barthes lived with his mother, chose to live with his mother all her life, a situation that our culture would conventionally see as requiring "discourse." Gabriel Josipovici, an English academic who lived with *his* mother all *her* life, wrote *his* memoir of his mother and his life with her. The title, *A Life,* refers to the inextricability of their lives, to their singular life. His mother, Sacha Rabinovitch, in one of those odd "coincidences" so pervasive of Barthes's story, made the English translation of the Blanchot essay on Orpheus that got Barthes rolling on the Orpheus myth. We know from *Camera Lucida* (the opening of the palinode) that Barthes was planning "to write a little compilation about her" (63), his mother; and with its use of photographs in the attempt to recover the dead, its recognition of the reversal of roles ("how inevitable") of mother and child at the end of the life as the child feeds his sick, dying mother, and in its writing in a period of evident ongoing grief after his mother's death, it is tempting to see Josipovici's book as a lot like *Camera Lucida* or the kind of book Barthes would have written had he been able to say more, had the book been more explicitly about his mother and less (ostensibly) about photographs.[50] *A Life* is above all an attempt to come to terms with the separation *and* the intrication of a mother's and son's lives. Josipovici is heterosexual. It is for this reason and more besides that I believe that this mother-love, pace Freud, has nothing to do with the gender of the projected sexual object-choice; for all that follows is *inconsequential*. Josipovici considers the Oedipal discourse that might surround their love, even quotes a poem by Sacha (who was a published poet as well as a translator) on the riddle of the Sphinx. He ultimately refutes such discourse:

> Was it my weakness that kept me by her? Had she, in her desire to protect me after what she felt had been the traumatic years of my earliest childhood, made me dangerously dependent on her? Or was the whole Freudian vocabulary and mind-set of devouring mothers and submissive sons a cliché by which the west had been enthralled? [Josipovici's mother is from the East, a Sephardic Jew.] I was certainly the best friend she had ever had, and she, to her surprise, had turned out to be the best friend I could have hoped for. Perhaps our relationship was a miracle which needed to be nurtured rather than denied. (186)

Or as he puts the explanation for their closeness more simply: "we found each other better company than anyone else" (159). Or, in response to the question of whether it was Josipovici's "weakness or my strength that had led to my making my life with her" (214), he quotes the closing lines of Sacha's poem on Oedipus: "Riddles are for asking. / They are better left unsolved" (224). Barthes was also aware of the psychoanalytic "discourse" that surrounded such love. In *Roland Barthes by Roland Barthes* the first autobiographical (author) photograph in the pages of photographs that begin the autobiography shows Barthes as a child in his mother's arms—captioned "The Demand for Love" (8)—already two-thirds the size of his mother (between seven and ten?), conventionally too "grown up" to be making a demand for such proximity, such holding: such *presque*. Yet in *Camera Lucida* Barthes somewhat defensively—rightly defensively—in terms very close to Josipovici refuses any discursive explanation of their proximity that has been dictated to by anthropology and psychoanalysis. "As if our experts cannot conceive there are families 'whose members love one another'" (74). The Winter Garden Photograph requires him to forget two social institutions—"the Family, the Mother" (74). He loves his mother looking back before anthropological and psychoanalytic conventions. He inverts the diagnostic syllogism he has been subjected to in his grief that imputes some blame for his melancholia with his staying too long with her. "It is always maintained that I should suffer more because I have spent my whole life with her; but my suffering proceeds from *who she was;* and it is because she was who she was that I lived with her" (75). Her being is the missed-out origin of his grief and his love, if one needs one.

It's a platitude to read in *Camera Lucida* a love letter or elegy to the dead mother, but what is it as both? What does it mean to proclaim one's love for one's mother—and such a limitless love as this—after she is dead, to a dead living in Barthes's melancholia? The pull of *Camera Lucida* is always from death to love, or love to death, as if Barthes were in love with death—or dead to love. (But what's the difference? Closing his journal "Soirées de Paris" and writing soon after his mother's death, Barthes despairs of finding love with another single other: "knowing it was over, and that more than O. was over: the love of *one* boy" [*Incidents* 73].) Love is soldered to death in *Camera Lucida,* and again one wants the French to convey this. The photograph is affixed to its referent with "la même immoblité amoureuse ou funèbre" (17): the same stillness of love or death. Classical phenomenology before *Camera Lucida* had never spoken of "désir ou deuil" (41), desire or grief; or Barthes kept with him like a treasure "mon désir ou mon chagrin" (42)—my desire or my sorrow. And from speaking of the desire in Mapplethorpe photographs at the end of the ode section of *Camera Lucida,* Barthes moves to immerse himself in his mother's death that begins the palinode section. Love and death, Proust, the great novel that Barthes never wrote—here in *Camera Lucida* are what Barthes writes he sees in photography: "l'amour et la mort" (115). In French (think the trio of the reading of the tarot cards toward the end of Bizet's *Carmen,* in which Carmen's friends are foretold love at the very same time she is prophesied death), the pronounced consonants ("l," "m") and the echoed assonances ("am," "ou"/"or") bring Barthes's repeated two words much closer—inseparable—than our contrasting Anglo-Saxon/Anglo-Norse sounds. As in most palinodes, it is sound, the echoes of the palin*drome,* that comes to put in motion what is most real, that which escapes the sense of language ("discourse") in this form that elides past and present, referent and self—music or sound that expresses the "coincidence"

(*Roland Barthes by Roland Barthes*) that is perhaps ultimately the best way to describe Barthes's relationship with his mother.

Is there a way to say—but in music or in photography—they simply coincided? In "One Always Fails in Speaking of What One Loves" Barthes writes that music as a space *"outside of language"* (*Rustle* 302) expresses love, generating a "kind of aphasia" (303). In *Camera Lucida* he compares the Winter Garden Photograph to "the last music that Schumann wrote before collapsing, that first *Gesang der Frühe* which accords with both my mother's being and my grief at her death; I could not express this accord except by an infinite series of adjectives, which I omit, convinced however that this photograph collected all the possible predicates from which my mother's being was constituted" (70). The "Song of Dawn" that Schumann wrote right before his death, a work of light as the composer was entering *his* darkness, constitutes another palindrome, another temporal contradiction that apparently is what moved Barthes about this piece. In an essay entitled "Loving Schumann" that he wrote the same year as *Camera Lucida*, Barthes, considering what the composer means to him, suggests that to love Schumann is to be out of time, not only in the sense of to contravene the preferences of his moment but also to be archaic, mythic in a way that takes the child back to an indissoluble connection with his mother. Schumann "is truly the musician of solitary intimacy, of the amorous and imprisoned soul that *speaks to itself*. . . in short of the child who has no other link than to the other." "This is a music at once dispersed and unary, continually taking refuge in the luminous shadow of the Mother (the *lied*, copious in Schumann's work, is, I believe, the expression of this maternal unity)." To love Schumann is "to assume a philosophy of Nostalgia, or to adopt a Nietszchean word, of Untimeliness, or again, to risk this time the most Schumannian word there is: of Night. Loving Schumann, doing so in a certain fashion *against* the age . . . can only be a responsible way of loving: it inevitably leads the subject who does so and says so to posit himself in his time according to the injunctions of his desire and not according to those of his sociality. But," Barthes continues and concludes the essay, "that is another story, whose narrative would exceed the limits of music."[51]

Indeed it does. And the desire that exceeds music is taken up in the essay on photography. In photographical palinodes as suggested by Barthes's analogy between *his* photograph and Schumann's last work to express what he at a crucial point cannot, music continues to be evoked as the *contrapunctum*, the counterpoint that puts in motion what exceeds, comes before or after language. But if music picks up what cannot be said in language—is as outside the space of the sign or code expressive of the inexpressible that is love—photography, when it can suspend even the limits of music, when it can freeze into the real the love that lies outside or before sociality, can point to this extreme "narrative." In the Winter Garden Photograph Barthes finds Benjamin's "flash" in history (30), the traumatic, the way to interrupt history that Benjamin suggests *is* history.[52] "I had discovered this photograph by moving back through Time. The Greeks entered into Death backward: what they had before them was their past" (*Camera* 71). The photograph "is a prophecy in reverse: like Cassandra, but eyes fixed on the past" (87). There is a madness in this history: Orpheus trying to retrieve Eurydice— Barthes "taking into my arms what is dead, what is going to die" (117). If history is the barrier that separates him from his mother—death, a generation, the mother as child, the mother as *wife*—what about conjuring a different narrative of history, one that moves not forward but backward, regressively, *palinodically*? "Is History not simply that time when we were not born?" Barthes asks (64). What does it mean to love one's mother so much one sees her, coincidentally, as one's wife? Such a prehistorical, impossible love, history has no name for, and myth names as incest, which is the very foundation of history, of time forward, of progress. Mythically there are different conceptions of history (this different conception of history is what myth is), nonlinear, cyclical, with a reversible quality to its time. Barthes, recognized as our deconstructionist of myth, ends up back in the greatest myth—living out Orpheus and the one that is before history. The recognition is something like Culler's, except I see that what Barthes has at stake in believing in the real of the myth of photography is absolutely exquisite and absolutely true. Only masks (veils, language) enable him to read photography, to talk about "photography" at all. And when the mask dissolves as it does in the Winter Garden Photograph the soul is left. Mary Bittner Wiseman suggests that photography is emblematic of postmodernism and yet returns to the primitive; for to be primitive and postmodern, as in photography, is to be out of time. Photographs for Barthes are like masks for primitives. Magical, photographs manifest the souls of ancestors. Seeking out the primitive in photography Barthes ends *Camera Lucida* by saying we have repressed the profound madness of photography, which is its mythic heritage.

In thinking about the significance of the palinodic organization of *Camera Lucida*, critics have suggested alternative influences on Barthes. Réda Bensmaïa finds in *Roland Barthes by Roland Barthes* a reference to the Kierkegaardian palinode. While she doesn't consider *Camera Lucida,* the insistence on becoming subjective and becoming mystical in the retraction of Kierkegaard's *Concluding Unscientific Postscript* surely continues as an influence in Barthes's final work.[53] Gary Shapiro thinks that Barthes's pal-inode rewrites that of *Phaedrus,* and indeed Barthes ends in a similar place to Socrates in his retraction, in love and (as) madness ("mon désir fou" [*La chambre* 166]).[54] But most significant for our contextualization of Barthes's palinode is a point that Lejeune makes in his elegy for Barthes—an elegy that like Derrida's is written in Barthes's voice ("ton sur ton"; "pastiche"). Lejeune writes that to name Barthes's form simply as "Palinodie" is to re-duce *Camera Lucida* to a Western logic: "la Doxa occidentale.[55] Why should photography be powerful to hold these extreme things after all? Because, *Camera Lucida* ends by telling us, the real for Westerners is now hidden. Death is not *in* modern society—is nowhere except in photography. Since the second half of the nineteenth century, with a crisis in religious belief that coincided with the invention of photography, death (the contact with death) has moved from religion to photography. Today, Barthes writes, we have renounced the mythic in photography, tamed it, dominating the world instead by the sign—especially in the United States, he insists, "where everything is transformed into images" and the sublimation in photogra-phy of the real into masks or signs "completely *de-realizes* the human world of conflicts and desires" (118). In his last chapter Barthes offers a critique of advanced societies and longs for a more naïve, a more primitive relationship to images. Incredibly he calls for an abolition of images and a contact with the real without mediation. The choice in conceiving photography he pres-ents as that between photography as madness (the real), or photography as tamed (the sign): photography's frozen stillness or its mediation; its silence or its narrative movement into language. Barthes chooses madness, silence, stillness. "I passed beyond the unreality of the thing represented, I entered crazily into the spectacle, into the image, taking into my arms what is dead, what is going to die, as Nietzsche did when [as he fell into madness], as Podach tells us, on January 3, 1889, he threw himself in tears on the neck of a beaten horse: gone mad for Pity's sake" (117). Yet in this embrace of death lies compassion: "la Pitié" (*La chambre* 179), a welling up of pathos in recognition of the void (and a very Kierkegaardian term as the object of a spiritual trajectory). Gone mad *for the sake of* pity. And this madness, this revelation of what's behind the curtains, forces Barthes to ask what he calls "the ethical question" of *Camera Lucida* (118), which this essay extraordi-narily poses in relation to photography: What is the status of the real in Western society when we choose to mask death?

By far the most outstanding (notable and incongruent) influence under-lying Barthes's palinode and enlightening of his mystical turn in closing are some works on Buddhism. Cited in the bibliography that appears only in the French version, *La chambre claire,* these constitute the text's intertextual *punctum.* Buddhism pervades Barthes's final works, is also in *Roland Barthes by Roland Barthes* and *A Lover's Discourse.* Barthes's most ostensible Buddhist text is *Empire of Signs,* from 1970. But his recognition of the emptiness of forms that *is* Buddhist reality is intellectual prior to *Camera Lucida* and stops short of the satori, of Zen. Death is strangely absent from *Empire.* This is notable because the Buddhist satori has impermanence, the nonexistence of the self—this is all going to change—at its essence. Photography is used briefly in *Empire* to evoke the emptiness Barthes idealizes in the haiku, that is the "trace," the "faint gash inscribed upon time," the "flash, a slash of light"—and, quoting Shakespeare— *"When the light of sense goes out, but with a flash that has revealed the invisible world."* The haiku is like the photograph one takes very carefully, "but having neglected to load the camera with film."[56] In *Camera Lucida* Barthes loads the film into the camera and works the analogy between photography and the haiku the other way round. Photography is now like the haiku because of its *"intense immobility"* (49). Looking back at photography, Barthes stays with the flash long enough to see that its slash of light reveals the zero degree as death. The lightness and playfulness of *Empire of Signs* contrast with the realization—and it is no longer intellectual but experienced, practiced—of *Camera Lucida.* One of the Buddhist texts that Barthes had been reading in writing *Camera Lucida, The Way of Zen* by Alan Watts, the conduit of Buddhism in the West in the sixties and seventies, emphasizes the centrality to Buddhism of the insight into loss thus: "It is precisely this realization of the *total* elusiveness of the world which lies at the root of Buddhism." Watts argues that forms—or signs—(Barthes's previous "empire") are conjured from the void to mask death. "The life of things is only conventionally separable from their death; in reality the dying is the living." And Buddhism sees that this truth is beyond form and language; Zen has "nothing to say."[57]

Barthes's realization of these central tenets of Buddhism in photography is a brilliant elucidation. In *Camera Lucida* the Lacanian real, the *This,* the *Tuché,* is also a Buddhist one—*tathata.* So that in the sentence following that in which Barthes defines the Lacanian real he performs this equation: "In order to designate reality, Buddhism says *sunya,* the void; but better still: *tathata,* as Alan Watts has it, the fact of being this, of being thus, of being so; *tat* means *that* in Sanskrit and suggests the gesture of the blind pointing" (5). The *punctum* is a satori for Barthes: "This *something* has triggered me, has provoked a tiny shock, a *satori,* the passage of a void" (49), and the definition of satori he gives is the *punctum* all over, "at once the past and the real" (82). The final word of *La chambre claire* (again absent from the English translation, lost taper) goes on the rear cover to that of another Buddhist writer, Chögyam Trungpa. The Tibetan Trungpa, who had just a few years before translated *The Tibetan Book of the Dead*, writes in his introduction there that "*Tathagata* literally means 'thus-gone,' which can be paraphrased as 'he who has become one with the sense of what is.' It is synonymous with *buddha* ('awakened')." With its journey to the underworld in its pilgrimage for the truth of the dead mother in her photograph, and with Barthes's becoming one with the sense of what has thus-gone, *Camera Lucida* is not unlike the Tibetan Book of the Dead, the Bardo Thötröl. *Camera Lucida*, too, like that prayer, is for the living as much as for the dead; singing to the dead "can show us how to live," Trungpa writes.[58] But what Barthes quotes on his rear cover is from another text by Trungpa, in which the lama discusses his lineage teacher Marpa's insight into the loss of his son. "Marpa was very upset when his son was killed, and one of his disciples said, 'You used to tell us that everything is illusion. How about the death of your son? Isn't it illusion?' And Marpa replied, 'True, but my son's death is a super-illusion.'"[59] Death is an illusion perhaps because we cannot grasp its real, because we can only view it like everything through the lens of our sense-perceptions. But the death of the one whom one loves the most is nonetheless real, and it becomes a super-illusion when our irremediable grief embodies their loss: as in a ghost, or even a photograph. As I think Barthes might take up Marpa's insight in relation to photography in the very last lines of *Camera Lucida*: "such are the two ways of the photograph. The choice is mine: to subject its spectacle to the civilized code of perfect illusions, or to confront in it the wakening of intractable reality" (119). Barthes's awakening is that he chooses to see super-illusion. It is a loss that coincides with our gain.

CHAPTER 2

CLAUDE LÉVI-STRAUSS'S
TRISTES PHOTOGRAPHIQUES

THE VIEW FROM AFAR

At the beginning of *Tristes Tropiques,* received to date as his most auto-biographical work, Claude Lévi-Strauss states his antipathy toward photographic texts by anthropologists or travelers. This book or lecture accompanied with slide show, which "enjoys a kind of vogue" at the time of Lévi-Strauss's writing in 1955, often takes the form of the "anthropologist's return" to his career's work "to reveal his precious store of memories."[1] Lévi-Strauss condemns not just the ways in which "actual experience is replaced by stereotypes" and "memories have to be sorted and sifted" (30). He condemns the hypocrisy of the enterprise: "photographs, books, travellers' tales" have taken the place of relics of the exotic that colonizers, those earliest explorers, brought back from their conquest, such as masks or *pau-brasil* ("Brazil-wood") from Brazil and from which Brazil was given its name (30). Both are part of a "quest for power" (32). But whereas the earliest artifacts at least acknowledged their conquest, their contemporary photographic equivalent mourns the cultures that its "monoculture" or "mass civilization" destroys (30). The modern narrative "pretends to itself that it is investing [primitive peoples] with nobility at the very time when it is completing their destruction" (33). When the anthropologist-traveler "brandishes before an eager public albums of coloured photographs, instead of the now vanished native masks," "Perhaps the public imagines that the charms of the savages can be appropriated through the medium of these photographs. Not content with having eliminated savage life, and unaware even of having done so, it feels the need feverishly to appease the nostalgic cannibalism of history with the shadows of those that history has already destroyed" (34). At the end of *Tristes Tropiques* Lévi-Strauss will propose Buddhism as an alternative to this model of knowledge as destruction of the other. As offering an enlightenment into the false divisions between self and other and an idealization of childlike unguardedness, Buddhism is "a return to the maternal breast" (498).

In 1994 some forty years later, Lévi-Strauss produces a book that would seem the embodiment of that repudiated photographic traveler's tale. Written, if not in extremis, then certainly since the anthropologist was already eighty-six in the twilight of his life, *Saudades do Brasil: A Photographic Memoir* collects 180 photographs in which Lévi-Strauss looks back on his travels in Brazil, the place that had begun and remained central to his career. From the 1930s, the photographs capture a way of life in Brazil that was then rapidly passing. This was before the substantial U.S. investment that began during the Second World War, the country still had a physical frontier, and its Indians in the interior were still primitive. Lévi-Strauss would discover "bravos" or savages in 1938 in the form of the Tupi-Kawahib, a group previously thought extinct, and record them on the cusp of abandoning their way of life in the Amazon and adapting (*Tristes* 316). Expensive and beautifully produced, translated from the French and then into English and Portuguese, *Saudades do Brasil* presents as a coffee-table guide for the armchair traveler. Moreover, since *saudades do brasil* in Portuguese means most closely "nostalgia for Brazil," Lévi-Strauss's last published book appears to literalize to the letter that act of nostalgic cannibalism. The turn is recognizably palinodic, and it comes in the form of a photographic memoir.[2]

In fact Lévi-Strauss's previous work had used photography—for the first time and most substantially before *Saudades* in *Tristes Tropiques,* where his criticism of photography in anthropology is made. But what's marked and constant in his oeuvre until the photographic memoir is that he doesn't recognize the distinctness of photography as a form: that is he doesn't see or articulate its ties to the real or even to the referent, and there are certainly no autobiographical photographs, or any revealed autobiographical investment in photography in line with the *punctum* that Barthes identifies in the essence of photography. Instead the photographs are used as code, or *studium,* in a way similar to Barthes's first engagements with photography. Indeed Barthes's distinction between message and code in his essay on photography "The Photographic Message" drew these terms from Lévi-Strauss's *The Raw and the Cooked*.[3] Lévi-Strauss is the key intellectual figure behind Barthes's structuralism, as Barthes's first structuralist analysis, *Mythologies*, derived its impetus from the structural study of myth proposed by Lévi-Strauss in *Structural Anthropology 1*.[4] The crisis of representation in the human sciences in the form of structuralist linguistics, the splitting of the signifier from the referent in which Barthes and Lévi-Strauss played foundational roles in their respective fields, allowed first Barthes via Lévi-Strauss and then Lévi-Strauss to see photography as code. Photographs are treated in Lévi-Strauss's structuralist work in a way consonant with his "ode," the system of structural anthropology that he founded. The crisis of representation allowed Lévi-Strauss to emphasize code and sign at the expense of the referent in his anthropology as much as in photography.

The kind of photographic anthropological narrative that Lévi-Strauss criticizes had been in existence since the middle of the nineteenth century, since anthropology and photography were invented simultaneously and immediately interwoven; for photography had an establishing function in anthropology.[5] Both forms were initially conceived as modes of observing and documenting reality. Anthropologists embraced photography for its apparent capacity for showing its referent unmediated: "for an anthropology deeply rooted in positivism, photography offered a tempting proposition: an objective vision and collection of 'facts,' facilitating systematic organization and analysis, in the service of scientific enquiry."[6] It was the documentary, superficial use of photography in previous anthropology that Lévi-Strauss rejected. His resistance to anthropological photography is consistent with structuralist tenets. He shows a distrust of the powers of the documentary, of the idea of reaching truth from the visible. Technology may one day record all native thought, yet even were it possible, he argues, documenting what is visible would not reveal significance: "The greater our knowledge, the more obscure the overall scheme. . . . it becomes impossible to visualize a system when its representation requires a continuum of more than three or four dimensions."[7] Structural anthropology exchanged the documentation of visible surfaces of cultures for a linguistic analysis of their deep structures, producing something like a cross-section of what is beneath the visible. The adaptation of Saussurean linguistics to conceive of culture as a language resulted in Lévi-Strauss locating meaning not in visible entities but in relations that because unconscious, remain hidden. Structuralism shifts from "*conscious* . . . phenomena to . . . their *unconscious* infrastructure; . . . [from] *terms* as independent entities . . . [to] the *relations* between terms; it introduces the concept of *system*" (*Structural Anthropology* 1:33). In the analysis of the myths of Brazilian Indians, in the first volume of the *Introduction to a Science of Mythology* tetralogy where we see this system best at work (for myths are key signifiers in this language), myths are said to reveal the "underlying structure" of culture (*Raw* 111). It was not enough to document; one must question the status of the referent, uncover the sign in the apparently referential, the connotative in the denotative—and culture therefore in the apparently natural. For Lévi-Strauss, because culture *is* language there is no presignifying, prediscursive, or natural stage. The paintings on the faces of the Brazilian Caduveo Indians, for example, are not mere ornamentation but signs that, like European heraldry, may be read to decode a system of class and rank and the elementary structures of kinship. The primitive or "savage mind" was a "science of the concrete" (*Savage* passim) as complex as the Western technique of structuralism that was therefore needed to decode it. Structural anthropology did not so much jettison the referent as transform it into code. Lévi-Strauss makes this the grounds on which to differentiate structuralism from its dematerializing cousin, formalism. Formalism in focusing on form—in the example of Vladimir Propp's approach to fairy tales—"destroys its object." Structuralism analyzes structure, which "is content itself, apprehended in a logical organization conceived as property of the real."[8]

How "real" can be used to refer to "structure" rather than referent or any other conception of real becomes clear in Lévi-Strauss's comments on photography in his art criticism, which reveal a distaste for the medium, for what Barthes calls its definitive "co-natural[ism] with its referent."[9] Even though he was using *the real* as a noun after Lacan had raised it to a psychoanalytic category, Lévi-Strauss's *real* is emphatically not Lacanian, disruptive of the symbolic, but absolutely consonant with code. Mirroring his own practice in structural anthropology, Lévi-Strauss was drawn to those pictorial artists who he believed encoded realism—such as even a surrealist, Anita Albus. His definition of realism as the artist's interpretation or encoding of the phenomenological object allows him to value the realism of painting over that of photography: "the physical constraints of the camera, the chemical constraints of the sensitive film, the subjects possible, the angle of view, and the lighting, allow the photographer only a very restricted freedom compared with the artist's practically unlimited freedom of eye and hand, as well as the mind."[10] When compared even to painting that is so realistic that it seeks to trick us into believing that the representation is real, trompe l'oeil, the mechanistic, reproductive inadequacy of photography is brought into greater relief:

Photographic realism does not distinguish accidents from the nature
of things. . . . It remains servile to a "thoughtless" vision of the world.
With trompe l'oeil, one does not represent, one reconstructs. . . . Trompe
l'oeil is selective; it does not seek to render everything about the model,
nor just anything. . . . With all its technical sophistication, the photographic camera remains a coarse device compared to the human hand and
brain. . . . As the term *snapshot* suggests, photography seizes the moment
and exhibits it.[11]

Lévi-Strauss thus dismisses the fear that photography will render realistic or
naturalistic painting obsolete, for the media are antitheses. Painting's creativity is associated with life; photography, in its lifeless reproductions, with
death. The only kind of painting Lévi-Strauss disparages in comparison to
photography is that modeled on photographs, the "miserable productions
of neofigurative artists who painted portraits or still lifes, not from life but
from color photographs they slavishly try to copy. Although they are said
to give new life to trompe l'oeil, the opposite is the case" (30).

As Lévi-Strauss's emphasis on the camera as "device" or machine suggests, it is particularly technology that gives photography the flaws he
identifies of lack of discrimination and artistic conceptualization. His
criticism of photography has a cultural association that can be drawn out
through reference to Walter Benjamin's correlation, in his "Short History
of Photography," of the development of photography with the increased
mechanization of the marketplace. Both photography and capitalism,
Benjamin writes, result in "the fragmentation of the aura": the unique
property of things.[12] The reproductive realism of photography is the
representational equivalent, because product, of the monoculturalization
against which Lévi-Strauss directs his entire anthropology and which he
predicts will result in cultural entropy. If photography is in this cultural
conception "the final culmination of a western quest for visibility,"[13] the
West's privileging of vision as a means to mastery of knowledge, Lévi-
Strauss implicitly aligns reconstructive realism with primitive societies,
and representational realism with postindustrial societies. The more tech-
nologically advanced a society, the more likely it is to reproduce an object
exactly as it appears because it can do so, yet in proportion does it risk aesthetic regression: "It has often been the case in the history of art that, as the
technical knowledge and skill increase, the aesthetic quality declines" (*Look*
163). If his ideal in art as in structuralism is "the promotion of an object to
the rank of the sign," primitive art most embodies this ideal.[14] Lévi-Strauss
writes that "preliterate peoples express themselves literally" (*Look* 178), by

which paradox he means not that primitive peoples reproduce realistically but that they create the literal before the technological means of reproduction. He exemplifies this literalism—supernaturalism really, for there is in the creation of the literal in the absence of the apparent capacity to do so something magical—with accounts of rituals that reenact myths and that must conceal their reenactive status, or statues carved in the likeness of dead love-objects. (The lost beloved wife of a chief who is reincarnated in the form of a cedar tree and who accounts for the origins of the beautiful cedars along Canada's Pacific coast resonates with the refusal to accept loss of the Orpheus myth.) The more lifelike the art—the more it can become or iconize the referent in the referent's absence—the more magical, "the more part of a supernatural order" (*Look* 181). "To have their art seen as lifelike was both their privilege and their obligation. . . . the purpose of the illusion created by a work of art was to attest to the ties binding the social to the natural order" (*Look* 184). Modern Western art that rejected realism altogether fell short on the other side of photography for breaking social or worldly ties, for failing the "collective function of the work of art" (Charbonnier 73). While it might seem contradictory given his objection to photographic realism, Lévi-Strauss also criticizes modernist aesthetics for their *"academicism of the signifier"* (Charbonnier 75). This kind of art abandoned the referent. Cubism "missed the object" (*View* 250), and Picasso is singled out as "much more an admirable discourse on pictorial discourse than a discourse about the world" (*Structural Anthropology* 2:277). Self-referential, missing the object, cubism appears in Lévi-Strauss's configuration the artistic correlative of formalism.

Photographs are treated in Lévi-Strauss's oeuvre not as reproductively realistic (referential) but as close as possible to reconstructively realistic; except, unlike primitive art, photographs *do* evidence that the referent has always been there. Photographs retain, indeed are defined by, the quality of technological reproduction of an object now in the past tense. Lévi-Strauss seeks to transubstantiate the referent of the photograph into code as he does with other visible surfaces in his structuralism—to free photography from its mechanical, thoughtless, and accidental limitations: to aesthecize it. When he publishes photographs before *Saudades,* they are interspersed with the drawings and diagrams that proliferate in his anthropology and that are a favored demonstration of his structuralist method. Tellingly, John Berger describes diagrams as the "metaphorical model of Cubism," since both treat "appearances as . . . signs."[15] In his diagrams Lévi-Strauss ends up repeating the "academicism of the signifier" of which he accused cubism; and indeed his photographs are no more referential than his diagrams. In *Tristes Tropiques* where Lévi-Strauss includes both photographs and drawings of the face paintings of the Caduveo, given that the drawings were produced by native informants and by one of the first anthropologists to record the Indians, the drawings may in this case have more authenticating power. Why Lévi-Strauss chooses to include both photographs and drawings especially when they are of the same referent is perplexing, until one realizes that most of what he represents in photographs is already in code. If photographs are evidence, his photographs evidence the referent as code. This criterion for selection informs Lévi-Strauss's use of photographs from first to last, *Tristes Tropiques* to *Saudades*. In *Structural Anthropology* 1, *The Savage Mind, The Naked Man, The Way of Masks,*[16] *The Story of Lynx,*[17] photographs of Indian art, artifacts, places, and people wearing native dress; and in *Look, Listen, Read,* photographs of Western pictorial art—all show the object was already sign—as, for example, in the design of a North American Indian mask.[18] And in all instances the writing coheres the photographs into a discursive, interpretative project. The photographs are subordinated to the text, in service as illustrative of the anthropology, or, in the case of *Look, Listen, Read,* of art criticism; they do not have any revelatory power beyond the text. Lévi-Strauss does not appear interested in the form of photography. If, as historians argue, photography in anthropology is now most useful as an analogue of anthropological history, and particularly and most recently its "raw histories . . . the unprocessed and the painful,"[19] photographs in Lévi-Strauss, his uses of them pre-*Saudades,* are symptomatic of structural anthropology. Photographs as those criticized "snapshots" "seize and exhibit" the oversights of structural anthropology. Lévi-Strauss writes that the "view from afar" is apposite for "expressing what I consider the essence and originality of the anthropological approach" (*View* xi). His photographs show how structural anthropology was able to emerge as a system of knowledge only in the "view from afar."

"Le regard éloigné" (the title of one of Lévi-Strauss's books reflecting on his methodology translated as *The View from Afar*) threatened to elide the referent. In order to see structure as a "property of the real," Lévi-Strauss needed to be far enough away from the referent, and his flattening out of the referentiality of photography into code, diagram, illustration is indicative. When we juxtapose the most famous structuralist diagram of a Bororo village appearing in *Tristes Tropiques* and *Structural Anthropology* 1 with a photograph of the same village not released until *Saudades,* the formulaic abstraction of the former is fleshed out by the two-dimensional actuality of the photograph. The dividing line through the village indicated in the diagram—which is constitutive of Lévi-Strauss's conception of moiety and

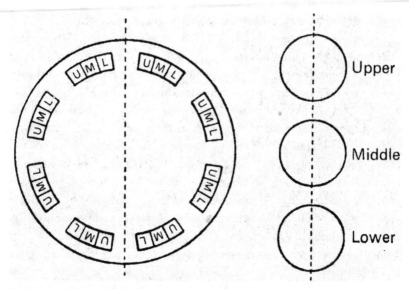

"A diagram illustrating the apparent real structure of the Bororo village." From Claude Lévi-Strauss, *Tristes Tropiques*. Reprinted with permission.

reciprocity and therefore central to the elementary structures of kinship and to structuralism—is "invisible" in the photograph, as he acknowledges in the photographic caption. The photograph returns something of the messy vitality at odds with the pure design of the original. The "unchanging" structure could be perceived only from the anthropologist's "panoramic view," high above the mêlée below. Structure is a property of the real only thence. The charge that Lévi-Strauss overlooked his referent—an overlooking in the sense both of surveying from so far back and of the omission resulting—is thus literalized by the photograph. Pierre Bourdieu highlights the importance of superiority. Lévi-Strauss "takes up a 'point of view' on the action, . . . stands back so as to observe it and, transferring into the object the principle of his relation to the object, conceives of it as a totality intended for cognition alone, in which all interactions are reduced to symbolic exchanges. This point of view is one afforded by high positions in the social structure, from which the social world appears as representation."[20] George Marcus and Michael Fischer write similarly of structural anthropology as "being too distant from the intentionality and experience of social actors."[21] In an essay, "The Scope of Anthropology," a title that like many (*A View from Afar* itself) betrays the essential place of distancing observational metaphors, Lévi-Strauss admits that it is only at a distance, in the laboratory out of the field, that a practice such as face-painting or an object such as a stone axe may be viewed as part of

"Perched on the roof of a cabin like the macaws the Indians bred for their plumage, I took a panoramic view of the unchanging structure of Bororo villages: the men's house in the center and family dwellings, owned by the women, in a circle around it. An invisible line of demarcation cuts across the men's house and divides the village into two halves. A man born in one half must choose a wife from the other half, and vice versa." From Claude Lévi-Strauss, *Saudades do Brasil*. Reprinted with permission.

a system: "it is conceivable that a stone axe could be a sign. In a given context, and for the observer capable of understanding its use . . . even the simplest techniques of any primitive society take on the character of a system that can be analyzed, in terms of a more general system" (*Structural Anthropology* 2:11). The transformation of the real into sign occurs "for the observer capable of understanding its use" and whose observation "has the privilege of being distant" (*Structural Anthropology* 2:28). This distance is emphatically not that of the native, for we should not "confuse the natives' theories about their social organization . . . with the actual functioning of the society" (*Structural Anthropology* 1:130). That would be to get too close up, to look through the microscope that Lévi-Straus rejects in a metaphor as too proximate to its object and hence blurring of difference (*Structural Anthropology* 2:34). The view from close up leads to the *"problem of invariance"* (*Structural Anthropology* 2:24); the metaphor for Lévi-Strauss's view is rather that of a telescope, the view that brings objects close but from afar. Yet it is an irony that "invariance" in the form of the invariants of the savage mind is precisely what the *tele* ("far") view produced. We see at work in Lévi-Strauss, especially when he is at his most structuralist and brilliant, a sometimes excessive reductionism. In his classic statement of structuralist method, "The Structural Study of Myth," he claims that it is possible to reduce "every myth" to a single algebraic formula: "$F_x(a)_y(b) \approx F_x(b):F_{a-1}(y)$" (*Structural Anthropology* 1:228). The mastery of knowledge is total, and it is ineluctable.

Until *Saudades do Brasil*, there are no photographs of Lévi-Strauss himself. And excepting those of face paintings all of the photographs are not taken by the anthropologist but are provided by museums—although *Saudades* is later to unearth a wealth of photographs taken by Lévi-Strauss. The omission of author photographs is true even of *Tristes Tropiques*, the memoir, which was nevertheless considered too autobiographical by some fellow anthropologists when it was published.[22] It was presumably to avert such criticism that *Tristes Tropiques* left out autobiographical photographs in the first place. The concerns about *Tristes Tropiques* as autobiography were expressed before publication of Bronislaw Malinowski's *Diary in the Strict Sense of the Term* in 1967 shocked the anthropological establishment with its revelations of an "I," and not coincidentally with an eye also. For Malinowski revolutionized anthropology through autobiography and photography together. *Participant observation,* the term he introduced into anthropology that has since become a staple, carries in its compound the twin exercises of autobiography and photography. Photographs in Malinowski's anthropology "are used to locate the anthropologist in his field."[23] While his *Diary* doesn't include photographs at all (the success of participant observation has led some critics to believe that the literal figure of the anthropologist-as-photographer was incorporated in the wholly textual figure of the anthropologist-as-participant-observer),[24] Malinowski is conscious there of how anthropology is a function of mediated looking that photography makes manifest: "Photos. Feeling of ownership: It is I who will describe them or create [the Trobriands]"—as if the act of not only taking the photographs but reflecting on it in the autobiography demands that the anthropologist confront anthropology as an exercise, like photography, in taking and creating life.[25] Lévi-Strauss rejected the participant observation of Malinowski in anthropology as too I-dominated (*Structural Anthropology,* vol. 1). In contrast to Malinowski, in *Tristes Tropiques* even those included photographs have an anthropological effect in excess of the personal view sometimes expressed in the memoir. While the body of the text may reveal a personal evaluation inconsistent with objective structural anthropology (for example, of the Tupi-Kawahib chief's primary wife, Kunhatsin, Lévi-Strauss writes in the text that she was—"the native view coinciding with that of the anthropologist—extremely beautiful" [430]), under the photograph of this same woman Lévi-Strauss's caption is now used to elide the personal: "Kunhatsin, Taperhi's chief wife carrying her child" (266). It as if the photograph were not taken by the anthropologist, were not his personal view (although we learn later in the republication of the photograph in *Saudades* that it is and where his personal evaluation is reinstated: "Of his four wives, Kunhatsin was the most beautiful" [194]). Structural anthropology in its methodology depended on a sublimation or elision of self: "the elimination of the subject represents what might be called a methodological need." And here, at the end of the *Introduction to a Science of Mythology* tetralogy in a volume called *The Naked Man,* where he finally reverts from the *nous* form he has used throughout to the *je,* Lévi-Strauss argues that it is only outside the structuralist work proper, in excesses such as prefaces or afterwords that the self can be acknowledged: "If there is a point at which the Self can reappear, it is only after the completion of the work which it excluded throughout."[26] He acknowledges that anthropology "is undoubtedly the only science to use the most intimate kind of subjectivity as a means of objective demonstration" (*Structural Anthropology* 2:15) and that the use of self as a medium to the other makes anthropology at first an autobiographical enterprise: "Every ethnographic career finds its principle in 'confessions' written or untold" (*Structural Anthropology* 2:36). This double paradox, contradiction, or "principle" (*Structural Anthropology* 2:39), as Lévi-Strauss successively calls it, he identifies through Rimbaud's "I is another" (36). This syntax Barthes would use as model in his autobiography, writing of himself in *Roland Barthes by Roland Barthes* in the third person. But Lévi-Strauss suggests that the autobiography or confession must remain untold in ethnography. In order to become anthropology the exercise must disavow autobiography: "To attain acceptance of oneself in others (the goal assigned to human knowledge by the ethnologist), one must first deny the self in oneself" (*Structural Anthropology* 2:36). Even the book intended as Lévi-Strauss's most personal is the story more of the work than of the self; Susan Sontag terms *Tristes Tropiques* an "intellectual autobiography" and—*le revers de la médaille*—Jeffrey Mehlman considers Lévi-Strauss's anthropological other the basis for an intrasubjective voyage.[27] Structural anthropology confused autobiography with biography—to produce *allo*biography: not the story of the self or the story of the other (or the story of the self in open exchange with the other) but the story of the self othered. This paradox or contradiction will become the palinode—as Barthes's initial recognition of a structural paradox in photography becomes his palinode—where, on completion of the methodology, in the photographic memoir, the self returns pictured in relation to the other.

Lévi-Strauss elides not only his self but the technological mediation of anthropology. Structural anthropology, like all anthropologies and photography, is a product of European epistemology at a particular aesthetic and technological moment, modernist and linguistic, or, as some have argued, cybernetic; and structural anthropology does resemble cybernetics's science of perfect control.[28] Myths are a symptom above all of structuralist thought, which was obsessed with mapping relations between textual signifiers and achieving mastery of systems. In a strikingly unreflexive moment in the autobiography during an account of how the Caduveo attempted to compel him to take photographs of them, Lévi-Strauss writes that, while anthropologists are taught that natives are afraid of being photographed and should be economically compensated, "The Caduveo had perfected the system: not only did they insist on being paid before allowing themselves to be photographed; they forced me to photograph them so that I should have to pay. Hardly a day went by but a woman came to me in some extraordinary get-up and obliged me, whether I wanted to or not, to pay her photographic homage, accompanied by a few milreis" (*Tristes* 197–98). Eventually he photographs them with his film unloaded for reasons of expense. Lévi-Strauss reflects not on how his behavior, the presence of his camera, and his anthropology—his technology—might have caused their behavior. Instead he continues anthropologizing even in relating the incident, reflecting that their response "represented the re-emergence, in a transposed form, of certain specific features of Indian society" such as the independence of women, performative behavior, and so on (198). He shows no awareness of his own technique of observation, literalized here by his camera, as mediating. In the "Overture" introduction to *The Raw and the Cooked,* he claims that "it is in the last resort immaterial whether in this book the thought processes of South American Indians take shape through the medium of my thought, or whether mine take place through the medium of theirs" (13)—but the medium surely shapes the message, if indeed it isn't wholly equivalent to it as some critics have braved. Edmund Leach is certainly suspicious of Lévi-Strauss's mastery: "He always seems able to find just what he is looking for."[29] For if pure structures are symptomatic of the primitive mind, they are also a reflection of the structuralist's mind. The structuralist, too, has a savage mind, and indeed in Lévi-Strauss's ideal of the "technique du dépaysement" (*Structural Anthropology* 1:117)—which translates as "homelessness" (1:118, Translator's note 23)—the anthropologist deracinates himself from his culture and seeks to become as primitive as possible in a bid to leave behind his *tekhnē,* his knowledge. Lévi-Strauss practices *dépaysement* in the "chronic rootlessness" of his life in Brazil, sleeping on the ground like the Nambikwara Indians, reduced to eating worm-infested meat and grubs in rotting tree trunks (*Tristes* 459). Becoming the other is the anthropologist's initiation rite into the savage mind he then ordains himself qualified to decode: "Leaving the country, his home, for long periods of time; exposing himself to hunger, sickness and sometimes danger; surrendering his customs, his beliefs, his convictions to a profanation to which he becomes an accomplice when, without mental restriction or ulterior motive, he assumes the forms of life of an alien society. The anthropologist practices integral observation, observation beyond which there is nothing except—and it is indeed a risk—the complete absorption of the observer by the object of his observation" (*Structural Anthropology* 2:15). The assumption of the other through observation has a double meaning in anthropology. The anthropologist can assume knowledge of the savage life because he has assumed (taken on) that life for himself. Yet past and Western self is not wholly absorbed. Lévi-Strauss admits that, especially when he is furthest away from home in the huge alien *sertão* or grassland plateaux of the Mato Grosso in central Brazil, instead of being absorbed by the sights, he hears, tellingly, music from Europe, replaying Chopin and Debussy in his head who "epitomize[d] all I had left behind" (*Tristes* 459).

Music and photography are forms to which time is intrinsic, in the making and experiencing of them. In contrast, in painting time seems almost superfluous, mostly forgotten. Music and photography need time in order to exist. Music and photography carry time's extremes or excesses, its movement and losses; they present us with all that has been left behind, either in the conventional sense of bringing back memories or in the Barthesian sense of *not* bringing back memory. Music, like photography, keeps time to the continual and irrevocable ebb of existence. But in Lévi-Strauss music and photography are, initially, peculiarly timeless forms. Music and myths are "machines for the obliteration of time," he writes (*Raw* 16). And his photographs, too, freeze history and perpetuate the presence of the past rather than acknowledging its loss, in the manner of the photographs criticized by anthropology's historians that manifest "anthropology's atemporal discourse," "presenting a timeless vision."[30] In treating photographs as diagrammatic codes, Lévi-Strauss removes the interaction between self and native from history, and in this his captions, the elision of narrative, are key. It is elimination of historicity that enables Lévi-Strauss to anthropologize, to freeze the real into structure. His captions to his photographs of Brazilian Indians in *Tristes Tropiques* insist on ongoing cultural representativity: "The siesta" (261); "The native method of carrying a baby" (261); "A Nambikwara smile" (262). The article generalizes as it atemporalizes. The native is still doing this, outside of time, has always done it—and yet is already part of the archive, like the artifacts (such as the photographs) that Lévi-Strauss brought back from Brazil. The captioning is consistent with Barthes's analysis in "The Photographic Message" where he wrote of captions: "Formerly, the image illustrated the text (made it clearer); today, the text loads the image, burdening it with a culture, a moral, an imagination."[31] The text is overwhelming in Lévi-Strauss, transforming the realness of photography into code—the raw into the cooked; "for anthropology, photography meant the *necessity* of caption."[32] Stasis in Lévi-Strauss is symptomatically structuralist. His predecessors' documentation of the surface differences of cultures often arranged those differences into an evolutionist narrative in which the primitive was our antecedent in a Darwinian line. Lévi-Strauss opposed narrative organization in anthropology, criticizing what he called "the archaic illusion"[33] or "pseudo-archaism" (*Structural Anthropology* 1:112). In the "Time Regained" chapter of *The Savage Mind*—for he saw structuralism as a Proustian recovery of time for the savage—he criticizes Western civilization's projection of its own origins onto primitive cultures as *"robinsonnades"* (264). Compounded of the romances *Robinson Crusoe* and *The Swiss Family Robinson,* this neologism meant a nostalgic construction of the other. Lévi-Strauss insisted on the simultaneity of the savage mind, and thus structuralism incorporates diachrony into synchrony and event into structure. Stasis was in part methodological for structuralism: "Evolutionism precludes any synthesis" (*Savage* 233). But methodology was also ethical, since Lévi-Strauss sought to bring the preliterate primitive into the linguistic present tense. Yet it backfired. Johannes Fabian singles out structuralism as the most complex contribution to the manipulation of time in his book subtitled *"How Anthropology Makes Its Object."* Structuralism preempts the problem of different times by "packing chronological Time into a spatial matrix."[34] Lévi-Strauss may not assign primitive cultures to archaic times in an evolutionary narrative, but the stasis he devises "to circumvent or preempt coevalness" works "to sustain the new, vast, anonymous, but terribly effective regimen of absentee colonialism" (69). It "calls for a native society that would, ideally at least, hold still like a *tableau vivant*" (67). Structuralism shows not the presence of the past inevitably lost as in a photograph, then, but treats the living scene as if it were already a photograph: the *tableau vivant* holds the natives suspended in what has been called an eternal, "ethnographic present" (Fabian 33).

There is an irony to Fabian's charge of "allochronism" (32) against Lévi-Strauss, though, and that is that Lévi-Strauss was among the first to make it against his predecessors, most famously in "Race and History," where he shows how time is a function of racism. In omitting this and other justifications Lévi-Strauss added to the practice of his structuralist theory, Fabian subjects Lévi-Strauss's structuralism to a similar kind of *tableau vivant.* In "Race and History" Lévi-Strauss shows how "false evolutionism" (*Structural Anthropology* 2:330 and passim) positions the primitive as recessive in a line of development culminating in the observer. Racism "often goes so far as to deprive the stranger of this last shred of reality by making him a 'ghost'" (*Structural Anthropology* 2:329). The ghost, as Derrida says, is "the dead other alive in me . . . a relationship of haunting which is perhaps constitutive of all logics"—and it is so of structuralism.[35] Lévi-Strauss sought to make the ghost live, to bring those who were conceived by his predecessors as dead or dying—"the primitives"—to life. Structuralism is a result of an anxiety about the narrative of progress. But the metaphors and analogies he innovates—spatial instead of temporal, structural instead of narrative—do not evade the problems of history, technology, or observer position of his predecessors. Rather his representation shows the inevitability of the previous frame of representation. Proposing that distinctions between primitive mythic/ahistorical peoples and progressive Western cultures might be rendered as those between "cold" and "hot" societies (*Structural Anthropology* 2:29; *Savage* 233), Lévi-Strauss thereby replaces the temporal metaphor with one drawn from energy. Or, from the discourses of surrealist art and science: primitive societies operate like the "bricoleur," recycling materials that are to hand and working "by means of signs"; the West, working in teleological fashion and "by means of concepts," operates like the engineer (*Savage* 20). And most famous, from the technology of travel: the histories of cultures may be analogized to the course of trains. If the other culture-train is travelling in the same direction as our own, it will appear to be progressing; if travelling differently, to be regressing. And it is only if we are travelling identically that we will be able to "see the faces of the passengers, count them, etc."—to read the culture (*Structural Anthropology* 2:341). While each pair is generated from an attempt to transcend the frame of his predecessors (narrative sequence, technology, and superiority of observer position), each borrows its metaphorical terms from the postindustrial cultures Lévi-Strauss was seeking to demote or at least stabilize in relation to the primitive. Like the too finely tuned cybernetic machine—say the thermostat of a central heating system in which the off and on temperature switches are so closely set that the boiler switches itself off at the very point when it comes on (for how to inhabit the "zero" degree?)—the attempt at perfect control is the system's own undoing.[36] The anthropologist ended up using the means of representation, the technology, that was the product of progress—and that he rejected in his predecessors' photography.

The image of the ghost, or more often of the shadow, encapsulates Lévi-Strauss's agonistic struggle with the frames of representation, and it haunts his writings. Like the ghost, the shadow is a revenant in relation to life: necessarily following and insubstantial.

> One deprives oneself of all means of understanding magical thought if
> one tries to reduce it to a moment or a stage in technical and scientific

evolution. Like a shadow moving ahead of its owner it is in a sense complete in itself, and as finished and coherent in its immateriality as the substantial being which it preceded. Magical thought is not to be regarded as a beginning, a rudiment, a sketch, a part of the whole which has not yet materialized. It forms a well-articulated system. (*Savage* 13)

The shadow that is finished and coherent in its immateriality; the shadow that *pre*cedes the substantial being from which it *pro*ceeded; the shadow that is not a sketch but a part of what is to follow: the oscillations of time, observer position and referentiality are dizzying. In the autobiography the paradox of anthropological representation—of how to capture an elusive, primitive past within contemporary thought, of how to put the real into his technology—is described in similar imagery of the shadow that flits beyond and before the solidity of his knowledge.

> For every five years I move back in time, I am able to save a custom, gain a ceremony or share in another belief. But I know the texts too well not to realize that, by going back over a century, I am not at the same time forgoing data and lines of inquiry which would offer intellectual enrichment. And so I am caught within a circle from which there is no escape. . . . I have only two possibilities: either I can be like some traveller of the olden days, who was faced with a stupendous spectacle . . . or I can be a modern traveller, chasing after the vestiges of a vanished reality . . . able to glimpse no more than the shadows of the past. (*Tristes* 36)

If the anthropologist "does not journey between the lands of the savages and the civilized [but] returns from among the dead," the question is how to make present, to represent the dead.[37] With his myths and music and his desire to recover lost time, Lévi-Strauss, too, is another Orpheus, as has been recognized.[38] For like Barthes, Lévi-Strauss conceives the choice between the madness of entering into the spectacle, or tameness, representation and code. The real or knowledge. Structuralism sought to avoid photographic texts that aimed "to appease the nostalgic cannibalism of history with the shadows of those that history has already destroyed"; for one cannot use a machine to record a ghost. Or can one?

THE NAKED MAN

The most startling photograph in *Saudades* shows Lévi-Strauss bathing amid the Nambikwara. The anthropologist is naked and uncovering his young white body for view. He looks vulnerable, self-exposed. This photograph must have been taken by someone else, or more likely on a self-timing mechanism by Lévi-Strauss himself, like the one labeled "Self-portrait" that appears on the rear jacket of *Saudades*. The natives in contrast have their back to the camera. They are not really the subject of the photograph, what the photographer or we look at. It is only the toddler's head, so precariously positioned, that covers Lévi-Strauss's total nakedness. The photograph reverses the conventions of anthropological looking. The *punctum* in *Saudades do Brasil,* the photograph encapsulates how this book is the *punctum* in the anthropological *studium* that is Lévi-Strauss's work.

There is much that is new and different in the photographic memoir. The self-exposure. *Saudades* is subjective, a self-declared memoir, the confession untold until this point—not even in the unsubtitled *Tristes Tropiques*. The prologue acknowledges the autobiographical investment: "Let it then be taken for what it is: a testimonial . . . to Brazil and its people more than half a century ago, to whom—as well as to my distant youth—I address a friendly and nostalgic salute" (23). The memoir is referential, revealing

From Claude Lévi-Strauss, *Saudades do Brasil.* Reprinted with permission.

the real place that had made his career, Brazil, his autobiographical investment in it, and making this place and his investment intrinsic to his photography. It was Brazil that made him a photographer. He was "not one until Brazil" and now "I no longer have the interest" (21). (The only other book of photographs Lévi-Strauss published is *Saudades de São Paulo,* a version of this book but focused wholly on São Paulo—and published only in Brazil.)[39] Even *Tristes Tropiques* had interwoven Lévi-Strauss's sojourns in India and Pakistan, retroactively since, taking place in 1950, they were not part of the origins of structuralist theory in Brazil between 1935 and 1939 that make up the entire material of this photographic memoir. In the return photography is embraced to reverse his previous use. Whereas in the oeuvre photographs are subordinated to the text, in *Saudades* the photographs outweigh the text that, after a prologue, is confined to captions and minimal intervening sections. Photography was rejected generically, at least in his art criticism, for its referential realism; Lévi-Strauss's criterion for a successful photograph of his own is reproductive precision. "I think that was our main criterion for a successful negative, for we never ceased to marvel how such a small format, when enlarged, could produce very precise details" (22). More startling in the memoir is the revelation that his father's profession was that of the painter who took photographs on which to base his subsequent portraits—"to guide him in the placement of their principal features" (21): precisely the kind of painting Lévi-Strauss had disparaged for taking the life out of trompe l'oeil. If we accept that the portrait painter was the one victim of photography, as Benjamin writes, we can understand Lévi-Strauss's previously expressed distaste for photography. Lévi-Strauss traces the legacy of the photographic art from nineteenth-century painters to his father, and then from his father to himself. Lévi-Strauss learned photography from his father, a family art. In Brazil, where his parents joined him in 1935, Lévi-Strauss *père et fils* seek out realism side by side, competitive reproduction: "Father and son competed to see who could obtain the sharpest images" (22). It is passed down the patriline. Claude's son Matthieu Lévi-Strauss made the prints for the book; his "decisions were critical" in the selection of the images and he should therefore be considered its "coauthor" (23).

The naked man image as with Bororo village is among 163 of the 180 photographs appearing in *Saudades* that were not previously published, but even those photographs previously published return an excess to the ode. They are "better reproduced, and often displayed differently" from before (9), made possible by new technology. And in the case of the seventeen of the twenty photographs appearing in *Tristes Tropiques* that are republished in *Saudades*, they are all enlarged in a way that undoes the cropping that we can now see was performed on the original. Enlargement, as Benjamin has argued, "does not simply render more precise what was, albeit indistinctly, visible 'anyway': it reveals entirely new structural forms of the subject matter"—or in excess of code/structure, we might say.[40] Subjects are no longer squarely positioned in the frames as they were; the photographs appear more accidental, more untamed. A Mundé woman balancing her child, for example, is now shown off-center, so we no longer necessarily look at the *studium* that Lévi-Strauss would previously have had us see (the eyebrows of the child waxed in preparation for plucking pointed out in the caption in *Tristes Tropiques*) but perhaps the *mato grosso*, the "vast scrub" out of focus and now an irreducible presence behind her (*Tristes* 263; *Saudades* 174). Or, now that it is enlarged, we can see that the odd rectangular object being carried in a Nambikwara Indian basket, catching the sun like a mirror (or sardine can), is a possession of the anthropologist: a fuel can that Lévi-Strauss acknowledges had become part of the Indians' personal possessions (*Tristes* 259; *Saudades* 156). In *Tristes Tropiques*, Lévi-Strauss had criticized the way in which the anthropologist glosses over his approach so as not to spoil our view of the primitives with his presence and that of Western technology, as happens in the photographic memoirs. But "the existence of the latter can be decoded by a practiced eye from small details in the illustrations, since the photographer has not always been able to avoid including the rusty petrol-cans in which this virgin people does its cooking" (31). Enlarging the mediating details in *Saudades* and pointing them out in the caption unlike in *Tristes Tropiques*, Lévi-Strauss turns the inadvertent, mechanical quality of photography and his own mediating presence in his photographs into the subjects of their second publication.

Most interesting, though, are the photographs that were omitted— because they were—and they interweave the eye and the I, the view with autobiographical desire. Many evidence the complex network of looking. In a photograph of a Bororo village ceremony, although the *studium* of the caption points to the villagers watching the spectacle—"At dusk, one part of the population sat down to watch the dance spectacle offered by the other part" (98)—in fact what catches our eye in the photograph are the figures in the foreground who are manifestly not watching the spectacle but watching the anthropologist—watching them. Their consciousness of his observation surely heightened by the presence of his camera, they are refusing wholly to comply with the activity under observation. Other photographs in *Saudades* draw attention to the imbalance and pain of anthropological observation. In *Tristes Tropiques*, Lévi-Strauss had written

"At dusk, one part of the population sat down to watch the dance spectacle offered by the other part." From Claude Lévi-Strauss, *Saudades do Brasil.* Reprinted with permission.

of an eye disease that had broken out among the Nambikwara during his observation of them, causing a very painful temporary blindness that could become permanent. The disease carries to the anthropologist's group, and the first to catch it is his wife, who is evacuated. New photographs in *Saudades* highlight the difference between an I that can be outside of the frame and the natives whose function is to be observed, to remain present. Devastating scenes show women and children lying on the dry earth, their hands raised to their eyes in pain. Lévi-Strauss writes ingenuously, "We witnessed some distressing scenes" (128), and we consider the status of this witnessing. Malek Alloula has written of how, when Western photographers encountered women of Algeria with their veils in the nineteenth century, the screen produced a kind of eye disease in the Western observer, "the symbolic equivalent of blindness: a leukoma, a white speck on the eye of the photographer and on his viewfinder."[41] Photography in the form of semi-pornographic postcards then resorted to stripping the women. Lévi-Strauss's Nambikwara women are already naked, and *they* have the eye disease. But here in returning to the images in his memoir,

Lévi-Strauss articulates his relation to that pain, not in abstraction from it. *Photographs* now makes visible the penetrating I of the anthropologist in his penetrating eye.

The photographs reveal the anthropologist's look as eroticizing, shaping with his desire. Many of the photographs are of naked young women and girls. Indeed, it's startling to realize how many of the photographs in *Saudades* are of naked women and girls; this degree of exposure had certainly not appeared before. The images have an unguarded, insouciant eroticism to them. Like Sally Mann's snapshots of her children, they make the viewer feel as if it were he and not the subject who projects sexual desire. Through his subjects the photographer-anthropologist is himself exposed, shown off guard. In the case of a photograph of a girl's breasts in which most of her head and torso are chopped off, the shot confronts us not so much with her (she's not a subject) but with him, because of what he is so unmistakably looking at. There is nothing of the anthropological *studium* in these close-ups of naked young women and girls, and the instantaneous, aleatory feel of the photographs wears down the edge of anthropological representativity. The significance is not so much that Lévi-Strauss took this photograph—accidents of course do happen in photography; what's significant is that Lévi-Strauss *publishes* the photograph, the exposure—of himself through the other—now the revelation. The photographic proximity to his subjects undermines his theory's insistence that he viewed from afar. In the autobiographical text, the possibility of a gap between the anthropologist's desire and the natives' culture had been suggested. Of the Nambikwara he had written: "During the amorous fondling in which couples indulge so freely and in public, and which is often quite uninhibited, I never once noticed an incipient erection. The pleasure aimed at would seem to relate less to physical satisfaction than to love-play and demonstrations of affection" (*Tristes* 344). But, he goes on, "It was difficult, for instance, to remain indifferent to the sight of one or more pretty girls sprawling naked in the sand and laughing mockingly as they wriggled at my feet. When I was bathing in the river, I was often embarrassed by a concerted attack on the part of half-a-dozen or so females—young or old—whose one idea was to appropriate my soap" (345). What did being *not indifferent* entail if not *being different*? This is not the ideal of the indifference of the structural anthropologist. Is it possible that Lévi-Strauss was made conscious of his difference—and embarrassed—by his own incipient erection?

So why produce a photographic memoir, why reveal such investment of self now? The turn, while it is implicit rather than acknowledged, is palinodic. For this is a form that Lévi-Strauss recognized—increasingly.

". . . most often merry . . ." From Claude Lévi-Strauss, *Saudades do Brasil*. Reprinted with permission.

Lévi-Strauss was fascinated by and was repeatedly drawn to write on others' palinodes and to ponder the reasons for returns; this helps us elucidate his reasons for his own return. He suggests a motivation for self-criticism that Durkheim the sociologist performs: "Properly speaking, Durkheim has not changed his attitude toward ethnography. The discipline he had criticized was not that one; at least it was not the same as the ethnography to which he was to rally" (*Structural Anthropology* 2:46). Publishing his photographic memoir in 1994, Lévi-Strauss had certainly seen changes not only in anthropology but also in the conception of photography. They had both moved from their documentary origins to the more linguistic emphases of the mid-twentieth century, when Lévi-Strauss, Barthes, and others were establishing structuralism; the linguistic turn that Lévi-Strauss innovated possibly sustained a suspicion toward photography in anthropology. Finally, photography and anthropology have come to rest in a more ethnographic and cultural point—they are autobiographical and descriptive again. In visual anthropology moreover, Lévi-Strauss saw the coming together of these changes to produce a new interdiscipline, literally a scope of anthropology. Visual anthropology has been described as "a turn from the linguistic to the pictorial, from the abstract to the embodied, from the collective to the individual, from the elaboration of general theory to the sensual evocation of the particular"; and if this is so it represents a recent turn away from Lévi-Strauss.[42] Proposed in the 1960s by John Collier, who came from the tradition of documentary photography which is to be explored in the next chapter, visual anthropology was initially documentary: "The memory of film . . . insures complete notation," Collier wrote.[43] But the most recent writings on visual anthropology argue that visuals should be used to develop a more self-conscious, a more self-reflexive anthropology. For Jay Ruby, the visual allows anthropology to address, literally, the "crisis of representation" that anthropology encountered in the form of first structuralism and then poststructuralism.[44] If we must ask how we look at anthropological subjects at the same time as we attend to the look (mediation) and its source (we), autobiographical visual anthropology proves an ideal hybrid medium for reflexivity, as two instances of self-reflexive anthropology that include photographs show: Nancy Scheper-Hughes's *Death without Weeping: The Violence of Everyday Life in Brazil,* and Marjorie Shostak's *Nisa: The Life and Words of a !Kung Woman* (by a photographer who became an anthropologist)—and Shostak's recent deathbed palinode to this, *Return to Nisa.*[45] Lévi-Strauss's palinode is certainly more in line with these disciplinary developments.

But, on revisions by the composer Rameau and the painter Poussin, he suggests another reason for return. He writes that the latter's return "may have resulted from the unconscious workings of his mind" (*Look* 21). Probably Lévi-Strauss's return is something of a middle way between these alternatives: that reflexive inclusion is made possible by a discipline is not, of course, divorced from the unconscious. He quotes, appropriately, the surrealist André Breton (who made the unconscious his discipline) responding to a critical pointing out by himself of a contradiction between Breton's works in an exchange of letters while the two writers were on board ship. Breton replies to Lévi-Strauss's rather pedantic observation: "Yes, naturally my positions have varied considerably since the first manifesto. One should understand that in such programmatic texts, which do not tolerate the expression of any doubt or reservation, and whose essentially aggressive character excludes all nuance, my thought tends to take on an extremely brutal, that is simplistic character, foreign to its real nature" (*Look* 148). Such doubt in the systematic Lévi-Strauss himself suggests as reason for his own self-reflexive returns; for Lévi-Strauss, like Barthes, was always engaged in a project of return. *The View from Afar* contains reflections on the earlier *Structural Anthropology* 1 and 2, and these are the most reflexive of his works (and he mentions he would have called *The View from Afar* "Structural Anthropology 3" if that didn't give the impression that he merely repeated himself [*View* xi]). "This 'anthropological doubt' does not only consist of knowing that one knows nothing, but of resolutely exposing what one thought one knew—and one's very ignorance—to buffetings and denials directed at one's most cherished ideas and habits by other ideas and habits best able to rebut them" (*Structural Anthropology* 2:26). The doubt of the anthropologist identified by Lévi-Strauss makes him analogous to Lejeune's autodidactic scholar who, in his method of palinodic revision, proceeds through a project of self-correction.[46] And it is with doubt embodied in photography that Lévi-Strauss actually begins *Saudades.*

TRISTES TROPIQUES

In fact, Lévi-Strauss states that he now views photography not as referential but as the real, as failing to recover the referent. The precision that he sought as he took the photographs is no longer their significance in publishing them. The naïve realism he had imputed to and rejected in photography is exchanged for Lacanian—or Barthesian—realism. He opens his prologue contrasting the capacity of his notebooks to bring back the reality of his memories with photography's failure to do this. Significantly, the notebooks return the past anyway not through writing (which is presented as not a means for recording memory in the famous writing lesson of *Tristes Tropiques*), not through their sight but through their smell. This smell, after a Proustian fashion, recalls things past; in *Tristes Tropiques* Lévi-Strauss had written evocatively of Brazil as an "olfactory intoxication," a mixture of "freshly cut tropical red pepper," the "black, honeyed coils" of a Brazilian homemade cigarette, among prime "fruity fragrances" (77–78). In *Saudades* he immediately replaces the smell of the notebooks, which alone have the power to bring back memories, with photographs that do not. There is "nothing Proustian about a photograph" (Barthes, *Camera* 82) for Lévi-Strauss either—

> When I barely open my notebooks, I still smell the creosote with which, before setting off on an expedition, I used to saturate my canteens to protect them from termites and mildew. Almost undetectable after more than half a century, this trace instantly brings back to me the savannas and forests of Central Brazil, inseparably bound with other smells—human, animal, and vegetable—as well as with sounds and colors. For as faint as it is now, this odor—which for me is a perfume—is the thing itself, still a real part of what I have experienced.

Is it because too many years have elapsed (the same number of years for both, though) that photography does not bring any of that back to me? My negatives are not a miraculously preserved, tangible part of my experiences that once engaged all my senses, my physical strength, my brain; they are merely their indices—indices of people, of landscapes, and of events that I am still aware of having seen and known, but after such a long time I no longer always remember where or when. These photographic documents prove to me they did exist, but they do not evoke them for me or bring them materially back to life.

Upon re-examination, the photographs leave me with the impression of a void, a lack of something the lens is inherently unable to capture. I realize the paradox of offering them again to the public, in greater number, better reproduced, and often displayed differently from what was possible within the format of *Tristes Tropiques,* as if I thought that, in contrast with my own case, the pictures could offer something substantial to readers who have never been there and who therefore must content themselves with this silent imagery, especially since, if they went to see it for themselves, this world would be unrecognizable and would in many respects have simply vanished. (9–10)

The paradox lies in producing a photographic memoir once he has recognized the failure of photographs to bring back memory—and beginning the memoir acknowledging this. The photographs are referents, for their evidence of the past is undeniable, as the use of the word *document* suggests: "these photographic documents prove to me they did exist." Yet the referents/memories have cut loose from the signs—so that they are "indices"—signs of lost referents. The Peircean term, *index,* instead of Saussurean *sign* or *code* (these two more common in Lévi-Strauss), suggests the loosening as more traumatic, since for Peirce *index* carries causal connection between referent and sign; Peirce's most frequently cited example is that *smoke* is an index of *fire.* The severing of index and referent is less arbitrary, then, less normalized, than in Saussurean signification. And this loss is not an incidental conception of photography. Rather Lévi-Strauss identifies loss as intrinsic to the camera. Upon his reexamination, upon his return, the photographs leave him with "the impression of a void, a lack of something the lens is *inherently* unable to capture." This inherent inability to capture—or the inherent ability to capture lack, void—is what defines the photographic relation for him now. The thing was there but is gone. *Ça a été; interfuit:* this is a Barthesian conception of photography (*Camera* 120, 121). Returning to photography after Barthes's loss, Lévi-Strauss grasps photography as a form that makes irrevocable the loss of the past. There is no evidence that Lévi-Strauss had read *Camera Lucida,* but since they moved in the same circles and this was the last and most personal work by Barthes it would seem unlikely that he hadn't. After borrowing "code" from Lévi-Strauss, Barthes had made very different kinds of connections between anthropology and photography: mythic, magical. In *Camera Lucida* he describes photography as "an anthropologically new object" because it "divides the history of the world" (88) and shows a world before culture. In looking at a photograph, he writes, "I am a primitive, a child— or a maniac; I dismiss all knowledge, all culture" (51). He writes similarly in *The Grain of the Voice* of photography as "a new iconic phenomenon entirely, anthropologically new," and that before the photograph, "I place myself in the situation of the naïve man, outside culture, someone untutored who would be constantly astonished at photography."[47] Photography locates Barthes in the place of the primitive, which is the native as well as the child. Lévi-Strauss is moved by the same astonishment, though it may be more of the primitive as native—as confronted with the supernatural art that can finally incarnate the ghost—than as child. Annette Lavers suggests that it was the negative reception that Barthes received from admired antecedents such as Lévi-Strauss that made Barthes turn at the end of his life from theory into trying to represent an unspeakable love for his mother, that drove Barthes back, therefore, to the myth that for Lévi-Strauss is foundational of all cultures.[48] If this is so, Lévi-Strauss receives back the gift of his student's work, finding himself in Barthes's same underworld: mythical, precultural, pre-encoded—and photographic.

The referent is gone in the first, most obvious sense because Lévi-Strauss can't correlate it in his memory to the sign. After a lapse of sixty years, he can no longer make contact with his memories through his photographs. This contrasts with the opening of *Tristes Tropiques* that establishes connection between self and experience. Written in 1955 and also retrospective, *Tristes Tropiques* looks back to the same time twenty years before; but here Lévi-Strauss writes that this lapse, "twenty years of forgetfulness were required before I could establish communion with my earlier experience" (37). A sublimation of autobiography into an account of structural analysis and a history of Brazil, *Tristes Tropiques* finds its generic unity in the travelogue. In this the other is remembered in the context, and as trophies, of the travels of the self. Travel, as we know from Lévi-Strauss's train metaphor, sees the place/culture as inextricable from time and the viewer's observation: "Travel is usually thought of as a displacement in space. This is an inadequate conception. A journey occurs simultaneously in place, in time and in the social hierarchy" (*Tristes* 86). Others are accordingly *retro-jected* (projection but backwards) into the past from the perspective of the present writing self. In this travelogue Lévi-Strauss follows the tradition of the anthropologist's traveler's tale he began by trying to avoid. Writing back, the *autos* is redeemed in the other's integral, better past to restore something missing in his own present. The recovery of past for present is nostalgic, and *Tristes Tropiques* has been identified as seminal for this most pervasive affect in anthropology. Derrida describes "an ethic of nostalgia for origins, an ethic of archaic and natural innocence" in the book, and Renato Rosaldo condemns its nostalgia as "imperial" and a way to "make racial domination innocent and pure."[49] Writing in 1950s New York after his arrival there in 1941, Lévi-Strauss sees prewar South America as offering the promise of the past lost from the postwar North. Critical of the mass communications and technology he believes are despoiling nature, he presents the Second World War as the catalyst of this monoculturalization and loss of diversity; but the war more intimately spelled the near loss of his own life. Brazil propelled him redemptively into his structural studies. Leaving Vichy France in 1941—as a Jew, "potential fodder for the concentration camp," escaping just in time (*Tristes* 12)—Lévi-Strauss ends up in New York after being refused a renewal of visa for Brazil (for bureaucratic but inexcusable reasons), where instead of living Brazil he writes it, in his first three books, the last of these *Tristes Tropiques*. Brazil comes to be cathected as a way to purify his own terrible time that had brought to an end many parallel lives—including Benjamin's. Brazil is recovered in *Tristes Tropiques* as Eden, which James Clifford identifies as "the ultimate referent" of all nostalgia.[50] On his arrival at his port of entry into Brazil, Santos, just south of the Tropic—"Crossing the Tropic" (92)—Lévi-Strauss remembers the land as "emerging on the first day of creation" (94). The landscape is subject to immobilizing; "the sense of time did not exist in the world I was now entering" (320). His anthropological research is described as going back to find wholeness: "To be the first white man, perhaps, to set foot in a still intact Tupi village would be to bridge the gap of four hundred years" (405). "I had wanted to reach the extreme limits of the savage" (402), he writes, and he finds in the Nambikwara, with their nakedness, their sleeping on the bare earth, and their open lovemaking, the "most primitive" nomads to be found anywhere in the world (327): "The Nambikwara had taken me back to the Stone Age and the Tupi-Kawahib to the sixteenth century; here [coming back from Amazonia] I felt I was in the eighteenth century. . . . I had crossed a continent. But the rapidly approaching end of my journey was being brought home to me in the first place by this ascent through the layers of time" (452–53). The depth of investment of his present self comes through in the language Lévi-Strauss uses to reflect on his anthropological researches. These are not "sequels to colonialism" but "an enterprise renewing the Renaissance and atoning for it" (*Structural Anthropology* 2:32); the modern anthropologist's "very existence is incomprehensible except as an attempt at redemption; he is the symbol of atonement" (*Tristes* 475). The repetition of *atonement*, in French, "expiation"—and with *La fête des expiations*/Day of Atonement as the most religious in the Jewish year—resonates given the burdens of Jewish survivorhood that possibly accompanied Lévi-Strauss, the grandson of a rabbi, from Europe. In describing anthropology as a "collaboration" with colonialism (*Tristes* 31)—or perhaps most pointedly himself as the "one to have brought back nothing but a handful of their [primitives'] ashes" (34) ("des cendres")—Lévi-Strauss bares the life of a French Jew who escaped the Vichy collaborating government and created his discipline out of the irreversible ashes of the Holocaust.[51] No wonder systematically the desire to freeze time, to subject the event to the eternal stillness of structure.

The notion of South America and particularly Brazil before U.S. investment and industrial development as restoring the lost past of the North shapes structural anthropology's conception of the continents. The tropics are *tristes* because they are rapidly passing; the title of *Tristes Tropiques*'s first British edition was *A World on the Wane*. In "The Lost World" chapter of *Tristes Tropiques*, Lévi-Strauss moves the history of American settlement back from the then assumed 5000 BCE to 20,000 BCE, and he does so by moving it south, to Brazil—and thus unifies the continents. With his relocation of the origins of American history in Indian Brazil, "The pre-Columbian history of America, like those Japanese flowers made of compressed paper which open out when immersed in water, has suddenly acquired the volume it lacked" (305). The image is straight from Proust: lost time recovered.[52] Written, then, by "an Americanist" (both in disciplinary and geographical affiliation) located in the North (*Structural Anthropology* 2:30), this nostalgic organization between North and South America pervades Lévi-Strauss's anthropology, particularly *Introduction to a Science of Mythology*. In the key transitional volume of the tetralogy that crosses the hemispheric divide, *The Origin of Table Manners*,[53] and in the final volume where North American myths are made to recapitulate those of South America in the first two volumes, *The Naked Man*, South America appears symmetrical to but inverting the North. Thus the loon woman myth of North America's Indians transforms the bird-nester of the Amazonians; the salt in the North is the refrain—but in reverse—of the function of sweet honey in the South. Lévi-Strauss thinks transcontinentally, so that, in places "separated from each other by millions of kilometers, speaking different languages," "there is only one myth" (*Naked* 56, 563). The equator is a temporal mirror. "The Double Inverted Canon" in *The Raw and the Cooked* presents South and North in their respective myths, plausibly because of astronomy, as "form[ing] a chiasmus" (239). In his autobiographical investment in Brazil Lévi-Strauss pursues a desire to inhabit this volumed-out lost past, paradise regained. As he writes of himself in the third person and of the moment of America's discovery: "He would have wanted to live then; indeed, he does so every day in his thoughts. And because, very remarkably, the Indians of Brazil (where I took my first steps in our science) could have adopted as a motto, 'I will maintain,' it happens that their study takes on a double quality: that of a journey to a distant land, and that—more mysterious still—of an exploration of the past" (*Structural Anthropology* 2:30–31).

In contrast, the transgeneric form of *Saudades* as a photographic memoir, photography in autobiography, severs past from present and does not reestablish connection. After a lapse three times that length, Lévi-Strauss can no longer make contact with his memories through his photographs. The captions evidence the I of the memoirist looking back and failing to join with the photographs taken by the eye of the young anthropologist. The photographs were taken in 1934–1939; the text—the captions and the prose interludes—returns to them after a full sixty-year gap (and what a gap). The captions now don't work the images into Lévi-Strauss's broken narrative of lost time. His captions begin in the past tense, with his arrival and acculturation in São Paulo in 1935 (a city which, "still a frontier town, was visibly turning into a financial metropolis" [*Saudades* 26]). As he journeys into the interior, where in photographs of *caboclo* (mixed Indian-Portuguese) farmers colonial "traditional life persisted" (49), and to the Indians and particularly the Nambikwara, though he shifts into the present tense, the subjects appear in the context of his past: "I knew the Nambikwara in the dry season, during a nomadic existence. At such times they live under flimsy shelters made of palm fronds stuck into the sandy soil" (118). Then at this nostalgic origin, Eden, he falls into ellipses that lose the verb tense and indeed the verb. Ellipses pervade the captions in *Saudades*. "Dreamy when the mood struck them . . ." (143); ". . . most often merry . . ." (144); ". . . mocking, provocative . . ." (145): the captions allow the photographs to float free of the anthropologist's project of cultural coding and explaining—and recalling. "The Nambikwara group on the move," in *Tristes Tropiques* (256), becomes, in *Saudades,* "I prevailed upon the Nambikwara to lead me to the site of their winter village. . . . We followed them on horseback" (156). "A Nambikwara smile" (*Tristes* 262) is now instead ". . . mocking, provocative . . ." (*Saudades* 145): all ellipses in original. The syntax of past and present cannot be crossed without omissions, without the syntax breaking down and forgetting, some loss. This elliptical, fragmented narrative is more lyrical (more musical) and suggests the loss of narrative. Clifford explains that nostalgia occurs as the excess when anthropology brings preliterate cultures into writing: "The other is lost, in disintegrating time and space, but saved in the text."[54] In the photographic memoir, in the failure of writing and the recovery of loss as loss, the photographs comprise the ellipses. Black and white, the photographs are imbued with loss. Of course, Lévi-Strauss could only have taken black-and-white photographs given that color was not introduced until 1942, but then the images are held back to be published in the 1990s and so clearly severed from their moment. In our age, color photography is so caught up with tourism it is possibly its principal reason, for the camera has made everyone a tourist, as Sontag writes.[55] Color photography is therefore a cause of the monoculturalization that Lévi-Strauss opposes. Like other contemporary collections, its black-and-white aesthetic appears a resistance to this middle-brow, popularized—domesticated—practice.[56] The stark black-and-white work, for example, of Brazilian photographer Sebastião Salgado in his portrait of his homeland in *Terra* or of the effects of globalization on the world's people in *Migrations,* is at an angle to the photographer-tourist driven by the desire to capture and consume on polychromatic film the others who offer him redemption from his increasingly monochromatic surroundings.[57] Barthes on color in an anthropological film: "colouring the world is always a means of denying it".[58] Lévi-Strauss in *Tristes Tropiques* had condemned brandishing albums of specifically *"colored"* photographs.

The fragmented form to capture loss is like a broken narrative of music, and is echoed in music. In the title of *Saudades do Brasil,* Lévi-Strauss borrows from a composition by Darius Milhaud (also a French-born Jew who fled France for America during the occupation and began his career in Brazil). Particularly in *his Saudades do Brasil,* which keeps disharmonious the African rhythms of Brazilian jazz, sambas and the melodies of Portuguese folk music, Milhaud opposed the systematization and classical mastery of his predecessors.[59] In the one written reference he made to Milhaud before his own *Saudades,* Lévi-Strauss had criticized some fugues Milhaud had composed around 1920 (the date of Milhaud's *Saudades*) as works that fail when they "try to step over the world and the manner of its representation" (*Look* 166). Lévi-Strauss in his musical tastes liked the baroque Rameau, in whose wrought harmonies and chords he had seen a forerunner of his own structuralism. Such music is a model because of its synchronization and encoding, and because it is exceptional in having no presymbolic, no natural referent. Music finds its material wholly in culture: "There are no musical sounds in nature, except in a purely accidental and unstable way; there are only noises," Lévi-Strauss claims, absurdly (*Raw* 19). In *The Raw and the Cooked,* where music is used most fully as Lévi-Strauss tries to write like music, myths and music are said to be "free from those representational links that keep painting in a state of subjection to the world" (22). His earlier conception of music was one that didn't acknowledge loss of the referent. Returning to name his photographs after the previously repudiated composer's desire and failure to join representation and world, Lévi-Strauss now lays claims as guiding to that fugacity. The fugue, literally "flight," is interwoven with loss. The polytonal fugue in its refrain constantly remembers and lets go, recalls and passes on, a melody in successive instruments or voices. In psychiatry, *fugue,* a kind of madness, describes loss of identity, occurring as a reaction to trauma (sometimes involving literal wandering from home). The idealized *dépaysement,* or "homelessness," results, then, not in indifference, but in *saudades*—which can also mean "home*sickness.*" Now, like Barthes comparing the Winter Garden Photograph to Schumann's last work (and the last works that Schumann composed as he went mad at the Endenich asylum were, with an exquisite coincidence, fugues), Lévi-Strauss returns to photographs as fugal images. The fugue captures the insanity of photography that is at once named after music and yet claimed "a silent imagery."

What is the death or loss, the *saudades,* that *Saudades* would speak, the silence it would imagize? *Saudades* is in the plural, and there are layers to Lévi-Strauss's retrospection that fail to integrate image into written text, photography into autobiography, and ultimately to redeem self through other. Most manifestly, the *saudades* is for the Indians. The book testifies to their world that has vanished dramatically since the taking of the photographs. For Lévi-Strauss the photographs do not recall their referents not simply because his *memory* is failing, but more importantly because the referents of the photographs really have gone; if we went to see their subjects for ourselves "this world would be unrecognizable and would in many respects have simply vanished." And hence the appropriateness of photography to evidence how the loss of referent became real. Lévi-Strauss's returns are generated from *real* loss. With each return, the photographic referent has receded and has thus become more exigent to show in photography, this form of "melancholy objects."[60] Lévi-Strauss returns to the photographs as if he can't get over the loss—traumatic repetition, not mourning. When Lévi-Strauss first took the photographs in the 1930s, he encountered Indians who had already survived four centuries of colonial decimation and displacement. The Indian population was just 4 percent of what it was in 1500 when the Europeans arrived. In the eighteenth and nineteenth centuries, the *bandeirantes,* or "pioneers," and gold prospectors perpetuated the colonial genocide. Publishing the images for the first time in the 1950s in *Tristes Tropiques,* Lévi-Strauss comments on epidemics and government policies regarding reservations that have continued the loss even in the twentieth century. And when he returns to the images again in 1994, he envisions new threats and further loss: "Before our eyes, a new cataclysm is dispossessing the Indians of this way of life" (16)—a new cataclysm namely in the form of globalization, made up of "giant agricultural conglomerates" (10), the "development of communications and the population explosion" (16), and the plundering of natural resources by the timber and fishing industries, real estate developers—and "organized tourism" (17). Beneath a photograph of a Karaja Indian making a toy for the tourist industry, Lévi-Strauss writes that tourism has expanded the native art but spoiled it, technological advance in proportion to aesthetic—and human—decline. "How can my old photographs fail to create in me a feeling of emptiness and sorrow? They make me acutely aware that this second deprivation will be final this time, given the contrast between a past I still had the joy of knowing and a present of which I receive heartbreaking accounts . . . ." (16). The gap between past and present has widened, the loss of the past now defining the present he would have us see—unclosable, irredeemable. Lévi-Strauss would have us see in his photographs not primitives, Edenic savages, but "wreckage" of earlier civilizations, what one colonial account cited in his prologue describes as "veritable cities . . . each city spread over several leagues along the banks of the river and comprised of hundred of houses of a dazzling whiteness. . . . A very dense population . . . fortifications adorned with monumental sculptures and the fortresses built on the heights. Well-maintained roads, planted with fruit trees, crossed cultivated fields" (11). The reason for Lévi-Strauss showing these photographs is not because he believes they will offer something present or integral to his readers. Quite the opposite. They will offer us loss of this substance. Here photography is embraced for its association with death—Barthes's "literal death"; for it is death, Barthes writes, that makes photography anthropologically new, the rites of death having transferred from religion to photography: "*Life/Death*: the paradigm is reduced to a simple click, the one separating the initial pose from the final print" (*Camera* 92). The loss is nowhere more shocking, more apocalyptic, than in the images of the Nambikwara who, naked and sleeping on the ground and with their eye disease, appear the embodiment of absolute human indigence.

> In those who, among the Indians, strike us as being most destitute, we must therefore see not examples of archaic ways of life that have been miraculously preserved for millennia but the last escapees from that cataclysm that discovery and subsequent invasions have been for their ancestors. Imagine, keeping everything in proportion, scattered groups of survivors after an atomic holocaust on a planetary scale, or a collision with a meteorite such as the one that, they say, caused the extinction of the dinosaurs. (*Saudades* 15–16)

The enjoinder to keep this holocaust in proportion can only be self-conscious and deliberately contrary, given the effect of the photographs (and the analogies) is to blow up the proportion.

Into the Indian loss Lévi-Strauss weaves not only his autobiographical loss, the *saudades* for Brazil and his own lost youth. In the loss Lévi-Strauss would have us see ourselves. Speaking "No longer as an anthropologist, but as a member of my civilization, I feel this dispossession profoundly" (19)—returning to the self after the methodology, Lévi-Strauss makes us the subject and would have us enter into the spectacle. Before the photographs, particularly of the Nambikwara, that most primitive of nomads, Lévi-Strauss would have us see our own losses. He writes that he could show pictures of contemporary Paris, Tokyo, New York in order to match the devastation of his past photographs of the Indians.

> As for progress, it is devouring itself. More and more, the advances of science and technology, including medical breakthroughs . . . have as their principal objective, often used as a pretext, the correction of harmful consequences of previous innovations. And when that end is achieved, further ill-fated consequences will result, for which it will be necessary to devise other inventions as a remedy. Dispossessed of our culture, stripped of values that we cherished—the purity of water and air, the charms of nature, the diversity of animals and plants—we are all Indians henceforth, making of ourselves what we made of them. (18–19)

We, our civilization, are the subject of loss. Now, at the turn of the century with globalization defining, it is we who are *tristes, our* world on the wane. And here, Lévi-Strauss produces a palinodic reversal of time. It is our civilization that has brought about the loss of theirs: our drive for progress has effected their regression, their loss. But now they, in the form of Lévi-Strauss's photographs from the '30s of a vanished world, bode our future. Brazil is no longer the North's past but our possible future. And new to Lévi-Strauss is a recognition in *Saudades* of the Indians as not simply elegiac but adapting to technology. The way of life in the photographs is almost gone, but, on the quincentenary in 1992 of the "discovery" of America, the Nambikwara travel as representatives of Brazil's Amerindians to Mexico City. "They went back home delighted by their trip and bringing with them transistors, which they said were cheaper than those available in Vilhena . . . where the shops are full of Japanese products" (10). In museums across the Americas, Indians place next to traditional masks a mask of Mickey Mouse. Even "the Amazon forest is not as 'primeval' as people liked to think," Lévi-Strauss admits here (13). At the mouth of the Amazon, evidence is being uncovered of multiple man-made flood defenses to protect cultivated fields covering 50,000 square kilometers and to maintain a population numbering seven or eight million—proof that there never was an Eden and the suggestion that this was the possible birthplace of technology in America. Photography's role in this temporal paradox is perfect. It brings apocalypse. New aerial photographs are being used to sell off and destroy more land, to forge unimaginable roads (the Trans-Amazonian highway) into the rainforest in order to encourage more prospectors—loss "caused by the development of communications" (16). But it is the same aerial photography (invented, by the way, by Nadar) that is helping to recover the prehistory of the Amazon. Lévi-Strauss's photographs from 1935 show "a prophecy in reverse—like Cassandra but with eyes fixed upon on the past" (Barthes, *Camera* 87). In evidencing the apocalypse that happened between this prehistory and the present, photography becomes a way, in Lévi-Strauss's photographs, to avert our own future apocalypse.

And this, then, is the reason for publication of these photographs now. Not nostalgic cannibalism of the other—for Lévi-Strauss can now show the true complexity of primal cultures *and* their loss: photograph ghosts— but consumption of ourselves and of the world resources (globalization, the form that world civilization takes, Lévi-Strauss describes as "a body without flesh" [*Structural Anthropology* 2:358]). The photographs urge our awakening to loss. For *saudades* is not equivalent to the backward-looking restorative and mournful nostalgia. It's significant that Portuguese has another word for nostalgia, *a nostalgia,* which *is* nostalgic mourning over a personal or a national loss—*as saudades da pátria, ou de casa, ou da família,* "mourning for country, home or family." The yearning in *saudades* is unqualified, immeasurable: foundational. *Saudades* is, as Lévi-Strauss says of the French *tristes* in his *Tristes Tropiques,* an untranslatable word (*Tristes* xix). *Saudades* acknowledges and sustains loss. Why the retraction of hated photographic memoirs in the past in *Tristes Tropiques,* then? Ultimately for ourselves. For our future.

CHAPTER 3

GORDON PARKS'S TAKING A LIFE

CHOICE OF WEAPON

If the unconscious of the anthropologist is revealed through photography, the photographer is also something of an anthropologist. Photography is in its origins a work of anthropological documentation, of curiosity about the world. Nadar was a documenter of Paris and its people, and Barthes writes that great photographers like Nadar, or August Sander in his photographs of Weimar Germany at the beginning of the twentieth century, are like mythologists because they give the face a mask, which for Barthes means they give the referent a signified—for "the mask is the meaning."[1] These photographers turn the photograph into a project of social and historical encoding. Works of photographic social documentation, instances of documentary photography then, treat photography as cultural record. From *documentum,* the medieval term for an official paper, "'document' means 'evidence,'" and documentary photography makes the photographic referent proof of a meaning.[2] This is why photography is intricated in the service of anthropology, for anthropology too reads from evidence code. Documentary photography emerged as a named genre as a kind of visual anthropology in which it cultivated an anthropological style. John Collier's term for photography as "visual anthropology" grew out of his training in the early 1940s with Roy Stryker.[3] Stryker was the head of the Farm Security Administration (FSA), where he had the effect of making photography *the* medium for social documentation. The FSA embraced photography as a chronicling of reality and canonized documentary photography as a mode of witnessing. Reflecting on the remit of the photographic project, Stryker suggests photography as a compilation of social facts. "I wanted to do a pictorial encyclopedia of American agriculture."[4] The FSA was premised on the belief that photography was the best form for that encyclopedic record, more transparent than any other medium, and that the photographer in the field could work as comprehensive recorder. Stryker often loaded his photographers up with "shooting scripts," which not only directed them to certain subjects but gave information about the profile, economic, political, and social context of their photographic subject.[5] Stryker believed that photographers should research a story thoroughly before shooting. The photographers, he said, "must be something of sociologists, economists, historians."[6] This total immersion was intended to subordinate the photographer as controlling auteur, to make invisible the photographer's subjectivity.

Recording life as it is, documentary photography appears to be a take on life, photography at its most realistic. Yet the aim of these photographs was not to record reality but to change it. Documentary photography was intrinsically political, its mythology national. The agricultural aid and resettlement unit of F. D. Roosevelt's New Deal program, the FSA was set up to combat the Depression specifically in the rural United States. It was directly sponsored by the U.S. government. Its brief was to support the Democratic president's New Deal, to justify his program of reforms and projects that sought to alleviate the plight of the U.S. poor. As Lawrence Levine has written of the documentary era, "Photography was not merely a mechanism for depicting these changes, it was simultaneously their product and their agent, their creation and their creator." As offering the rationale for and producing rather than transcribing social change, documentary photography romanticized and idealized certain subjects. What got to count as real in Roosevelt's New Deal United States was politically overdetermined. People were selected as representative, in this case of Depression America, and the entire documentary tradition, both photographic and literary, is bound up with mythologizing the masses. U.S. writers and artists documented this side of the United States because they "preferred the struggling poor to the genteel affluent: the former were more 'real.'"[7] Documentary photography did not portray victims then; it created them. The photographs have a point of view, that of myth-making, and this nonneutrality is what makes a good documentary photograph. The successful documentary photograph convinces us of its vision. Propaganda works by direct appeal to the viewer, and by seeking to effect this documentary photographs were not unmediated. The documentary was not such at all: "Many people would now acknowledge that a work of social documentary, whether or not they agree with its message, is, or originally was, propaganda."[8] The point of the photographs was to propagate in the viewer approval for the New Deal in support of the U.S. government. There is a paradox of time here. In order to justify social change, documentary photography had to present in a rosy, nostalgic light the very conditions it suggested as outdated and in need of change. It had to present a harrowing experience, but not in so alienating a glare that the viewer immediately turned away. Documentary photographs had to convince us that the suffering were worthy of redemption, that there was nobility even in abjection. In this documentary photography bears comparison to the contradictions of photography in salvage anthropology condemned by Lévi-Strauss as consuming the people the combination of forms sought to preserve. The missionary role, the zeal of documentary photographs is also undeniable.

In this moment of the 1930s also lies the nationalization of the genre of documentary photography. Roosevelt was himself something of an inveterate documenter, relying on factual reports for all his political changes. The notion of documentary traditions and above all photography as the best means for bringing about change to U.S. reality (U.S.-)Americanized documentary photography. The form enabled ideals the nation had about itself. Recent work has begun to unpick the ideologies and constructions that lie behind documentary photography.[9] Dorothea Lange's "Migrant Mother," one of the most famous documentary photographs and the archetype not only for this moment but perhaps of a turning-point in American modernity, worked because of its apparent unmediatedness, because the viewer is supposed to have an immediate and compassionate political response to the distressed-looking mother and her three filthy, reticent children. But the revealed context of Lange's taking the photograph compromises documentary photography's claims to attest to the real on several fronts. It shows Lange's construction of and distance from her subject. Lange selected this image of the family because it fit the social subject (poor U.S. farmworker in need of aid or resettlement, migrant mother without father) that she was being directed to see by the FSA. She chose the most devastating shot from her roll of film and left unpublished many others that showed the family smiling, more relaxed, and considerably less harried. And Lange's comments on taking the photograph, that she just happened on her subject and did not ask her name or any information about the family, undermine the anthropological ideal of Stryker's informed sociology and reveal the photographer as opportunist. More than any this photograph made Lange's career. The photograph tells a story, but it may be more of the life of the photographer and less of her subject's. The photographer controls the subject as image, and the purported real in the photograph may consist in the photographer's autobiography. One of the most problematic aspects of documentary photography is that by definition it occults the photographer's (autobiographic) investment in her subject, as opposed to the pictorial tradition in which the point of the photograph is the photographer's conceit. As Clive Scott has written, documentary photography is voyeuristic, "breaking down responsibilities connected with the *continuity* of experience and *one's own visibility;* the camera, one comes to believe, conceals the photographer." In this documentary photography "dramatizes our problematic relationship with photography generally," by keeping out of the picture the location of viewers in relation to subjects.[10]

Gordon Parks is the key documentary photographer of African American lives. Parks followed other, more famous FSA photographers, such as Lange and Walker Evans, in travelling the United States and documenting the American oppressed, but Parks's main concern is African Americans. Parks has photographed crucial moments in the history of African American life in the second half of the twentieth century, including the rise of the civil rights movement and the Black Muslim movement. He has also photographed the quotidian details of ordinary African American lives, what he calls "moments without proper names."[11] His signature photograph, entitled "American Gothic" (1942), shows an African American woman, "Mrs. Ella Watson, Government Charwoman," in front of a huge U.S. flag in the federal government offices she cleaned. In the juxtaposition of this thin woman, holding her bathetic mop and broom, and the grandeur of the Stars and Stripes, Parks evokes in a small human document, with irony, the place of African Americans in the U.S. institution. Parks's documentary skills had been honed by his training starting out as a photographer with Roy Stryker and the Farm Security Administration in the early 1940s. He then worked for the Office of War Information, which was what the FSA became after the Second World War broke out and, as is obvious from its name, was the war's propaganda unit. During this time Parks produced a photographic project, *Midway: Portrait of a Daytona Beach Neighborhood,* which is perhaps his most anthropological. Like the anthropologist, Parks with his camera provided a meticulous record of all aspects of a Florida community, an encyclopedia of this time African American life.[12] He also innovated and made his own the technique in which he would focus a series on one person or a small group of people to tell, in a kind of biography, a broader story of humanity. His series in 1948 of Red Jackson, a Harlem gang leader, or of the Fontenelle family in Harlem in 1968, both first published in *Life* magazine, are exemplary and as such were landmarks in documentary photography.[13] Parks was the first African American photographer at *Life*, where he worked for over twenty years. It was at this magazine that his documentary photography really came to fruition. *Life* was the institution that inherited the documentary tradition in photography and conveyed it to the larger public in the form of photojournalism—the telling of a current-events story in photographs. Famous documentary photographers had contributed to *Life* before Parks, such as Margaret Bourke-White and Lange. Parks was inspired to become a photographer when he found a photojournalistic magazine while working as a waiter on a Pullman train and saw photographs of dispossessed migrant workers in the Dust Bowl and California. Lange's and Evans's are among the images, and while Parks doesn't mention its name, given that it led both in publishing FSA photographs and in the U.S. photojournalistic market in the 1930s, more than likely the magazine was *Life*. Parks's project of representation and representativity has extended to other media. He is known as a filmmaker and directed the seminal and popular blaxploitation film *Shaft* in 1971, an attempt, he has said, to give blacks a positive role model. He also wrote and made a film of *The Learning Tree*, his previously written autobiographical novel.[14] Parks's style across his oeuvre is consistently documentary. Michael Torosian has termed his crisp, clear prose "telegraphic," its short, punchy sentences serving to communicate in minimal form a powerful message apparently culled from reality.[15] It is not insignificant that Parks's greatest writerly influence—and the work to spur him to write—was Richard Wright, with his *Twelve Million Black Voices*. A collection of documentary photographs of African Americans made in 1941, this greatest of mid-twentieth-century African American realist writers used the FSA files.[16]

Parks's photographic witnessing of African Americans is enabled by his conscious use of his identity as an African American; he is an observer who is nevertheless participant. Photography is significant for African Americans because, as bell hooks writes, "For black folks, the camera provided a means to document a reality that could, if necessary, be packed, stored, moved from place to place. It was a documentation that could be shared, passed around" and that thereby "offered a way to contain memories, to overcome loss, to keep history."[17] Portable, migrational even to the most uninhabitable of communities, yet allowing a record or testimony of those conditions to be made, the camera for African Americans was a "choice of weapons" against poverty and bigotry, to use one of Parks's own descriptions.[18] With Parks's work the camera passes from the anthropologist to the native—or rather the native becomes a self-reflexive and political anthropologist, documents his own life to record and challenge adversity. Parks's oeuvre repeatedly seems to stem from his proximity to and involvement with—identification with—his subjects. He was able to photograph intimately, because he was actually with, the family of Malcolm X the night the activist was assassinated. He photographed—while sharing a hotel room with him—Muhammad Ali on the night he became heavyweight boxing champion of the world. He was invited by Eldridge Cleaver to join the Black Panthers as "Minister of Information" on the strength of his photographs, though he refused because of his commitment to "objectivity" in documentary photography.[19] Nicholas Natanson argues that Parks's work represents the most sustained engagement with African American subjects in documentary photography. Parks was exceptional in the documentary tradition in his intimate photographs of African American subjects because, "consistently able to gain his subjects' cooperation for close-in, low-angle shooting, [he] achieved a considerable degree of immediacy." But in line with the FSA's "photographic 'constructing'" of reality, Parks "fell short of a full documentary encounter with urban conflict and change," precisely because of the national mythologies in which documentary photography was enmeshed and in whose tradition Parks followed: "these shortcomings reflected a long-standing weakness in FSA documentation of the deepest class and race divisions in American society, the fissures that could not be healed with New Deal initiatives."[20] Parks's photographs do not live up to the ideals the photographer himself might have had about race and equality in the nation but are instead co-opted by the institutions and cultural frameworks in which documentary photography was produced and distributed—mythologies not altogether realized in the consciousness of the photographer. In his analysis of the series of images surrounding Parks's "American Gothic," Natanson reveals that Parks rearranged certain objects in the surroundings in order to intensify the impact of the photograph, and he argues that this compromises the photograph's documentary quality and objectivity. Parks in his autobiography *Choice* writes of posing Mrs. Watson with broom and mop and admits that he "overdid it." And his initial request to photograph her pops out because he can think of no way to help: "I was escaping the humiliation of not being able to help."[21] Photography is the inadequate and artificial recompense for help. Like the anthropologist whose mission to bear witness to threatened lives is inextricable from those lives, the documentary photographer is inevitably entangled with and adjusted the lives of those he photographed, however subtly and unconsciously.

For Sontag, the photographer is "an extension of the anthropologist" not so much because he can live up to the ideal of recorder—"The whole point of photographing people is that you are not intervening in their lives, only visiting them"—but because he fails.[22] "To photograph people is to violate them," to turn them into "objects that can be symbolically possessed" (14). The "predatory" aspects of photography are that, although the photograph records for posterity, it at the same time steals—"loots and preserves" (64). This is particularly so in America, she suggests, where links between photography and tourism meant that pushing back the frontier and the genocide of North American Indians were coincident with the popularization of the camera. Nature was domesticated, and the primitive or original "cannibalized" in photography: "In America, every specimen becomes a relic" (65). The loss in photography is similar to that she has already recognized in Lévi-Straussian anthropology, which she calls a "necrology," since it, too, is implicated in the death it seeks to recover its subjects from.[23] Documentary photography may be similar to anthropology in this much more problematic sense. It opens up the language of what it means to "take" or "shoot" a photograph, the terms we use for capturing on camera that bring to the surface the injurious effects even in documentary photography. Or, in the French *tirer,* which means not only "to draw," "to draw back" (as in curtains), and "to photograph" but "to take away." Portuguese for taking a photograph of a person has even more resonance. In *Tristes Tropiques* Lévi-Strauss describes some young boys in Brazil who urge him to "Tira o retrato! Tira o retrato!" of them instead of begging money from him.[24] *Tirar* has the sense of the French *tirer* of "to take away," "to take out forcibly"—but also "to earn." *O retrato* is "a portrait" but also "a likeness," "an effigy"—the essence, as if it were the life itself that is taken. It is this same primitive conception of photography—living in the myth as reality; not making the myth and controlling code—that leads Barthes to write that "young photographers who are at work in the world, determined upon the capture of actuality, do not know that they are agents of Death." Apparently preserving life, they take it: "in this image which produces Death while trying to preserve life . . . the simple click."[25] The primitives' belief about photographs stealing the soul seems to be borne out in the case of Parks's most famous subject, celebrated in his day but now forgotten—taken. But as to whose life the camera takes, and where life has particular resonance given the role played by *Life* magazine, is unclear, in this two-part, extraordinary story of the involvement of a photographer in his subject's life.

EVIL EYE

Parks had been given an assignment for *Life* magazine in 1961 to document poverty in Latin America. The original plan was to get Parks to represent poverty by one photo in seven separate Latin American countries. The mandate to Parks on setting out was "Find an impoverished father with a family of eight or ten children. Show how he earns a living, the amount he earns a year. Explore his political leanings. Is he a Communist or about to become one? Look into his personal life, his religion, friends, his dreams, frustrations. What about his children—their schools, their health and medical problems, their chances for a better life?"[26] This proves too impersonal for Parks. Parks actually finds as his single subject Flavio da Silva, a twelve-year-old boy who lives in a Rio slum *(favela)* with his family of seven other children, an out-of-work father who sells kerosene, and a mother who

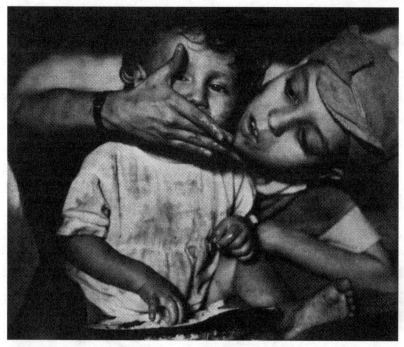

Gordon Parks, "Flavio Feeds Zacarias" (1961). Copyright Gordon Parks. Reprinted with permission.

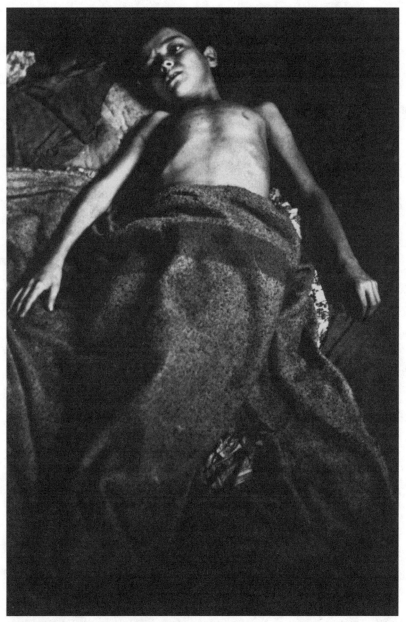

Gordon Parks, "Flavio da Silva during an Asthmatic Seizure" (1961). Copyright Gordon Parks. Reprinted with permission.

washes clothes, immigrants from the northeast of Brazil. Sick with bronchial asthma and malnourished, Flavio according to Brazilian doctors is on
the point of death. This seems to be Parks's initial draw to Flavio: "Death
was all over him" is one of the first things Parks notices about Flavio (14).
Parks's photographs bear all the signs of Stryker's training. They use classical documentary techniques to represent and attest to reality. Their theme
is social, that of poverty and starvation, recalling documentary photographers' favorite subjects of thirties United States. It is embodied in a human
subject. Parks's close-ups reveal a detailed realism, so that we see the dirt
in the child's clothes, the roughness of the blanket, the thinness of Flavio
in his rib cage. The social context is given, as the unremittingly poor shack
on the Catacumba ("Catacomb") *favela* is shown cluttered among other
makeshift homes but crouched symbolically beneath the Cristo Redentor
("Christ Redeemer") of the Corcovado hill, Rio's most famous landmark.
And the assignment is marked by Parks's trademark biography. He moves
from *Life*'s instruction to represent poverty generically to representing
Flavio biographically. Flavio's story is told as representative, with occasional statistics about poverty in Brazil given in parentheses in the text
accompanying the photographs. The series follows a day in Flavio's life,
from getting out of the bed that he shares with his parents and four other
children, to doing chores, to preparing the supper and struggling to feed
the other children. Though clearly the sickest, as the eldest child Flavio is
his family's mainstay. The photographer's proximity to his subject creates
an intimacy. The point of view the photographs want us to have is that of
compassion, to feel involved and empathetic. They idealize their subject's
unquestioning fulfillment of duty and hard work. The photograph of
Flavio in his bed, originally captioned "Sick and exhausted from week's
care of the family . . . ," iconizes the boy as a Christ-like figure with his
arms outstretched, like the Cristo Redentor, who Flavio's father says has
deserted the *favela*. The layout and caption similarly manipulate this response in us. The photograph of Flavio sick in bed appears on a page facing
that of an actual dead child—as if this is what Flavio could be. And the
caption goes on, presenting Flavio as martyr: "'I am not afraid of death,'
he explained to Parks. 'But what will they do after?'" The chiaroscuro
style of the photographs emphasizes the dark more than the light involved
in photography; the photographs enter into a horrifying, very dark underworld. Parks's account of taking the photographs, excerpts from his diary
at the end of the series entitled "Photographer's Diary of a Visit in Dark
World," works to draw out the Hadean journey.[27]

    If social change is the aim of documentary photography's recording of

Gordon Parks, "The Catacumba *Favela,* Rio de Janeiro" (1961). The da Silva shack is near the top, just beneath the Christ figure (Cristo Redentor). Copyright Gordon Parks. Reprinted with permission.

reality, this is what the publication of Parks's photographs in *Life* magazine achieved, perhaps more dramatically and more completely than any other documentary photography. As a result of the photographs' publication, *Life* received and three weeks later reported back on a "uniquely urgent and moving response," in the form of donations and letters from its readers.

Among some of the letters it publishes: a widow promises Flavio an allowance from her monthly sum; offers are made of a home and an education for Flavio; money has been collected in a school, and other children have arranged a yard sale to contribute; there are gifts of bicycles, of an inhaler for Flavio's bronchial asthma—and most crucially the pledge of a complimentary place for Flavio at the Children's Asthma Research Institution and Hospital in Denver. At the bottom of the page *Life* announces that it is setting up a "Flavio Fund," calls for further donations, and suggests that with the money Flavio would be brought to hospital for treatment and the Da Silvas relocated from their slum.[28] Combined with the initial donations, this call produces what amounts to an unprecedented flood of $30,000 from readers. Channeled into the fund, the money allows Parks to return to Brazil and collect Flavio to be brought to the Denver asthma institute. There is no doubt in *Life*'s mind that Parks's photographs and the response of *Life*'s readers have saved Flavio's life. Another two weeks later shows how effective the original documentary photographs were. "Flavio's Rescue: Americans Bring Him from Rio Slum to Be Cured," the July 21, 1961, cover of *Life* beams, with new Parks photographs of Flavio in new, clean pajamas and proper, clean bed. The color images of Flavio the smiling boy relocated in the United States in this issue are in stark contrast to those of him reprinted here in its "Story of the Week" in his dirty bed in a "Rio de Janeiro hovel, wasted by malnutrition and bronchial asthma, with only a few years to live": "Today he is in Colorado, and his smile, his new clothes, his Hopalong watch flopping down his skinny wrist and his chance to live—all are the work of hundreds of generous, compassionate Americans." The juxtaposition dramatizes the transformative effects of this relocation. In this issue we see Flavio in his first shoes, Flavio in Denver learning English ("such basic American words as 'baseball,' 'television,' 'food'"). He "symbolized the enormous problems of Latin America's impoverished millions." His family, too, have been relocated, and the issue includes photographs of the Da Silvas moving from the shanty town to a proper, stone house.[29]

Flavio spends two years in the United States at the institute. His bronchial asthma is treated and apparently cured, and he grows eight inches and gains twenty-two pounds. But his treatment is as much psychological and cultural as physical. On arrival and repeatedly during his stay, he undergoes intelligence and psychological tests; there's apparently one theory that asthma has psychosomatic dimensions. He's found—and repeatedly—to be maladjusted and falling short. He's seen to have emotional and social problems. After his asthma is resolved, according to one report Flavio remains "belligerent, resistant to discipline, and uncontrollable," although Parks senses in his withdrawal, silence, and lack of communication that he is depressed because he is isolated and misses his family (*Flavio* 102). He becomes a social experiment, and the cure corrective. He is taught the wrongness of stealing, better eating habits, and correct table manners. He undergoes cultural assimilation as part of his improvement, is given an ideal American life. He lives with a Portuguese American family, and his foster mother, Kathy Gonçalves, an American married to a Portuguese, teaches him not simply English but better Portuguese, instead of the *favela* slang they think he comes speaking. The photographs of this two-year period, when he is out of Parks's life, show Flavio experiencing Thanksgiving turkey dinner with his new family, his first Christmas, his first fishing trip with the Gonçalves boys, all of these taken by foster father José Gonçalves. These photographs are family snapshots and they paste Flavio firmly into the family album, a form that does not reflect family life but, as Marianne Hirsch has written, "perpetuates family myths while seeming merely to record actual moments in family history."[30] The white nuclear family was a particularly favored subject of *Life*'s: it "symbolized the United States," was an "imagined community" for the nation.[31] Flavio is a tabula rasa according to Kathy—"He's like dry soil soaking up everything around him" (*Flavio* 105). He is a symbol or metaphor—better yet, given that in the eyes of North American readers his existence originated in and is confined solely to photographs, an emanation of Brazil. So his eventual adjustment to his new life is seen as successful Americanization. "We'll soon have a number one American boy at Willens," his house parent at the institute promises (111–12). Not surprisingly, the result of this adjustment is a gap for Flavio between his Brazilian past and his U.S. present. He rejects all things Brazilian, refuses to speak Portuguese and insists on only English, stops writing to his mother, and loses touch with his family. "I don't want to go back" (131). *Life*'s involvement not only with Flavio but with his family and the *favela* of Catacumba may have exacerbated these rifts. With part of the Flavio fund, *Life* not only relocates the Da Silvas out of the *favela* to a suburban house, bringing about a remarkable and immediate—and very photogenic—transformation, as the family are kitted out with new toys, clothes, and furniture—courtesy of Sears Roebuck. *Life* helps create a means of work for the father, in trucking. The *favela,* too, undergoes a project of development, with access to drinking water provided and a process of building and the introduction of services such as power supply and waste disposal. These adjustments result in differences in degrees of poverty and security and introduce the sense of envy and alienation:

between the Da Silva father and his eldest son, between the Da Silvas and their neighbors, and between Catacumba and surrounding *favelas*. Flavio's "rescue" from Brazil is so successful that "Flavio da Silva had, after twenty months, grown to love America. It had given him more than most children around the world ever get—a small fortune, a house for his family, a chance to learn, love, and to live a full and healthy life. It was a place where he had been close to complete happiness, and he did not want to leave it" (130). Dread of return to the *favela*—that underworld—and the recurrence of the illness and everything that had characterized Flavio's life there, hangs over the whole episode—for Flavio and for Parks.

Why the unprecedented generous response by *Life's* readers to the original Flavio photographs, and what lies at the heart of the episode? The event is a good deal less redemptive and more appropriative than may initially seem from the story of compassion and salvation. The historical moment is key. The episode is actually in line with postwar American policy, spread from McCarthyism to inform foreign policy—toward Korea, Latin America, and soon Vietnam—an expression of containment of the subversion of communism. *Life's* readers are not seeking to eradicate poverty for its own sake but are responding inextricably to *Life's* presentation of Flavio's poverty in the context of the fear of communism. As so strongly but oddly indicated in Parks's initial instructions from *Life* ("Find an impoverished father. . . . Explore his political leanings. Is he a Communist or about to become one?"), his assignment for *Life* is thoroughly embedded in U.S. politics toward Latin America. Parks's photographs appeared as part of a five-part series in *Life* in the summer of 1961, entitled "The Crisis in Our Hemisphere"/"Crisis in Latin America." The exchange in titles between what appears on the cover and what appears inside the introductory issue suggests how U.S. anxiety about the fifth column within its own borders in the fifties extended to the continent in the south in the sixties. The titles and headlines in the series are equally evocative of the Red Scare in Latin America of the moment: "The Menacing Push of Castroism" (front cover: "Exclusive Photo Report Shows How Castro and the Communists Are Working to Seize Latin America"); "Freedom's Fearful Foe: Poverty" (front cover: "Shocking Poverty Spawns Reds"), in which Parks's Flavio photos appeared; "Bolivia: U.S. Stake in a Revolution"; "Latin America's Story of Turbulence"; "Prisoners of Our Geography—The Races and the Terrain, a Mixed-Up Inheritance."[32] In the early 1960s at the height of the cold war and after the Cuban revolution of 1959 (but populist reforms in Guatemala had already caused U.S. concern about communism in Latin America), Latin America, the United States' own "backyard," was the main battleground between the "Christian free world" (capitalism) and the threat to the free world (then, communism). The year 1961 when Parks published his photos and the Latin American series ran was particularly pivotal. In April the buildup of tensions between the United States and Cuba resulted in the failed, U.S.-sponsored invasion of Cuba, the Bay of Pigs fiasco. And in March President Kennedy had announced his Alliance for Progress in the Americas, a policy to develop continental links as another strategy to combat communism, the goal to eradicate the poverty that "produces" communism. In the words of one history of the messy U.S. politics toward Latin America, in adherence to the Monroe Doctrine of right to intervention in Latin America that has characterized U.S. policy for almost two centuries, following Cuba "Latin America's economic development became an obsession in Washington."[33] The Alliance for Progress echoed the political intervention hiding behind economic and cultural development in F. D. Roosevelt's "Good Neighbor Policy" in the thirties and forties; and the Good Neighbor Policy was itself an exportation abroad of Roosevelt's New Deal at home, with all its attendant national mythologies about poverty and social and economic stability.

Brazil was particularly significant to the United States. Historically it had been the only Latin American nation that had fought for the Allies in the Second World War; and in its geography it was equivalent to the United States without Alaska, as comparisons of the time repeatedly stress. But Brazil was most important politically in the bipolar vision of communism-versus-the-free-world of this moment. The Kennedy government desperately wanted new Brazilian President Jânio Quadros's regime to succeed, since the suicide of longtime dictator Getúlio Vargas in 1954 had produced a series of fast-shifting and unstable governments in Brazil that swung the pendulum with regard to cooperating with their relations in the north. The forces of communism and nationalism often formed uneasy alliances in Latin America and always resulted in anti- (North-) Americanism, as they were in Brazil especially in the late 1950s-early 1960s, its modern period of greatest political uncertainty—and possibility. The United States was willing to pour finances into the Brazilian government to ensure stability and friendly relations—in other words, anticommunism and openness to U.S. corporate investment. In May 1961, weeks before Parks published his photographs, a communiqué from the U.S. government announcing loan arrangements to Brazil "emphasized that Brazil's future was vital to the future of the hemisphere and that the maintenance of free government in Latin America was dependent upon the success of Brazil's economic development."[34] In the early 1960s, the United States was the biggest foreign investor in Brazil, begun in industrialization in the Second World War. Half of foreign investment in Brazil was from the United States. By 1961, a summer of what turned out to be a period of transition but not crisis in Brazil, Quadros (described by *Life* as "radical")[35] both played the United States for financial support *and* courted the new Cuban government. He visited Cuba in March 1960 and in August awarded the Order of the Southern Cross, Brazil's highest honor, to the Cuban-Argentinean Che Guevara, refusing to comply with the U.S. demand for sanctions against Cuba. While he accepted their aid, Quadros was less pro-American than any Brazilian president since the Second World War, preferring instead to pursue "independent foreign policy" alliances with other Third World countries.[36] This autonomous, ambivalent policy so far as the United States was concerned would only end with the right-wing military coup in Brazil in 1964, which would rule Brazil and suppress democracy for the next twenty years. The coup delighted Washington. The U.S. government supported the coup militarily, dispatching warships to Brazil in March 1964, and financially, skyrocketing aid to 600 percent after the coup's success. Brazilian police, who proved so efficient at rounding up intellectuals, left-wing activists and anyone who objected to the military regime, continued to be trained at the Washington Police Academy through the 1970s even once the brutality of the regime was internationally well known. "Clearly involved in the military overthrow of the constitutional and democratic government of Brazil, the United States became intimately associated with the military dictatorship that followed." In the summer of 1961 when *Life* magazine ran its stories and when the United States "bore the brunt of [Brazil's] attack on imperialism,"[37] it was crucial for the United States to justify its ideological and economic investment in Brazil and to portray a cause-and-effect relation between poverty and communism. In the concluding editorial in the last of the *Life* series, *Life* journalist Robert Coughlan argues in support of Kennedy's Alliance for Progress that pouring money into the continent would battle anti-U.S. stance and communism.[38] And if we have any doubt about how anticommunist belief insidiously informs the overwhelming response of *Life*'s readers to Parks's photographs of Flavio, the letters page provides adequate testimony. "Let us first beat the Russians to the distant star in Flavio's eyes," as one reader manages to put it both whimsically and bellicosely.[39] In writing of his decision to focus in on a Brazilian *favela* in his assignment, Parks initially saw his story within the anticommunist remit: "During a trip to Rio de Janeiro several years before, I had seen poverty at its worse in the infamous favelas ringing the city. The poor there were a large part of those already ripening for the sharpest danger facing the Western Hemisphere, a Communist take-over" (*Flavio* 58). Flavio's fund is "With President Kennedy's Alliance for Progress as a model . . . a pilot *project for progress*" (91). Flavio's life becomes the choicest weapon in this moment of the cold war.

   Life was particularly significant in the nationalist politics of the moment and the war against communism. John Tagg insists that to evaluate documentary photographs' realism we need to look at the "institutional frameworks within which they are produced and consumed," for documentary photography functions "within certain ideological apparatuses."[40] *Life* magazine was a propagandistic institution, inheriting the mantle of documentary photography in unabashed function as a U.S. nationalist mouthpiece. Conceived as the United States' first truly national magazine, it was targeted at every American, and it decided America's issues. Its emergence and success were interdependent with the emergence and success of U.S. technology and economy. Technology made possible not only good media photographic reproduction but the mass distribution of *Life*—first nationally, then globally. Economically, *Life* was funded initially and at different points sustained by advertising revenue from expanding U.S. companies.[41] Coughlan goes on to underline the part that communications should play in similarly priming the U.S. population for the government's message: "merely to make the facts available—as our present information agencies mostly do—is far from enough. What are needed are the tactics of full-scale psychological warfare, for we are dealing not simply with an information gap but with an empathy gap, the production of long condition and deeply set emotional attitudes."[42] *Life* explicitly performed this function. The publisher's mission statement for the magazine, in the first of the series on Latin America and thus in the issue just before Parks's initial photographs of Flavio, presents *Life* as a nationalist tool, not merely reflective but creative of national goals. "For the next 25 years, therefore, what better dedication could there be for *Life* than the fulfillment of National Purpose and the pursuit of excellence in our American civilization? . . . LIFE dedicates itself to being a lively instrument of the National Purpose, to helping the people of America recognize their deepest aspirations and work increasingly toward that fulfillment." The "National Purpose" is summarized as twofold. "1) Win the Cold War. 2) Create a better America."[43] *Life* magazine was proclaimed the "pictorial window on the world" by Henry Luce, its founder and head of media empire that also included *Time* and *Fortune*; but "The outlook was relentlessly American. . . . Time[-Life] was more an exporter of American ideas than a global publisher."[44] From his initial vision to "get the photographers into the byways of America"[45] when the magazine was set up in 1936, Luce, by 1941 in his famous editorial essay "The American Century," was writing that the United States "must undertake to be the Good Samaritan of the entire world," which meant exporting not just economic aid and American ideals but a system of free economic enterprise led by America and American technical and cultural expertise. Noting that American artifacts were the one thing world communities had in common—the one thing that could unify the world in a time of division, of self versus other—Luce dreams, under the guise of America as global redeemer, globalization, *avant la lettre*.[46] As William Stott puts it ironically, "Our [U.S.] sympathy had grown beyond all boundary."[47]

It was impossible for *Life*'s photographers or journalists to be critical of the United States. *Life* photographer, German Edwin Rosskam's challenge to the U.S. position in Puerto Rico previously had only resulted in "incurring the wrath of *Life*'s conservative editors."[48] And the pattern was repeated, for even Barthes remarks of *Life* that its editors rejected the images of one photographer "because, they said, his images 'spoke too much'; they made us reflect" by distracting us from the message that *Life*'s editors would have us see, something other than the authorized code.[49] *Life* had served a major propagandistic function in Brazil before. In 1941 its editors helped launch a South American version of *Life, En Guardia,* under the auspices of the Office of Inter-American Affairs (OIAA) during the war and at the time of Roosevelt's Good Neighbor Policy. This office sponsored the work of Parks's closest predecessor in Brazil, U.S. photographer Genieve Naylor, who was sent to Brazil with a mandate by the OIAA to convince North Americans that Brazil was a "Good Neighbor," a trustworthy ally. Her recent commentator suggests that *she* deliberately failed in this duty, and in accordance her photographs are a good deal more open in their meaning, less nationalist in their mythologies—and therefore less documentary than Parks's.[50] The Office of War Information where Parks began his documentary career effectively made irrefutable the political bonds of documentary photography. And then it got too much even for its chief proponent: "When the object of the pictures changed from essential 'truth' in the old FSA sense to the outright manufacture of propaganda for the OWI, it became offensive to Stryker."[51] In war and especially in cold, virtual ones, photographs are ammunition. Photographs of the Cuban boy Elian Gonzalez, which recently played a similar role to Flavio's, demonstrate this. Photographs released, first in the U.S. press of Elian waving an American flag, and then by the Cuban government of him happily reunited with his Cuban national father, caught the boy in a crossfire of information/

disinformation.[52] Flavio was subjected to a similar propaganda battle. On initial publication of Parks's photographs, the Brazilian magazine *O Cruzeiro*, recognizing the documentation of Brazilian poverty as politically laden, "rushed one of its own photographers to New York City to do a similar story on a Puerto Rican family in the Wall Street district, and it depicted a sleeping child with cockroaches crawling over its face, and another child crying from hunger" (*Flavio* 91). *Time*, sibling to *Life* in Luce's media empire, quickly countered and revealed the *O Cruzeiro* story as fabrication. Parks remarks the irony that "O Cruzeiro had felt it necessary to go to such lengths. If it had gone to New York's Harlem or Chicago's South Side, they could have found a story as genuinely tragic as the one of the Catacumba" (*Flavio* 91–92). Or it could have gone to Parks's own rural Kansas.

Life's photojournalistic format is key to its place as propagandistic institution. *Life* is celebrated for taking documentary photography into a photojournalistic format, and its combination of photographs and text was groundbreaking at its launch. Photojournalism sought to bring to a mass audience a reflection of current events in photographs with few words—to report through pictures. *Life* was the most successful of photojournalistic magazines from the 1930s because in its photographs, apparently "for the first time, the real world was depicted realistically, aided by rapid technological advances"; and its minimal prose narrative catered to the U.S. public's perceived lack of time to read the news in full, as story.[53] In its quarter-centenary anniversary issue, in which the mission statement appears and which serves as an introduction to Parks's photographs, *Life* announces that it has revamped itself in order "to quicken and sharpen communications between printed page and reader's eye." The publisher touts his magazine's attributes and makes clear what is different about photojournalism: "In its first 25 years LIFE has dedicated itself to enlarging communication among the American people through the revealing power of picture journalism."[54] *Life*'s editors rightly attributed its success to its "'new picture-and-word editorial technique' which 'makes the truth about the world we live in infinitely more exciting, more easily absorbed, more alive than it has ever been before.'"[55] The text-photograph combination that was the hallmark of *Life* ensured both the apparent comprehensiveness of the picture—we seemed to be seeing the facts, the event itself—and yet at the same time a narrow, even coercive, what Barthes called a coded point of view, the meaning. The photographs enlarged the details. The text underwrote these with the national line. And the combination of forms gave a sense of instantaneity in keeping with modern mass media, of making issues alive and bringing them home, of news in the making or changing. Prose was factual but typically emotive. The whole focus was on simplification, on direct and unmediated communication. In his autobiography *A Choice of Weapons*, Parks recounts that in his training Stryker insists that text must "underscore" photographs,, that images and words must be "fitted together properly." The text and photos should appear to literalize each other, so the reader has instant apprehension and instant response. Stryker looks at Parks's initial prose and rejects it: "you have to simplify all this material. It would take many years and all the photographers on the staff to fulfil what you have put down here."[56] Parks studies other documentary photographers—Lange, Collier, Evans—and realizes that what he must aim for is conveying contemporary disasters literally, with no ambiguity about their message. *Life* magazine as photojournalism spelled the end of an era of documentary photography because it was undeniably propaganda, making a parody of whatever documentariness there was in documentary photography. The documentary photograph had a title. Photojournalism provides the photograph with a caption and accompanying editorial text, with the result that the meaning of the photograph is anchored down. And captions or editorial text are often used in photojournalism as part of the image, turning photographs into mythologies.

Thus in the introductory issue of the Latin American series, a whole page is given to the hideously enlarged eyes of Fidel Castro, dark-ringed, out of focus, with nothing else of the face visible. Text is used not only to underscore but as part of the face. "The editors of LIFE present a New Series"—and then massively enlarged, too, and in between and below the eyes instead of the face, "CRISIS IN LATIN AMERICA." The lower part of the page is used to literalize the image: "The messianic eyes of Fidel Castro," as the text declares, preside over what determines the content of later *Life* issues. He is the "face of the troubles of Latin America."[57] In the upcoming issues *Life* would show photographs of banners of Castro surrounded by firebrands at protest rallies across Latin America—as if Castro's face was incendiary, prefigurative of continental communist revolution—and add other faces, among them that of the popular land reformer Francisco Julião from northeast Brazil, who was organizing the first landless movement in Brazil and who suggested the Cuban Revolution as precedent. And in Flavio *Life* finds another face that, as "poverty always has a human face" the presentation urges, could become Castro's if his poverty was not alleviated. Faces are given masks, meaning, especially with the success of Parks's own technique in photobiography which is exceptional in these issues in representing poverty instead of through several Latin American countries by a single boy in Brazil. After his contravening their instruction, *Life* initially decided to reduce Parks's photographic-biographic record to a single photograph. But then, with a transitoriness that is how photojournalism works, the magazine changed its mind when Dean Rusk, Kennedy's secretary of state who worried that Quadros was making a populist Peronist turn in Brazil, made clear the inexorably engendering relationship of poverty to communism, warning that very week in the *New York Times* "that if our government didn't give immediate and sizable aid to the poor of Latin America, Communism would surely spread rapidly throughout the hemisphere" (*Flavio* 65). This pronouncement is key to why the story does get published, and Parks personally writes to thank Rusk. Under the title "Freedom's Fearful Foe: Poverty," the colon making simplistically clear that what precedes it is equivalent to what follows it—that "freedom's fearful foe" or communism is a result of poverty, that there is a direct causal relationship—Flavio's story in photo-text format expresses Rusk's worst nightmare. But the effect of Parks's photographs of boy Flavio fulfilled unwittingly the propagandistic remit beyond Rusk's or even Coughlan's and *Life*'s editors' wildest dreams. Embodying his theme in a single boy, Parks makes Flavio a symbol of poverty and saving his life a test case for the U.S. war against communism. From leaving Brazil until Denver—when he made the cover of *Life* magazine—Flavio is according to Parks the most celebrated, mediatized boy in the Western Hemisphere. For a moment.

According to the good old contradictions of the U.S. immigration service and with the very success of the experiment (the U.S. courts reached similarly contradictory decisions regarding Elian Gonzalez's patriation, first that America should save him from Cuba, and then that he should be sent "home" to his father), Flavio is eventually compelled into leaving the United States. Parks seems to sense the contradictions of prematurity and belatedness, the limitations of the project: "we had dreams for Flavio da Silva that were hopelessly beyond his reach. It was as if we expected abundant fruit from a sapling already gone barren" (142). Returned to Brazil in the summer of 1963 when the increasingly left-wing and nationalist successor to Quadros, President João Goulart, was busy fostering new alliances "between the undeveloped nations of Latin America, Africa, and Asia" and pointedly ignoring the United States—when Brazil was most on the verge of a popular social democratic revolution[58]—Flavio no longer serves a useful, elucidatory role for North Americans and the media circus vanishes. Yet Flavio, though back in Brazil, cannot go home again. Initially sent to a boarding school in São Paulo as a kind of halfway house between U.S. affluence and his *favela* poverty, even then Flavio says "America is the only place to be. Brazilians are awful and this school is awful" (159). He is expelled from the school. Attending another school in Rio, his desires for America alienate him from neighborhood boys. He rows with his father and invokes *Life* as a buffer or salvation in his arguments. Flavio's visit to the Time-Life building in New York—where he saw an image of himself and asked for a job—inserted him into the heart of the institution. And his family's experience is no longer the fairy-tale world of *Life*'s rescue. The family still owns the house, but it is a shambles and in disrepair. The contrast between what was and what is Flavio finds traumatic, experiencing "embarrassment at his family's situation" (155–56). And when Parks returns in 1976 after Flavio inherits the remainder of the *Life* fund at twenty-one, we see the horrible irony, the provisionality and regression of the whole project. The mother ends up back washing clothes, the father loses his trucking business, and Flavio feels like they are back in the *favela* again: "Fifteen years of failure showed there beneath a dripping wash. The throwback to a state so close to their former one was hard to accept" (189). Parks "felt as if I were escaping a disaster" (189). Even on Parks's return when Flavio is living poorly but in employment and supporting his family, Flavio is still hankering after a return to America as a way to rescue him from problems—even at the airport as Parks leaves for his flight: "'I think almost every day about going to America, Gordon, to see the places that I once passed and to find all the friends that I know. It would be so good to have a job and live there again. Please, Gordon, see if you can get me back there.' The longing in his eyes was unbearable" (197). Parks wants to say, stop dreaming, those places are passed, but instead is still making promises. "His yearning was honest, poignant. He would go on believing that only in America could he have another chance" (186).

At the time of 1961–63, only José Gallo, a Brazilian working for *Life* in Rio and thus at the border of two national mythologies, recognizes the current of bereavement, of deprivation underlying the whole project—although Flavio's father is suspicious and distrustful of *Life* all along. When Flavio returns to Brazil Gallo "complained that some of the Americans had done more harm than good by spoiling Flavio. He hoped that no one from the States would write him, and that Flavio would forget his whole experience there" (152). *Life* produces no real follow-up story though, amazingly, continues to publicize its role. Flavio-as-Christ is reproduced in a 2000 edition of *"Life" Classic Photographs,* in which we are told that a house was purchased for the family in Brazil and that, in 1986, Flavio had steady jobs, his own house, and a color TV: "Thank God," Flavio is quoted as saying, "dreaming isn't prohibited."[59] There's a shocking editing-out of the dilapidation of the Da Silva house, the failure of the father's job and the reversions that Parks finds in '76. We do not see the loss or the failure to realize dreams that Flavio himself will realize by 1998, when British newspaper the *Guardian* found Flavio to do an update on the boy. At last, he has given up his driving wish and no longer wants to return to the United States. Thirty-seven years later, he is unemployed, divorced, and living in a shed in the back of the house bought for him by *Life's* readers. The house is now a slum: "he has slipped back into the poverty from which *Life's* readers thought they had saved him. His life has come full circle." Flavio recognizes that, instead of being given a life, he has had his life taken from him. "As well as feeling he was a foreigner in his own country, Flavio's sense of disillusionment and disorientation was accentuated by having seen the prosperous western world and knowing that he would probably never see it again." He returned home a foreigner. He could no longer speak Portuguese—"I could hardly speak to my friends. . . . I felt that everything had been stolen from me"—and he talks now in broken sentences of English and Portuguese. The trauma was that of being extirpated from his community and thrown back. The Da Silva family talk about how Parks's book *Flavio* was not translated into Portuguese—they never knew what was written. The *Guardian* correspondent (who lives in Brazil) uses the story to deconstruct Western mythology held even to the present day. "Far from being a symbol of how to help the third world, Flavio is perhaps a better example of the difficulties—some may say irresponsibility—of spontaneous acts of charity."[60]

When Parks first takes his camera to the slum, the *favelados* (*favela* inhabitants) seek to dodge his lens. His informant tells him that they believe the camera is "an evil eye that brings bad luck" (28), and in *Flavio* Parks reveals how, in the destructive potential of his "choice of weapon," it does. Flavio as symbol or sign does not get a better life. As foster mother Kathy Gonçalves says, "he couldn't even realize what he was meant to symbolize" (133). The most remarkably interventionist effect of Parks's photographic witnessing is that Flavio is removed from his family and sent to a Denver institute and home for two years. While this might clinically save his life, it also steals his cultural life, and the sacrifice of the son takes on other, irremediable dimensions. When he is taken from his family home, Flavio's mother, Nair, views his departure as loss and, enclosing him in her arms, weeps in grief: Pietà. Ultimately what Parks's photographs "take" from Flavio is Brazil; his photographs initiate the (U.S.) Americanization of Flavio. Flavio is led the American way, which is not so different today. There are always losses entailed in manifest economic and political redemption. With

Flavio's ingenuity, it is likely that he would have got out of the *favela* himself, given evidence of his hard work, as he holds two jobs for years. Perhaps he would even have got further. These *favelas*, historians of Brazil have written, are set up as a route for migrants to better things, to improvement; people struggle out. But what does it mean to photograph someone's life and to change it? What of self-consciousness and after-effects—remorse, atonement for sacrifice of other—in the photographer?

GHOSTS OF MY OWN PAST

The other intriguing aspect of the story concerns the other player in it. What was Parks's role, and especially why the return to write about it seventeen years after taking the photographs? By 1978 Brazil had a change in government, with a military dictatorship in power. The gap between rich and poor had grown and there were new *favelas* sprouting around the country. But the United States is no longer interested to the same extent. The Carter years beginning in 1976 practiced a deliberate policy of nonintervention in Latin America following post-Vietnam remorse (though it was not to last long—Reagan in the 1980s, in the Iran-Contra affair, reverted to U.S. custom). Parks discusses none of these political changes. His decision to go back is made, according to *Flavio,* apparently on impulse. In '76 he decides to visit Brazil and seek out Flavio on a trip back from Argentina, when asked by a clerk in a Buenos Aires shoe store about Flavio's current welfare. The return to Brazil may be to satisfy his curiosity. But one doesn't write a book—and indeed what is a biography—on impulse, or to satisfy one's own or a reader's curiosity. Instead "confusion and guilt" (51) seem to be at work. Guilt is one of the most repeated affects of Parks's text, a regret tied up with displacement, dislocation, and Americanization. A photographic memoir, what *Flavio* adds to the original assignment is, in fact, autobiography, the life of self interwoven around (in exchange with) the story of the other in photographs. Released from a photojournalistic context, *Flavio* is less a simple social document of Flavio's life than it might initially seem. Only the middle section is mostly documentary, in the account of Flavio's life in America for two years when he's at the institute and not part of Parks's life—when Parks is out getting a life, getting assignments, and getting known as a result of the Flavio story. Even then Parks writes of his guilt for not giving Flavio personal attention. In the tradition of documentary photography the impression is of an omniscient camera with the photographer invisible. In the photographer's autobiography Parks includes his self, his presence as part of the story of his subjects' lives, and perhaps in terms of revelations this is his most autobiographical text. The chronic distance on the assignment allows Parks's anxious reflections to come to the fore. Retrospective as well as self-conscious and reflective, Parks's palinode *Flavio* encourages Parks to assess his own role in the story. Like Lévi-Strauss he returns, in relation to photography, to the problems of witnessing and observation. *Life* magazine has gone, made obsolete possibly by television, Parks thinks. From this point on, Flavio "would be keeper of his own memoirs" (168). Yet Flavio is not so, and Parks continues to record and to entangle Flavio's life in his own—and to write Flavio's memoir. What is at stake in the autobiographical element of this entanglement? In the return, in the palinode, the photographer expresses doubts about his profession. *Flavio* is more about himself and the subsequent effects of his photography. *Flavio* shows how Parks becomes too involved in Flavio's life. The realization and renunciation are perhaps not always conscious, but they are what come back belatedly.

What returns in *Flavio* is the remarkable intrusion of a photographer's self into his subject's life far in excess of the participant observation of his documentary photography. Parks writes in *Flavio* of how his engagement with Flavio quickly moves beyond that initial photographic assignment to record and beyond politics. He recognizes that as a photojournalist he should be emotionally disinterested. "I tried to be objective. The fact that I had become deeply attached to Flavio was irrelevant. After all, his real importance was not this personal bond, but the fact that he was the medium through which I could show the ugliness of poverty to millions of people. For a moment, I was like the man who is proud of his inability to shed a tear—free of any sentimental attachment to an experience. I would be a tougher, better reporter for this" (51). But he experiences real conflict. After three weeks, New York *Life* is concerned about his silence, and he is concerned that perhaps they'll feel he's changed the story and got too close to it. His account of taking the photographs is a paradox: "Flavio's predicament was my story" (24), but he can't simply witness the predicament. The point is that he can't leave Flavio simply as a story. How wonderful to change the life: to rescript the story. Becoming more and more immersed, he enters into that other world—that underworld. We see the contrast between Parks's world and the photographed, as Parks is increasingly unable to spend time at his Copacabana hotel—with its food and perfection and beauty and the size of his room—after the shack. He goes to the *favela* at night, ignoring advice not to risk his life thus. He enters into their lives. He holds Flavio when he coughs, he removes a nail from the younger child's foot, he stops the children fighting and brings them gifts of food concealed in his camera case so as not to upset the economy. But he does upset the economy, and on their moving the Da Silvas incur the wrath of the other *favelados*. They need to move because of the effects of outside intervention, because they have no answer to the others' question: why not us?

And at the time of taking the photographs in 1961, although he had been at *Life* magazine some twelve years, when the editors of *Life* decided to publish only one photograph of Flavio in keeping with their initial instruction and limited space—and then opposite a fashion shoot—Parks compromised his career. Furious and emotional, he dashes off his letter of resignation. He was prepared to give up his professional life at *Life* magazine over Flavio's representation, no negligible sacrifice given how hard he had struggled as the first African American photographer there. And even after he realized that with his initial visit he had fulfilled his assignment as a photojournalist, Parks nevertheless wants to save and intervene in that life but is constantly drawn up short by his ability and the ethical rectitude of his attempt. The regret and guilt follow him even seventeen years after the assignment—for planting the dream and then realizing its impossibility.

> I couldn't respond to his desire to return to a place that only existed in his memory. I felt that I had already shuffled his dreams too much. Those of us who had in some way touched his life witnessed an incredible experience. But now I was asking myself what that experience really meant. The miracles of energy that took place on Catacumba were dissipated; it was as though they had never been. The Da Silva family was better off, but their experience was precarious, in fact tragic. Flavio had survived the Catacumba. But it looked as if he had gone as far as he could go in his lifetime. Now that his life had been saved, I hoped that he would not waste it chasing a futile dream. (197)

One situation illustrates the remarkable intervention and shuffles Parks's own dreams. Wracked by the guilt of his distance from the situation he is photographing, he travels one night from his beachfront hotel to the *favela*. It is well past midnight but, he writes, he lets himself into the Da Silva one-room shack, where the family sleeps crammed on one bed, and settles down to watch, not photographing but an observing presence. "I sat in the strange darkness watching the embers cooling and falling into ashes, unable to find my place in such an experience" (49). He remembers the dream he had in the shack—and it is remarkable as the one dream in *Flavio*. The passage continues: "Eventually I fell into a nightmare of sleep. The great concrete statue of Christ tumbled backward into the favela crumbling the hills and its shacks into a river of terror. There were coffins filled with garbage and human limbs" (49). He had visited the Corcovado that morning, intending to photograph it but unable to because it was covered in a heavy fog; he returns in the afternoon to Flavio, whom he does photograph and who becomes his subject. Flavio, the substitute Christ symbol, is here destroyed by the Christ of suffering and redemption so important to the book—the Cristo who not only hangs over the *favela* but figuratively over the whole narrative. About the destruction by a Christ who is meant to be a redeemer—*redentor*, this zenith of redemption—the dream suggests the disturbing effect of redemption, of intervention on the *favela*. Does the dream betray Parks's anxiety about the potentially devastating effects of his own "evil eye"?

With Parks focusing on the boy, instead of the father as he was instructed to do by *Life* magazine, at first Flavio seems like Parks's surrogate son. Parks is a substitute parent in place of negligent parents too distracted by poverty or their own suffering. Flavio asked Parks to keep him as a son before returning, and Parks even considers adopting Flavio. In a slip in the text he refers to Flavio as his natural father José da Silva's "troublesome stepson" (168). (A current Web site states that Parks, in effect, adopted Flavio and still calls him in Brazil "to this day").[61] Driving back and forth from his hotel in Copacabana to the shack in Catacumba, Parks forms, in his account of the assignment in *Flavio,* a potential paternity: "I could not help but compare the good fortune of my own children with the fate of these others. Fate might have so easily reversed the circumstances" (51). Parks's dedication of *Flavio* to his own daughter seems to underline these lines that cross and diverge in the narrative but only by chance. Yet more profoundly there is a generational slip. It suggests his continuing uncertainty about his autobiographical place in relation to his photography. Parks himself begins with a life almost identical to Flavio's, that had a good deal more in common with the Da Silvas' fight for survival in a Rio *favela* than does his own children's comfortable middle-class life on their Long Island home. Parks's mandate from *Life,* "Find an impoverished father with a family of eight or ten children. Show how he earns a living, the amount he earns a year" could be an instruction to return to his own past. Parks departs early on, to make a better life from a poor Kansas childhood, a family of fourteen brothers and sisters, and an apparently uncaring father for whom he appears to have as little sympathy as he does for José da Silva. He experiences periods of homelessness and moves into the ghetto in Harlem during the Depression where he describes being surrounded by squalor. In his account of Flavio's circumstances, he constantly interweaves his own identification. His own poverty and Harlem and Chicago's South Side seemed "pale by comparison" to the poverty and hunger of the *favela* (19). His desire to

make things different for Flavio is to fulfill, he says, the wishes in this child
he himself had as a child for things he could never have. His *Choice of
Weapons* chronicles in detail the context of exclusion faced by a young boy
and his family growing up amidst segregation and lynchings in the United
States, with Parks torn between absorption by national mythologies and
opposing them. "I stood before the cracked mirror in our house and wondered why God had made me black, and I remembered the dream I once
had of being white, with skin so flabby and loose that I attempted to pull it
into shape" (8). "At fourteen, in the black-and-white world of Kansas, anyone whiter than I became my enemy" (8). The struggle is in identification.
In *Moments without Proper Names* he reveals autobiographical origins for
photographs. "I was born to a black childhood of confusion and poverty.
The memory of that beginning influences my work today. It is impossible
for me now to photograph a hungry child without remembering the hunger
of my own childhood. Time has taught me that it is not enough to look,
condemn, or praise—or to be just an observer. I must attempt to transcend
the limitations of my own experience by sharing, as deeply as possible, the
problems of those I photograph. . . . We must give up silent watching and
put our commitments into practice" (7). And the point is that his photographs are beyond testimony and that he can't just watch. As if, as another
critic writes of a documentary photographer who was a precedent for Parks,
"The story that seeks to 'know' through what it can 'see' of the other finds,
not the other, but itself."[62]

Parks punctuated his work with reflections on his photography and
makes repeated returns to consider his own place in relation to his subjects.
His oeuvre is marked by serial autobiography, which suggests something
unworked-through about the life and his career. He wrote his early life
as "a novel from life" first in 1963, later as a screenplay for the film *The
Learning Tree* in 1968; this was recast as autobiography in *A Choice of
Weapons* in 1965, and part two followed as *To Smile in Autumn: A Memoir*
in 1979. Finally—but is it?—the life was integrated in *Voices in the Mirror*
in 1990. Such repeated revisions constitute constant self-assessment and
betray anxiety about self-representation and self in relation to representation.
Born Black for instance, a collection in 1971 of assignments Parks took for
Life magazine between 1960 and 1970, intercalates moments from Parks's
life with classic photographs, not as if they were identical but as if he were
trying to close the gap between self and other, personal and career: past
and present.[63] Parks personally got involved with and tried to help several
of his subjects, long after he took their pictures. Next to Flavio the most
prominent story is that of the Fontenelles. The Fontenelles were a poor

African American family living in Harlem whom Parks photographed for *Life* magazine after Flavio. Assuring the family the community would benefit from the photographs, Parks was allowed to live with the Fontenelles and to photograph them for one month. Parks faces the same struggle over objectivity and remaining outside. "It was difficult not to immediately, being in my position, take money in, take food in, to ease their situation. Because the minute you do that you've lost your story. So you pray and hope that you can get your story over as quickly as possible, and that there will be a response from the public." There was a response and with readers' donations again *Life* enables the Fontenelles in '68 to move to a house on Long Island. But this help, too, might be seen as containment, since *Life*'s editor had asked Parks to explain why black people were rioting through urban areas and *Life*'s answer once again is economic. The father came back drunk one night, caused a fire—and died in the fire with one child. The end of it all, at least for Parks, is that the mother wants to go back to Harlem, and Parks pays for the mother's funeral. "The whole family was destroyed," Parks sighs. "The problem in documenting a family like that," he explains, "is that, you wonder, in the end, whether you should have touched the family, or just left them alone."[64] This assignment in turn becomes cause for anxious return, a canvas for many of the same ph/autographical doubts that surround Flavio—"Perhaps I shouldn't have touched that family, I thought to myself"; "it's impossible to detach yourself. You become a part of the family. They become a part of you. I am still a part of the Fontenelles."[65] Indeed it is the Fontenelles who are evoked at the beginning of *Flavio*—"a private tragedy at once very public—and I became caught up in their struggle to survive it" (7).

But although the Fontenelle story is more dramatic—a literal loss of life for which Parks cannot exonerate himself—and has more in common with his own black rural Kansas childhood, Flavio's is the most returned to and elucidated, for himself, the most returned to, compulsively, irrepressibly. After initial publication on June 16, 1961, was followed up by an update on July 21, 1961, Parks made a film of his assignment in 1964, shown on NBC in 1966.[66] In 1974 his collection *Moments without Proper Names* republished Flavio's images embedded in a poem. In 1978 we have *Flavio*, his autobiographical memoir account of photographing. And in 1990 Parks reflects on Flavio in two chapters in his latest autobiography, *Voices in the Mirror*. What is a puzzle is why it should be Flavio who becomes vehicle for Parks's palinode, why he should devote to him his only book-length account of photographing one subject. Flavio is the one white subject and the one non-U.S. subject whom Parks has focused on in his documentary photography (he photographed some fashion models for *Vogue* and poverty in Portugal in the fifties before joining *Life*). The choice might seem all the more surprising given that the book *Flavio* itself opens not with Flavio's story but an account of the Fontenelles. In the foreword to *Flavio*, which considers photojournalism as destructive, Parks suggests why this Brazilian boy fascinates. There are two stories, the Fontenelles and the Da Silvas. Parks tries here to differentiate the Da Silva story from the Fontenelles, the success of the first in contrast to the disaster of the second—but *Flavio* contains precisely doubt and uncertainty about the involvement of the photographer. *Flavio* begins with an autobiographical reflection on a photojournalist career—and regret: "As a photojournalist I have on occasion done stories that have seriously altered human lives. In hindsight, I sometimes wonder if it may not have been wiser to have left those lives untouched, to have let them grind out their time as fate intended" (7). He sets out his belief that "The condition of anyone hopelessly ensnared in such misery and poverty could only be helped, I thought, by its exposure in such a great magazine" (8). He then takes his photography into his self and expresses uncertainty about its beneficial role. "From the outset of each assignment to its very end, I reported objectively. But in the end, my emotions, which are by nature subjective, took over. Disguising these emotions in objective clothing I dug deeper and deeper into the privacy of these lives, hoping, I realize now, to reshape their destinies into something better. Unconsciously, I was perhaps playing God. I hold a fierce grudge against poverty because I was so desperately poor when I was young" (9). And it is in giving his account of this assignment that in his autobiography *Voices in the Mirror* he explains his autobiographical involvement in his photographic subjects thus: "I have for a long time, worked under the premise that everyone is worth something; that every life is valuable to our own existence. Consequently, I've felt it was my camera's responsibility to shed light on any condition that hinders growth or warps the spirit of those trapped in the ruinous evils of poverty. . . . To me, they were ghosts of my own past" (179–80).

In confessing in his autobiography that he photographs ghosts of his own past, Parks finds in the image not only not the other and his self but his past self; the images are ghosts of his own past, and in this sense the photographs are a haunting of the present by the past (the dead past self of me alive in the other). It casts documentary photography as a much more ominous—and literal—taking of a life. The racial and national complexities of African American photographer identifying more with the white Brazilian boy than other poor African Americans might be the key to the conundrum. Parks remarks more than once in *Flavio* that his assignment and his photographs are facilitated by his "dark skin" (42), which allows him to blend in with the Brazilian poor amongst whom Flavio lives and who are themselves mostly black. A local television cameraman, blond, comes to film Parks photographing Flavio. Oddly Parks feels the need to "shield" Flavio and the Da Silvas from the local filming (41). Some *favelados* notice the white cameraman and rough him up. African American Parks is seen as insider and the (white) Luso-Brazilian as an outsider/ intruder. But Parks feels shame: "I felt deeply ashamed to have been spared their spittle. My dark skin had saved me—and I wasn't very proud of it" (42). When marked out as different among the white Da Silvas, in his initial account of his assignment, Parks is seen not as black but as American. He gives the children cruzeiros, and they still want more money, forcing their hands into his pockets: "Americano, mawny, mawny, mawny, Americano!" Here, it is his language and his camera that set him apart, not his skin—as American.[67] Unconsciously but inevitably perhaps, he is drawn into a history of African American ambivalence toward Brazil, which has mythologized itself as a color-blind nation, whose central mythology perhaps is that it has no color line.[68] One can be definitive of, represent, the nation, but at the expense—in sacrifice—of what? Why, after all, does Parks choose a white subject when *favelados* tend to be darker than most Brazilians, and certainly darker than the apparently white *Luso* Flavio?[69] Is it to encourage identification among *Life*'s readers? One wonders if the same amount of money would have flowed in had Flavio been in Brazil *and* black. There is a deep irony in Parks's disturbing of Brazil in *Flavio*, given his critique of America and his combating of racism and poverty in the United States—and at this time he was photographing the rise of Black Nationalism in the United States. This irony corresponds to splits in racial and national institutions in Parks's life. He achieves a Rosenwald Fellowship which starts his career photographing Chicago's South Side and African Americans. But to fund this work he photographs fashion assignments and white society ladies. As a *Life* photographer he documents racism. But out on *Life* assignments he is himself confronted with racism and segregation. Writing in a collection that brings together his classic photographs of African American life, Parks wonders if his career has required him to leave black culture. "I wondered whether or not my achievements in the white world had cost me a certain objectivity. I could not deny that I had stepped a great distance from the mainstream of Negro life, not by intention, but by circumstance. In fulfilling my artistic and professional ambitions in the white man's world, I had had to become completely involved in it."[70] While Parks's identity with his subjects enabled his photographs, his success in institutions interposed a distance. It is in relation to Flavio that the contradiction between outsiderness and opposition, and belonging and assimilation is dramatized. He is most insistently Americanized in this assignment, not only part of the national mythology. The publication of these photographs, in *Life* magazine, makes Parks purveyor of the national mythology. Caught up in *Life*'s propagandistic machine, in his Flavio assignment Parks's eye is strategically white, his I—worried, regretful. Flavio represents his palinode as an inverted (negative) reflection of his own departures. Photography has propelled Parks into a white man's world; Flavio as a poor white boy living in Brazil is a ghost of his own past. The text *Flavio* is less an attempt to recover the life than, through retelling Flavio's loss, the echo of a melancholic doubt, not till then expressible about his subjects, about whether Parks saved the life and indeed lost his own. Flavio's story repeats his own loss—but without the mythology of redemption of *Life* magazine. *Life*'s photographs took a life. But as to whose life has been taken and in what sense they have taken a life remain—open.

In one of his reflections on Flavio in his collection *Moments without Proper Names*, Parks writes a poem about a stranger watching a sick boy.

> A stranger, uninvited but expected,
> Coming from a distance
> That only a mind could travel
> Sat silent outside the door,
> Patiently feeling the pulse
> Of this stilt-leg house,
> This minute scrap
> On a mountain's festered side.
>
> Inside, crumpled in his fevered bed,
> A boy lay, silent too, thinking,
> Trying not to remember much,
>
> Knowing that there wasn't much to remember,
>   only that
> His knees stood just above the weeds,
>   only that
> His shadow still slanted short
> Beyond the hot glow of late suns that
>
> Cut across steaming paths
> (Dung paths of man and dog alike)

Where only beasts should have to climb.
Why then, asked this boy of so few moments,
Should this stranger have come so soon
To sit uninvited at his door?[71]

We only know that the boy who tries not to remember too much is Flavio because the poem is reproduced amid images of Flavio. But there is confusion about who the uninvited observing stranger is. By the end of the poem it turns out to be death, who then waits for another night. But at the beginning of the poem the reader, especially the one who knows the Flavio story and *Flavio*, thinks that the stranger could be the photographer. Does Parks's encounter with Flavio rescue Flavio from the underworld or condemn him to it? Does Parks's involvement with his subjects represent the photographer's redemption from his underworld or his return to it? Is it coincidental that, since *Flavio*, since about the late 1970s, Parks has retreated from his career as a documentary photographer and laid aside that weapon increasingly to take photographs instead of nature—more painterly and abstract images, consciously poetic and less realistic? He has also worked on his music as well as his poetry, for he learned piano from his mother, and has gone on to compose a symphony, sonatas, concertos, and a ballet on the life of Martin Luther King. In interview in 1998, Parks, then almost of an age to rival Lévi-Strauss's venerable years, states "You know, the camera is not meant just to show misery. You can show beauty with it; you can do a lot of things. You can show—with a camera you can show things that you like about the universe, things that you hate about the universe. It's capable of doing both. And I think that after nearly 85 years upon this planet that I have a right after working so hard at showing the desolation and the poverty, to show something beautiful for somebody as well. It's all there, and you've only done half the job if you don't do that. You've not really completed a task."[72] This trajectory, from photojournalism to art photography, tells of disillusion with documentary photography and the approximation of a poetic conception of photography, one that doesn't insist on revealing truth or perhaps offers a different kind of truth—allusive, lyrical, missing: losing. In one of Parks's latest books, *Arias in Silence* published in 1994, his foreword draws our attention to the fact that this is a collection of photographs not of crime, racism, and poverty but of nature.[73] "Arias in silence" also poignantly suggests the necessary limits on speech and the powers of communication. Nevertheless, like photography conceived through music as silent imagery, there is a paradoxical and rather mad recognition—the recognition of the palinode—of the need to say this.

The final chapter of *Flavio* is where Parks really confronts what has been the effect of his photographs. He returns in 1976 with the adult Flavio to the site where he first photographed the boy. Skirting the Lagoa or "lagoon," where in 1961 "the lovely sweep of water . . . divided the shacks of the favelados from the radiant white homes of the rich" (191), Parks writes that now as he looks to the Catacumba the *favela* has gone along with all *Life*'s improvements to it. Closed by the state governor Carlos Lacerda who used funds from the Alliance for Progress, for his "Battle of Rio" declared that the *favelados* needed to be evicted "before the Communists get to them"[74]—or moved to other parts of Rio depending on the extent of your vision—the Catacumba hill in 1979 opened as a park with sculptures. For Parks, the *favela* and its struggles had reverted to an original state of nature. "I got out and looked skyward. Cristo Redentor was still there, strongly silhouetted against the darkening clouds. Now I looked just below it. The favela of Catacumba was no more. Where once there had been thousands of shanties clinging to the mountainside, there were now only acres of unkempt tropical foliage. It was staggering" (192). They climb. "The silence of those who had died on Catacumba mingled with the silence of those who had escaped it. . . . And why had we come back to this tomb of bad memories, other than to recall its misery?" (193). Why indeed resurrect this tomb of the Catacomb, ascend to a place to which one ought in the scheme of things descend—a world as topsy-turvy as Toni Morrison's Bottom at the top of a hill?[75] Actually, it's as if the slum had never been there. "As we drove away I turned for one final look, still amazed at how nature had so thoroughly reclaimed the poisonous mountainside" (194). The closing motif, Parks tries to see this forgetting as hopeful and to take the story forward, to the next generation. He concludes that, if we are unsure about the success of Flavio's life, the juxtaposition of Flavio adult with Flavio's own son, Flavio junior—enabled by a photograph of the new Flavio falling out of a billfold Flavio senior gives him before Parks boards his plane and placed next to an old Parks photograph of Flavio at the same age—provides the movement of desire, of Parks's desire: "I stared at the two faces for several moments, realizing suddenly now what the point of Flavio's story was—it lay in this boy" (198). The mood is propulsive but the direction of *Flavio* has been all retrospective, to take us back. The most poignant photograph in the republished *Flavio* is perhaps the final, of adult Flavio looking at photographs of *himself* as a child taken by Parks. I'm not sure that, in *Flavio*, Parks lays to rest his own ghosts. And certainly in his adulthood Flavio remains haunted by his past experience and by Parks.

CHAPTER 4

ELIZABETH BISHOP'S ART OF LOSING

LOOKING FOR SOMETHING, SOMETHING, SOMETHING

In her explicitly autobiographical poem "In the Waiting Room" (the only place where she names herself), Elizabeth Bishop describes the sense of loss that comes from looking at photographs in the *National Geographic* magazine. What the child Elizabeth "carefully / studied" are the ethnographic photographs, particularly of "black, naked women with necks / wound round and round with wire / like the necks of light bulbs. / Their breasts were horrifying." The child reads the magazine straight through, "too shy to stop." In the poem's lack of narrative transition our eye travels with Bishop's. "Suddenly, from inside, / came an *oh!* of pain." The cry, which Bishop first thinks comes from Aunt Consuelo but then is surprised to discover comes from her own mouth, appears to issue from inside those photographs. Bishop writes of the effect of the moment as "I—we—were falling, falling, / our eyes glued to the cover / of the *National Geographic*, February 1918." The "we" must include the women in the magazine. In the midst of "the sensation of falling off / the round, turning world," Bishop realizes "you are an *I*, you are an *Elizabeth*, / you are one of *them*"; but *what* this is she scarcely dare look at. She knows that "nothing stranger / had ever happened / that nothing / stranger could ever happen." What the child awakens to, in the real of the photographs, is the loss of mastery that underlies every moment of self-knowledge.[1]

Throughout her life Bishop was reluctant to be photographed or to send photographs of herself. In a letter to a photographer renowned for her work of authors, Bishop shied at once from photographical and autobiographical exposure. "Maybe one has no right to one's own life or looks."[2] Bishop's reservations about the autobiographical, tied here to the photographical, distinguish her poetry. Her contemporaries of the 1950s and '60s—Robert Lowell, Sylvia Plath, Anne Sexton—took themselves as subjects. Whereas the confessionalists went public with the private, ironically a trajectory that goes from inside to out, Bishop moved from the outside in: from geography to the self as in "The Waiting Room" to produce a geography of the self. She can seem the more introspective and self-reflective poet. She insisted that her poems were "almost invariably just plain facts" about a place (*One Art* 621). Yet like the twice misreferencing of photographs that critics found her doing in "The Waiting Room" and after (there are no photographs of African women or babies in the February 1918 issue of the *National Geographic,* nor in the subsequent issue as Bishop claimed in interview),[3] it is the wavering around the referent, the *almost* invariably that is striking. Can facts ever be variably plain? Can the photograph, this most referential of forms, represent something that's not only no longer there but that's never been there? At issue is how forms such as poetry and photography capture fact. Can one ever represent the facts of a place, of a life, above all in poetry, which is surely the most mediated literary form, the most linguistically self-conscious: one that—particularly as Bishop practiced it as an expert and committed metrician—depends on the "mastery of . . . art"?[4]

The visual, long recognized by critics as prominent in Bishop's poetry, is an attempt to get at the facts but with an awareness of mediation. Bonnie Costello calls Bishop's "a poetry of looks." Harold Bloom says of the "reality of Bishop's famous eye" "it confronts the truth." And Adrienne Rich finds that in Bishop's poetry "the eye of the outsider" enables an identification with other outsiders—but this is too unmediated, as the shifting, thwarted glances and the broken phrasal lines of "In the Waiting Room" show.[5] The perspective that Anne Stevenson notes in Bishop's poetry, what she later calls Bishop's quality as a "word painter," needs to be taken literally and therefore meticulously and poetically.[6] Bishop saw herself as more visual than most poets; she was flattered by the early comment that she was a poet with a painter's eye.[7] Her painterliness has been brought out by the recent publication of her watercolors, which are characterized by their minuteness of observation and self-consciousness of perspective.[8] Like her poetry they show the facts and the problems of representation. *Anjinhos* ("Angels") is inspired by the drowning of a young girl in Rio de Janeiro. As a collage it is made up of detritus of the fact, flotsam of the real: a sandal, shells, a child's dummy, dead butterflies. But these objects are framed in a glass box, Cornell-like: "Objects and Apparitions," as Bishop titled the poem she translated by Octavio Paz about Joseph Cornell. *Cabin with Porthole* similarly documents a ship's cabin during a journey—suitcase, notebooks; fan, flowers—with an exactitude and simplicity of the primitives she so admired, like Gregorio Valdes (who did his best work copying from photographs).[9] But the open porthole again inserts a frame and suggests the difficulty of distinguishing inside from out. In her notebooks Bishop wrote that on board ship, especially with the cabin's lens-like window, travelling produced "some physical shift . . . in one's self," and because of the round porthole the sensation is "of being in a box-camera, of being 'exposed' to the sea & sky—*(camera obscura)*."[10] In the dark room of the ship's cabin an acutening—or rather an *acutance* (photographic sharpening)—in the self's consciousness takes place. We might compare this click or shift to "that sense of constant readjustment" which is loved by the acutely self-conscious early "Gentleman of Shalott" and found throughout Bishop's poetry. The poems like the artwork see the thing but never quite fixedly and never finally. Of oil hitting water Bishop searches out the best way to describe the color produced, and the poem becomes a record of not resolving that search—adjustment in punctuated aside: "like bits of mirror—no, more blue than that: / like tatters of the *Morpho* butterfly." Substitution, or repetition (the latter anaphora), is typical of Bishop. An art of self-correction, it suggests not approximation of perfection but the failure of getting it right. The thing itself, like a butterfly, just escapes. Doubt is intrinsic to Bishop's unbelieving art.[11]

As the cabin/camera analogy suggests, the lack of settling representationally is enfolded in Bishop's work with an unwillingness to settle geographically. Travelling is what shifts perspective. The other place makes you look, makes you notice things, Bishop is remembered by friends as discussing.[12] The visual text that is the consistent analogy for and often subject of Bishop's poetry is the map. Mapping transcribes real space into cartographic representation. As she says in the opening "lessons" of *Geography III* just before "In the Waiting Room," the map is "A description of the earth's surface," "A picture of the whole or a part of the / Earth's surface." But mapping as a form of mastery loses the real. The *National Geographic*, for which mapping remains a principal vehicle of representation, casts its masterful eye over the world. (In its hallmark shots in the vault of Bishop's memory, "Thousands of young boys viewed female breasts for the first time in its pages, a display considered, curiously, not indecent, because they belonged to women of another race."[13] In her letters Bishop called the *National Geographic* "silly"—although she says "I'll buy it just for the photographs" [*One Art* 341].) In *Geography III* in the epigraph, Bishop's proliferating questions override any didactic conclusions we can draw from the opening lessons of her mock childhood primer: *Geography III.* Travelling posed questions for Bishop in excess of answers. Her volume of poetry *Questions of Travel* begins with an awareness that there is a "childishness" in rushing "to see the sun the other way around," to shift perspective through travel. Her notebooks remark on how this desire can become "the god-like ambition to see what something looks like from *there*—or what 'here' looks like from 'there.'" But it is also possible in the process of travelling to find oneself as exposed as a child, inside that camera, not mastering the other but feeling uncertainty about, even losing, the self. "One holds on to the child's sides of one's berth—as if one were going somewhere," Bishop notes, still on board ship. And on arrival in her strange city she writes this is how the world must seem to a child. The child's sense of wonder, seeing for the first time, doesn't translate the seen fully.

Questions of Travel is Bishop's book of poetry about Brazil and this is where she was headed, for the first time when writing these notebooks. To "see the sun the other way around" is of course to cross the equator, which Bishop did, in her voyage from Brooklyn to Brazil in 1951. Brazil especially brought out her "acutance" of observation and compelled her to ask questions. She found a culture overwhelmed by detail to which she, as an outsider, was attuned: "a good place for the keen observer. It is teeming with particularities," as a friend who also spent much time there commented.[14] Settling in Brazil—at least the longest she settled anywhere in her life—Bishop translated a child's narrative, Helena Morley's *Minha vida de menina* (My Life as a Little Girl). What she liked was Helena's precision of observation; as she puts it in the introduction, "*it really happened*; everything did take place . . . just the way Helena says it did."[15] She later attributed realism as a Brazilian characteristic (*One Art* 434). Marianne Moore, the poet with whom Bishop had most in common in her precision of observation, in her review said that Bishop as translator was attracted to qualities she shared with her Brazilian subject, in particular a "hyperprecise eye."[16] *Minha vida* was also an autobiographical work: both the original narrative and Bishop's act of translating it.

Brazil drove Bishop at this later stage of her life to recollect her own childhood. *Questions of Travel* contains in a section titled "Elsewhere" poems about her early life in Nova Scotia. It was also in Brazil that she wrote many of the prose pieces about her childhood, including "In the Village" that sits between the "Elsewhere" and "Brazil" sections of *Questions of Travel,* neither separating nor connecting them. If Brazil posed travel as a question for Bishop, she never quite answered fully, and the significance of that "almost invariably" is that she doesn't close the gap between origin and destination—though her desire is surely there and evident. *Questions of Travel* begins with poems that see Brazil through the self-conscious, self-questioning tourists' arrival. Geography is the subject but mediated. The most realistic poem, "The Burglar of Babylon," retells an event from the *favelas* of Rio: the police shooting of a young *favelado.* When it was originally published the poem was prefaced by Bishop's insistence that everything in it, "often word for word," is true.[17] Bishop watched the episode through binoculars and included this detail in the poem: "Rich people in the apartments / Watched through binoculars." Hers is *a* perspective, not necessarily *the.* Her longest poem accumulates other voices including that of the burglar, his aunt, residents—and the soldiers who shoot him.[18] In the form of a ballad moreover with its origins in the folk song, "Burglar" is particularly responsive to its probably illiterate subject. (Bishop had the poem published as a book for children.) In other Brazil poems Bishop describes Brazilian realities with similar consciousness of perspective. In "The Squatter's Children" the children at first are "specklike" from the point of view of the "sun's suspended eye" suspended in the lines below them. In "Going to the Bakery (Rio de Janeiro)," the moon's gaze takes us down a columnar poem to the "glazed white eye" of the sickly cakes on sale in inflation-stricken, rationing Brazil.

If painting is an analogy for mediation of reality in Bishop's poetry, photography as in "The Waiting Room" draws our attention to what gets lost in mediation, what can't be caught; for that "almost" of the invariable proves a chasm. Photography appears elsewhere in Bishop's poetry and prose. In "First Death in Nova Scotia," one of the poetic returns to childhood enabled by Brazil, little cousin Arthur is "laid out" dead by *her* mother, beneath the chromographs (early color photographs) of the current royal family. At the end of the poem they "invited Arthur to be / the smallest page at court," to enter *into* the photograph. For the child Elizabeth the photograph is the place where the dead go. In a childhood prose memoir again written in Brazil, "Memories of Uncle Neddy," the arrival in Rio of two painted portraits of her uncle and mother as children, "these ancestor-children," sends Bishop back to the family album to compare "tintypes" (photographs on tin plate)—"And although she has been dead for over forty years," to look at photographs of her mother as a child.[19] For less metropolitan Brazilians, she writes of the arrival of photographs, "all portraits apparently strike them as being of dead people" (*One Art* 346). Photography sets up another encounter with death and dying, and tellingly more explicitly this time her dead mother. Her memories of Neddy are recollected in place of those of her mother, because her mother's madness and confinement to a mental institution when Bishop was five meant her early and final absence from Bishop's life. Bishop never saw her mother again. But she lived until Bishop graduated from college. Finally in a poem translated by Bishop but included in her own *Complete Poems*, "Retrato de Família" ("Family Portrait") by Carlos Drummond de Andrade, the photograph is not simply frozen in lost time but its personages could still fly from the portrait, hide. The portrait does not communicate. It does not distinguish the living from the dead. There is only through it "the strange idea of family / travelling through the flesh."

Bishop worked on two collections of photographs in her life. One was published, the other not. When the photographer turns to poetry he retreats from documentary truth. What happens in the inverse? Why would the poet turn from her most linguistic medium of poetry to this message without a code? Bishop likened her observational eye to her intently focused "Sandpiper": "Yes, all my life I have lived and behaved very much like that sandpiper—just running along the edges of different countries and continents, 'looking for something.'"[20] If she never quite found it—probably a home inside and outside herself: a geography of the self—or if, rather, she found she had repeatedly lost what she'd found, her engagement with photographs propelled her each time more deeply into that missing.

WHY NOT TELL THE TRUTH?

Seen as an authentic representation of Brazil and an addition to Bishop's oeuvre if read superficially; shunned as superficial and incongruous with the oeuvre when read thoroughly: Bishop's published volume of photographs, *Brazil*, has had a mixed critical fate.[21] Appearing with Time-Life publications in early 1962, it was the one book she regretted in her life. As late as 1977 two years before her death, she said she chose not to remember much of the book.[22] She had troubles with the form, particularly with the journalistic brief. "Probably no one reads the text, anyway, just looks at the photographs. . . . that kind of writing is hard for me to do and I have to cover the whole country . . . *everything*, even if superficially" (*One Art* 399). She also hated the institution of *Life*. The reason for her taking on the project is that they could afford to pay her as no publisher could for her poetry. She received $10,000 plus expenses, three complimentary weeks in New York, and an excuse to travel in Brazil. "I don't like the magazine and don't like *them* much—these high-pressure-salesman types—but I am doing it for the money—and I do know a lot about Brazil by now, of course, willy-nilly" (399). What she feared is that they would put her knowledge "through their own meat grinder, lawfully, and it will come out sounding like them no matter what I say"; "It is really more like manufacturing synthetic whipped cream out of the by-products of a plastic factory than anything remotely connected with writing—even journalistic writing" (399). It turned out as she feared. After the New York trip to do the final editorial work she was exasperated beyond redemption: "I wouldn't work for them again for $50,000 a book—honestly. . . . And the poor little book isn't going to please anyone—me, LIFE, nor the Brazilian friends I did hope to please—don't judge my prose style by it, for heaven's sake—and I am awfully disappointed in the photographs, too—after all their boasting they had almost none when I got there—and I fought a bloody fight for everyone you will see" (400). Though we are right to read *Brazil* as contentious, we are wrong to read it as Bishop's. We recover Bishop's voice, the significance of *Life's* manufacture, and the bloodiness of their fight if we go back to Bishop's drafts and her correspondence.

The form of the book is superficial and generalizing. *Brazil* closes down questions of travel. "That *Life*-slicked book" (413), as Bishop execrated it, took its place in the Life World Library series. It was the book version of *Life* magazine—or rather it moved the news stories of *Life* toward the geographic overviews of the *National Geographic*. The *National Geographic* began publication, also in America (the "national" was U.S. American), in 1888, but it was only successful when twentieth-century technology made possible travel to ever remoter places and the reproduction of photographs. In a slogan that would be harnessed by *Life* decades later, it was declared by its founders "America's first window on the world"; yet as one of the most profitable publishing companies and the largest purveyor of maps and globes in the world, the *National Geographic's* camera lens like that of *Life's* has been less than transparent. The *National Geographic* was as much an advance arm of globalization as *Life*; it brought the world to America and, by mediating every corner of the globe, exported America to the world.[23] The invention of the illustrated magazine, as one astute contemporaneous commentator said in a criticism that anticipated those made by Lévi-Strauss and Benjamin, was "a strike against understanding"; for illustrated magazines made the world mass reproducible and instantly accessible.[24] The Life World Library cast its standardizing eye on others. Before beginning writing, Bishop was advised to peruse as models those in the series on Japan and Germany. Intended as authoritative, comprehensive and for mass distribution ("sold through the mail" as her literary agent Carl Brandt conveyed the commission to Bishop), *Life* was looking for something that "would, in a sense, sell the country here," and it shouldn't be too factual. The follow-up from Oliver Allen, editor of Life World Library with whom Bishop would have an increasingly antagonistic and eventually furious correspondence over two years, elaborates that the text is neither a guidebook nor exactly a history, a "textbook." It is instead meant for the reader who is "extremely intelligent but not necessarily very well informed, who has a consuming desire to understand the important countries of the world but who may never have the opportunity to visit more than one or two of them." It is in short the ethnography for the armchair traveler scorned by Lévi-Strauss. Above all *Life* want "a readable . . . picture," "for the country to come alive on the pages."

The combination of photographs and text makes *Brazil* a readable picture. The photographs were not Bishop's. She wrote the prose, and the photo-essays inserted between her prose were written by someone else, the book's publication information tells us. The photo-essays, along with intermittent boxes of data about language, history, geography (Allen's idea), emblematize how Brazil is turned into immediate, digestible nuggets. *Brazil* deploys photography in the manner of *Life* magazine as in Parks's assignments. In a photo-essay summing up the Amazon the compressions produce a single, hackneyed message: "the Amazon forest rises, inhuman and repellent, an appendage of wilderness occupying almost half the area of Brazil" (32). This is clearly not Bishop's voice. Contrast Bishop's Amazon in "Santarém," where the "dazzling, watery dialectic" makes this a place from which the poet "really wanted to go no further." The outsider's perspective is embodied in the retiring head of Philips corporation "who wanted to see the Amazon before he died" but, of the wasps' nest admired by the poet and given her by a pharmacist ("small, exquisite, clean matte white"), can only ask: "What's that ugly thing?" The photo-essays echo but monotonize Bishop's prose. It was here that she lost most control. But the process of writing over her in relation to the photographs is typical of the whole book. The photographs-plus-prose format produced confusion from the beginning about the authorship of the book. While Allen says in his commissioning letter that her text is the "guts" of the book (his word) and that Bishop would appear to be the author, what the reader sees on opening the book are the pictures. Allen promised "you can correct us at any stage," and this covered both prose and photographs. In her copy of the letter Bishop underlined and put a check by this assurance. In fact she lost control of both aspects. By the end of the project Allen will acknowledge that what lies behind their misunderstanding is the book's joint byline. Bishop would be so unhappy with *Brazil* that she rued even that her name came first in the dual authorship declared on the title page: "by Elizabeth Bishop and the Editors of *Life*" (3).

The photographs were an important part of the appeal for Bishop. At the beginning she gave Allen a list of "ABSOLUTELY IMPORTANT PICTURES" of what she wanted to show—"new" material including wildlife, such as parrots, monkeys, a toucan, the ant-eater, termite nests, the Brazilian Morpho butterfly; as well as slaves and "Indians with pets." In her choice she wants to give the reader "a fair and up-to-date picture" of Brazil and to avoid the "ephemeral and flashy." They mostly ignored her suggestions and at the same time managed to include what she didn't want. On the cover they placed a photograph by Dmitri Kessel, the fashion photographer whose work Parks refused his photographs of Flavio to appear opposite and who is credited with many of the photographs in *Brazil*. Bishop specifically stipulated that she didn't want a picture of the Sugar Loaf, but their choice of Kessel's of the Rio bay includes it. Their photographs skim off the most obvious of Brazil's geography, contemporary society, architecture. They also ignored her request to write captions. She wanted to "point out the thing that is interesting to have *seen* . . . and avoid *clichés*, preconceptions." Her increasing anxiety about the photographs was not helped when Allen wrote to her toward the end of the project, in an apparent attempt to reassure her in the face of the erratic photographers they were sending out to her in Brazil, that he as picture-editor had final say: "I not only have complete supervision of all copy but of all pictures too." This proved true yet in complete contradiction of his earlier promise that she would be able to make final revisions. For Allen as editor of the Life World Library series it was essential that they produce *Brazil* as readable picture. He stated they needed to strike a balance between pictures that "are purely spectacular, with not very much content" and photos that "are extremely meaningful but perhaps not very appetizing photographically." His commitment to balance was not so ingenuous. Even from this stage in his correspondence we can see on which side *Life* truly weighted the scales: "We feel we must not put out a book that is uninteresting to look at."

One of the few photographs that make it into *Brazil* that Bishop did suggest is Parks's *favela*/Corcovado shot, which in a handwritten postcript to one of her responses to Allen she calls "superb." Clearly she must have seen this issue of *Life* magazine. The juxtaposition in Parks's photograph would have appealed to her. In the notebooks for *Brazil* Bishop remarks on a similar yoking of the beautiful and the terrifying in the film *Black*

Orpheus: "the horror concealed lightly decorat[e]d," she writes of this re-telling of the myth of Orpheus set during the Carnival in Rio's *favelas.* The paradoxes of Parks's photograph have been flattened by the final version of *Brazil.* Where she and we and Parks might see at once the redemption and trauma, the beauty and horror, *Life* overwrites the irreconcilable real with their code. Their caption would have us read simply that "The BLIGHT of poverty, increasing in spite of industrial growth, is taxing the capabilities of free institutions" (138). The caption is remarkably similar in meaning to those that accompanied Parks's photographs and that produce equivalence between poverty and political threat to freedom, in other words commu-nism. That Bishop's book of photographs of Brazil for *Life* was published at this particular moment, in 1962, so soon after Parks's *Life* magazine assign-ment in 1961, is not coincidental. As Bishop is written over in the process of producing *Brazil* a theme emerges that is the same as that underscoring Parks's photographs. The theme, a political one, is that Brazil is a "land of unfulfilled promise"—as Allen proposed it in his commissioning let-ter (every book has to have a theme, he said). At the same time he offered topics that would enable the theme's progression, enclosing sample chapter outlines from two other Life World Library books.

The photographs with the editors' captions narrate the theme of promise. *Brazil* reenlists several photographs published previously in *Life* magazine. The notion of how "RADICAL MOVEMENTS" "feed" on poverty is embodied in two now-facing images that appeared in *Life* June 2, 1961. One of "MILITANT MARXIST, Francisco Julião" speaking to workers, another of Castro's face on a banner held aloft at a demonstration again suggest an incendiary political situation (142–43).[25] At the same time the book must evidence potential for fulfillment, the open-endedness of the words of the title of the last chapter that Brazil is "A Nation Perplexed and Uncertain." Toward the end of the book, particularly in the photo-essays, the narrative becomes entirely futural, speaking of the "critical role ["the new middle class"] will play in the new Brazil" (119). The tense of the book is that Brazil is emergent but not enough, that progress is incipient: that Brazil is "under-industrialized" (97). We are not surprised then when the book concludes with a direct appeal for financial aid, which we are told will lead to strong, in other words U.S.-friendly government. Brazil is presented as developed and stable enough to deserve financial aid but undeveloped and unstable enough to need it. Particularly in the northeast and with the grow-ing *favela* problem, poverty is related causally to communism: a narrative that can be redirected given sufficient financial investment. The rewriting of Brazil's contemporary history for the United States is the rationale of the book. This theme—and its theme is its *studium*—is revealed in the introduction to the U.S. edition by John Moors Cabot, a former U.S. ambassador to Brazil. Sounding suspiciously like the mission statement that preceded Parks's photos in *Life,* Cabot emphasizes Brazil's importance— and *Brazil*'s importance—in achieving the current U.S. administration's "inter-American ideals" (7). "The magnificent picture essays [and] . . . Miss Bishop's brilliant text . . . bring the reader a better understanding of our South American sister republic. . . . For . . . understanding and co-operation between Brazil and the United States were never more necessary than they are today" (7). This introduction is quite different from that to the British edition that, by a British professor of Portuguese, presents *Brazil* as helping redress readers' poor knowledge of Brazil.[26] Bishop says Cabot's introduction resembled nothing that Cabot wrote (*One Art* 405).

In fact particularly Bishop's last two chapters resemble nothing *she* wrote, at least not in the records we have. And in her list of corrections to the revised galleys that she got back from *Life,* chapters 9 and 10 are most subject to her rejections of their revision, rejections that were not accepted of their revisions that therefore eventually got published. *Brazil*'s narrative and its politics are not hers. The titles of the last two chapters were published as "Struggle for a Stable Democracy" and "A Nation Perplexed and Uncertain." In Bishop's drafts her title for chapter 9 was first "A Golden Age of Republicanism," later changed to "The Republic"; she had no title for chapter 10. Her chapter 9 is designed to give a much fuller, more complex, less linear account of the politics of contemporary Brazil embedded in the context of the history of the Empire and Republic. While in the published version some of the historical material has been moved to an earlier chapter that would now be recognized by *Life*'s readers as "historical," most of Bishop's writing has been omitted or condensed. In the place of the excision the editors reduce four to five pages of detail to a platitudinous sentence: "Although the young republic had yet to produce a body of statesmen, matters gradually improved" (128). What was not included from Bishop's drafts complicates the politics of the book. An account of the politicization of communism in Brazil, "which provided the pretext for setting up the Vargas dictatorship," is much reduced in the final version. Bishop's drafts call Vargas's regime a dictatorship with consistency. While *Life* occasionally use the word *dictator,* they mostly perform substitutions: "Vargas era" for instance (130). Bishop is much more critical of the brutality of Vargas's rule and reveals its political allegiance. They cut her description of his crushing communism "with great severity" and its effect on intel-lectuals of arrest and exile. By the same token *Life* inserts into her prose for

Vargas's opponents the labels "Communist" and "hard-core Communists," which would seem to justify his nondemocratic government (147). And whereas she says that Vargas allied himself with the fascist party during the Second World War and was forced to fight against the Axis powers only after popular demonstration, they say he made "friendly gestures to both sides" (130). "Under the name of the 'New State,' fascism began in Brazil," Bishop wrote. Allen deletes and inserts passages that describe how with the help of U.S. aid, Vargas "laid the foundations on which a strong economy could eventually be constructed" (131).

Far from the theme of financial aid in current U.S. relations with Brazil, Bishop is *critical* of loans. In the drafts she speaks against the concentration of policy on financial aid. She writes that it is not just money Brazil needs—"far from it"—and suggests that U.S. aid to build Brasilia fed a cycle leading to inflation. Allen's inserts are thus all the more brazen: "To alleviate the ills besetting it and to enable it to maintain its economic growth, Brazil needs financial aid" (147–48). Her chapter 9, on recent politics in the context of Brazil's history, is open-ended: "It is still too early to foresee the results of the change." Their substitution draws the chapter to an alarming close by connecting Brazil's increasing foreign debt, inflation, and the need for electoral reform. Crucial in the difference is a passage from chapter 9 discussing the awarding of the Order of the Southern Cross to Che Guevara by Brazil's President Quadros, which had just taken place. This passage is entirely missing from Bishop's draft where there is simply a gap and a red question mark. Allen notes that Bishop promised to cable a new version of the Guevara passage later but they never received it. Yet in her later correction notes on the galleys Bishop charges them with leaving out the word *communist* for Guevara, which indicates that she did at one point produce the passage, whether from Brazil or written in New York. If Guevara, just given Brazil's highest prize, was a communist, then Quadros too would appear communist and *Life* had to be careful in justifying the worthiness of financial aid about making Brazil seem too red. At the same time Goulart, the replacement populist president, *Life* presents as regarded as leftist. Bishop writes that he was regarded by military heads as leftist. These subtle changes—variations—are crucially loaded. She foresees problems with the military that are again cut: "the very expression, ["spirit of compromise" between the left and right] like 'land of unfulfilled promise' is almost a red flag to a Brazilian at present." If the former phrase had always meant the excuse for a military coup, and the latter an excuse for foreign intervention, Bishop in one sentence speaks against both and warns at the dangers of relying on truisms. While it is not true to say that Bishop's and *Life*'s anxieties about Brazil's future lay in antithetical directions, certainly Bishop's drafts evidence that her political outlook is less fixed and secure than the published version would have us believe.

In Bishop's drafts the "theme" is how the United States looks at Brazil. Though *theme* is the wrong word since she says in conversation that unlike many she has no theories of Brazil.[27] The published book, therefore *Life*, stress how a shift to the left in Brazil "would have far-reaching repercussions throughout South and Central America" (146). Bishop in her corrections insisted that they make the change back to her original, that it would have "repercussions for the USA." Allen replaces all of the comparisons Bishop makes to the United States with "any other part of the world" or "any other country" (146, for example). But this is not Bishop's point. She's working as a comparative Americanist. They repeatedly neutralize the concerted and evident effort she makes to perform comparisons at almost every turn. In her notes for chapter 10 for example, she writes that Brazil is "Undoubtedly the most important country for us to deal with." In her corrections she accuses *Life* of being "pretty condescending" about Brazil and clearly her desire is to highlight this lack of U.S. knowledge. She calls for more education of Americans in relation to Brazil. She begins her draft of the contentious chapter 10 with lack of perception on both sides: "The United States and Brazil have many things in common. . . . It is time we got to know and appreciate each other better; time that the United States gave more to Brazil than loans and those less attractive features of our culture that, rightly or wrongly, are thought to be 'Americanizing' the world. The United States and Brazil have more in common than coffee and Coca Cola."

Bishop's comparisons result in a sometimes impassioned and certainly prescient criticism of the United States. She hopes that the "harsh industrialization" of the United States may be avoided by Brazil. The "United States should be careful of what it exports." And she recollects all that the United States doesn't know about Brazil that may be a precedent for the United States. She presents the "Indian problem" as better managed in Brazil (as it might have been then) and likewise racial problems following slavery. Her *Brazil* contains a good deal more on racial mixing (one can imagine how this would have gone down in civil rights–riven United States) as definitive of Brazil and she is keen to detail racial typology—"caboclo," "claro." Allen is determined to whitewash this with his substitution—"With each new census an increasing proportion of the total population is classified as white" (114). Bishop details an advertisement for a gas range of a black cook kissing her white mistress, which for her illustrates Brazil's characteristic racial tolerance and which she states would never have been shown in the United States. When this description was first published in her article on Rio for the *New York Times* in 1965, she was dragged over the coals by a Brazilian critic for being patronizingly American by treating Brazil as a country of underdevelopment awaiting U.S. development.[28] But the passage was omitted from *Brazil,* one imagines, for suggesting the opposite and what Bishop had intended—that Brazil was progressive in race politics compared to the United States. Bishop's suggestions of what the United States can learn from Brazil cut from publication are consistently subversive: Brazil has no death penalty, no real enemies, has never had a war of conquest, atomic bombs ("and so far has never expressed any desire for them") and "no industries that circle the globe." She is much more critical of tourism, capitalism, and commodification. "Progressive" and "modern" appear in quotation marks in her drafts, removed for the published version, with the attitude to development a big difference between her and Allen. Allen's inserted calls for financial aid seek to further industrialization and building in the interior. Surviving in *Brazil* is Bishop's discussion of the effects of commercialization on the sambas. Radio technology and Hollywood have homogenized their poetry, she writes, producing from Carnival a monoculture. And—although she doesn't seem to have any self-consciousness when she writes this; or none survives—photographers, including tourists, interfere and change the nature of the activity by trying to get good shots. In her criticism journalism is implicated in this commodification, for Bishop writes that in Brazil writers must often resort to journalism for financial reasons, to "deadening effect" and the "deterioration of writing": again, of course, cut.

The notion of perspective and the sense of where we're looking from so important to Bishop are cut from the published version even on the level syntax. Allen has replaced every "we" in Bishop's drafts to produce passive sentence constructions or simple statements—no longer "we think" but "it is." Predicates: every subjective has been objectified out. Her personable "you" addressed to the reader has also been cut. In this "you" she had conjured her reader into perspective in Brazil. Her notes for chapter 1 multiply points of view so that "you see" Brazil from various times and places, as she asks us to make one "shift in angle of vision and imagination" after another. She describes Rio de Janeiro as it would be seen by "A foreigner lying in the old Strangers['] Hospital" (where Bishop had been to dry out, placed there by her partner Lota for whom she decided to settle in Brazil); and from a plane; and from a skyscraper penthouse; and from a boat approaching part of a coast that had barely changed since 1500, reliving the sensation of the Portuguese as they approached it for the first time:

a complicity of perspectives Bishop would take up in her "Brazil, January 1, 1502" poem. The whole draft is much more like *Questions of Travel,* with the writer indicating that this is what "the average North American" would see, parenthetical asides reminding us that these are an outsider's observations of Brazil and therefore limited and subject to adjustment—pointers to what has been left out which have all been deleted by Allen. This loss of perspective is perhaps what Bishop means when she accused them of "telescoping" her sentences. In radical revision of Bishop's descriptions of paintings of Portinari compared both with the actual Brazilian landscape and what the stranger on arriving in Brazil might be struck by, *Life* cut the double frame, making Portinari's images simply reflective of Brazil. They do this by compressing her sentences, flattening her focal shifts. They slide together her perspectives on Brazil to produce generalization and cliché—forcing them into one another like the tubes of a hand-telescope; or, taking the view from afar but using the telescope, eliding or belying the distance. Bishop, who writes the anecdote without generalization, the quirky concrete without conclusion, somehow manages to be closer up while indicating her viewing distance.

Bishop's protest—"Why not tell the truth?"—comes in response to *Life*'s leaving out "communist" for Guevara. They are "*lying* like RUGS" she wrote to friends (*One Art* 400). Their suggestion had been "communist-leaning" and eventually they decided on the awkward and dangling "believed to be a Communist" (133) (by whom? Again perspective is cut). "It is a very severe thing, Elizabeth, to call someone a Communist," Allen scolds. "How would you define the truth in this instance?" In response to Bishop's accusation on their tiptoeing around the Vargas regime that they were "whitewashing dictators," Allen wrote that although she may find it hard to believe there was no editorial slanting in an "operation" run by "Time, Inc." These political details are important because as Bishop's draft recognizes they set the stage for Brazil's volatile contemporary politics. For Bishop in the draft, Vargas's suppression of left-wing activity was an excuse to bolster his own dictatorial powers. It was to be—and Bishop's insistence on the perspective of political and other judgments is historically farsighted—a precedent for the military dictatorship that would justify its coup of 1964 by pointing to the increasingly socialist politics of first Quadros, then Goulart. The political changes in Brazil in turn set the stage for Bishop's life. The key connection for Bishop is Carlos Lacerda (the same governor of Rio and Guanabara state whose effects are encountered by Parks and who was himself a newspaper man), in whose circle Bishop increasingly moved in the '50s and early '60s. An assassination attempt on Lacerda in 1954 was the main factor in bringing the end of Vargas's regime. Lacerda had eyes on the presidency himself, but after the coup he capitulated to the military government.[29]

At the end of 1961 Bishop went to New York to do the final revisions on *Brazil*. The trip was already three months late and what is clear from Bishop's drafts is that the book, particularly those all-important chapters 9 and 10, was patchy and incomplete. She apparently didn't have time to check that final chapter. In the dispute that continued even after the project Allen says that it was because Bishop was "unable to do the revisions on chapter 10" that he did them himself—and apparently therefore almost conjured the chapter from scratch and in the course turned the book into its plea for American governmental financial aid for Brazil. What happened in late 1961 that Bishop proved unable to finish the project, particularly that final chapter, the most important and the one that surely most led to Bishop's repudiation of the book? In 1961 Bishop's Brazilian partner, Lota de Macedo Soares, an architect, received a job from Lacerda to direct the design of a park for the poor on the reclaimed Flamengo landfill, something of a counterbalance in Rio to the Lagoa for the rich besides which rises the hill of Catacumba and (before Lacerda) its *favela*. At the time Lacerda was speaking out against communism, Castro, and in support of the U.S. invasion of Cuba. Relations between him and the then president, Quadros, who had just decorated Guevara, were strained, a tension that did not make Lota's work on the park any easier. Bishop's letters, which were responsive initially to Lacerda's obvious intelligence, found him increasingly the political opportunist, egoist and hysterical. Conversely she at first didn't trust Goulart and his politics but then admired his calm. When Bishop was supposed to be finishing *Brazil,* Lota was preoccupied with the park and increasing bureaucracy. Bishop's letters in turn are preoccupied with Lota. Work on the park would change Lota and their relationship irreversibly. The park with its backdrop of the changing politics in Brazil would not only prove key to thwarting Bishop's work on *Brazil*. It would carry over as trauma from this photographic book on Brazil to the next one.

Bishop notoriously hated politics, and in extensions of the Brazilian journalist's criticism of her previous representation of Brazil she has been charged with being patronizing and even racist, as having a detached if not reactionary stance. But new readings of Bishop complicate the received idea of her as conservative. Camille Roman argues that Bishop moved to Brazil in part because she dissented from U.S. cold war militarism and she seeks to highlight dissenting politics in her poetry. The paradox is that Bishop had not escaped the military conflict at all but becomes more immersed in it, with Lota's park, Lacerda, the military coup—and *Brazil*. For Roman's reading as for Sandra Barry's, it is important that Bishop is outside of American culture.[30] She was not of course U.S. American but three-quarters Canadian, born in Nova Scotia, and only moved to the United States when her mother was institutionalized. Her mother was diagnosed permanently insane and confined to a public sanatorium in Nova Scotia, moreover, after the death of Bishop's father—who was half American—removed from her mother the right to U.S. citizenship and the private treatment she had to date received. In the notes for *Brazil* Bishop was consistently critical of nationalism. Her articulated comparisons of Brazil with America make us conscious of the limitations of national perspectives. Bishop was certainly not cognizant of the contemporary U.S. propagandistic context in which her prose would appear. At the beginning of the project she is telexed from *Life*'s New York office to ask if she'd ever been a communist, which at this point causes her much mirth and incredulity. Yet *Life*, she intuits in her letters, behaves exactly as does the U.S. embassy in Brazil (*One Art* 400). It may look like conjuring a conspiracy theory to suggest the connection between Allen's cuts/substitutions and contemporary U.S. politics toward Brazil but they do produce a consistent line. And we can't believe it is just the process of edition as Allen tells Bishop.

Bishop can't tell the "almost invariable" truth in their format. The different political conceptions of truth intersect with truths in different genres: narrative, prose, and photography lined up as documentary or absolute on one side; fragments, poetry, and a notion of photography as more variable and losing on the other. Truth fixed and revealed versus a form that allows truth to escape, or rather recognizes truth as that which escapes. The joint authorship of Bishop and the editors of *Life* was a remarkable mismatch. He is full of flattery for her writing when he commissioned her but one wonders if Allen had ever *read* Bishop. She's an appalling choice for this book given that she was a poet not a journalist, that she had published very little, and that she was terrible at meeting deadlines and letting go her writing. He gave her very little time to write the book, commissioned as it was in June and with the bulk of it expected by September. The pace of the project was so against Bishop's nature. Her notebooks for *Brazil* are telling. One titled *"to be used"* is empty other than a single address on the first page. In another, scrappy and fragmented, one phrase is repeated throughout and concerns a *Life* photographer with whom Bishop was apparently drawing a contrast to the traveler—something that a traveler could do or see "(always excepting / a LIFE photographer)." As not prose and thus not usable in *Brazil* the poem is working out her frustration with, rather than furthering, the *Life* project. Bishop's drafts submitted to *Life* suggest she struggled with the writing. "I gave up here," she hand-annotates the end of one chapter draft.

Bishop anyway found prose more difficult than poetry. In correspondence with Lowell she wrote that poetry allows her a truth that prose doesn't: "somehow—that desire to get things straight and tell the truth—it's almost impossible not to tell the truth in poetry, I think, but in prose it keeps eluding one in the funniest way." Lorrie Goldensohn comments that it is precisely the ellipses and gaps of poetry that allow Bishop to shape a truth.[31] Whereas taking prose to its most prosaic, *Brazil* demanded that she document everything and do so in a narrative with a theme. It is significant in this regard that Bishop objects to Allen's use of the term *verse* as interchangeable with what she had written, *poetry*. *Verse*, from the Latin for the turn that comes at the end of the line of the plough and now synonymous with that line, is more narrative than *poetry*, from the Greek for doing, making. Bishop's voice is heard in *Brazil* most recognizably when she speaks about the untranslatability of nineteenth-century Brazilian romantic poets. She evokes their "*saudades* (melancholy yearnings)" (103)—though in an earlier draft she had glossed this as "nostalgia tinged with despair," struggling to translate as if to emblematize this non-translatability. In interview soon after her anthology of translations of Brazilian poets, Bishop said that Brazilians were given to depression;[32] her biographer believes she equated melancholia with homesickness, but her balancing both terms in the drafts suggests she wanted to keep open a gap—a gap that *saudades* perhaps occupies (but doesn't fill).[33] Bishop rejected the line about "unfulfilled promise" in a letter to Allen. She acknowledges this to be true of Brazil but wants to make it secondary, include other things, less line. Her early drafts after the notebooks make clear what these other things were. Her *Brazil* would have been much more fragmented, more like her poetry with the gaps showing. She wanted not a unifying picture but a broken, composite collage, holding at a distance certain generalizations about Brazilians: "familiarity" and "laziness" appear in her chapter outline in quotation marks. She wanted to illustrate Brazil through the anecdotal, as depressed but humorous, made up of quirky details and quotations—bumper stickers ("Woman, still the best Brazilian product"), sambas (which she called "a real living poetry of the people"), folklore, jokes, and sayings, which do make it in but thinly. Bishop's book on Brazil would have been much more pointed, much more in perspective.

Allen also changed her prose style and this is why *Brazil* reads so clunkily and it's obvious that this isn't Bishop. Reading the drafts one realizes that in the cutting of details all the life has gone. There's very little call for this because though they are clearly written fast the later drafts are as coherent as Bishop's prose ever is. The cuts matter because Bishop cared so much about *le mot juste*. She agonized over precision, over every aspect of production, finding the act of writing very painful, and alternated between putting her writing away, destroying it, and rewriting it.[34] Bishop was the arch self-critic. "I supposes no critic is every really as harsh as oneself" (*One Art* 146). When asked if she thought someone had too many defenses she responded, surprised, "Too *many*? Can one ever have *enough* defenses?"[35] As *Life* make prosaic, the beautiful balance and rhythm of Bishop's prose that reads more like poetry is thrown off. "A hand's-breadth is often more than a day's work" on the art of Portuguese women's lace-making becomes Allen's "A hand's breadth often takes more than a day to do" (84). Allen U.S.-Americanized Bishop's prose. "Manioc" becomes "tapioca"; "sweets," "candy"/"confections" (54). *Life* wanted to render the other perfectly translatable, to master. In debates with Lowell about translation Bishop said that, though one must be faithful to the original, the translator can never get it exactly: "probably at least 50% is always lost, in another language."[36] While there's no record of whatever Allen and Bishop agreed in person in their meeting in New York, the violence of *Life*'s overwriting can be felt in her response to the galleys sent her once she had returned to Brazil. "Please don't put in that cliché," she begs, accusing them of "ignorant chauvinism" toward Brazil. And repeatedly she writes "I corrected all this in N.Y.," "I remember correcting this satisfactorily in N.Y." She was a distressed reader of the galleys and became more so, particularly of the crucial chapter 10, with question marks and underlinings and asterisks culminating in a frustrated *"No!"* and a plea: "Please . . . my words and phrases." Of the photographs apparently Bishop didn't see these with the proofs at all.

In response to her corrections Bishop received back from Allen's office a telegram rejecting them, defending their changes, and turning the criticism back on beleaguered Bishop, even to grammar; key for them is narrative, transition, down to sentence: "PLEASE DONT CALL US IGNORANT CHAUVINISTS . . . WHAT YOU TERM CLICHE IS RESULT OF MY ATTEMPT TO SHORE UP TRANSITION AT THAT POINT AFTER YOU CONFESSED INABILITY TO DO SO." This was followed by a nine-page letter. Beginning with none-too-carefully-disguised impatience at how "fascinating and challenging assignment it was for us all. Each one of these books turns out to be exasperatingly different from the last, and each one turns out to be a great deal more difficult than we had anticipated, and all that was particularly true in the case of *Brazil*"—Allen goes on: "It came as something of shock to me to read, 'I beg you not to change my words any more. If necessary omit phrases but please don't distort or iron out what little life they have left.'" He proceeds to give her "a point-by-point explanation" of why they failed to meet her request that they not make changes. Given that the book was now in final proofs and was anyway beyond change, particularly Bishop's, it is hard to understand why Allen undertakes this, other than to pour out his defensive, at turns offensive, stream. It must have been a crushing letter for Bishop to receive. Allen is at turns "amused," "confused," "surprised," "irritated," "puzzled," and "disagreed" with her reaction to their changes, which he would "defend vociferously." His refusal to meet her requests saved her from foolish errors, he writes, and he throws back at her the charge of "condescending," which they fixed through their editing and revising. He simply understands meaning not style. Though the style was changed, he says, to put in transitions, the meaning was not changed. "But for goodness sake [sic] what difference does it possibly make?" he writes, illustratively. For him they are "bickering over these microscopic points." Yet for her they had telescoped her in style, views, perspective and hence in her Brazil. She, like the sandpiper, wants the detail.

Bishop came out of the battle absolutely ambivalent about revision. She clearly wanted to wash her hands of Time-Life. In her letter to Lowell coinciding with the book's publication she writes, "Well, as Ginsberg put it so brilliantly: 'Are you going to let your emotional life be run by *Time* magazine?'—it seems to me I have been, lately" (*One Art* 406). She uses *Time* magazine as exemplary of the globalization happening all over the world, which she sees as leading to the "dying out of local cultures . . . one of the most tragic things in this century" (408). In her old home of Great Village, Nova Scotia—as in her new home of Rio de Janeiro—"trucks arrive bringing powdered milk . . . and *Time* magazine" (408). U.S. Americanization is taking place in the continent north and south and *Time* is inculpated. Yet what's striking is that in the same letter Bishop does not wholly disown the *Life* book. She is still wanting her readers to go to it, to get something of her ideas about Brazil. "The *Brazil* book is awful; some sentences just don't make sense at all. And at least the pictures could have been good. Maybe, if you can read it at all, you will find a trace here & there of what I originally meant to say" (405). Before Bishop signed a copy of *Brazil* for at least one friend she went through the book, "every line of every page making changes in the text back to the way she originally had written it," obsessively looking to return her work to her work to regain some sense of her truth lost from representation. Yet when Time-Life asked her to revise and update certain sections formally for a second printing in the autumn of 1962, she flatly refused.[37] What's marked about the *Brazil* drafts in fact is the very little correction that appears on them. Bishop was in her poetry a serial reviser. It took her sometimes decades to perfect a poem, and her numerous drafts and corrections show her struggle with completing, show that for her writing was struggling. "Nature repeats herself, or almost does: / *repeat, repeat repeat; revise, revise, revise*," Bishop wrote in "North Haven." But unlike Lowell, for whom "North Haven" is an elegy, Bishop never revised her poems once they were published, the only exceptions being when she had been pressed too soon to a deadline. Nature almost repeats herself. Like the "almost invariably" the almost makes all the difference and makes for not a repetition but a return.

Repeat, repeat, repeat; revise, revise, revise

Three years after publication of *Brazil,* in a letter of 1965 Bishop writes to Lowell about a notice of a Rockefeller award she had received. The Imaginative Writing and Literary Scholarship required initial nomination by a committee, to be followed up by an application from the candidate, and Lowell, who was then an adviser for the Rockefeller Foundation, had put forward Bishop as he did for many of her fellowships and appointments. Saying that she guessed he had something to do with it, Bishop declares that she was "delighted" to receive the invitation.

> If you can—I know you're in Maine—will you tell someone or other that I do want one (desperately, but don't say that!) It fits in so well with a scheme I've been working on lately—I haven't time to go into details now, but I want to put a book together—prose pieces—about Brazil—and in order to do it I shall have to make a good many rather expensive trips by air and boat. I think writing on S[outh] A[merica]—and Brazil—has declined sadly since the days of the great naturalists—for a 100 years, that is—and the run-of-the-mill book is written, badly, by someone who has been here three months. . . . I have three pieces more or less done— before I heard from the Rockefellers.—My idea is to mix places, a few life-stories, short stories more or less, a piece on Aleijadinho probably— perhaps popular music, etc.—and the places will be those where the journalists don't go, or rarely—Where life is pretty much unchanged but bound to change very fast very soon. I shall try to do all this, of course, in the most beautiful prose imaginable—and with photographs—for which I shall have to buy a new camera;—& films are very dear now, etc. . . . So

far I'm calling it (all this was in the works, so to speak before I heard from the Rs at all, so it isn't made-up specially) the old title I wanted to use before: BLACK BEANS AND DIAMONDS; (tentatively).[38]

From 1966 to 1968 Bishop received $12,000 from the Rockefeller Foundation, successful with the full amount she requested for the full time. Her application outlines in more detail what she had in mind in putting together this other book on Brazil. She begins by mentioning Lévi-Strauss's *Tristes Tropiques* as the exception to her century's writing about Brazil that is "vulgarly written, extremely superficial, and frequently inaccurate as well." She, in contrast, "fond enough of the people to have made a home here" for fourteen years, knows the language and has visited most of the better-known sights. And with the money and the time she planned to travel further, to the more inaccessible parts of the country, to see the upper Amazon and the Rio São Francisco. She had already "completed, partly completed, or outlined" a dozen chapters: an account of a voyage down the lower Amazon, another to the Amazon delta; an essay on Aleijadinho, Brazil's greatest artist; an article on St. George's Day in Rio; a study of Noel Rosa, the most famous of samba composers, the life story, "a typical one, of a servant of mine from the northeast, etc." She also planned to include some poems "that would seem to go better in such a book than in a volume of verse." And she wanted to use her own photographs to illustrate the book. She already had a few "considered good enough to use for reproduction." The book would be 400–500 pages. She was sure that she could complete it and had a publisher already interested.

Undoubtedly Bishop had been planning such a book on Brazil for many years. Her letters reveal the trail. Even before *Brazil,* in 1960 she had written to Lowell—and this may have planted the seed in his mind for the nomination—"Rockefeller has long been interested in South America, and I have an idea for getting money to see more of it and finish up a book of stories about Brazil" (*One Art* 383). In 1956 she noted that she had "planned out a special book of travel sketches about Brazil" (327). And in 1946 even before she went to Brazil she wrote to her publishers Houghton Mifflin seeking an advance for "a book of travel essays about certain parts of South America" (142). She didn't get it, but the request raises the question of to what extent she went to South America with such a book in mind. Hence when she wrote to Lowell about his nominating her for the Rockefeller fellowship in 1965 that "It fits in so well with a scheme I've been working on lately," the scheme was late not so much in the sense in which she meant it of "recent" as late in "already overdue." It was also overdue following *Brazil,* for what is clear is that this was going to be corrective if not retractive, to replace not only "the run-of-the-mill book . . . written, badly, by someone who has been here three months" but also her own previous book on Brazil, and its "places will be those where the journalists don't go, or rarely." This critical comment reveals that Bishop had obviously been smarting since her involvement with *Life* and that she bucked against the journalistic directive of *Brazil.* The "working title" she proposed in her application, "Black Beans and Diamonds," is at the pivot of this old-but-new, originary but revisionary project. Bishop considered "Black Beans and Diamonds" at one point as the title for her *Minha vida* translation. (She sent her introduction to *Diary of Helena Morley* as a sample of her prose about Brazil with her grant application, and she sent her translation of *Helena Morley* originally to publishers with photographs) (*One Art* 301). But the words also appeared together in the drafts of *Brazil* in a passage about *"futebol"* that is among those that get cut. In some lovely, lyrical details Bishop writes that the Brazilian team in the 1958 World Cup were allocated a supply of black beans, the staple dish of Brazil. Pelé, who changed the face of world football (and race in the football world),[39] was known as the "Black Diamond." When proposing "Black Beans and Diamonds" as a title for *Minha vida,* Bishop was aware that she would have to wait and "see what the publishers think" of it (*One Art* 316). Obviously they didn't think very much. "Black Beans and Diamonds" would appear to have been dropped from both projects as being untranslatable, not recognizable. In choosing it as title now Bishop redeemed something of that untranslatability and made it her subject.

The title "Black Beans and Diamonds" also captures the mosaic nature of the book. Its fragmentedness, ellipses, or compressions were instrumental in making Brazil *un*translatable in this work. *Black Beans and Diamonds* was to be unapologetically not a narrative. "This may sound like a grab-bag sort of book—and that is really what I have in mind," she wrote in her application. Made up of fragments and observations, not only in different genres but different media—text and photographs; prose and poetry; memoir, essay, and fiction—the book would have been multiperspectival. For all its fragmentedness much of the material Bishop promised is remarkably complete. Even the more sketchy pieces give us a consistent sense of her shifting perspective, not only from piece to piece but within pieces. Translated newspaper quotations jostle alongside sambas. A recipe for the beautifully named Brazilian sweet *baba de moça* ("maiden's drool"), with grated coconut, sugar, egg yolks, cinnamon, wonderfully intersplices the political history of sugar in an account of plantations given by Gilberto

Freyre. As non-narrative but also photographic-textual *Black Beans and Diamonds* was to be *Brazil*'s mirror image. (The only other transmedia text Bishop had produced was *Brazil*.) The photographs were again fundamental. In a 1966 interview given at her home in Brazil and much about Brazil but that conspicuously fails to mention the *Brazil* book, Bishop says *Black Beans and Diamonds* is to be "a combination of a travel book, a memoir, and picture book. I am quite interested in photography. I'd like to make Brazil seem less remote and less an object of picturesque fancy."[40] Part of the reason why she needed so much money, she writes in the budget section of her grant application, is the expense of a camera, the film, and development.

That Bishop budgeted for and did indeed take her own photographs shows a very different relationship to photography from that we have seen her take in *Brazil*—to others' photographs, detached, written over by *Life*, apparently objective. Bishop's letters reveal that she took photography into her life, from 1938 when she enclosed her "best snapshots" of Key West and planned to take still "many more pictures" of local life (*One Art* 67). Once she was in Brazil references to enclosed photographs increase, presumably because she was further away from her correspondents but also perhaps to convey the real difference of her life there. Her written comments on the rear of many of her photographs, about the mechanics of a water supply or the exact location of a perspective, as well as annotations and arrows on the front indicating what she wanted her recipient to notice, show she used photography to detail the facts about a place. Or rather the almost facts of a place, because that she couldn't quite cede text in her annotations suggests that she didn't quite trust photography to do the truth-telling. Yet her photographs are remarkable on initial viewing because they corroborate her poems of *Questions of Travel*. It really did happen just as she wrote it. There really are "too many waterfalls" in her home with Lota, Samambaia, Petrópolis; there really are "clouds putting pressure on the mountaintops." In an ornate birdcage one can see the "whittled fantasies of wooden cages." There, in a canoe, is the "riverman"—though Bishop had yet to go to the Amazon when she wrote this poem. Bishop's collection holds a wealth of slides and photographs, a wealth not only in quantity but quality. She was a prolific and good photographer, not surprisingly given her eye in painting and poetry. She cared about photography as form. In her letters she remarks on a man who could write about Brazilian flora and fauna, "although he was a dreadful photographer, you'll see" (*One Art* 280). In what appears to have been at the time just a happy juxtaposition, in that same 1960 letter in which she first mentions her plans for a book via Rockefeller on Brazil, Bishop writes excitedly to Lowell of her growing photography collection: "Did I tell you that I have been taking photographic slides? . . . I have a small Amazon lecture and a small Cabo Frio lecture, etc. Lota does the machine part. . . . Who is ever going to look at these, and when, I can't imagine" (383). The excitement is contagious to any researcher looking at the photographs now. This is particularly the case with the slides, which one must view through Bishop's own projector, since their frames now measure too large for modern projectors; we take the machine part of Lota. The plans for *Black Beans and Diamonds* suggest that Bishop had found a place for her photographs.

Several of the prose accounts that Bishop planned to include and wrote show how she would have punctuated her writing with her photographs. She notes when and where she took photographs with regularity, often then with these placed in her typescript into handwritten parentheses, as if in a later drafting the photographs would replace notes. On her promised

Elizabeth Bishop, photograph taken in the Amazon, February 1960. From Special Collections, Vassar College Libraries. Reprinted with permission.

account of her trip to the Amazon finally made in February 1960, she details taking photographs in Manaus, the Amazon's main port, of the fountain in the city's square, the Praça de Matriz; and we see it just as she describes it, "a magnificent affair" with its life-sized cherubs and hexagonal base pool. We see described and photographed the poorer section of the town, the bright colors of shutters, the men with their white pants sitting outdoors eating dinner, with *cafezinho* cups arranged on bright, oilcloth table covers—photographs that are painterly for, as Bishop says, the scene is "all very much like Brazilian primitive paintings." We recognize the hub of that city's life, the huge elegant *Mercado* or market on the docks with its wrought iron and glass roof (designed by Eiffel and based on Les Halles). She records in writing and photography the traffic of the river, villages passed through, the process of their boat taking and in return receiving supplies. She notes and photographs their boat being loaded up with meat, great hunks of raw carcass carried by brown-skinned boys red against the verdant shore. And we recognize the huge open seas of the Amazon itself with all its life. "I have never seen a lovelier wild sight," Bishop writes of a flock of 150 white herons, luminous with an "electrical effect" against a sky darkening with an Amazonian storm. Released from her photojournalistic context like Parks in *Flavio*, Bishop produces a form that is photographic travel memoir, with the I and the eye, the perspective returning. In an account of another river trip better drafted this time and (with notes to herself about editing) clearly for publication, "A Trip on the Rio São Francisco," the personal journey is interwoven with a history of navigation that she was obviously reading at the time. She visited this river in 1967, alone this time on the advice of Lota's doctor. Bishop says the voyage acted as "a sort of eraser" for the political and personal turmoil of the moment (*One Art* 463). On a boat named Wenceslau Braz of which she has a photograph, she evokes the quietness of the stern-wheeler, the way in which it seemed to be symbiotically blended in with the river life through which it passed: It went "*ppph . . . ppph . . . ppph . . .* softly, rather like a seal coming up for air." The simile puts one in mind of Bishop's comparably cross-species seal of "At the Fishhouses." *Black Beans and Diamonds* would have been—as she noted in her notes for a plan of one chapter—a "sort of prose poem."

Bishop's eye in writing and photography notes quirky details. Her observation making its way from the foreground of her poetry to behind the camera, the photographs contain none of that lumpen, *studium* quality of the photos of the *Brazil* collection. She is conscious of perspective, angles, shapes, movement, juxtapositions. At Pirapóra (which means "'jumping fish' in the language of the Cariri Indians"), she photographs the fishing nets she had seen used on the São Francisco, interested in how the light she describes as fading creates from the nets silver patterns against the water and soft sand. In Ouro Prêto where Bishop bought her own house as things began to get difficult with Lota in Rio and Petrópolis, she photographs the baroque architecture that she so loved, particularly the town's famed churches and its terra-cotta-red roofs. She took many photographs of the sculptures by town artist Aleijadinho ("little cripple"), their bodies with oversized heads startlingly vital and misshapen as though picking off his own crippling deformity. Bishop asks questions in photography, catches the *punctum*. Two boys squat in a road. The shadows are long, the light soft and golden. Is it evening? The street is almost deserted; a woman walks away from the camera, a man walks toward it. Here is no theme, no revealed message. In a photograph that looks like a Bishop watercolor—actually better than one—a rust-colored wall sprouts a dark, ivy-like plant with red, perpendicular flowers. Next to it a cracked, red-brown wooden door has been

Elizabeth Bishop, photograph taken during travels in Brazil, 1960s. From Special Collections, Vassar College Libraries. Reprinted with permission.

decorated with pink flowers in the shape of a cross. In other photographs women and children stand in long queues. In the poor northeast? Or somewhere in Minas? An old woman dressed in a large mackintosh holds a red flag with "Scotch" written on the side. The flag appears homemade. Scotch what? Is this a public ritual? Or the private habits of an eccentric? Behind an old man are some political posters. He carries a massive tray of—parasols? political streamers? These are places journalists and *Life* photographers don't go. Like paintings, like poetry, they are mediated. Unlike them the photographs catch a reality that we can see really *was* there—but that still goes unanswered.

In many of the photographs Bishop's subjects return her look. They are conscious of the photographer's presence and she is interested in this. Back in the *praça* in Manaus Bishop photographs a photographer photographing. He has his back to us. A woman to his right, and a girl to the left in a turquoise dress giggling self-consciously, look back at Bishop and us. Bishop writes that the photographer was annoyed because he had wanted

Elizabeth Bishop, photograph taken during travels in Brazil, 1960s. From Special Collections, Vassar College Libraries. Reprinted with permission.

to photograph her. She finds her "beady-eyed" proxy in him. Nowhere in Bishop's unpublished prose is self-consciousness of what it means to look at Brazil better caught than in her account of a trip to Brasilia in August 1958. "A New Capital, Aldous Huxley, and Some Indians" was rejected by the *New Yorker*—not to her surprise: "the material just didn't go together," she realized (*One Art* 369). In fact the forty-five pages of completed typescript constitute a wonderful poised memoir that is also an essay on the building of Brasilia and its effects. It is exemplary of the kind of work that might have been included in *Black Beans and Diamonds*. One of the few critics interested in *Black Beans and Diamonds* searched for but didn't find this piece, writing that "Hundreds of pages of prose about Brazil have never been found; unless one includes her drafts toward *Brazil*, the extant material amounts to few dozen pages."[41] It is quite likely that Victoria Harrison mistook this piece for a draft of *Brazil*, since Bishop's annotations written over the typescript show where she culled from it for material on Brasilia in *Brazil*, taking all the facts, shucking like corn the variation, the memoir. The design of the essay was to show how the material it describes doesn't go together. How to reconcile, even see side by side, the development of Brazil's new capital in the interior with the survival of the Indians surrounding it? The founding of Brasilia and the industrialization of which it was the most visible symbol promised to alleviate poverty and bring workers from the northeast to stem the tide of migration into *favelas* like those in Rio. But the government "Palaces" are erected by workers who camp in a "free city" of wood shacks that themselves are growing like *favelas*. The pool at the presidential palace is bigger than an Olympic pool. But the builders and the employees are housed inadequately below ground, the architect Niemeyer "like a lazy housewife shoving household gear out of sight under a deceptively well-made bed." Above all the development has brought the selling and development of Indian lands much closer to the Mato Grosso where the Nambikwara live. Bishop's account travels from the most modern and extravagantly designed city in the world to "the most primitive people left in the world."

Or putatively, because Bishop doesn't reconcile and narrate since she's so conscious of where she and we are looking from. Writing for an audience of which she demands greater responsiveness to nuance, she unravels expectations we might have of both an overreaching South American government and "primitives." Bishop ends with a comparison between Anthony Trollope's cynical remarks about the development of Washington in the United States in the middle of the nineteenth century and

Elizabeth Bishop, photograph taken during travels in Brazil, 1960s. From Special
Collections, Vassar College Libraries. Reprinted with permission.

what Americans might think of Brasilia now. This time her comparativist
approach—English author/United States; American perception/Brazil—
stands. Traveling in an international party Bishop is as much about observing them as observing the sights; this generates the greatest juxtapositions.
From others' reactions to Brazil she produces satire: the Polish countess
who, on her hunting trip, thinks Brazilians have the killing instinct; the
English Cambridge anthropologist studying the effects of contact; the
reserved Huxley and his Italian wife, Laura. Their looking is as prismatic
as all the glass Bishop describes has been used to build Brasilia. Images of
tools of observation pile up, not only in the descriptions of that glass that
acts as an "aquarium" (though who exactly are the fish?). Huxley is key to
her looking at looking, accruing as he does an entourage—her included.
She notes how he was fascinated by instruments of observation, with
his magnifying glass, miniature telescope and special lensless spectacles
("These, he told us, were an ancient invention of the Chinese, useful for
both near-sighted and far-sighted eyes. Laura remarked that she also found
them very useful for going to sleep, and when we finally got on the plane

she put them on and promptly did so"). Huxley's book on vision, *The Art of Seeing*, though not mentioned by Bishop, shows the extent of philosophical, psychological, and cultural investment her writerly other recognized in looking.[42]

The inclusion of photographs in the piece above all reveals mediation and in the process the loss of the real or primitive. The appearance of cameras, hers and Laura's, highlights the canniness of the Indians—this most "primitive people left in the world" are already touched. When Laura takes pictures with her Polaroid "these Indians knew all about cameras and were happy to pose, in rows, with their arms about each other's necks." One Indian in pants and a shirt when asked to pose for a photograph "politely removed his clothes," and puts his trousers back on to cook the lunch (the sausages they'd brought). "The Indians loved the Polaroid pictures (in fact a Polaroid camera and a large supply of film should see one through the jungle), almost tearing them apart to see the results." Bishop photographs Laura preparing to take a photograph among the Indians. With Huxley discreetly in the rear, the Indian woman with the child, and the young white woman on the right (probably the Huxleys' interpreter whom Bishop mentions) all looking off in the same direction possibly at some Indian activity, the focus of the photograph is not obvious. It is in fact, *Las Meninas*–like, the photographed camera's lens. Only Laura looks back at Bishop. Laura the photographer mirrors Bishop the photographer. The effect is endless reflection, and the white woman photographer (both of them) is the subject rather than the Indian woman—who somehow becomes at the edge. Bishop's self-consciousness in shifting perspective includes, in her prose too, the Indians. From the Indians' point of view "Huxley did appear, not homely, but exceedingly long, white, refined, and misplaced."

Bishop too was intrigued by optical instruments. Living in Key West before she went to Brazil she worked in a factory that made lenses for binoculars—a job that, ironically, gave her eyestrain. She read Newton's *Opticks*, and when given a pair of binoculars by her doctor Anny Bauman she wrote, "The world has wonderful details if you can get it just a little closer than usual."[43] The interest in optical instruments that we also saw in "Burglar" makes it elsewhere in *Black Beans and Diamonds*. In "Rio de Janeiro, 1565–1965," two pages of rough typescript that promised to reinstate that overlaying of historical moments and of perspectives cut from *Brazil*, she borrows a pair of binoculars from an officer as she returns to the coast of Brazil by boat. But she says here she is "far-sighted" and could anyway see miles and miles, a beneficial hypermetropia (the inverse of myopia) remembered by friend;[44] she uses them to confirm what she

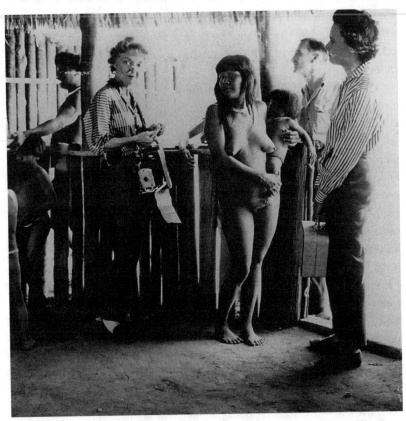

Laura Huxley (with camera), Aldous Huxley, and their interpreter, visiting Xingú
Indians, August 1958. Photograph by Elizabeth Bishop. From Special Collections,
Vassar College Libraries. Reprinted with permission.

can already see and knows after living there for fourteen years. Bishop
then passes them to a Tasmanian passenger who in contrast sees nothing.
"One's heart sinks," Bishop writes. "This was the first time the Tasmanian
who had been twice around the world and was now half-away around for
the third lap—and this was all he cared to know, apparently, of Brazil."
Though syntactically fragmented, the piece promised to develop a criticism
of tourism questioning the official line that it meant improvement to social
conditions. In "Another American," undated and also unfinished, Bishop
similarly connects tourism with optical instruments and their mediation.
An American couple have "been all over . . . the world, almost! . . . five countries in six weeks," including "San Pollo," the woman tells the protagonist.
The husband carries "a movie camera and under that arm a copy of TIME,
a two-days-in advance copy." Since they're in the Amazon it's more likely

he's an employee of *Time* than a subscriber. The narrative observes that "If one had been collecting Americans like butterflies" he especially is a species worth netting. The shift in perspective—who constitutes the wildlife in the Amazon?—is reversed as the short story removes even this ground. The woman watches the protagonist in the mirror, initially mistaking her for a Brazilian, looking for something foreign in her. But from cringing withdrawal the protagonist suddenly realizes her own "irrational self-pity of the self-exiled" and identifies with the Americans—and thereby identifies herself. "Then ~~she~~/I told ~~herself~~ not to be a snob. After all, they were interested in seeing the world . . . and that was what was so wonderful about ~~her~~ race and ~~her~~ country, after all—their energy, the curiosity." The protagonist is of course herself "Another American." What's interesting about what we get to see of the drafting is that Bishop was considering point of view formally. Her handwritten annotations on her typescript include revision and juxtaposition of *I* for *she*, the first person for the third for her protagonist. Bishop was clearly wondering about where to render perspective from. It's quite possible that her inability to resolve point of view—the main edits to the draft—were what made her leave the piece unresolved.

The concern with mediation extends to newspaper translations, where we see Bishop's attachment to documenting reality but documenting oversights. Her promised account of the St. George's Day parade in Rio (dated 1963) begins with a newspaper quotation that segues into what the newspaper leaves out, details that strike the poet's eye. Other newspaper translations home in on her interest in relations between Brazil and America, the significance of U.S. financial aid, and occasionally but incrementally the effects of the military dictatorship, the restrictions on her friends' movement in contrast to her own freedom as an American. Translations from the Brazilian daily *O Globo* in 1967 through to the early 1970s concern the distribution by the U.S. Navy of cookies, tea, and chewing gum to *favelados;* a Janis Joplin concert in Rio thwarted because authorities fear the huge crowds of young people she would draw; and the identity papers or *carteiros* increasingly required. As she travels in perspectives she shifts between genres and forms. In "Suicide of a (Moderate) Dictator—A Report in Verse & Prose," Bishop treats to prose and poetic versions the facts of Vargas's suicide following the demand for his resignation after the scandal of the Lacerda assassination attempt. The poem, dedicated to Lacerda (surely ironically: "Perhaps truth is a shadow, Carlos," she has handwritten), heightens the contrasts with images of the ephemerality of media truths that will "rub off on our fingers / like the ink from unproof-read newspapers / crocking the way the unfocused photographs / of crooked faces that soil our coats," versus those of the scene of dogs being walked along the beach "as usual," a rainbow, and two boys flying kites. Another unfinished poem, "A Baby Found in the Garbage," catches in its incisive circularity the cold detachment of reporting, beginning with the still-breathing baby "Wrapped in the very newspaper / whose headlines she would make that day" when at the end of the poem she dies. At the same time Bishop's witnessing of social situations is mixed with the imaginary to convey empathy for events beyond the media's brief. The account promised of the "servant of mine from the northeast" might be among the 78 people who have been traveling for 8 days in the back of a truck to Rio. Already three people have died, and only one (a baby) could be buried when they stopped at night. Now a girl lies about to die, supported by her family, her body held by and uniting them all. The story's title is the truck's bumper sticker: "Farewell Teresa." Or from pathos to satire, it could come in the account of northeast immigrant to Rio who makes good and returns home to find it provincial, "Grand Opening." In prose, poetry, in memoir, fiction, in photography—in the incomplete processes of translation—Bishop reaches out to unearth Brazil. "A Trip to the Mines—Brasil" searches out for the graves of slaves now hidden in the obsolete gold mines they worked. Its several unresolved drafts don't unearth them.

Among Bishop's notes currently filed under *Brazil* is one page headed "Introductory Note." Like the newspaper translations and annotations that are also filed here, the introductory note is written too late to have been for inclusion in *Brazil*. Bishop states here that she stayed in Brazil for sixteen or seventeen years, so this would take us to a point at or after 1967 when she left Brazil for the United States. Bishop writes that her immersion in Brazil meant that she saw the country "from a double point of view—perhaps more than a traveler or tourist would see, or the Brazilians themselves." The note goes on that the work that follows is to be autobiographical as well as documentary. "This collection random collection of stories (true stories, mostly, travel sketches essays, poems, and a selection of th selections from the hundreds of newspaper clippings I saved over the years is partly a thank-you note for the hospitality I enjoyed, to the friends I made and lost and made." With her changes emphasizing that the work is non-narrative (*random* collection), Bishop's note echoes the generic multiplicity foreground in the Rockefeller application. We are reading the introduction to *Black Beans and Diamonds*. It also presents this work, like Lévi-Strauss in his prologue to *Saudades do Brasil*, as a valediction to Brazil interwoven with personal losses.

The explanation of those interwoven losses at the heart of *Black Beans and Diamonds* comes in a letter to the Rockefeller Foundation explaining why she hadn't finished the book. Dated October 16 with no year given but probably 1968 since her grant terminated that summer, Bishop writes what she calls a "very frank letter," totally unnecessarily given that all the foundation had asked for was her "informal evaluation of the assistance received." The letter flies in the face of professional correspondence, of all her professional correspondence. "Because of a series of unusual and unhappy occurrences in my personal life" she begins, "my answers to your questions will have to be very different from what they would have been if I had spent that time, as I had intended to, in working almost exclusively on my project: a book of prose pieces about Brazil. But I sustained a great loss, the prolonged illness and death of my closest friend & the breaking up of my Brazilian home of seventeen years, followed by three illnesses of my own." She is still planning on finishing the book, "trying hard to make up for the unavoidably lost time." But her losses meant her departure from Brazil and incompletion of this work. Her biographer, Brett Millier, says that Bishop was unable to complete her travel prose collection as opposed to her travel poems about Brazil because she was unable to generalize.[45] But there's more to it than that, or rather we see what's at stake in generalizing: the loss of the ability to express loss without mastery.

Bishop's incompletion of *Black Beans and Diamonds* traumatically repeats the events of late 1961 when she hadn't been able to complete properly and do the revision on *Brazil*. It hinges, as traumatic repetition does, on the same unresolved cause. Then Lota's involvement in the building of the park had meant Lota's immersion in her growing workload and Bishop's distraction from completion. Now Lota had a breakdown and Bishop found the project of completion impossible. While Bishop and Lota approved the military coup in 1964, like most people in Brazil they had no idea how it would turn out. After the coup in which Lacerda would be a principal actor knowing about it in '63, there was increasing tension between Lota and Lacerda. The new President Branco and his government grew uninterested in funding the park. Lacerda and Lota had different politics. Lacerda wanted to reclaim other public land around Rio for an international hotel, which would have provided him with a lucrative deal. Lota defended land for public use. The effect on Bishop's and Lota's relationship was immediate and inexorable. From 1964 on Bishop records in her letters Lota's worsening nervous exhaustion and says, in what may be a manner of speech but proves prophetic, that she doesn't want the park to "kill" Lota (*One Art* 427). By 1967 when she writes of wanting to escape "the violence" in Brazil (457), it is not clear whose violence she is referring to—of Lota or towards

Lota of politics—probably the enmeshed both. Struggling with her own work and illnesses, in July Bishop flew to New York, against her wishes but on the advice of Lota's doctors. Here Bishop was to bring together the *Black Beans and Diamonds* pieces—the second Brazil book. In September and this time against doctors' advice, Lota begged Bishop to be allowed to join her in New York. The night she arrived Lota took an overdose of valium. Though it looked at first as though she was going to survive she died five days later. In her account, fictional but based on research of documents and interviews, Brazilian novelist Carmen Oliviera has gotten at this traumatic chain of events, the ellipses and elisions from politics to the personal, from '61 to '64 to '67 as no one else has previously.[46] Bishop's photographs of Lota's park and the development along Rio's seafront somehow catch the same overshadowing and connection. In one photograph, so different from Kessel's which is taken at the most obvious angle, Bishop has photographed not from the customary east of the bay looking at the skyline but from the west looking out to the beach from the skyline. An evening photograph with the sun setting in the west, the skyscrapers themselves are not shown, but their long shadows on the white sands leave their ghostly mark.

After Lota's death Bishop decided she could no longer live in Brazil and in 1968 moved to San Francisco. (Her letter to the Rockefeller Foundation was written from here.) From '66 to '69 Rockefeller asked her to nominate other writers for the same award. One can imagine the guilt, the self-doubt and self-berating that Bishop must have gone through with each reminder of her own incompletion. But at least up to the mid '70s she was still planning to finish the book. In a letter to photographer Mariette Charlton written in 1970, Bishop seems to have given up the idea of her own photographs and now wants to commission others. Back in Ouro Prêto ("the worst mistake in my life" she realizes, the belief that she could return to Brazil) (*One Art* 510), trying to sell the house and move permanently to the United States, Bishop suggests to Charlton that "you might possibly, possibly like to come here and do some pictures for my 'book.'" She offers to pay fee plus expenses. "The book is away behind—three years or so!—but that wouldn't matter—because the pictures have nothing directly to do with the text. I just want GOOD ones, and not the usual ones at all—in fact I know what I want, exactly, but just can't take them myself, and I am sure you could. . . . Perhaps even saying 'exactly' is rude to a photographer, since you must know what would make better pictures than I do—and a lot must depend on luck, just as in poetry, but I'd give you my LIST."[47] And still in 1973 she was speaking, to Howard Moss, her longtime editor at the

New Yorker, of the "several hundred pages of my long-procrastinated book on Brazil on hand."[48] But *Black Beans and Diamonds* was never finished.

There's a way in which Bishop moves more fully into loss at the end of her life or rather awakens to it. In her final decade she was trying to finish several things. Among them was an elegy for Lota. Called "Aubade and Elegy"—like Schumann another dawn to an end, an awakening to death—Bishop left enough of its bones for us to see that she blamed politics for Lota's death. The notes in preparation for the poem remember

the beautiful colored skin—the gestures (which yo[u] said you didn't have) / . . . the door slamming, plaster falling—the co[o]k and I laughing helplessly on the other side of the door / And oh the dream—t[h]e house, the desire . . . / and oh the co[u]ntry's ingratitude—misunderstanding— WASTE / . . . and courage courage to the last, or almost to the last— / Regret and guilt, the nighttime horro[r]s.

Bishop wrote several drafts of the poem, the best of which reads in part:

Perhaps for the tenth time ~~today~~ already
and still early morning I wake it's like waking
wake and go under the black wave of ~~your death~~

.   .   .   .

the smell of the earth, the smell of the black-roasted coffee
as fine as fine humus as black

no coffee can wake you no coffee can wake you no coffee
can wake you.

Another work that went unfinished, dating from the Brazil period, was entitled "Homesickness." Worked on for fifteen years, "Homesickness" was about Bishop's mother and *her* homesickness. David Kalstone was the first among critics to isolate as "the unspoken fact of Bishop's childhood: an absent mother."[49] This was a mother who went mad because, as Bishop renders it in "In the Village," she could not give up her mourning for her father; her scream hangs over Nova Scotia as the dressmaker tries to get her out of her mourning dress.[50] This was a mother who never recovered from loss. Bishop's mother was the first—though not the last—among Bishop's ghosts. (In an uncanny coincidence Bishop read *A Lover's Discourse* probably the year she herself died.)[51] While she was finishing "In the Village" and deciding to make her home in Brazil, she wrote in her letters: "It is funny to come to Brazil to experience total recall about Nova Scotia—geography must be more mysterious than we realize, even" (*One*

Art 249). Was Bishop at home enough in Brazil to become a child because of *saudades*, because of *its punctum*? For Bishop's was a childhood punctuated with loss and suffering. She herself suffered depression and twice took an overdose. It was in her childhood that she developed asthma, which she acknowledged could be connected to her depression and which her biographer believes was one of the forces behind her travelling: she went "in search of air she could breathe."[52] It was only with later losses that Bishop could realize *saudades*—look at the earlier losses. As Lloyd Schwartz writes in his reminiscence of Bishop in Brazil, "Having given up Brazil, she could finally become a Brazilian."[53]

Bishop's last finished book, her most abbreviated and formally exquisite as a butterfly wing, is predominated by poems about loss. A Crusoe now repatriated mourns his Friday but doesn't get over him (no *robinsonnades* here). A proto–dream house on a beach turns out to be boarded up. In the "Enormous morning" of "Five Flights Up" is discovered a "yesterday . . . almost impossible to lift." And of course there is initiation into loss, in the photographs of the *National Geographic,* in the first poem "In the Waiting Room." Bishop's seminal poem about loss, and one of the touchstones for telling loss, also appears here. "One Art" is an art, in how not to master loss. While critics have debated endlessly the source of the poem—who is the "you" addressed in this possible moment of "even losing you"?; it could be more Lota, or it could be the partner who stood by Bishop after Lota's death until Bishop's own[54]—the point is the catalogue of losses, as the adult now looks back on the child of "The Waiting Room," including that of her mother in "my mother's watch." Losses pile up ("two cities . . . / some realms I owned, two rivers, a continent"), counted but really incalculable. A villanelle, the poem's form is associated with mourning[55] and counting. The distinguishing feature of the villanelle is calculated repetition. Two one-line refrains must be repeated in each of the five triplet stanzas, before being brought together in the last two lines of the closing quatrain. Of poetic forms the villanelle requires most mastery.[56] Bishop's has been much admired by critics: "in the writing of such a disciplined, demanding poem lies the mastery of loss"; "One Art" is indicative of the way in which "writing is a way, not to overcome, but to come to terms with loss."[57] Yet while the poem's *studium* states that mastering loss is possible, even easy, that in the reiterated line-ends "the art of losing isn't hard to master" and "loss is no disaster," the poem's poignancy is to demonstrate the opposite. The *punctum* comes in a repetition, a return in the last line: "the art of losing's not too hard to master / though it may look like (*Write* it!) like disaster." The double *like* in the closing line is a giveaway of the failure to meet, masterfully, the intervening parenthetical injunction to *write* the loss. It is the point where, syntactically, the speaker loses it. Yet the repetition realizes loss better than anywhere in Bishop (in poetry?). Art of loss without mastery. For its own visions and for the perspective it would add to Bishop's canon, it's tempting to edit and publish *Black Beans and Diamonds*. But that would be to perform an art of mastering that she herself proved so fine in losing.

CHAPTER 5

MY SECOND SKIN

O R MY FIRST SKIN? I waver over what to call this return to my first book, which was called *Second Skins*. Especially since in saying "second skin" we cannot come any closer in language to embodying our corporeal skin. There is no idiom consisting of a first or original skin. "Under the skin" seems to me to be saying something different, something altogether more visceral, exposed: skin*less*. "Second skin" carries the greatest proximity to our literal skins. It is the metaphor closet to the skin we are in.

There's something like this equivocation in timing at work in the palinode. The palinode is a doubling back, a return to the ode. Yet in recovering what the ode left out the palinode makes its subject what should have been in the first. Indeed it goes back before the original. The palinode is take two but more authentic than take one. And as a return the palinode creates a new kind of text. The palinode is not among the customary modes for responding to one's errors. It is not a defensive turn against the reader in which the author accuses you of misreading and goes on to restate imperiously or painstakingly the argument (most common). Nor is it a full-scale retraction, an exercise in self-abnegation (I take it all back: for obvious reasons rarer). The palinode is rather a return that realizes that realization could only come with loss from the original. It may be a model of learning without deliberate self-advancement. As Hal Foster writes in the different context of his *Return of the Real*, a history of avant-garde art that may itself be read as a palinode since the author criticizes the linguistic turn in art theory for which he confesses he is in no small part responsible, the figure of return can disrupt a relentlessly evolutionary model of intellectual history in which one must abandon projects to take up new ones, always and fully break with the old.[1] The palinode creates something new in the repetition. It returns to expose the former surface, for there is in this exercise of turning in on oneself (although not turning on oneself) something gently self-excoriating: "scab-picking" as John Updike describes a tendency in much contemporary autobiographical writing.[2] The palinode picks at the first skin in order to lay open—but also to heal—the wounds remaining in the second.

Skin was very important to me in my book *Second Skins* (ode to my palinode here), as its title suggests. *Second Skins: The Body Narratives of Transsexuality* used transsexuality to bring back the materiality of sex that I argued theories of gender performativity current in gender studies left out.[3] Skin represented the most literal aspect of the body in transsexuality's "body narrative." As the largest and most visible bodily organ, yet also our interface between self and world and for many of us subject to psychic investment, skin literally incorporated identity. It is moreover the material through which transsexuals most substantially change sex, gender reassignment surgery consisting most visibly of a manipulation of the surface tissues of the body—and skin can run quite deep. Skin helped me move, so I thought, from *gender performativity* to transsexuality's *body narrative.* It contained the sexed referent that could anchor the free-floating gender signifier. And narrative (for my analysis consisted of reading the representation of sex in transsexual narratives) moved sex/gender on from the endless repetitions of gender performativity. In *really* changing sex I argued, transsexuals concluded a body narrative. With transsexual narratives I hoped to have wrapped up the plot of sex.

If I was aware then of the importance of skin as the literalization of the body of my body narratives, I was not aware to what extent photography carried the conclusion of but actually interrupted my narrative. It was in my epilogue that I finally turned to photographs. There I looked at how photographs of transsexuals evidenced the transitions of transsexual narratives, the intertwined transitions of sex and the story. The photographs presented visibly, really the evidence of sex as referent. The apparent referentiality of photography, its distinctive feature for showing its referent unmediated, seemed to me to correspond perfectly to the referentiality of sex at the end of transsexual narratives; it was a correspondence too perfect to forgo. So absolute was my faith in photography as presenting the referent of sex that I ended *Second Skins* with my own photograph. "I blow my cover," I wrote in my greatest moment of self-unveiling, "and embody my narrative with this photograph" (234). This sole autobiographical photograph in the book was supposed to literalize *my own* completion of a transsexual narrative as a female-to-male transsexual—now a man—and also simultaneously to complete my book. That was my last sentence. The photograph evidenced my point of no return. But the preceding, penultimate photograph was more important—the most important included in my book I now think—for literalizing the materiality of sex that I sought to recover through transsexuality (through photography). This photograph was an incredible close-up of a female-to-male's genitals before surgery but after hormone treatment. The photograph shows, I argued, my friend Zachary Nataf "as no longer female . . . but neither as a genetic male." Of a "clitoris-turning-penis," the photograph captured "this flesh as the referent of his narrative" (234). "Transcock," as it was retroactively named by photographer Del La Grace, seemed to encapsulate (literally: I was a real literalist) the substance of my work. Adamantine, huge, and irreducible, particularly when I projected it in slide shows at talks publicizing *Second Skins,* it had the effect, at least initially, of shocking my audience to see the referent I sought to make irrefutable. It was also the most cutaneous of my photographs.

My faith in photography as referential turned on a reading of Barthes's *Camera Lucida*.[4] In retrospect I realize this was a misreading: a failure to factor in what Barthes leaves out. Barthes of course crucially *doesn't* publish the most referential photograph for him, the Winter Garden Photograph of his mother. Amazingly I failed to mention this fact. Instead, seizing upon Barthes's initial setting up of the referentiality of photography, my reading remains confined to the first part of *Camera Lucida*. I didn't show (didn't see then) how *Camera Lucida* moves backward into the loss of the referent; I overlooked its palinode. *Camera Lucida* establishes reference only to show how photography loses it: *Ça-a-été;* the thing *was* there. The referent becomes irrevocable; the referent becomes real. Reading the referent back into the real, mistaking the latter for the former, I found presence in the lost past of the photograph. Thank goodness I managed at least to mention that *Camera Lucida* was Barthes's quest for his dead mother. Yet at the very moment I did so, I turned, through my etymological wordplay—through a performance of signifiers!—the absolute singularity of Barthes's relation to *his* photograph into gunshot for my cannons lined up against the linguistic turn and the rise of the signifier in gender theory. "Sifting through photographs of her, he looks for her flesh and blood *being*, a way to fill the absence of her body. From structuralism to poststructuralism to this

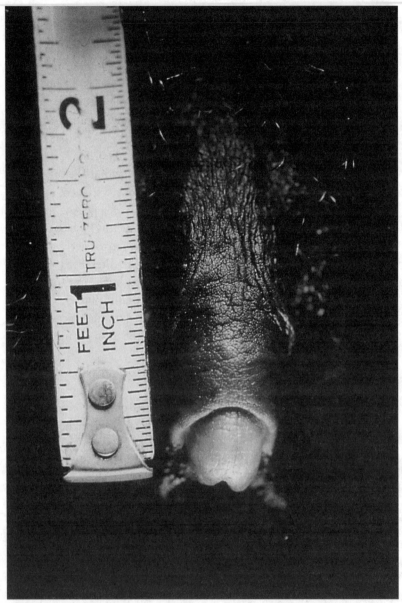

Del La Grace Volcano, "Transcock 1" (1996). Reprinted with permission.

signing off with the referent, the personal, and the search for his mother's presence (mater, matter): is there not something of an allegory in the final trajectory of Barthes's writings, a story for our specific theoretical time?" (211). I just couldn't get beyond that word "allegory," even though it took me away from the referential direction in which I sought to go, toward the figurative and further signification. I was even conscious at the time that Judith Butler, against whom I most directed my criticism of gender performativity, had used the base of this very word, in "allegorization," as a way to describe the performative relation of signifying drag to apparently natural heterosexual gender.[5] But, *faute de mieux,* I used the vocabulary and hurried on. In that sentence in which I sought to urge the importance of our doing so, I couldn't get *underneath* language.

In making Barthes allegory at the denouement of my narrative I didn't notice how Barthes's photograph stops narrative. In lieu of presence, the absence of Barthes's photograph interrupts his quest for his mother and sends him into palinodic decline—and silence: "nothing to say about the death of one whom I love most, nothing to say about her photograph" (93). I however, bustling onward and upward, had everything to say: about photography, about transsexuality. I read the linguistic-like codes in the photographs, the *studium* and never the *punctum,* responding to where the photographer, or the textual context, would have me look in my haste to close out anything accidental, anything that might stop my narrative. This is especially obvious when my reading was determined wholly by the captions of photographs, as it most often was. As Barthes had made quite clear in the earlier essay "The Photographic Message," captions along with layout and photographic composition are a crucial way in which photographs direct their reading or *studium:* the study of that which is most obvious about a photograph. These features constitute the "connotation procedures" through which the photograph connotes its message. They comprise photography's language and hence, Barthes writes of this medium that is really distinct as a message without a code, are "not strictly part of the photographic structure."[6] In response to a self-portrait of Loren Cameron for instance, I focused on the verbal frame of the image and read the photograph as "literally fram[ing] the viewer's gaze, reflecting back that look of fascination, objectification and desire s/he may cast" (230). In my opening image of a female-to-male transsexual at his desk with a pipe and pen, I dutifully noted the prominence of the props of pipe and pen, along with a beard, as evidence of the achievement of that body narrative. And it was the arrangement of four photographs of a male-to-female transsexual on a single page that enabled me to claim that they documented her sex transition. Even the putatively most referential photograph for me, "Transcock," relied on the code of the measuring tape for my reading, as many in my audiences tripped over each other in the eagerness to point out once they had recovered from the initial shock of the image.

To think now that I thought I could recover the referent even through *that* photograph! Without the brilliant enlarging techniques of La Grace's photography and the juxtaposition of the tape measure that encodes the image with size as a penis, the genitals would not, I must admit, be seen as a penis. In attempting to represent the referent, to symbolize it, I made it something else—part of the symbolic—and hence the referent *qua* referent escaped me.

But in mitigation Barthes *does* say that particularly with captions and text it's easy to fall prey to reading connotation in looking at photographs. Connotation uses the apparent referentiality of the photograph "in order to pass off as merely a denoted message which is in reality heavily connoted" (*Image* 21). You can see why I might have embraced the "passing off" of connotation procedures in transsexual photographs as the real (sexed) thing: read the clothing for the naked skin, the signifier for the referent. For if I read the *studium,* whose *studium* did I read and for whom? If I read the image according to how the photographer or the subject represented wanted me to see it, this had everything to do with where I was reading from. The return of the real that is a reaction against the postmodern "inflation of text and image" that Foster traces in his history of avant-garde art comes in two forms: first of all through the body, "through the violated body and/or the traumatic subject"; and second through autobiographical or ethnographic work in which the artist becomes representative of their community, "a turn to the referent as grounded in a given identity and/or a sited community" (xviii). My approach combined both of these turns against a postmodern inflation of text, for this is surely where I was writing from: as a transsexual; from and for a violated body; from that "as a" position Nancy K. Miller has called "representativity"—though she urges that we seek to avoid it in part by foregrounding our own bodies.[7] But how to avoid representativity when there is no (authentic) representation of oneself, in the combined imagistic and democratic senses of the word? Or more to the point, how to avoid reading oneself into the other when what one sees represented *is* oneself, when there is no real identity difference between who's represented and who's reading? In response to transsexual narratives but especially in relation to the photographs of transsexuals, I succumbed to a process of what I later discovered Susan Rubin Suleiman had just called "autobiographical reading": that is "the autobiographical imperative [that] applies not only to writing about one's life but to reading about it; reading *for* it; reading, perhaps *in order to* write about it."[8] Autobiographical reading, Suleiman writes of her own experience of reading memories of concentration camp survivors, "independently of any appreciation for the author's style or depth of vision, is shamelessly, unsophisticatedly, referential" (205). Crying not only on first but second reading of these memoirs, Suleiman realizes that what she's reading for her is herself: "What exactly am I looking for, and finding in these works? . . . I recognize the stories all too well. They could have been my own" (207). And although she doesn't theorize it as such, Suleiman seems to suggest that autobiographical reading, or at least the kind of autobiography that she reads and writes, is, like photography, caught up with the "shameless" and naïve desire for the "referential." One reads autobiographically because what one reads, what one wants to write autobiographically, is ultimately just out of reach of narrative's recovery: "the only kind of autobiography I find truly essential to read *or* write . . . is the kind that tries to recover, through writing, an irrevocable absence" (214). Reading and writing for transsexuality's absence, reading in the struggle to make it present, not surprisingly I got caught up in the connotation codes of transsexual photographs. Reading only with and for transsexuals, I read for my life.

Even so. How could I have missed Barthes's ultimate encounter with photography as wound? "I wanted to explore it not as a question (a theme) but as a wound," he writes undisguisedly in *Camera Lucida* (21). Buckling down to the *studium* in my ode, my first study, I covered over the *punctum*, "this wound, this prick" that for Barthes *is* the essence of photography (26), embodied in the Winter Garden Photograph and the reason he doesn't publish it: "(I cannot reproduce the Winter Garden Photograph. It exists only for me. For you, it would be nothing but an indifferent picture. . . . at most it would interest your *studium:* period, clothes, photogeny but in it, for you, no wound)" (73). But how to expose that wound, how to hold off the compulsion to re-dress it: a redressing that may cover but doesn't necessarily heal the wound? Barthes had actually left an explanation, and thereby made a prediction for his own future return, for how the connotation procedures are shattered off the real of the photograph, how the *punctum* or wound breaks through the *studium* that is strictly exterior to the structure of the photograph. At the end of "The Photographic Message" he had written that if "pure denotation, a *this-side-of-language*" is possible, it is "at the level of absolutely traumatic images. The trauma is a suspension of language, a blocking of meaning" (30). This insight (which will become Barthes's second sight and his second skin) accords with Lacan's sense of how the real returns, how we make contact with "what resists symbolization absolutely": "The function of the *tuché*, of the real as encounter—the encounter in so far as it may be missed, in so far as it is essentially the missed encounter—first presented itself in the history of psychoanalysis in a form . . . of trauma."[9] Yet Lacan emphasizes that the real depends on an initial loss. Although the real is all presence ("there is no absence in the real"; "the real is absolutely without fissure"),[10] the return of the real requires our missed encounter: the first time around; originally. Barthes's description of the *punctum*—"it is what I add to the photograph and *what is nonetheless already there*" (55)—follows this same temporal deferral. The *punctum* is what we miss in our reading of the photograph, what is already there but which wounds us only on return (when we shut our eyes). It is what we see when someone brings "an oil-lamp into a dark place, so that those with eyes could see what was there."

In his *Return of the Real* Foster follows Lacan's theory to suggest that the splitting of the sign from the referent has left us with a notion of reality that can only be traumatic. After its loss the referent could only return as real. There has been a *"shift from reality as an effect of representation to the real as a thing of trauma"* (146). Foster's concept of *"traumatic realism"* (130–36) in our apprehension of the representation of reality both confuses what's representation and what's real, and mixes up what's created and new with what's reproduction and subsequent: first with second. Reading Warhol photosilkscreens of car crashes—where the reproduction with light-sensitive chemicals on a screen of the original photographs makes the wounded skin of the parties especially visible—Foster writes: "repetition in Warhol is not reproduction in the sense of representation (of a referent) or simulation (of a pure image, a detached signifier). Rather repetition serves to *screen* the real understood as traumatic. But this very need also *points* to the real, and at this point the real *ruptures* the screen of repetition" (132). The deferred trajectory of the real (like the palinode and photography it requires an original missing) may perhaps best be understood by that word "screen," which Foster uses in a carefully doubled sense. In the first sense Warhol's silkscreens actually veil the real. But the real then returns with unexpected force to break through or wound the screen of representation in that second sense that is on the contrary the visual display of the object. Slavoj Zizek, who has made this shift from reality to the real a key theme of his work, has also identified the same ambiguity of representation as screening out the real and simultaneously blowing up its screening: "Herein lies the fundamental ambiguity of the image in postmodernism: it is a kind of barrier enabling the subject to maintain distance from the real, protecting him or her against its irruption, yet its very obtrusive 'hyperrealism' evokes the nausea of the real."[11] Both Foster and Zizek moreover describe our confusion over the real as melancholic. Foster writes that "In recent intimations of postmodernism . . . the *melancholic* structure of feeling dominates"

(165). And in an image of cut skin that, like Foster's, corporealizes the idea of the readable surface of reality as a skin, Zizek suggests that "the inherently painful dimension of our contact with reality"—our desire to touch the real but our inability to hold it since every encounter, "even the most benevolent, *cuts into* the world"—renders our archetype Tim Burton's cinematic protagonist Edward Scissorhands. Edward Scissorhands, whose every attempt at contact results in unbearable wounding both to himself and others, "epitomizes the postmodern subject: a melancholic subject" (59). As Lynda Hart writes movingly of sadomasochistic scenes (I know: I'm piling up the texts when I should be getting real; layering skins when I should be peeling back my own skin)—but in a context that continues the image of our desire to touch the real as cutting through the other's and our own flesh—we have a "yearning for something that rips through the fabric of reality. We could think of it as a mourning for referentiality, the grief expressed for the loss of something one never had. . . . death is the referent, the moment when time stops—the present."[12]

What is this repeatedly invoked power of cut skin, particularly in a visual representation, to cut through the skin of representation and return the real? Perhaps transsexuality resonates for our moment, and I could equate it with the presence of the referent in *Second Skins,* because the process of surgical reassignment seems to offer a literalization of the traumatic loss of the referent and our attempt to regain it through trauma. Like Edward Scissorhands we cut *ourselves* up in the attempt to recover the referent of sex. Refusing to accept the loss of something we never had—a real sex; and this refusal brings transsexuality closer to melancholia than mourning—we turn in on our own skin. The hope is that surgery will provide us with immediate access to the referent—like photography. Indeed the two procedures of surgery and photography have been compared. For Walter Benjamin writing in an essay that sees in the photograph a demotic approximation to the referential, photography is like surgery because it "diminishes distance . . . and penetrat[es] into the patient's body."[13] For Barthes also, in *Camera Lucida* having one's photograph taken is like being subject to a surgery: "to become an object made one suffer as much as a surgical operation" (13). And with his history of TB Barthes would have had considerable experience of medical photography, of its ability to function like surgery in penetrating the body. X-rays cut through the body with sight, turning into an outside photographic skin a representation of what's going on inside (often traumatic) the otherwise opaque skin.

What's painful about photography and gender reassignment surgery both is that, in spite of how close they are to reproducing the referent, to making it present (and I emphasize they are our best means of approximation), they ultimately fail. Reading transsexuality and photography as referential (my photographic epilogue was entitled hopefully—but also tellingly—"Fielding the Referent": who, really, was out in left field?), I missed this loss. Now in an unbidden encounter I turn to see the lost referent return as real. Gender reassignment surgery fails most obviously in the case of female-to-male transsexual reassignment, which has found no way, half a century after its invention, of reproducing a functioning penis. It is almost impossible to develop a penis one can piss through without it developing disabling fistulas or complications. It *is* impossible to develop a penis with which one can have penetrative sex without first having to "pump it up" or insert a stiffening rod into the head (which may well shoot out during intercourse). And still one must chose between these "options," between *either* pissing *or* having sex—as if life could be decided between urinary or sexual function. And one makes this decision knowing (1) that *neither* will be fully successful and (2) that the end result will anyway leave severe scarring, the loss of flesh in the donor body part sometimes so shockingly large as to leave that part dysfunctioning. Literally, to have a penis one must give an arm and a leg. And then—sorry: but the trauma goes on—years after the surgery, the penis (often misshapen and ugly and looking nothing like a penis) can still fall off. Believe me, it happens. For male-to-female transsexuals, although by no means to the same degree, there is also some trace, some remnant, something that returns that can't be realigned or reassigned: a voice, height, hands, or, as was made traumatically evident in the recent experience of a dear friend of mine who was sure that at least in this way she passed perfectly, even postreassignment genitals. This failure to be real *is* the transsexual real.

This transsexual real is there in some of the photographs I showed in my book, although it's often not immediately or even completely apparent (the *punctum* is the partial detail that ruptures the *studium*). The *punctum* in the transsexual image is literally traumatic: the wounds of transsexuality, the scars from surgery or the physical traces that sustain this body as differently sexed. The scars or traces—for me it is an absence of parts—won't allow a prereassignment history to pass into, to pass as the apparent referentiality of a reassigned sex. In the Loren Cameron self-portrait the real is the scar that runs across the wall of the chest. One can barely make it out here (one of the reasons I chose this image), but in other photographs in *Body Alchemy* where Cameron is straightened up the scars are evident, unavoidable. What the scars make evident is the constructedness of transsexuality, the splitting of gendered sign from the sexed referent. For surely even if it does become possible to produce a perfectly reassigned sex in the future (tissue engineering is perhaps the way as I suggested—hoped—in my book, although what government health service or private insurance is going to fund this for transsexuals?), the irony will always remain that this referentiality was achieved only through the latest forms of technological construction. Here's the paradoxical deferral at work in the real: transsexuals can approach the referent of their sex only through reconstruction—a history that transsexual scars make evident. As reconstruction, transsexuality, too, like the palinode and photography, is an attempt to return, to get back the lost referent—the *ça-a-été* of sex, the body that should have been. And the scars on the skin are, like the photographs that don't hide them, that terrible thing: the return of the dead: they show the sex that was never really alive. In fact in many of his self-portraits Cameron leaves this trace of reconstruction in the form of the shutter-release bulb he holds quite visibly. The bulb, with its wire trailing outside of the frame of representation, points to the process of photographic construction. Emblematic of the brave facing up to the absence of the referent that *is* Cameron's photography, as it is *his* transsexuality (the *punctum* is subjective, stresses Barthes), the visibility of the technology means that the photograph does not try to pass itself off as referential, unmediated, but makes evident that it is a representation, a reconstruction. Cameron himself reads the shadow of the bulb as a metaphor for his path of self-construction as a transsexual: "People have asked me, however, why I don't try to conceal the bulb in my photographs. . . . I am creating my own image alone, an act that reflects the transsexual experience as well."[14]

The palinode like photography returns the real as ineffable. Flying to Brazil where I first presented this palinode as part of a seminar series that began my return to photography (my Brazilian colleagues, bless them, afterwards *congratulated* me on my transsexuality; they had a new and extraordinary response to loss, as I was to discover), I was reminded by a friend and my travelling companion of a footnote that had appeared in an early draft of my book but that had not made it through revisions into the final draft. This footnote, the existence of which I had completely forgotten, consisted of a discussion of a self-portrait by Cameron that appeared two years before publication of *Body Alchemy* in a female-to-male transsexual support journal.[15] Checking the journal to make sure I discuss the right image, I am startled to discover as true something I realize in retrospect I had already unconsciously known. This photograph did not make it into Cameron's final version of *Body Alchemy*. Like my footnote for me it proved unreproducible. Here's my footnote on Cameron's photograph,

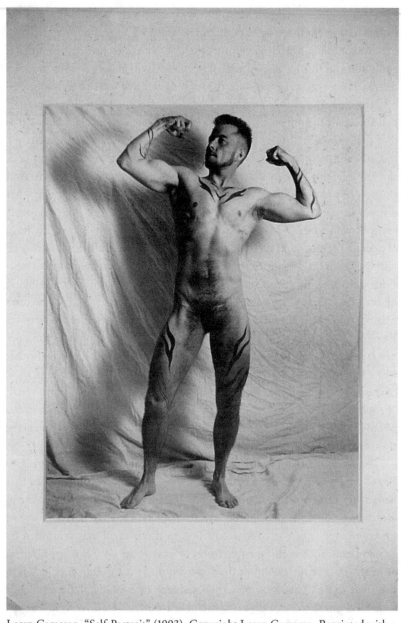

Loren Cameron, "Self-Portrait" (1993). Copyright Loren Cameron. Reprinted with permission.

finally found on a computer disk of discarded writings, written in 1994 at a crucial, decisive point in my transition. It appeared originally embedded in a discussion of German photographer Bettina Rheims's photographs of male-to-female transsexual Kim Harlow:[16]

FTM Loren Cameron's photographic self-portraits might be juxtaposed with Rheims's photographs of Harlow on this subject: the repetition of that splitting in self-representation. Although Cameron's photographs emblematically do not reverse or cover up the history of his transsexuality in the way that Rheims's portraits of Harlow do (quite the contrary), they strike me as being subject to something of that same splitting or doubling dynamic. Many of Cameron's shots are nudes. When the inscription of transsexuality on his body is occulted, that is, when he passes (i.e. as not transsexual), he appears as an integrally gendered subject. But when he represents his transsexuality, when he makes it visible, a splitting of the subject (and for me as viewer the split takes place in looking and looked at subject) seems to occur as a matter of course. The look/my look is drawn and fixed to what might be thought of as the transsexual markings on his body, as it tries to reconcile these markings with the remainder of the body. The splitting in viewed and viewer takes place precisely because of a (my?) failure at reconciliation of these parts/past. Cameron's stylized *(passing)* masculinity—his muscular chest and shoulders and the beautiful tattoos spread across them—only makes visible what is excessive or absent from the picture: what doesn't pass. My girlfriend's immediate reaction to these photographs voiced what I thought but couldn't say: "But he has no penis!" While Cameron's photographs are brave and brilliant testimony to the fact that transsexuality is certainly not unrepresentable, they do suggest that transsexuality exceeds the limits of (gendered) representation and, for me (at least for now), remains profoundly unreadable, irreconcilable within these limits.

One reason why I must have cut this footnote is that for a footnote it is ridiculously long. But there was an ample supply of long and abstruse footnotes in my book and the explanation doesn't seem sufficient. What really proved so necessary to cut, essential to overlook about this footnote for me, as perhaps Cameron's photograph was for him? Obvious to me now is that Cameron's photograph and my footnote are about the cutting and splitting in transsexuality, which were for me unspeakable. I couldn't name the nature of the splitting that took place both in the photograph and in the viewing subject; I am conspicuously vague here—"*that* splitting . . . *that same* splitting." The splitting that I was trying to describe was between what was representable (seeable, showable: the conjoining of the sign to the referent) and what was not (the real: the cut). This cutting in representation corresponded absolutely to the sexed splitting in the photograph. Simply, maleness, what can be shown in the image of Cameron's passing as a man, everything integral to that, proved speakable. What can't be reconciled with the apparently male subject in the photograph, what cut integrity, proved unspeakable. Or rather I should quickly particularize and say speakable/unspeakable *for me,* for my then girlfriend (at that point anyway) what *I* found unspeakable *she* spoke in her very first response to the photograph. I made this absolutely clear at the time: "My girlfriend's immediate reaction to these photographs *voiced what I thought but couldn't say: 'But he has no penis!'*" What she spoke and what I wrote and then cut was the unspeakability of transsexuality for me. Was this failure of Cameron's body to be genetically male-ly referential (and I emphasize this failure not just as his but as universally inevitable) speakable for my girlfriend because she was not transsexual? I was doubtful of this even at the time (evident from that questioning "my"? in parenthesis), that the lines of what could be seen and spoken of transsexuality were firmly pasted onto the division between nontranssexuals and transsexuals. And in retrospect as my girlfriend found *my* transsexuality increasingly unspeakable (literally: she couldn't speak about it for three years after we split, and is only starting to be able to discuss it and its role in our split now that she is with a genetic male, a man with a penis), I am certain that the division is not so correspondingly neat. As my final sentence in that note suggests, perhaps something about transsexuality remains not only unspeakable for me but for us all, irreconcilable—the referent unsuturable with the signifier, can I say?—within gendered representation.

What this unspeakability is I am trying to suggest (insane drive of the palinode: to speak the unspeakable; to recover the irrevocable) is the failure of us all, transsexuals and nontranssexuals alike, to achieve the real however much we desire to; indeed our failure to achieve it perhaps in proportion to our desire. Good old Lacanian conceit that I've only really understood for myself in return: it is loss in the real that engenders our desire for it, that engenders desire: photography, writing, transition. It's important, I think, that in this photograph Cameron does not show the shutter-release bulb. (Was this therefore taken by another photographer? Or, like Lévi-Strauss's self-portraits, on a self-timer? Probably the latter, since Cameron's career as a professional photographer has kept course with his transition as a transsexual, has apparently been determined by it.) This photograph is one of the few self-portraits of Cameron I've seen, and certainly the only full-length nude of him, that does not foreground, make visible as trace, the processes of technological (photographic/medical) construction. *For why the need to do so when the full frontal itself makes these processes of construction irrefutably evident?* What do we *not* see in this image except a genetic male? And my difficult placing of the "not" here is advised, because I think quite possibly we see everything in this photograph *but* a genetic male. We see a transsexual, a transsexual male, a self-constructed man, a body that is no longer woman but once was; we see the trace of a woman . . . The photograph itself—and surely this is where the eye is drawn: to what's not there, that absent male bodily referent—makes evident the missing penis. It can't be represented because indeed it's not achievable. I can hardly speak it.

But lose the referent and the real comes back. The return to what's missing impels a (self-) realization. Cut footnotes perhaps only serve to create the preconditions for a palinode: for what is the palinode if not an article-length footnote? In precedents of palinodes in theory what returns with startling consistency is an overlooked body part, often in a visual encounter—as frozen and clear as a photograph. For the writers of these palinodes the returning body part is typically a symbol of identity difference, the means to their realization of their own identity difference. But the body part is more than a symbol: in visual screenings—largely in photographs—it is literal too. And as literal *and* symbolic, not only moving between first and second texts but seeming to motivate them both (covered over in the first, remembered in the second), the body part somehow breaks free of the splitting between referent and signifier required of signification. These recurring body parts work a bit like Lacan's transcendental signifier: which is, of course, the phallus. In her palinodically titled "Afterthoughts on 'Visual Pleasure and Narrative Cinema' Inspired by *Duel in the Sun*," Laura Mulvey returns to her classic statement on Hollywood to consider, through film stills from *Duel in the Sun,* what she had left out of her previous account of cinematic narratives. In her concern with showing how Hollywood narrative is driven forward by a phallic gaze that castrates women in the film for a male audience ("subjected to her image as bearer of bleeding wound: she can exist only in relation to castration and cannot transcend it"), Mulvey realizes she had missed the female spectator's response.[17] She had thus missed her own pleasure in Hollywood narratives, cut her desire, which was symbolized in her earlier essay by the Lacanian phallus: "my own love of Hollywood melodrama . . . shelved as an issue in 'Visual Pleasure.'"[18] Recovering her pleasure now as she recovers herself, her own partiality to the phallus punctures, if it doesn't entirely reverse, Hollywood narrative. In an essay that makes clear its debt to Mulvey's first thesis on Hollywood's fetishization of women, Kobena Mercer criticized the photographs of Robert Mapplethorpe for similarly fetishizing—and feminizing—black men by fixating on their penises. Returning likewise out of doubt in the certainty and self-abstention characterizing his own first formulation ("I now wonder as I wander back into the text"), he recovers, too, his own pleasure: as a gay man he too loves penises. His desire makes him participant in the same "fantasy of power and mastery which I said was the projection of the white subject."[19] But perhaps the apparent coincidence of remembered or dis-membered body parts with deferred realizations in visual scenes is less arbitrary and more inevitable than may appear.

Perhaps the coincidence is classically uncanny. The model for deferred realization—Mulvey's and Mercer's and Lacan's and indeed from where the term comes to us—is Freud's case history on fetishism, that of the Wolf-Man.[20] A series of early sexual encounters had spurred the Wolf-Man's expected Oedipal conception of the female genitalia as a wound, in characteristic boyhood denial of women's sexed difference from his phallic own. Instead of pulling through the Oedipal plot and getting on with Freud's narrative, however, he had got stuck in and repeatedly returned to this moment. His adult life had been punctuated by a castration complex, channeled into a series of neuroses. Many were sexual: he alternated between sadism in which his penis was a weapon against women and masochism in which it was a target, on the point of becoming wound, mainly for other men. Some of them were not. Perhaps the most public way in which he acted out his horror in the uncertainty of sexual difference was by taking out a mirror to inspect repeatedly what he thought of as a wound in his nose: a hole—not visible to others—after he had picked a pimple on his skin. In analysis Freud goes back, goes back with the Wolf-Man to uncover the neuroses as the deferred realization or action of the castration complex: *nachträglichkeit* (189). Through a childhood dream along with other "screen memories" (163)—including the child Wolf-Man's account of being shown a picture book—the wound becomes readable on a screen. The crucial dream had consisted of a number of wolves sitting in a tree staring at the dreamer. Freud writes that three features continued to haunt the Wolf-Man about the dream: its immobility (the "perfect stillness and immobility of the wolves"); the power of the gaze (the "strained attention with which they looked at him"); and its enduring realness (the "lasting sense of reality") (177). The dream has a preternaturally photographic quality (stillness, gaze, reality); preternatural because it is a dream and unconscious, but also because it forms the projected surface for what is formative (pre-), primordial about the Wolf-Man's identity. At its exposed center is a primal scene, which Freud believes the Wolf-Man had encountered at eighteen months: possibly his first memory, but Freud here leaves undecided whether the scene was really witnessed by the child or whether it was solely fantasy. The dreamer associates the dream with a story he had been told just before he had the dream, of a maimed wolf: a wolf that had its tail docked. Suturing the dream with this story—and the Wolf's lost tail with the Wolf-Man's tale—Freud unlocks the castration complex screened in the dream but cloaked by repression into the neuroses.

After Freud had read his dream and his life the Wolf-Man never got back to a point before his trauma. He reentered analysis subsequently, with Freud and others. But he was considered sufficiently recovered, by himself and Freud, to lead a different life from that which had impelled him into analysis in the first place. Perhaps there is something that grows back around wounds and that's the skin. One of the remarkable properties of skin is its ability to regenerate: to produce second, even third layers when wounded. The palinode, though tied up with loss and belatedness—like transsexuality an attempt to get it right this time—is ultimately restorative in realizing loss. In his seminal palinode in autobiography theory, Philippe Lejeune captures this paradox. His expression of the palinode's recovery in loss borrows the Freudian fetishist's syntax of realizing wrongness: "I know but." "'I was wrong—but I was right to be wrong!' Undoubtedly self-criticism, like autobiography, is an impossible undertaking." "In spite of the fact that autobiography is impossible, this in no way prevents it from existing."[21] So: in spite of the fact that transsexuality is impossible this in no way prevents it from existing. Indeed, as with self-criticism, a similarly impossible undertaking, I would do it over again.

There is a recurring belief in photographs as a kind of skin. It is the most metaphysical and yet at the same time the most corporeal image of the photograph we have, and it goes back to a mystical conception of photography—to an ideal of photography that existed even before the chemical invention of photography. In it the photograph is the ghost of the photographed body, a revenant of the referent's lost skin. The image appears in the nineteenth century in the work of Oliver Wendell Holmes—a writer who was also a doctor—who embraced photography at its moment of birth for "its miraculous nature" which, even then, he claimed, "we forget . . . as we forget that of the sun itself, to which we owe the creations of our new art."[22] Holmes traces his cutaneous faith in photography back to an ancient assumption that our bodies are "continually throwing off certain images like themselves . . . subtile emanations" (72). He may have got it from Democritus, a 4 BCE traveling mystic who in his work on visual perception, *On eidola,* argued that we see objects only because they slough off membranes which then impinge on our eye; or more likely since this and all of Democritus's writings are lost, Holmes got it from Lucretius, who adopted the theory in his *De rerum natura* when he wrote

> there exist what we call images *(simulacra)* of things; which, like films drawn from the outermost surface of things, flit about hither and thither through the air; it is these same that, encountering us in wakeful hours, terrify our minds, as also in sleep, when we often seem to behold wonderful shapes and images of the dead . . . lest by chance we should think that spirits escape from Acheron or ghosts flit about amongst the living. . . . I say, therefore, that semblances and thin shapes of things are thrown off from the outer surface, which are to be called as it were their films or bark, because the image bears a look and shape like the body of that from which it is shed to go on its way.[23]

But with the power of technology to capture light, Holmes claims, for the first time photography had realized these "Forms, effigies, membranes or films"—fixed this lost *"cortex"* (72). In its unprecedented incarnation of the photographic instant, the photograph "has fixed the most fleeting of our illusions" (73), the "incidental glimpses of life and death" (79) that the artist typically leaves out but that the accidents of photography make their subject. These accidents themselves may be marked literally by vestiges of the skin. If we look at a photograph of a particular cottage in Stratford-upon-Avon, Holmes writes, "It is not impossible that scales from the epidermis of the trembling hand of Ann Hathaway's young suitor, Will Shakespeare, are still adherent about the old latch and door, and that they contribute to the stains we see in our picture" (80). Holmes embraces the epidermalization that carries over from the skin of the dead referent to the photograph, even though it means—as Benjamin will say a century later of photography's effect on the aura—loss of vitality from the original. Instead of going to a real place or making contact with a real object, with the invention of the new art, Holmes predicts, we will look at photographs and "call for its skin or form": "Every conceivable object of Nature and Art will soon scale off its surface for us. Men will hunt curious, beautiful, grand objects, as they hunt the cattle in South America, for their *skins,* and leave the carcasses as of little worth" (81).

This extraordinary notion of photograph-as-skin returns a few decades later, at the turn of the twentieth century, in Nadar's memoir, with the idea of the body shedding skins traced by a photographer this time back to Balzac.

According to Balzac's theory, all physical bodies are made up entirely of layers of ghostlike images, an infinite number of leaflike skins laid one on top of the other. Since Balzac believed man was incapable of making something material from an apparition—that is, creating something from nothing—he concluded that every time someone had his photograph taken, one of the spectral layers was removed from the body and transferred to the photograph. Repeated exposures entailed the unavoidable loss of subsequent ghostly layers, that is, the very essence of life.[24]

And with this description of the translation of bodily ghost to apparitional photograph, you won't be surprised to hear that Barthes's bibliography indicates that he read Nadar's memoir; for the photograph-skin recurs in *Camera Lucida*. And it is in *Camera Lucida* that we realize finally how much a faith in photography as *real* in spite of the loss of the referent was indebted to the *skin*. If for Barthes the "photograph is literally an emanation of the referent," a revenant of "a real body, which was there" (80), it is because the instant of photographic illumination produces a cutaneous connection between photograph and subject. This skin is protective, maternal; in Barthes's image the photograph is almost (not quite) womblike; it is the closest the child can get to the envelope that sustained him now he is outside his mother: "A sort of umbilical cord links the body of the photographed thing to my gaze: light, though impalpable, is a carnal medium, a skin I share with anyone who has been photographed" (81). In this medium whose *eidos* is death, suddenly, in the image of skin, there is birth after.

In one of the footnotes I *did* include in *Second Skins* (I wish I hadn't), I promised my next book would be about skin. Perhaps in writing this book on photography I've come close to that book on skin. What the image of the photograph as a skin brings to the surface and makes almost palpable is that the mystical realness of photography comes only with the loss of reality in the original. The photograph incarnates *because* it takes the body of the referent. Here's the trade. I may never recover my first skin. But the realization of that loss *is* my second skin.

THE REALIZATION OF LOSS

A THERAPIST ONCE TRIED TO PERSUADE ME to read old journal entries and bring in old photographs as a way to get over losses. I resisted. The exercise seemed far too literal for what I imagined of my psyche, and anyway as far as I could see I had no major losses.

Reading diary entries now of my first time in Brazil, I'm annoyed I didn't record what I remember as significant. After I'd presented some slides from my first book, I was approached by a member of the audience. He was in tears and embraced me. He embraced me for my sense of loss, he said. I hadn't known my talk was about loss.

Saudades is "endemic melancholy," two cultural commentators on Brazil recently suggest.[1] It is intrinsic to Brazilian self-conception. It is native, national, loss: the realization that we are born into loss; that it inheres in the human condition.

It was the first time I'd fallen in love with a notion or a nation. It was the first time I'd stayed with loss. I knew then I'd return.

I'm looking at Bishop's slides of Brazil at Vassar. I'm looking at Bishop's slides *with* Bishop at Vassar. At least, that's what it feels like. The curator of the Bishop Special Collection tells me that her photographs are rarely consulted, her slides even less so. I'm not surprised. To view them one must retrieve from the dark rooms of storage her slide projector. This is a cumbersome, antiquated piece of equipment from the 1960s. But it ran for me yesterday smooth as gliders.

Here is Bishop's Brazil unmediated. And yet . . .

> Is it right to be watching strangers in a play
> in this strangest of theatres?
> What childishness is it that while there's a breath of life
> in our bodies, we are determined to rush
> to see the sun the other way around?
> The tiniest green hummingbird in the world?
> To stare at some inexplicable old stonework,
> inexplicable and impenetrable
> at any view,
> instantly seen and always, always delightful?
> Oh, must we dream our dreams and have them, too?[2]

On July 4, I take a break from the library and visit Kykuit, Hudson home of the Rockefellers. The Rockefeller family was the first philanthropic dynasty, the prototype for making a family profession out of giving away the fortune. Yet their philanthropy was inextricable from, because made possible by, their also being the first multinational monopoly: the start of globalization. The source, John D. Sr., made his money from kerosene. He bought out—or shut out if they refused to join him—oil companies throughout the United States and from them formed his massive Standard Oil. Through this conglomerate he controlled much of the oil industry and, with the help of his sons, sought to influence international politics in the mid-twentieth century. His son Nelson helped steer the U.S. policy toward Latin America as a cold warrior in the '50s—and he visited Brazil for this purpose in the '50s and '60s. Nelson's more retiring brother, John D. Jr., turned giving into the family's raison d'être, in part as a way of making restitution midst the accusations of Rockefeller control and untrammeled incorporation.[3]

Taking the train alongside the Hudson from Tarrytown back up to Poughkeepsie, I'm put in mind of the Amazon. Immediately you know you're on the same continent. The breadth of the river. The hills on the opposite side, with their thick, huge-leafed foliage. Where else in the world such abundance: such wilderness? This, I say to myself with an Old World confidence, is America.

I'm reading Bishop's "A Cold Spring." At that exact moment, I look up and see that we're passing through Cold Spring station. Her poem is about the weather anyway, not the place. The weather now is positively Amazonian; a tropical rainstorm sheets it down. Nevertheless, it's the same uncanny feeling you get when the radio says the exact word you're saying or thinking, like "death." These coincidences often seem to hang on death. Ghosts coincide with the real.

I dream up a trip to Brazil that will take in all the sites and sights of my Brazilian photographers. Would the referent meet the real, I wonder? My trip will take me from the divided wealth of Parks's Rio; to the baroque, gold-mining towns and lunar landscapes of the state of Bishop's Minas Gerais. And back to Lévi-Strauss's Amazon.

In Rio, I decide against the *"favela* tour" that is now on offer, according to the tourist bumph they leave in your hotel room. Escorted by a local tour operator and with a stop-off so you can take photographs of the "spectacular views of Rio," you can see this other side to Brazil from the safety of your tour bus: the "real Brazil," they say. The bumph also urges that you not miss the Sugar Loaf, and advises on the most expensive restaurants in Rio.

Instead, I go with a Brazilian friend, who drives me round the developments of the wealthy Lagoa. On one side I recognize the Catacumba, the park where Flavio's *favela* once was. It's no longer the wilderness of Parks's visit. Yet *favelas* in Brazil do tend to be in wildernesses—to *be* wilderness. They perch like fabulous, mythic settlements atop their seemingly uninhabitable rocky outcrops. From planes, they look deceptively beautiful and ancient. In cities outside of Rio, they dot the wasteland between airports and the city's limits, shortening the space between: the space between the wealthy and poor; the urban and the rural. *Favelas* are one of the first and most frequent things you see in Brazil.

I've been warned by guidebooks and friends (even Brazilians) about the chasmic differences in wealth in Brazil and the provocative conspicuousness of affluent northern tourists. I'm fully prepared to be robbed in Rio. Instead I lose only my glasses in the Atlantic—my own fault (I'm trying to peer at something *under* the ocean, to see in the sea). The rest of my week is a blur—oddly reassuring though. This is my second time in Rio.

Ouro Prêto is very picturesque. It's all shapes and color, hills of tapestried landscapes forming the background to steep cobbled streets. The town is famous for its numerous churches, and these comprise a palette of yellows and whites and blues: all baroque. I take lots of photographs here in Minas. I photograph Aleijadinho's sculptures. His "lions" look more like monkeys, apparently because living in Brazil in the eighteenth century he hadn't seen a lion and didn't know what they looked like. A. had leprosy and progressively lost parts of his body. Working with more and more elaborate prosthetic extensions attached, he transferred his monstrosities from his beleaguered body to his lions.

Standing before Bishop's Casa Mariana I have a powerful sense of déjà vu, because of course I've already studied it in her photographs. As she recorded it with such painstaking precision while it was under construction though, and as her inscriptions on the back and front of her photographs offer detailed commentary on this process, Bishop's photographs seem more real than the scene before me. Redundantly, I take my own photographs anyway. Afterwards I'll have to peer at them and I'll still have trouble distinguishing which is Casa Mariana.

In the Amazon I'm not sure *what* to photograph because not sure quite what to focus on. What's surprising is that, in spite of all that green or maybe because of it, it feels like you're in black and white. I have no trouble at all identifying the Amazon from Lévi-Strauss's sixty-year-old photographs of his trips upriver here.

On the way to our base lodge, the space becomes less and less inhabited, and less and less touched. From a petrol station that is clearly recognizable as such, in the middle of the rivers when they're still oceanic sized. To churches and even a cemetery. Schools. "Farms"—of a sort—of zebu cattle, with their humps and their horns. Then of water buffalo which, better adapted to the flooding here, have since the '80s been gradually replacing the cattle. Farmers are given tax breaks to raise livestock. This has led to the so-called grass rush, the slash-and-burn techniques of forest clearance that are amongst the most destructive of recent impacts on the Amazon. Huts. And eventually just the walls of the green forest, closing in on either side of the narrowing river channels.

Then, suddenly, dolphins: freshwater dolphins. River dolphins are far less common than their marine cousins. (The only other places they can be found are the Yangtze in China and the Ganges in India: like the Amazon, their countries' holy rivers.) River dolphins are also much more humanoid in their shape than sea dolphins, with demarcated heads and *necks*.[4] And they're pink: positively, pleasurably pink.

The presence of the dolphin here suggests how the Amazon came to be formed. During the Pleistocene era (the Ice Age)—that is between 11,000 and 1.8 million years ago—ice sheets covered much of the Americas, as they did much of the world. In the interglacial periods of warmth, the ice covering the highlands (in South America, particularly the Andes) melted and the sea level rose, scouring the river channels and producing the Amazonian floodplain. The Amazon sediment resulting preserves a piece of this world from millennia ago. It is this, it is thought, that makes its ecology rich and life-giving.[5] The Amazonian tropical climate is also a leftover of a previous tropical climate that has not adapted to our drier climes.

No one's really sure how the dolphins got here but—since it's agreed they find their species origin in the sea—they, too, seem like vestiges of that previous world. The *"boto,"* as the Brazilians call the river dolphin, is the most mythicized inhabitant of the Amazon. Yet this river god (as Bishop's "Riverman" recognizes) is now threatened with extinction.

That evening as I arrive at our lodge, I'll trust the assurances about the generic passivity of piranhas and the nocturnality of caimans and swim with the pink dolphins.

One of the strangest things I see in the Amazon is the point where the black waters of the Rio Negro meet the white waters of the Rio Solimões, to form the River Amazon. What's weird is that the rivers meet but don't merge. You can still see the white in the black, the light in the dark. Or is it the other way round?

I take two photographs here. I have to admit later they're spectacular. When I have them framed and hung, people will mistake them for watercolors. But maybe it's the frames.

The first Brazilian opera tells the story of the myth that originated the waters' meeting. In Carlos Gomez's *O Guaraní,* an Amazonian Indian falls in love with a Portuguese girl. Their encounter is depicted in the opera house in Manaus. This is a spectacular and somehow very Brazilian affair, with its marble brought from Italy, its cast iron from Scotland—and the wood of *pau-brasil* from upriver.

Bishop, who also visited the joining of the waters of Solimões and Negro, left a draft of a poem "On the Amazon" that also speaks of encounters:

> crossing over
> the dark blue line
> and the river
> erases it all
> the world, all pink
> has dissolved at last
> and is going somewhere
> under a rainbow, too—

Rio Negro meeting the Solimões to form the Amazon. Photograph taken by the author, August 2000.

the rainbow has taken shape, but the world, all pink, strange to say
has dissolved at last
    and is going somewhere at last—
so *that* is the color of the world all together—

Another unfinished poem "Crossing the Equator" begins:

We imagine an horizon, & it hardens
into faultless definition: the horizon.
It begins to illustrate imagination.
Other things that are imagined
are not often so obliging.[6]

Myths imagine an integral world before divisions. Before loss.

Crossings figure a lot in discussions of the Amazon:

1. As we enter the third millennium, it's being proposed, we stand at a cross-roads over the future of Amazonia.[7] The route choice we face is between continued corporate extractivism (the extraction of resources for corporate profit), leading to some kind of meltdown. And, in the other direction, careful, ecological, and sustainable management of the forest under local people. Chico Mendes, an Amazonian ecologist and rubber-tappers' union leader who was murdered in the late '80s for his activism, suggested—in support of environmentalists' plans against deforestation—"extractive reserves" as an economic alternative to forest exploitation.[8] In extractive reserves, workers live in the area they use and so are less likely to destroy it. They use it, but don't lose it.

Development in the Amazon began properly in the 1960s, though this continued the work of industrializing Brazil that was initiated under the Getúlio Vargas regime. After its successful coup in 1964, the military government undertook the project to colonize Brazil's massive interior. This was in part to deflect political unrest and to avoid making real social change elsewhere in the country. In the increasingly impoverished, drought-ridden northeast, the "landless" were causing problems. They were campaigning for the redistribution of land outside its concentration in *latifundia:* "large estates" held by landowners or companies. And at the same time, they were swelling the *favelas* in the newly prosperous, urbanized southeast. The military government also wanted to make Brazil a leading nation in the rapidly industrializing world. As containing the country's richest resources, the Amazon beckoned. The new general president promised the Amazon as "a land without people for a people without a land."[9] The Amazon was to be paradise regained. Its development would run hand in hand with industrialization, militarization, and globalization. Paradise lost.

Current figures for rates of deforestation inevitably vary. From 11 million acres; to 2 million hectares—that is, 5 million acres; to 17,000 square kilometers per year. My head spins anyway at such numbers. But imagine something like Switzerland being lost every year. By 2020, in the worst scenario, 40 percent of the Amazon will be lost; in the best case, 25 percent will have gone. The three major causes of deforestation are, in order: industrial logging; land clearing for livestock; and extraction of raw materials in the form of minerals and ores for export to global markets.

Key to the colonization of the Amazon has been the construction of the Trans-Amazonian highways.[10] The new road system opened the Amazon to trade routes leading to major urban centers in Brazil, and from there to the rest of the world. The road project was planned under the military government. But the actual building was made possible with the help of funds from the World Bank and Inter-American Development Bank. In return foreign companies investing in the area got concessions or investment deals at favored ("banana": falsely depreciated) prices. The loans that Brazil took to implement this project of industrialization have left it with the largest debt of any Third World country. Indeed, the largest debt of any country, after the United States.

The road building project continues to this day.[11] Aerial photographs reveal the extending, spaghetti-like tentacles of this arterial network and at the same time make possible new incursions into an otherwise seemingly unmappable and impenetrable forest.

The Amazon is now a literal crossroads.

2. An alternative crossroads, an alternative story. In the form of its cities such as Manaus, the rainforest is already a global frontier zone. Manaus was designated a free trade zone in the '60s (of course by the military government). Its visitor today will be struck by the numerousness of electronics stores selling the latest gadgets from Asia, Europe, and the United States at cut prices. They're higher here proportionally than in Hong Kong, Tokyo, or New York. Manaus is where Brazil comes to do its hi-tech shopping. The Nambikwara don't *have* to travel to North America anymore to buy cheap transistor radios.

Such rainforest cities are "technopoles" at the vanguard of globalization. They comprise another, more global, less material kind of crossroads—a crossroads for signs: "technological crossroads that link specific activities to global circuits of information and exchange."[12]

3. The crossroads of Amazonia is also for the rest of the world as well as Brazil. Why do we care about the Amazon's loss after all? Why should we care about the Amazon's loss?

Because the Amazon is our most precious preserve. It contains over half of the world's rainforest, and most of this is in Brazil; Brazil holds 40 percent of the remaining rainforest in the world. It is the world's largest and most diverse forest. It is home to one in five birds on all earth. Nowhere else do so many birds live—both in total number and in diversity of species. Its plants form the basis for many of the latest pharmaceuticals used to treat our current ills—leukemia treatments, antibiotics, antivirals, and anesthetics for example. And many of its plants, birds, and animals are as yet uncatalogued. Even unseen. There's so much bird life up in the forest canopies that, as one naturalist graphically puts it, "The observer can well break his neck trying to see up there and identify a bird whose voice he isn't familiar with."[13] And it contains one-fifth of the world's water supply, our most vital and increasingly scarcest resource.

For the Amazon is not simply a place of conservation, a vault for storing what's gone or soon to be gone. It sustains and gives life to the world's current ecological system. The destruction of the rainforest in South America has already been shown to have immediate and precise consequences on the North—to affect the rainfall in midwestern states, for example; to exacerbate, in the contribution of deforestation to climate change and global warming, the flooding and droughts that increasingly take place across our world today.[14] It's not an exaggeration to say that Brazil holds the determinants of our future.

And for the future of the Brazilian Amazon the latest research foresees not only continued but accelerating loss.[15] A conference of climatologists, environmentalists, and scientists just ending in London as I write this concluded that with the Amazon's deforestation we would see the collapse of the climate system.[16] Or rather we would not be here to see it.

The lung of the world. El Dorado. The Last Frontier. The Original State. The destruction of the Amazon would entail nothing less than the apocalypse of the world.

The Rio Negro is terrifying in its blackness. It really *is* black, the result of a vegetation that, because it is so rich, as it decomposes releases very high levels of tannin into the water. The tannin prevents light from penetrating the water, and this in turn produces an inordinate amount of oxygen in the river. The oxygen means less fish, therefore less birds—less life than in the "light" waters. The riverbanks of the Negro actually look more vital then, but the river is relatively impoverished compared to other Amazon tributaries.

The locals call it the "dead" or "silent" river.

Our jungle trek in the morning is an education. Our guide, G., shows us biodiversity in action. He points out *how* the relationship between plants and parasites is symbiotic. A termite nest balancing like a huge bulb on the top of a tree serves to sustain the life below it. The termites recycle the bacterial and vegetable matter, cleaning the plant and allowing it to reabsorb its sterilized decompositions in the form of nutrients. Parasites work like antibiotics work for us: to preserve the life of the biota.

In spite of its appearances, the Amazon's ecology is actually very fragile. Or rather it is strong only in its ecological complexity and exclusivity. It's a self-contained system. It is only biodiversity—the symbiosis on every level: between floodplains and terra firma, between plant and parasite; between the *living* and the *dying* here—that sustains the life system. The basis of the Amazon's ecology (of any ecosystem really) is, of course, light, but in a certain combination with darkness. Photosynthesis, which literally means a "making by light," is the process whereby plants synthesize organic matter from inorganic substances that are present in solar light. This process can only take place afterwards, in the dark. Insects, fish, and animals, which cannot use the sun's energy as a direct life-source, depend upon vegetation—these "autotrophers" or producers of energy—for our life-sources. Animals, birds, and fruit-eating fish in the Amazon have propagated and sustained the autotrophic forest by dispersing its seeds. The plants' seeds have in turn adapted and become resistant to the destructive elements present in these secondary trophers' gastric enzymes.

And what do humans do? Humans are far down in the trophic chain. We consume.

Life on earth depends on photosynthesis. It all comes down to this: plants' ability to transform light in the darkness.

You can't, after all, magic the recovery of the Amazon. Reafforestation, which *is* undertaken, has so far worked with nonnative species. Native species grow too slowly and are too diverse to be replicated. Nonnative species change the ecology anyway, and reafforestation with them takes between 100 and 150 years. Although, there are stories of the forest beginning to grow back, where the roads have been barely used, and reclaim the land of its own accord. But once the land is cleared, the forest never really recovers. The Sahara, too, was once a forest. Then there's more light than we can see, with no shade at all.

The story of the progress of the human species is the story of the destruction of forests.[17] The achievements of culture have been at the loss of nature. Monoculture—whether in the form of agriculture, industry, or national culture—spells the end of biodiversity. Farming in the Amazon produces floods, then, ironically, as the land loses its ability to absorb and hold water and erodes, drought.

The external, nonindigenous exploitation of the forest began, in a precursor of the dynamics of globalization, with research on some rubber trees conducted by an Englishman, via Kew. His efforts led to the transportation of the entire rubber industry to Malaya and, as a result, by the beginning of the First World War, the collapse of the Brazilian rubber market. In the period following the First World War, coinciding with the growth of the U.S. economy and *its* industrialization, the U.S. government sought to revive the Brazilian rubber industry in order to sustain its own cheap supply of rubber. The U.S. Rubber Company made deals under the Vargas regime to get concessions in return for investment. Henry Ford was among those who got exemption from taxes to cordon off large chunks of the Amazon into rubber plantations. In the lower Amazon he built Fordlândia, a city to complement his plantations and house their workers, and a narcissistic extension of himself. With its whitewashed wooden houses, its front gardens and fire hydrants, Fordlândia is a piece of small-town America: America *in* Brazil. At the start of the Second World War, when rubber was in its most critical short supply, the U.S. Department of Agriculture and Office for Inter-American affairs poured funds into Brazil to prop up its rubber industry. But then after the Second World War the logic of the "free market" of global capitalism took inexorable hold. Asia became the world's indomitable supplier and Brazil's rubber industry again collapsed—leaving just a few rubber-tappers in the Amazon to eke out a survival.[18]

But there's much hypocrisy, even imperialism, in the environmentalist arguments for conserving the Amazon. Up until the last decade, the U.S. and U.K. governments were still pressuring Brazil to exploit the forest. And multinational companies based in the United States and the United Kingdom continue to invest in development there. Now that we near exhaustion of resources in our own territories, have lost—or shrunk to parks—our own wildernesses, we place an imposition on Brazil to redeem us from our ills.

(National parks in the United States, by the way, originated under Theodore Roosevelt, who recorded how impressed he was with the Brazilian wilderness after his trip there in his book *Through the Brazilian Wilderness.*)[19] It is our desire for tropical hardwoods, for hamburgers and the extensive, unjustifiably expensive use of crops required to produce a single hamburger, that, after all, are ultimately behind the destruction of the Amazon. It is our gas emissions—harvest of our overconsumption—that lie behind the climate change for which we now demand the preservation of the Amazon as restitution. Of the carbon credits program, agreed in 1997 under the Kyoto Protocol to reduce greenhouse gases (which was vetoed by the United States), while there's much to be said in favor its intention, in practice it perpetuates economic exploitation of Southern Hemisphere countries that is globalization's form of colonialism. The program provides an escape route from our own excesses rather than demanding that we radically curb them. In exchange for their pristine environment, poorer nations can earn money by "absorbing" the pollution of wealthier nations. (But where exactly does that waste go? Not "to" the Amazon, literally.) In environmental protectionism resides imperial nostalgia.

The defensiveness of the Brazilian government is therefore not surprising. Their responses to the latest research, which is mainly undertaken by U.S. researchers and published in U.S. journals, see in it an undercurrent of ongoing imperialism. They argue that such research overlooks indigenous Brazilian projects that are underway. The Brazilians recognize in the above situation the economic colonialism that is typical of the global capitalism going under the name of "free trade." The latest loans from the International Monetary Fund ("essentially a covert arm of the U. S. Treasury") compelled Brazil into stalling a project to save the Amazon.[20] Brazil's "loans" (at extortionate rates of interest) and its "favored" designation as supplier of raw materials—in return for absorbing some of the surplus of consumer goods that swamp the developed world—compel it into undertaking rapid industrial development for economic reasons, simply to play catch-up with their neighbors in the North. The Brazilian government reminds northern conservationists that the Amazon is already inhabited and that it has a responsibility towards these people for improving their economic conditions. Environmentalists are hypocritical in demanding the "immobilization" of Brazilian economic development, from the affluence of their own developed countries. The Brazilian government's program for development, which includes the Amazon and entails its mass industrialization, is called "Avança Brasil": Go ahead Brazil; advance; don't hold back.[21]

Brazil's government contests the latest statistics about deforestation and claims that the losses are greatly exaggerated. The true extent of deforestation, it insists, is revealed by satellite photographs. Brazil has the largest and most advanced technological program in the world for monitoring forests from space, INPE, the National Institution of Space Research. Its Sino-Brazilian satellite beams images of the Amazon back to the world and to the World Wide Web.[22] It is upon photographs that the figures spin, and the future of the world turns.

Nevertheless, part of the "Avança Brasil" program consists of "The Project to Recover Altered Areas of the Amazon": a plan for reversing environmental degradation. But can you ever get back what's lost? Meanwhile, the hi-fis spill out onto the barely paved streets of Manaus as I catch my boat upriver.

Since Darwin's *Origin of Species,* the writing of the history of nature has served both to oppose and compound the creationist myths of religion, which are vestigial in the environmentalists' argument for preserving the original, the autochthonous. The latest natural histories of the Amazon argue that it's not virgin at all. The so-called virgin forest has actually been managed for millennia, and at the end of the Pleistocene riverine settlements were probably the most densely populated. What we experience as original is a crafted, human—produced—product.[23] It used to be held that the Amazon had been a more-or-less stable feature of our world over these past million years. But the rainforest's impenetrability—its apparent virginity—has deferred its archival exploration. Geologists are now even finding, beneath the riverine sediment, deposits of windblown sand. What is now rainforest may for a time have been—a desert. Maybe what was lost *does* grow back.

Posing a direct challenge to the former-held notion of indigenous cultures in the Amazon as inhabiting a "counterfeit paradise," the Amazon is now unearthing some of the first agriculture, culture, and technologies in the New World.[24] At Monte Alegre, a modern city positioned between Manaus and Belém, archaeologists are examining the ghostly traces of Paleo-Indian inhabitants. Alongside campsites and areas of apparent forest clearance and cultivation, they left painted caves—including one containing "an inverted figure with rayed head."[25] The cave paintings are evidence of a people who sought to represent their world and one of the markers of a sophisticated, artistic culture. They are proving key to the dating of these first settlements. And it's the new science of luminescence, which, by shining lights into their dark rooms, makes the history of the caves readable—and the culture of the Amazon thereby with them.

Monte Alegre, alongside the revelations/realizations of Monte Verde in Chile at the very tip of South America, suggests that South America may have been the birthplace of technology in the Americas. Archeological research at the turn of the millennium is revoking the theory long held that American occupation began with the crossing of the Bering Strait into *North* America. The dominance of this Clovis culture argument by U.S. archaeologists, and the consequent ignoring of research conducted by Latin Americanists until very recently, represents another kind of imperialism—an archaeological imperialism, as if the settling of the Americas was "the first great [U.S.] American invention—the Ice Age equivalent of the spread of Coca-Cola or baseball caps."[26] The North American Clovis settlement is typically dated to somewhere between 11,000 and 13,000 years ago. At possibly as much as 50,000 years old, the Monte Verde remains are beyond doubt pre-Clovis. And there's a chance that their inhabitants did not come here via land crossing into North America but direct from another continent, by Paleolithic boat. Curiously, the supposition that the first Americans were from Asia, which would seem much rockier than the dating of the settlements, still generally stands. One of the first skeletons in Brazil has even been matched genetically to some found in a cave in China.

The debates about the hemispheric location and historical dating of settlement in the Americas entail a fight over origins. Who was first? Who belated?

How do you move in the world without losing it?

Where does America begin, where does it end?

When an asteroid hit the planet 65 million years ago and killed off 80 percent of existing species, it very nearly wiped the slate of the world clean. Six months of darkness followed the blast of light: a nuclear winter. It was an apocalypse. The first one. But this end was also a beginning. For nature loved the vacuum. And it came to create life as we know it. As we've come to live it.

Right before the asteroid made its impact—its "ground zero" was North America; actually the very furthest southern tip of North America, in Mexico to be precise—the continent of South America was gradually drifting toward North America. "Indeed, it probably made land contact just before Ground Zero. After this brief continental kiss South America began to waltz—at about eight millimeters per year—to the south-west, out into the Pacific. Whatever connection had earlier appeared between the two continents was now lost."[27] But then a dry land connection did open at some point later, the Isthmus of Panama, probably as long as 2.8 million years ago. This thin string of land still joins the continents, a kind of umbilical cord—though no one's dared which was first. Once rejoined, South America became the refuge for many species that were driven out of the north by the successive waves of immigrants—most dramatically by humans—over the last 13,000 or so years. Peccaries and tapirs traveled south. A range of cats. Camels and llama. Deer, skunk, and horses. All, originating in the north, made the trek south. Ironically, birds were one of the most widespread genera to make use of the land bridge. The one thing that these refugee birds have in common is that they're all now migratory land-birds. Flycatchers and warblers, for instance. But when they migrate each year they're not so much flying south in the winter as, when they fly north in the summer, going home. Some species went the other way, from south to north, most predictably perhaps the notoriously slow and evolutionarily backward sloth. Creosote bushes also crept north. Its toxins would prove very useful, millennia later, for northerner anthropologists travelling south again in preserving their notebooks from overly cooperative termites, and just a bit later, for bringing back their memories of Brazil.

What is the relation between two continents that have so much in common in evolutionary terms, where so many life forms are prodigious and peculiar to them? North America's latest and most extensive natural historian believes there may be an ecological principle that will come to explain their inextricable connection. Currently it is unrealized, so as he writes he "can only put it down to coincidence. Yet it is a coincidence as great and seemingly portentous as that which resulted in the sun and the moon appearing to be the same size in our skies."[28]

Bird-watching in the afternoon.

> Egrets. Tropical cormorant. Ducks *(irerê)*. Plenty of tern, wheeling.
> A kingfisher.
> A hummingbird I couldn't believe I was seeing, it was so tiny—
> green-throated, crimson breast, orange wings. The Crimson Topaz,
> rightly named: a jewel.
> Flocks of green parrot and blue macaw. And the golden parakeet,
> which with its yellow body and green flash on wings is dressed
> in the colors of Brazil.
> Toucans, comically heavy-billed, raucous and sociable.
> Kinds of cuckoos (apparently).

It was a show. Evening when the sun started to go down and the heat turned off was when the star performers took over.

> Scissor-tailed nightjar, with its streamer kite-like tail: fly catching.
> And a glorious, regal, fishing white hawk.

But around Vassar I see animals I've never seen before and that are extraordinary to think of running under lecture halls here and past north New York State's dilapidated factories. Still in America. Woodchucks, for example: flat-tailed and foolish, their fear at your approach fixes them in place. Lots of birds native to the continent. New World blackbirds, flashes of red wing startling on black body. Mockingbirds, which are much tamer and more common than I thought they'd be. They're arresting singers. They can now imitate car alarms. I look out for the confusion of car-owning residents.

The treasure, though, is a skunk I see in someone's front garden. Like Bishop's chain-mailed Brazilian armadillo scrambling to escape the bursting festival fire balloons of an encroaching city, it's an American atavism. Snuffling underneath the bird table, it was right at home but at the same time looked very, very strange. Black with a white wig running its entire length, like a body-sized toupee. Andy Warholish. The assistant curator said I was lucky I didn't scare it; otherwise its spray would have got me barred from the library.

This evening to G. and L.'s (G.'s French girlfriend) home for a slideshow of her photographs (she's a photographer) and G.'s talk on the history, ecology, and politics of Amazonia. The relationships of biodiversity and symbiosis are fascinating and far-reaching.

They argued that only ecotourism can save the forest. Ecotourism is the one industry apparently that can realistically sustain the local population while maintaining the environment largely unspoiled. We, who come from the most developed and wasteful societies in the world, to the best-preserved and most primitive, hold the solution. Here's the paradox at the heart of *saudades*. Our realization of loss provides the initiative—and the possibility of a revocation.

G.'s girlfriend came here originally as a tourist, to take photographs. Doubtless the camera will have a role to play whatever path we take.

This is the zero degree, the world at its origins: the real before the symbolic.

I sit in the dark room of G. and L.'s wooden house on the river and look at the slides.

This afternoon canoe trip with G. alone. The sounds surrounding us are more intense than the sights. Howler monkeys and capuchins. And birds, birds, birds. "We must listen to the wheat growing," urges Lévi-Strauss, in his plea for diversity.[29] You should hear the Amazon. It's total exposure to your senses—all of them open. And you become all receptacle. No self.

I put my camera aside. Right here in the canoe, I'm in the photograph. For once, or maybe longer, I'm all present.

NOTES

INTRODUCTION

1. Walter Benjamin, *Illuminations* (London: Fontana, 1992), 219.

2. Susan Sontag, *On Photography* (London: Penguin, 1977), 54, 154.

3. Roland Barthes, *Camera Lucida: Reflections on Photography* (London: Vintage, 1993), 77.

4. Simon During, *Modern Enchantments: The Cultural Power of Secular Magic* (Cambridge, MA: Harvard University Press, 2002).

5. Helmut Gernsheim, *A Concise History of Photography* (New York: Dover, 1986).

6. Robert Temple, *The Crystal Sun: Rediscovering a Lost Technology of the Ancient World* (London: Random House, 2000).

7. David Hockney, *Secret Knowledge: Rediscovering the Lost Techniques of the Old Masters* (London: Thames and Hudson, 2001). Philip Steadman makes a similar argument, about Vermeer, in *Vermeer's Camera: Uncovering the Truth behind the Masterpieces* (Oxford: Oxford University Press, 2001).

8. Hal Foster, *The Return of the Real* (Cambridge: MIT Press, 1996), 130, 165.

9. Dylan Evans, *An Introductory Dictionary of Lacanian Psychoanalysis* (London: Routledge, 1996).

10. Jacques Lacan, *The Four Fundamental Concepts of Psycho-analysis,* ed. Jacques-Alain Miller, trans. Alan Sheridan (New York: Norton, 1981), 53.

11. John North, *The Ambassadors' Secret: Holbein and the World of the Renaissance* (London: Hambledon and London, 2002).

12. Benjamin, 230.

13. Jacqueline Rose, *Sexuality in the Field of Vision* (London: Verso, 1986).

14. Sigmund Freud, *The Interpretation of Dreams,* trans. and ed. James Strachey (New York: Basic, 1965), 574.

15. Freud, *Moses and Monotheism: Three Essays,* in *The Origins of Religion,* trans. and ed. James Strachey (London: Penguin, 1990), 374.

16. Lacan, 47–48.

17. Hélène Cixous and Mireille Calle-Gruber, *Hélène Cixous: Rootprints; Memory and Life Writing,* trans. Eric Prenowitz (London: Routledge, 1997), 179, 189.

18. Michael Ondaatje, *Running in the Family* (London: Picador, 1984), 161, 162.

19. Gabriel Josipovici, *A Life* (London: European Jewish Publication Society, 2001), 7.

20. Tim Lott, *The Scent of Dried Roses* (London: Viking, 1996), 36.

21. Timothy Dow Adams, *Light Writing and Life Writing: Photography in Auto-biography* (Chapel Hill: University of North Carolina Press, 2000).

22. Linda Haverty Rugg, *Picturing Ourselves: Photography and Autobiography* (Chicago: University of Chicago Press, 1997), 9, 238.

23. Paul de Man, *The Rhetoric of Romanticism* (New York: Columbia University Press, 1984), 69.

24. Nancy K. Miller, *Bequest and Betrayal: Memoirs of a Parent's Death* (New York: Oxford University Press, 1996). Marianne Hirsch, *Family Frames: Photography, Narrative and Postmemory* (Cambridge, MA: Harvard University Press, 1997). Annette Kuhn, *Family Secrets: Acts of Memory and Imagination* (London: Verso, 1995).

25. Philippe Lejeune, *On Autobiography,* ed. Paul John Eakin, trans. Katherine Leary (Minneapolis: University of Minnesota Press, 1989), 115.

26. Roland Barthes, *Roland Barthes by Roland Barthes,* trans. Richard Howard (New York: Farrar, 1977), 56.

27. J. Gratton, "*Roland Barthes par Roland Barthes:* Autobiography and the Notion of Expression," *Romance Studies* 8 (1986): 57–58.

28. Paul John Eakin, *Touching the World: Reference in Autobiography* (Princeton: Princeton University Press, 1992), 21, 4.

29. Patricia Berrahou Phillippy, *Love's Remedies: Recantation and Renaissance Lyric Poetry* (Lewisburg, PA: Bucknell University Press, 1995).

30. Plato, *Phaedrus,* trans. James H. Nicols (Ithaca, NY: Cornell University Press, 1998).

31. Saint Augustine, *The Retractions,* trans. Sister Mary Inez Bogan (Washington, DC: The Catholic University of America Press, 1999).

32. Geoffrey Chaucer, *The Complete Works,* ed. F. N. Robinson (Oxford: Oxford University Press, 1985), 265

33. Friedrich Nietzsche, *The Birth of Tragedy* (London: Penguin, 1993).

34. Søren Kierkegaard, *Concluding Unscientific Postscript to Philosophical Frag-*

ments, vol. 1, ed. and trans. Howard V. Hong and Edna H. Hong (Princeton: Princeton University Press, 1992), 621.

35. Kierkegaard, *Repetition: An Essay in Experimental Psychology,* trans. Walter Lowrie (London: Oxford University Press, 1942), 6.

I. ROLAND BARTHES'S LOSS

1. Colin MacCabe, "Barthes and Bazin: The Ontology of the Image," in *Writing the Image after Roland Barthes,* ed. Jean-Michel Rabaté (Philadelphia: Pennsylvania University Press, 1997), 72. Daniel Ferrer, "Generic Criticism in the Wake of Barthes," in *Writing the Image,* 217.

2. Jacques Derrida, *The Work of Mourning,* ed. Pascale-Anne Brault and Michael Naas (Chicago: University of Chicago Press, 2001), 50. First published as "Les Morts de Roland Barthes," *Poétique* 47 (1981): 269–92.

3. Roland Barthes, *Camera Lucida: Reflections on Photography,* trans. Richard Howard (London: Vintage, 1993), 9.

4. Tzvetan Todorov, "The Last Barthes," trans. Richard Howard, *Critical Inquiry* 7 (1981): 449.

5. Jonathan Culler, *Barthes* (Glasgow: Fontana, 1983), 116, 122, 124.

6. Elaine Hoft-March, "Barthes's Real Mother: The Legacy of *La chambre claire,*" *French Forum* 17 (1992): 62

7. J. Gerald Kennedy, "Roland Barthes, Autobiography, and the End of Writing," *Georgia Review* 35 (1981): 397.

8. Nancy Shawcross, *Roland Barthes on Photography: The Critical Tradition in Perspective* (Gainesville: University Press of Florida, 1997), 119.

9. Barthes, *La chambre claire: Note sur la photographie* (Paris: Gallimard, 1980).

10. For the former see Marianne Hirsch, *Family Frames: Photography, Narrative and Postmemory* (Cambridge, MA: Harvard University Press, 1997); for the latter see Kathleen Woodward, "Freud and Barthes: Theorizing Mourning, Sustaining Grief," *Discourse* 13 (1990–91): 93–110.

11. Sigmund Freud, "Mourning and Melancholia," trans. James Strachey, in *On Metapsychology,* vol. 11, *Penguin Freud Library,* ed. Angela Richards (London: Penguin, 1991), 262.

12. Paul John Eakin, *Touching the World: Reference in Autobiography* (Princeton: Princeton University Press, 1992), 20.

13. Ralph Sarkonak, "Roland Barthes and the Spectre of Photography," *L'Esprit Createur* 22 (1982): 48–68. Louis-Jean Calvet, *Roland Barthes: A Biography,* trans. Sarah Wykes (Oxford: Polity Press, 1994).

14. Chantal Thomas, "La Photo du jardin d'hiver," *Critique* 423–24 (1982): 799.

15. Barthes, "The Great Family of Man," in *Mythologies* (1957), trans. Annette Lavers (New York: Farrar, 1972) 100–102. Barthes, "The Rhetoric of the Image,"

in *Image Music Text*, ed. and trans. Stephen Heath (London: Fontana, 1977), 35. Barthes, *Roland Barthes by Roland Barthes*, trans. Richard Howard (New York: Farrar, 1977).

16. Barthes, "The Photographic Message," in *Image*, 16.

17. Barthes, *The Rustle of Language*, trans. Richard Howard (Oxford: Blackwell, 1986), 148.

18. Barthes, *S/Z: An Essay*, trans. Richard Miller (New York: Farrar, 1974).

19. Philippe Lejeune, *On Autobiography*, ed. Paul John Eakin, trans. Katherine Leary (Minneapolis: University of Minnesota Press, 1989), 22.

20. See respectively Mary Bittner Wiseman, *The Ecstasies of Roland Barthes* (London: Routledge, 1989); J. Gratton, *"Roland Barthes par Roland Barthes*: Autobiography and the Notion of Expression," *Romance Studies* 8 (1986): 57–65; and Patrizia Lombardo, *The Three Paradoxes of Roland Barthes* (Athens: University of Georgia Press, 1989).

21. Jane Gallop, *Around 1981: Academic Feminist Literary Theory* (London: Routledge, 1992).

22. Susan Sontag, "Writing Itself: On Roland Barthes," in *A Barthes Reader*, ed. Sontag (London: Cape, 1982), xviii.

23. Barthes, *The Grain of the Voice: Interviews, 1962–1980*, trans. Linda Coverdale (Berkeley and Los Angeles: University of California Press, 1985), 282–83.

24. Antoine Compagnon, "Who Is the Real One?" in *Writing the Image*, ed. Rabaté, 197.

25. Culler, 12.

26. Stephen Ungar, *Roland Barthes: The Professor of Desire* (Lincoln: University of Nebraska Press, 1983).

27. Lejeune, 134.

28. Barthes, *Writing Degree Zero*, trans. Annette Lavers and Colin Smith (London: Cape, 1967), 81.

29. James Beighton, "Le Texte Symptomal? Evidence of Depression in Barthes's Later Writings," unpublished essay, MA in English (University of Leicester, 1999). Lewis Wolpert, *Malignant Sadness: The Anatomy of Depression* (London: Faber, 1999) is one such study that Beighton uses.

30. Julia Kristeva, *Black Sun: Depression and Melancholia*, trans. Leon S. Roudiez (New York: Columbia University Press), 9, 40, 42.

31. Barthes, *Incidents* (Berkeley and Los Angeles: University of California Press, 1992), 73.

32. Maurice Blanchot, "Orpheus' Gaze," in *The Siren's Song: Selected Essays*, ed. Gabriel Josipovici, trans. Sacha Rabinovitch (London: Harvester, 1982), 179, 181.

33. Barthes, *Critical Essays*, trans. Richard Howard (Evanston, IL: Northwestern University Press, 1972), 268.

34. Barthes, *A Lover's Discourse: Fragments*, trans. Richard Howard (New York: Farrar, 1978), 98, 98.

35. Beryl Schlossman, "The Descent of Orpheus: On Reading Barthes and Proust," in *Writing the Image,* ed. Rabaté, 156.

36. Ovid, *The Metamorphoses,* trans. Mary M. Innes (London: Penguin, 1955), 225, 226.

37. W. K. C. Guthrie, *Orpheus and Greek Religion* (Princeton: Princeton University Press, 1993).

38. In chronological order: Roland L. Champagne, "Between Orpheus and Eurydice: Barthes and the Historicity of Reading," *Clio* 7 (1978–79): 229–38; Claude Reichler, "L'ombre," *Critique* 421–22 (1982): 767–74; Réda Bensmaïa, *The Barthes Effect: The Essay as Reflective Text,* trans. Pat Fedkiew (Minneapolis: Minnesota University Press, 1987); Lombardo (1989); Wiseman (1989); Schlossman (1997).

39. Reichler, 767.

40. Freud, *Civilization and Its Discontents,* trans. and ed. James Strachey (New York: Norton, 1961).

41. Wiseman, 181.

42. Schlossman, 150.

43. Daniel Grojnowski, "Le Mystère de *La chambre claire,*" *Textuel* 34 (1984): 92.

44. Diana Knight, "Roland Barthes, or The Woman without a Shadow," in *Writing the Image,* ed. Rabaté, 138.

45. Calvet, 247. Essay translated in Barthes, *Rustle,* 296–305.

46. Barthes, *Barthes Reader,* 461, 465, 465.

47. Marcel Proust, *Swann's Way,* book 1 of *Remembrance of Things Past* (New York: Penguin, 1992), 217, 218.

48. Barthes, *Rustle,* 279, 280.

49. Kennedy, 395.

50. Gabriel Josipovici, *A Life* (London: European Jewish Publication Society, 2001), 281.

51. Barthes, *The Responsibility of Forms: Critical Essays on Music, Art, and Representation,* trans. Richard Howard (New York: Farrar, 1985), 293–94, 298, 298.

52. Eduardo Cadava, *Words of Light: Theses on the Photography of History* (Princeton: Princeton University Press, 1997).

53. Bensmaïa, *Barthes Effect.* Søren Kierkegaard, *Concluding Unscientific Postscript to Philosophical Fragments,* vol. 1, ed. and trans. Howard V. Hong and Edna H. Hong (Princeton: Princeton University Press, 1992).

54. Gary Shapiro, "To Philosophize Is to Learn to Die," in *Signs in Culture: Roland Barthes Today,* ed. Steven Ungar and Betty R. McGraw (Iowa City: University of Iowa Press, 1989), 3–31. Plato, *Phaedrus,* trans. James H. Nicols (Ithaca, NY: Cornell University Press, 1998).

55. Lejeune, "Le Roland Barthes sans peine," *Textuel* 34, no. 44 (1984): 18, 13.

56. Barthes, *Empire of Signs,* trans. Richard Howard (London: Cape, 1982), 82, 83, 83.

57. Alan W. Watts, *The Way of Zen* (1957) (London: Penguin, 1990), 63, 90, 97.

58. Guru Rinpoche according to Karma-Lingpa, *The Tibetan Book of the Dead: The Great Liberation through Hearing in the Bardo*, trans. Francesca Fremantle and Chögyam Trungpa (Boston: Shambhala, 1992), xxxxiii, xxvii.

59. Trungpa, *Cutting through Spiritual Materialism* (1973), ed. John Baker and Martin Casper (Boston: Shambhala, 1987), 49.

2. CLAUDE LÉVI-STRAUSS'S TRISTES PHOTOGRAPHIQUES

1. Claude Lévi-Strauss, *Tristes Tropiques*, trans. John and Doreen Weightman (New York: Random House, 1997), 4, 5.

2. Lévi-Strauss, *Saudades do Brasil: A Photographic Memoir*, trans. Sylvia Modelski (Seattle: University of Washington Press, 1995).

3. Roland Barthes, "The Photographic Message," in *Image Music Text*, ed. and trans. Stephen Heath (London: Fontana, 1977), 15–31. Lévi-Strauss, *The Raw and the Cooked*, vol. 1 of *Introduction to a Science of Mythology* (London: Random House, 1994).

4. Louis-Jean Calvet, *Roland Barthes: A Biography*, trans. Sarah Wykes (Oxford: Polity Press, 1994). Barthes, *Mythologies*, trans. Annette Lavers (New York: Farrar, 1972). Lévi-Strauss, *Structural Anthropology*, vol. 1, trans. Claire Jacobson (London: Penguin, 1993).

5. Christopher Pinney, "The Parallel Histories of Anthropology and Photography," in *Anthropology and Photography, 1860–1920*, ed. Elizabeth Edwards (New Haven, CT: Yale University Press, 1992), 18–31.

6. Terence Wright, "Photography: Theories of Realism and Convention," in *Anthropology and Photography*, ed. Edwards, 20–21.

7. Lévi-Strauss, *The Savage Mind* (Oxford: Oxford University Press, 1996), 89.

8. Lévi-Strauss, *Structural Anthropology*, vol. 2, trans. Monique Layton (Chicago: University of Chicago Press, 1983), 132, 115.

9. Barthes, *Camera Lucida: Reflections on Photography*, trans. Richard Howard (London: Vintage, 1993), 76.

10. Lévi-Strauss, *The View from Afar*, trans. Joachim Neugroschel and Phoebe Hoss (Oxford: Blackwell, 1985), 249.

11. Lévi-Strauss, *Look, Listen, Read*, trans. Brian C. J. Singer (New York: Basic Books, 1997), 29–30.

12. Walter Benjamin, "A Short History of Photography," in *Classical Essays on Photography*, ed. Alan Trachtenberg (New Haven, CT: Leete's Island Books, 1980), 209.

13. Pinney, 74. Western mastery of vision is explored in Martin Jay, *Downcast Eyes: The Denigration of Vision in Twentieth-Century Thought* (Berkeley and Los Angeles: University of California Press, 1994).

14. G. Charbonnier, *Conversations with Claude Lévi-Strauss*, ed. and trans. John and Doreen Weightman (London: Cape, 1969), 125.

15. John Berger, *The White Bird* (London: Chatto and Windus, 1985), 176.

16. Lévi-Strauss, *The Way of Masks,* trans. Sylvia Modelski (Seattle: University of Washington Press, 1982).

17. Lévi-Strauss, *The Story of Lynx,* trans. Catherine Tihanyi (Chicago: University of Chicago Press, 1995).

18. Or, in the untranslated and single-printing first book, *La Vie familiale et sociale des indiens Nambikwara* (Paris: Musée de l'Homme, 1948)—which was an extracted journal article and later incorporated into work on the elementary structures of kinship—photographs of Indian family life.

19. Elizabeth Edwards, *Raw Histories: Photographs, Anthropology and Museums* (Oxford: Berg, 2001), 5. The argument about photography as revelation of the history of anthropology is also made in Edwards's collection, *Anthropology and Photography,* and in Anna Grimshaw, *Ways of Seeing in Modern Anthropology* (Cambridge: Cambridge University Press, 2001).

20. Pierre Bourdieu, *Outline of a Theory of Practice* (Cambridge: Cambridge University Press, 1977), 96.

21. George E. Marcus and Michael M. J. Fischer, *Anthropology as Cultural Critique: An Experimental Moment in the Human Sciences* (Chicago: University of Chicago Press, 1999), 29.

22. Marcel Hénaff, *Claude Lévi-Strauss and the Making of Structural Anthropology,* trans. Mary Baker (Minneapolis: University of Minnesota Press, 1998), 255.

23. Roslyn Poignant, "Surveying the Field of View: The Making of the RAI Photographic Collection," in *Anthropology and Photography,* ed. Edwards, 42.

24. Edwards, *Anthropology and Photography;* Grimshaw.

25. Bronislaw Malinowksi, *A Diary in the Strict Sense of the Term,* trans. Robert Gutterman (Stanford, CA: Stanford University Press, 1989), 140.

26. Lévi-Strauss, *The Naked Man,* vol. 4 of *Introduction to a Science of Mythology,* trans. John and Doreen Weightman (London: Cape, 1981), 268, "Translator's Note" 265, 630.

27. Susan Sontag, *Against Interpretation* (London: Vintage, 1994), 72. Jeffrey Mehlman, *A Structural Study of Autobiography: Proust, Leiris, Sartre, Lévi-Strauss* (Cornell, NY: Cornell University Press, 1974).

28. James Clifford, *The Predicament of Culture: Twentieth-Century Ethnography, Literature, and Art* (Cambridge, MA: Harvard University Press, 1988).

29. Edmund Leach, *Claude Lévi-Strauss* (Chicago: University of Chicago Press, 1989), 13.

30. Edwards, *Anthropology and Photography,* 7.

31. Barthes, *Image,* 26.

32. James C. Faris, "A Political Primer on Anthropology/Photography," in *Anthropology and Photography,* ed. Edwards, 255.

33. Lévi-Strauss, *The Elementary Structures of Kinship,* trans. James Harle Bell, John Richard von Sturmer, and Rodney Needham (Boston: Beacon Press, 1969), 84–107.

34. Johannes Fabian, *Time and the Other: How Anthropology Makes Its Object* (New York: Columbia University Press, 1983), 58–59.

35. Jacques Derrida, *The Work of Mourning,* ed. Pascale-Anne Brault and Michael Naas (Chicago: University of Chicago Press, 2001), 41–42.

36. Alan Watts takes apart cybernetic control in *The Way of Zen* (London: Penguin, 1990).

37. Lévi-Strauss, "Diogène Couché," *Les Temps Modernes* 110 (1955): 1217; my translation.

38. George Steiner, "Orpheus with His Myths," in *Claude Lévi-Strauss: The Anthropologist as Hero,* ed. E. Nelson Hayes and Tanya Hayes (Cambridge: MIT Press, 1970), 170–83.

39. Lévi-Strauss, *Saudades de São Paulo* (São Paulo: Companhia das Letras, 1996).

40. Cited in Eduardo Cadava, *Words of Light: Theses on the Photography of History* (Princeton: Princeton University Press, 1997), xxix.

41. Malek Alloula, *The Colonial Harem,* trans. Myrna Godzich and Wlad Godzich (Minneapolis: University of Minnesota Press, 1986), 7.

42. Paul Henley, "Fewer Words, More Pictures," *Times Literary Supplement,* February 2, 2001, 27.

43. John Collier, *Visual Anthropology: Photography as a Research Method* (New York: Holt, Rinehart and Winston, 1967), 4.

44. Jay Ruby, *Picturing Culture: Explorations of Film and Anthropology* (Chicago: University of Chicago Press, 2000), 4–5.

45. Nancy Scheper-Hughes, *Death without Weeping: The Violence of Everyday Life in Brazil* (Berkeley and Los Angeles: University of California Press, 1992). Marjorie Shostak, *Nisa: The Life and Words of a !Kung Woman* (1981; Cambridge, MA: Harvard University Press, 2000). Shostak, *Return to Nisa* (Cambridge, MA: Harvard University Press, 2000).

46. Philippe Lejeune, *On Autobiography,* ed. Paul John Eakin, trans. Katherine Leary (Minneapolis: University of Minnesota Press, 1989).

47. Barthes, *The Grain of the Voice: Interviews, 1962–1980,* trans. Linda Coverdale (Berkeley and Los Angeles: University of California Press, 1991), 357.

48. Annette Lavers, *Roland Barthes: Structuralism and After* (London: Methuen, 1982).

49. Derrida, *Writing and Difference,* trans. Alan Bass (Chicago: University of Chicago Press, 1978), 292. Renato Rosaldo, "Imperialist Nostalgia," *Representations* 26 (1989): 107.

50. Clifford, "On Ethnographic Allegory," in *Writing Culture: The Poetics and Politics of Ethnography,* ed. Clifford and George Marcus (Berkeley and Los Angeles: University of California Press, 1986), 113.

51. Quotations in French from Lévi-Strauss, *Tristes Tropiques* (Paris: Librarie Plon, 1955), 426, 31.

52. Marcel Proust, *Swann's Way*, book 1 of *Remembrance of Things Past* (New York: Penguin, 1992), 59.

53. Lévi-Strauss, *The Origin of Table Manners*, vol 3. of *Introduction to a Science of Mythology*, trans. John and Doreen Weightman (Chicago: Chicago University Press, 1990).

54. Clifford, "On Ethnographic Allegory," 112.

55. Sontag, *On Photography* (London: Penguin, 1977).

56. Bourdieu, *Photography: A Middle-brow Art*, trans. Shaun Whiteside (Oxford: Polity Press, 1998).

57. Sebastião Salgado, *Terra: Struggle of the Landless* (London: Phaidon, 1997); *Migrations: Humanity in Transition* (New York: Aperture, 2000).

58. Barthes, *Mythologies*, 94.

59. Darius Milhaud, *Saudades do Brasil*, Leonard Bernstein, cond. Orchestre National de France, EMI CDC-7 47845 2, 1978.

60. Sontag, *On Photography*, passim.

3. GORDON PARKS'S TAKING A LIFE

1. Roland Barthes, *Camera Lucida: Reflections on Photography*, trans. Richard Howard (London: Vintage, 1993), 34.

2. Graham Clarke, *The Photograph* (Oxford: Oxford University Press, 1997), 145.

3. John Collier Jr., *Visual Anthropology: Photography as a Research Method* (New York: Holt, Rinehart and Winston, 1967).

4. Roy Emerson Stryker, "The FSA Collection of Photographs," in *In This Proud Land: America, 1935–1943, as Seen in the FSA Photographs*, ed. Stryker and Nancy Wood (London: Secker and Warburg, 1974), 7.

5. F. Jack Hurley, *Portrait of a Decade: Roy Stryker and the Development of Documentary Photography in the Thirties* (New York: Da Capo Press, 1972), 56.

6. Stryker, cited in Alan Trachtenberg, "From Image to Story: Reading the File," in *Documenting America, 1935–1943*, ed. Carl Fleischauer and Beverly W. Brannan (Berkeley and Los Angeles: University of California Press, 1988), 61.

7. Lawrence W. Levine, "The Historian and the Icon: Photography and the History of the American People in the 1930s and 1940s," in *Documenting America, 1935–1943*, ed. Fleischauer and Brannan, 40, 56.

8. William Stott, *Documentary Expression and Thirties America* (London: Oxford University Press, 1973), 22

9. The following criticisms are Levine's and Clarke's respectively.

10. Clive Scott, *The Spoken Image: Photography and Language* (London: Reaktion Books, 1999), 31, 96.

11. Gordon Parks, *Moments without Proper Names* (London: Secker and Warburg, 1975).

12. Parks, *Midway: Portrait of a Daytona Beach Neighborhood* (Daytona Beach, FL: Southeast Museum of Photography, 1999).

13. Both reprinted in Parks, *Harlem: The Artist's Annotations on a City Revisited in Two Classic Photographic Essays*, ed. Michael Torosian (Toronto: Lumiere Press, 1997).

14. *Shaft*, MGM, 1971. *The Learning Tree*, Winger, 1969. Parks, *The Learning Tree* (New York: Ballantine, 1963).

15. Michael Torosian, introduction and interview, in Parks, *Harlem*, 13.

16. Richard Wright, *Twelve Million Black Voices: A Folk History of the Negro in the United States of America*, with photographs by Edwin Rosskam (London: Lindsay Drummond, 1947).

17. bell hooks, "In Our Glory: Photography and Black," in *Picturing Us: African American Identity in Photography*, ed. Deborah Willis (New York: New Press, 1994), 43–44, 48–49.

18. Parks, *A Choice of Weapons* (St. Paul: Minnesota Historical Society Press, 1986), 260.

19. Parks, *To Smile in Autumn: A Memoir* (New York: Norton, 1979), 210.

20. Nicholas Natanson, *The Black Image in the New Deal: The Politics of FSA Photography* (Knoxville: University of Tennessee Press, 1992), 183, 183, 186–87.

21. Parks, *Choice*, 231.

22. Susan Sontag, *On Photography* (London: Penguin, 1977), 42.

23. Susan Sontag, *Against Interpretation* (London: Vintage, 1994), 73.

24. Claude Lévi-Strauss, *Tristes Tropiques*, trans. John and Doreen Weightman (New York: Random House, 1997), 20.

25. Barthes, 92.

26. Parks, *Flavio* (New York: Norton, 1978), 14.

27. *Life*, June 16, 1961: "Freedom's Fearful Foe: Poverty," 94, 95; Parks, "Photographer's Diary of a Visit in Dark World," 96–98.

28. "A Great Urge to Help Flavio: Special Report," *Life*, July 7, 1961, 15–16.

29. "Flavio's Rescue: Americans Bring Him from Rio Slum to Be Cured," *Life*, July 21, 1961, 1+.

30. Marianne Hirsch, *Family Frames: Photography, Narrative and Postmemory* (Cambridge, MA: Harvard University Press, 1997), 7.

31. Wendy Kozol, *"Life's" America: Family and Nation in Postwar Photojournalism* (Philadelphia: Temple University Press, 1994), 78.

32. *The Crisis in Our Hemisphere: Crisis in Latin America*, part 1, spec. issue of *Life*, June 2, 1961, 1+. *Shocking Poverty Spawns Reds: Latin America*, part 2, spec. issue of *Life*, June 16, 1961, 1+. *Bolivia: U.S. Stake in a Revolution: Latin America*, part 3, spec. issue of *Life*, June 30, 1961, 1+. *Latin America's Story of Turbulence: Latin America*, part 4, spec. issue of *Life*, July 14, 1961, 1+. *Prisoners of Our Geography: Crisis in Latin America*, part 5, spec. issue of *Life*, July 28, 1961, 1+.

33. Lars Schoultz, *Beneath the United States: A History of U. S. Policy toward Latin America* (Cambridge, MA: Harvard University Press, 1998), 357.

34. Thomas E. Skidmore, *Politics in Brazil, 1930–1964: An Experiment in Democracy* (London: Oxford University Press, 1967), 195.

35. *Life*, June 2, 1961, 88.

36. Skidmore, 199.

37. E. Bradford Burns, *A History of Brazil* (New York: Columbia University Press, 1993), 444, 424.

38. Robert Coughlan, "The Staggering Problem," *Life*, July 28, 1961, 52A–58.

39. *Life*, July 7, 1961, 16.

40. John Tagg, *The Burden of Representation: Essays on Photographies and Histories* (Minneapolis: University of Minnesota Press, 1988), 157, 160.

41. A. J. Van Zuilen, *The Life Cycle of Magazines: A Historical Study of the Decline and Fall of the General Interest Magazine in the United States during the Period 1946–1972* (Uithorn, Netherlands: Graduate Press, 1977).

42. Coughlan, 57.

43. C. D. Jackson, "The Aim of *Life*," *Life*, June 2, 1961, 1.

44. Richard M. Clurman, *To the End of "Time": The Seduction and Conquest of a Media Empire* (New York: Simon and Schuster, 1992), 19, 38.

45. Stott, 130.

46. Henry Luce, "The American Century," *Life*, February 17, 1941, 65.

47. Stott, 138.

48. Natanson, 64.

49. Barthes, 38.

50. Robert M. Levine, *The Brazilian Photographs of Genieve Naylor, 1940–1942* (Durham, NC: Duke University Press, 1998).

51. R. J. Doherty, *Social-Documentary Photography in the USA* (Garden City, NY: American Photographic Book Publishing, 1976), 86.

52. Julian Borger, "The Photo War," *The Guardian*, G2, April 26, 2000, 12–13.

53. John Tebbel and Mary Ellen Zuckerman, *The Magazine in America, 1741–1990* (New York: Oxford University Press, 1991), 227.

54. Jackson, 1.

55. Stott, 130.

56. Parks, *Choice*, 227.

57. *Life*, June 2, 1961, 81.

58. Burns, 432.

59. John Loengard, *"Life" Classic Photographs: A Personal Interpretation* (Boston: Little, Brown, 2000).

60. Alex Bellos, "Exposed to a Doubtful Dream," *The Guardian*, G2, June 4, 1998, 2.

61. http://www.pbs.org/newshour/bb/entertainment/jan-june98/gordon _1-6.html (accessed April 17, 2002).

62. Paula Rabinowitz, "Voyeurism and Class Consciousness: James Agee and Walker Evans, *Let Us Now Praise Famous Men*," *Cultural Critique* 21 (1992): 166.

63. Parks, *Born Black* (Philadelphia: Lippincott, 1971).

64. http://www.pdngallery.com/legends/parks/mainframeset2.shtml (accessed April 17, 2002).

65. Parks, *Born*, 68; *Harlem*, 10.

66. *Flavio*, NBC, 1966

67. *Life*, June 16, 1961, 96, 98.

68. David J. Hellwig, ed., *African-American Reflections on Brazil's Racial Paradise* (Philadelphia: Temple University Press, 1992).

69. The census just before Parks's intervention cites blacks and *"pardos"* ("mulattoes") as constituting 68.6 percent of Rio's *favela* population compared with 29 percent of the total city population. Julio César Pino, *Family and Favela: The Reproduction of Poverty in Rio de Janeiro* (Westport, CT: Greenwood Press, 1997), 48.

70. Parks, *Born Black*, 28.

71. Parks, *Moments*, 101.

72. *Half Past Autumn*, *NewsHour* transcript January 6, 1998, http://www.pbs.org/ newshour/bb/entertainment/jan-june98/gordon_1-6.html (accessed April 17, 2002).

73. Parks, *Arias in Silence* (Boston and London: Little, Brown, 1994).

74. Pino, 138.

75. Toni Morrison, *Sula* (London: Chatto and Windus, 1973).

4. ELIZABETH BISHOP'S ART OF LOSING

1. Quotations of published poems from Elizabeth Bishop, *The Complete Poems: 1927–1979* (New York: Farrar, 1999).

2. Bishop, *One Art: Letters*, ed. Robert Giroux (New York: Noonday Press, 1995), 329.

3. Bishop makes the later claim in conversation with George Starbuck, in *Elizabeth Bishop and Her Art*, ed. Lloyd Schwartz and Sybil P. Estess (Ann Arbor: University of Michigan Press, 1983), 318. Lee Edelman discusses the misreferencing in "The Geography of Gender: Elizabeth Bishop's 'In the Waiting Room,'" *Contemporary Literature* 26 (1985): 175–96.

4. Paul Fussell, *Poetic Meter and Poetic Form* (New York: McGraw Hill, 1978), 175.

5. Bonnie Costello, *Elizabeth Bishop: Questions of Mastery* (Cambridge, MA: Harvard University Press, 1991), 6. Harold Bloom, "Foreword," in *Elizabeth Bishop and Her Art*, ed. Schwartz and Estess, x. Adrienne Rich, "The Eye of the Outsider: Elizabeth Bishop's *Complete Poems, 1927–1979*," in *Blood, Bread and Poetry: Selected Prose, 1979–1985* (London: Virago, 1987), 124–35.

6. Anne Stevenson, *Five Looks at Elizabeth Bishop* (London: Bellew, 1998). The description comes in Gary Fountain and Peter Brazeau, *Remembering Elizabeth Bishop: An Oral Biography* (Amherst: University of Massachusetts Press, 1994), 274.

7. George Monteiro, ed., *Conversations with Elizabeth Bishop* (Jackson: University Press of Mississippi, 1996), 24.

8. Bishop, *Exchanging Hats: Paintings*, ed. William Benton (Manchester, England: Carcanet Press, 1997).

9. Bishop, "Gregorio Valdes," in *The Collected Prose,* ed. Robert Giroux (New York: Noonday Press, 1984), 51–60.

10. Quotations of all unpublished material unless otherwise indicated from the Special Collections, Vassar College Library, with permission. I have proofed obvious spelling or typographical errors and omitted Bishop's drafts before her corrections unless making a point about changes. All ellipses my own; any exceptions will be noted.

11. Robert Dale Parker, *The Unbeliever: The Poetry of Elizabeth Bishop* (Urbana: University of Illinois Press, 1988).

12. Fountain and Brazeau, 182.

13. John Tebbel and Mary Ellen Zuckerman, *The Magazine in America, 1741–1990* (New York: Oxford University Press, 1991), 229.

14. Ashley Brown, "Elizabeth Bishop in Brazil," in *Elizabeth Bishop and Her Art,* ed. Schwartz and Estess, 223.

15. Bishop, trans. and ed., *The Diary of Helena Morley* (London: Bloomsbury, 1997), xxvi.

16. Schwartz and Estess, 194.

17. Schwartz and Estess, 305.

18. Maria Lúcia Milléo Martins, "Elizabeth Bishop and Carlos Drummond de Andrade: Verse/Universe in Four Acts" (Ph.D. diss., University of Massachusetts, Amherst, 1999), 170.

19. Bishop, *Collected Prose,* 229, 233, 233.

20. Cited in Brett C. Millier, *Elizabeth Bishop: Life and the Memory of It* (Berkeley and Los Angeles: University of California Press, 1993), 517.

21. Bishop and the Editors of *Life, Brazil* (New York: Time, 1962).

22. Schwartz and Estess, 312.

23. Howard Abramson, *"National Geographic": Behind America's Lens on the World* (New York: Crown, 1987). Catherine A. Lutz and Jane L. Collins, eds., *Reading "National Geographic"* (Chicago: University of Chicago Press, 1993).

24. Siegfried Kracauer, quoted in Eduardo Cadava, *Words of Light: Theses on the Photography of History* (Princeton: Princeton University Press, 1997), xxvi.

25. Originally published in *Life,* June 2, 1961, 82–83, 88.

26. C. R. Boxer, introduction to Bishop, *Brazil* (London: Sunday Times World Library, 1962).

27. Monteiro, 80

28. Bishop, "On the Railroad Named Delight," *New York Times Magazine,* March 7, 1965, 30–31, 84–86. The Brazilian criticism—and Bishop's response—is discussed in Victoria Harrison, *Elizabeth Bishop's Poetics of Intimacy* (Cambridge: Cambridge University Press, 1993), 167.

29. Thomas E. Skidmore, *Politics in Brazil, 1930–1964: An Experiment in Democracy* (London: Oxford University Press, 1967). Skidmore, *The Politics of Military Rule in Brazil, 1964–85* (New York: Oxford University Press, 1988).

30. Camille Roman, *Elizabeth Bishop's World War II–Cold War View* (New

York: Palgrave, 2001). Sandra Barry, *Elizabeth Bishop: An Archival Guide to Her Life in Nova Scotia* (Nova Scotia: Elizabeth Bishop Society of Nova Scotia, 1996). Bettsy Erkkila considers the leftist possibilities of Bishop's poetics in "Elizabeth Bishop, Modernism, and the Left," *American Literary History* 8 (1996): 284–310. Renée R. Curry charges Bishop with racism in *White Women Writing White: H. D., Elizabeth Bishop, Sylvia Plath, and Whiteness* (Westport, CT: Greenwood Press, 2000).

31. Lorrie Goldensohn, *Elizabeth Bishop: The Biography of a Poetry* (New York: Columbia University Press, 1992), 228.

32. Monteiro, 75.

33. Millier, 87.

34. Fountain and Brazeau, 98, 111–12.

35. Monteiro, 44.

36. Quoted in Schwartz, "Elizabeth Bishop and Brazil," *New Yorker,* September 30, 1991, 93.

37. Fountain and Brazeau, 173.

38. Bishop, letter to Robert Lowell, July 6, 1965. Reprinted by permission of the Houghton Library, Harvard University; shelfmark *bMS Am 1905 (226).* The first ellipsis is Bishop's own. Thanks to Maria Lúcia Milléo Martins for bringing this letter to my attention.

39. Alex Bellos, *Futebol: The Brazilian Way of Life* (London: Bloomsbury, 2002).

40. Monteiro, 29.

41. Harrison, 172.

42. Aldous Huxley, *The Art of Seeing* (London: Chatto and Windus, 1943).

43. Quoted in Costello, 63.

44. By Ashley Brown in Schwartz and Estess, 223.

45. Millier, 287.

46. Carmen L. Oliveira, *Rare and Commonplace Flowers: The Story of Elizabeth Bishop and Lota de Macedo Soares,* trans. Neil K. Besner (New Brunswick, NJ: Rutgers University Press, 2002).

47. Bishop, letter to Mariette Charlton, June 15, 1970. Reprinted by permission of the Houghton Library, Harvard University; shelfmark *bMS Am 2001 (12).* I am once again indebted to Maria Lúcia Milléo Martins. Bishop's ellipses.

48. Cited in Harrison, 172.

49. David Kalstone, *Becoming a Poet: Elizabeth Bishop with Marianne Moore and Robert Lowell,* ed. Robert Hemenway (London: Hogarth, 1989), 5.

50. Bishop, "In the Village," in *Collected Prose,* 251–76.

51. Susan McCabe, *Elizabeth Bishop: Her Poetics of Loss* (University Park, Pa.: Penn State University Press, 1994), 104.

52. Millier, 75.

53. Schwartz, "Elizabeth Bishop and Brazil," 97.

54. For the former see Goldensohn, and Thomas J. Travisano, *Elizabeth Bishop:*

Her Artistic Development (Charlottesville: University Press of Virginia, 1988). For the latter see Millier and Harrison.

55. Stephen Matterson and Darryl Jones, *Studying Poetry* (London: Hodder Headline, 2000), 87.

56. James Fenton, *An Introduction to English Poetry* (London: Penguin, 2002), 20.

57. Millier, 513. McCabe, 1.

5. MY SECOND SKIN

1. Hal Foster, *The Return of the Real: Avant-Garde Art at the End of the Century* (Cambridge: MIT Press, 1996).

2. John Updike, *Self-Consciousness: Memoirs* (London: Penguin, 1990), 44.

3. Jay Prosser, *Second Skins: The Body Narratives of Transsexuality* (New York: Columbia University Press, 1998).

4. Roland Barthes, *Camera Lucida: Reflections on Photography*, trans. Richard Howard (London: Vintage, 1993).

5. Judith Butler, *Bodies That Matter: On the Discursive Limits of "Sex"* (New York: Routledge, 1993), 237.

6. Barthes, "The Photographic Message," in *Image Music Text*, ed. and trans. Stephen Heath (London: Fontana, 1977), 20.

7. Nancy K. Miller, *Getting Personal: Feminist Occasions and Other Autobiographical Acts* (New York: Routledge, 1991), xiii.

8. Susan Rubin Suleiman, *Risking Who One Is: Encounters with Contemporary Art and Literature* (Cambridge, MA: Harvard University Press, 1994), 200.

9. Jacques Lacan, *Freud's Papers on Technique, 1953–1954*, ed. Jacques-Alain Miller, trans. John Forrester, book 1 of *The Seminar of Jacques Lacan* (New York: Norton, 1991), 66. Lacan, *The Four Fundamental Concepts of Psycho-analysis,* ed. Jacques-Alain Miller, trans. Alan Sheridan (New York: Norton, 1981), 55.

10. Lacan, *The Ego in Freud's Theory and Technique of Psychoanalysis, 1954–55,* trans. Sylvana Tomaselli, book 2 of *The Seminar of Jacques Lacan* (New York: Norton, 1991), 313, 97.

11. Slavoj Zizek, "Grimaces of the Real, or When the Phallus Appears," *October* 58 (1991): 59.

12. Lynda Hart, *Between the Body and the Flesh* (New York: Columbia University Press, 1998), 163.

13. Walter Benjamin, "The Work of Art in the Age of Mechanical Reproduction," in *Illuminations,* ed. Hannah Arendt, trans. Harry Zohn (London: Fontana, 1992), 217.

14. Loren Cameron, *Body Alchemy: Transsexual Portraits* (Pittsburgh, PA: Cleis, 1996), 11.

15. *FTM Newsletter* 27 (April 1994).

16. Kim Harlow and Bettina Rheims, *Kim,* trans. Paul Gould (Munich: Keyahoff Verlag, 1994).

17. Laura Mulvey, "Visual Pleasure and Narrative Cinema," *Screen* 16 (1975): 6.

18. Laura Mulvey, "Afterthoughts on 'Visual Pleasure and Narrative Cinema' Inspired by *Duel in the Sun,*" in *Feminism and Film Theory,* ed. Constance Penley (New York: Routledge, 1988), 69.

19. Kobena Mercer, "Reading Racial Fetishism: The Photographs of Robert Mapplethorpe," in *Fetishism and Cultural Discourse,* ed. Emily Apter and William Pietz (Ithaca, NY: Cornell University Press 1993), 320. The first essay, reprinted here, was published in *Photography/Politics: Two* (London: Comedia/Methuen, 1986), 61–69.

20. The Wolf-Man, *The Wolf-Man by the Wolf-Man, with the Case of the Wolf-Man by Sigmund Freud and a Supplement by Ruth Mack Brunswick,* ed. Muriel Gardiner (New York: Noonday Press, 1991).

21. Philippe Lejeune, "The Autobiographical Pact (bis)," in *On Autobiography,* ed. Paul John Eakin, trans. Katherine Leary (Minneapolis: University of Minnesota Press, 1989), 134, 131–32.

22. Oliver Wendell Holmes, "The Stereoscope and the Stereograph," in *Classic Essays on Photography,* ed. Alan Trachtenberg (New Haven, CT: Leete's Island Books, 1980), 73.

23. Lucretius, *De rerum natura,* cited in Robert Temple, *The Crystal Sun: Rediscovering a Lost Technology of the Ancient World* (London: Random House, 2000), 259.

24. Nadar, "My Life as a Photographer," trans. Thomas Repensek, *October* 5 (1978): 9.

EPILOGUE

1. Robert M. Levine and John J. Crocitti, eds., *The Brazil Reader: History, Culture, Politics* (Durham, NC: Duke University Press, 1999), 469.

2. Elizabeth Bishop, "Questions of Travel," in *The Complete Poems, 1927–1979* (New York: Farrar, Straus and Giroux, 1999), 93. Further references to Bishop's published poems are to this book.

3. *The Rockefellers, American Experience* transcript, PBS 2000, http://www.pbs.org/wgbh/amex/rockefellers (accessed November 1, 2002).

4. F. N. and Susan Johnson, *The Dolphin Story: An Introduction to the Biology of Dolphins* (Carnforth, England: Castlerigg Publications, 1976).

5. Nigel J. H. Smith, *The Amazon River Forest: A Natural History of Plants, Animals, and People* (New York: Oxford University Press, 1999).

6. Quotations of unpublished Bishop material from the Special Collections, Vassar College Library, reprinted with permission.

7. Anthony Hall, ed., *Amazonia at the Crossroads* (London: Institution for Latin American Studies, 2000).

8. Chico Mendes, *Fight for the Forest: Chico Mendes in his Own Words,* trans. Chris Whitehouse (Birmingham, England: Third World Publications, 1989).

9. Neil MacDonald, *Brazil: A Mask Called Progress* (Oxford: Oxfam, 1991), 32.

10. R. J. A. Goodland and H. S. Irwin, *Amazon Jungle: Green Hill to Red Desert? An Ecological Discussion of the Environmental Impact of the Highway Construction Program in the Amazon Basin* (Amsterdam: Elsevier Scientific Publishing, 1975).

11. John Vidal, "Road to Oblivion," *The Guardian,* June 13, 2001, G2 6–7.

12. John Browder and Brian Godfrey, *Rainforest Cities: Urbanization, Development and Globalization of the Brazilian Amazon* (New York: Columbia University Press, 1997), 13, 14.

13. Helmut Sick, *Birds in Brazil: A Natural History,* trans. William Belton (Princeton: Princeton University Press, 1993), 7.

14. David Werth and Roni Avissar, "The Local and Global Effects of Amazonian Deforestation," LBA [Large-Scale Biosphere-Atmosphere Experiment in Amazonia, a special section of the journal], *Journal of Geophysical Research: Atmosphere,* series D, 107, no. 55 (2002): 1–8.

15. William F. Laurance et al., "The Future of the Brazilian Amazon," *Science* 291 (2001): 438.

16. Bianca Jagger, "Threat to the Trees of Life," *The Guardian,* G2, November 6, 2002: http://society.guardian.co.uk/societyguardian/story/0,7843,833969,00.html.

17. Warren Dean, *With Broadax and Firebrand: The Destruction of the Brazilian Atlantic Forest* (Berkeley and Los Angeles: University of California Press, 1995).

18. Dean, *Brazil and the Struggle for Rubber: A Study in Environmental History* (Cambridge: Cambridge University Press, 1987).

19. Theodore Roosevelt, *Through the Brazilian Wilderness* (London: John Murray, 1914).

20. Chalmers Johnson, *Blowback: The Costs and Consequences of American Empire* (New York: Henry Holt, 2000), 210, 213.

21. "Plans for the Sustainable Development of the Amazon," February 2001, Brazilian Embassy in London, http://www.brazil.co.uk (accessed November 1, 2002). "Avança Brasil" has a Web site at http://www.abrasil.gov.br.

22. Tony Reichhardt, "Brazil's Space Programme Comes of Age," *Nature* 398 (April 1, 1999): 10. The satellite photographs are relayed from São José dos Campos's Global Resource Information Database Web site at http://www.grid.inpe.br.

23. Colin McEwan, Cristiana Barreto, and Eduardo Neves, *Unknown Amazon* (London: British Museum Press, 2001).

24. Anna Roosevelt, ed., *Amazonian Indians from Prehistory to the Present: Anthropological Perspectives* (Tuscon: University of Arizona Press, 1994), 4.

25. Roosevelt et al., "Paleoindian Cave Dwellers in the Amazon: The Peopling of the Americas," *Science* 272 (1996): 374.

26. Thomas D. Dillehay, *The Settlement of the Americas: A New Prehistory* (New York: Basic, 2000), xvi.

27. Tim Flannery, *The Eternal Frontier: An Ecological History of North America and Its Peoples* (London: Heinemann, 2001), 34–35.

28. Flannery, 139.

29. Claude Lévi-Strauss, *Structural Anthropology,* vol. 2, trans. Monique Layton (Chicago: University of Chicago Press, 1983), 362.

INDEX

Jay Prosser is lecturer in the School of English at the University of Leeds. He is the author of *Second Skins: The Body Narratives of Transsexuality* and coeditor of *Palatable Poison: Critical Perspectives on "The Well of Loneliness."*

Youth Development
and Critical Education

● ● ● ● ● ● ● ● ● ● ● ● ● ● ● ● ● ● ● ●

SUNY Series, Democracy and Education

George H. Wood, Editor

Youth Development and Critical Education

The Promise of Democratic Action

• • • • • • • • • • • • • • • • • • •

Richard D. Lakes

State University of New York Press

Cover photo by Louie Favorite: Moving in the Spirit. National Tour Explosion. Dancers: Carey Wheeler, Michael Bowman, Valenna Spikes, Corissa Castle, LaQuanda Gibson, and Atiya Jones.

Cover design: Charles Martin

Published by
State University of New York Press, Albany

For information, address State University of New York Press,
State University Plaza, Albany, N.Y. 12246

Production by M. R. Mulholland
Marketing by Fran Keneston

Library of Congress Cataloging-in-Publication Data

Lakes, Richard D.
    Youth development and critical education : the promise of
democratic action / Richard D. Lakes
        p.   cm. — (SUNY series, democracy and education)
    Includes bibliographical references (p.   ) and index.
    ISBN 0-7914-3349-8 (alk. paper). — ISBN 0-7914-3350-1 (pbk. :
alk. paper)
    1. Community education—United States.   2. Critical pedagogy—
United States.   3. Socially handicapped youth—Education—United
States.   I. Title.   II. Series.
LC1036.5.L35   1996
370.11'5—dc20   96-21038
                                                              CIP

10 9 8 7 6 5 4 3 2 1

To Len, my muse
To Pat, my love

● ● ● ● ● ●

Contents

Illustrations

Preface

In 1994 my edited anthology, *Critical Education for Work: Multidisciplinary Approaches*, was published, advancing the notion of industrial and economic democracy through a transformative vocational education. In the Afterword to that book I interviewed Len Krimerman, a friend, scholar, and workplace activist, who emphasized democracy-building actions generated in various locales by a variety of critical educators involving teens and children in grassroots social change. Len spoke to me about how existing progressive coalitions in low-income areas were transforming neighborhoods through educational reconstructions aimed at microenterprise development. Some of these bottom-up revitalizations were targeted to job creation and vocational training for teens. He told me about the educational programs of REAL Enterprises (Rural Entrepreneurship through Action Learning) in Georgia and EDTEC (Education, Training, and Enterprise Center) in New Jersey, two nonprofit organizations providing curricular materials and limited funds for business start-ups. He told me about the Natural Guard in New Haven, Connecticut, a social justice organization founded by folk singer Richie Havens that helps kids to build community gardens while researching the ecology of their own neighborhoods—making connections between environmental racism, toxic dumping, and urban decay, *and doing something positive to change all that*. Then Len gave me a short list of addresses and contacts for the kinds of youth projects he was talking about and directed me to find out exactly what these grassroots actions offered in the way of educational reconstructions.

I took his advice. Seriously. Three years ago I began researching the variety of organizations engaging youths in intergenerational partnerships devoted to community economic development. I gathered a wide variety of information from the scholarly literature related to teen issues and prevention education, as well as from field notes and site visits, interviews with project staff, published curricular materials and instructional resources, newspapers and magazines, evaluation reports, and policy papers, among others.

Presented in these pages are my investigations of social projects for economically disadvantaged inner-city youth engaged in neighborhood revitalizations in low-income communities scattered around the country. Children and teens are highlighted as they participate in a variety of interesting non-school initiatives, such as operating a credit union, working a community garden, planning and starting businesses, and assisting with neighborhood housing rehabilitation. The analysis of these programs broadly examines young people working in coalitions with adults to achieve a level of economic and political self-determination and community control, as well as personal fulfillment coupled with healthy adolescent growth.

I do not attempt to draw out connections between these youth projects and ongoing school-based reform efforts; I have not provided in-depth analysis of individual programs or participants in order to assess outcomes and competencies. My purpose in this book is singular: to illuminate sites of production, that is, educational reconstructions where loving and caring adults enter into intergenerational learning communities that follow the Freirean dictum to reify history, culture, and struggle. These adults—call them critical educators, cultural workers, or youth workers, if you prefer—create a realpolitik that brings them into coalitions and alliances with local players in building democracy from the bottom up.

By engaging in real-life projects that address their lived realities, youthful participants and caring adults voice their concerns, frame the problematics of their oppressive circumstances, articulate the images, thoughts, and feelings of their marginalized subgroup, and choose strategies which engage peers in neighborhood activities that are positive, meaning-making events. With proper adult guidance, youths have the potential to design, plan, and organize projects for social change in learning communities that give voice to ongoing cultural struggles. I am reminded once again of Len's imperative for democratic praxis: "We are trying to turn our communities around!"

I owe a debt of gratitude to many people consulted in the preparation of this book. My ideas about translating critical educational theory for sustainable community development have been refined in discussions with Jon Abercrombie, Cliff Glasberg, Mel King, Marita McComiskey, Doris Perryman, Jerry Poole, Maria-Luz Samper, Margery Swann, Gerald Taylor, Shirley Thomas, Andre Turnipseed, and Susan Wefold. Robin Lakes, my sister, established initial contacts for site-based visits in Chicago. Fred Otte, friend and colleague, first provided me with a resource list of mailing addresses for community-based organizations that set me on the research process.

I am grateful to the many youth workers who gave to me their valuable time and attention in (a) responding to letters of request and telephone exchanges about the projects; (b) giving me program brochures, curriculum manuals, press clippings, photographs, videos, and additional supplementary printed resources; (c) agreeing to a site visitation, whenever our schedules permitted; and (d) reviewing portions of my written text as needed. Special thanks go to: Doug Ackley, Carol Aranjo, Bill Batson, John Bell, Ron Bieganski, David Coolidge, Gary Daffin, Rodney Dailey, Paul DeLargy, Diana Edmonds, Ryan Eliason, Maria Ferri, Greg Gale, Phil Gauthier, David Gershon, Michael Gilbreath, Robert Ginn, Pat Gray, Olivia Gude, Cheryl Hughes, Mr. Imagination, Pa Joof, Fronita King, Kitty Krupat, Gil de Lamadrid, Maureen LaMar, True Lawrence, Kelly Lindquist, Turbado Marabou, Dana Marschalk, Chuck Matthai, Tony Melton, Fernando Morales, Jan Nagaj, Omar Ortiz, Genene Pittman, Jon Pounds, Karen Prince, David Reid, Rose Reyes, Ocean Robbins, Arthur Robinson, Joshua Sage, Cherylyn Satterwhite, David Schein, Anthony Thigpenn, George Waters, and Sev Williams.

Several portions of this book have appeared elsewhere in a different form. I would like to thank Alan Jones for publishing "Reclaiming Community: Social Projects for Youth Development," in *Educational Foundations* (1995), 9(4): 41–56; and Paula Cordeiro for including my chapter contribution "Moving in the Spirit: A Dance Ministry for Urban Youth," in her edited book *A Changing Conception of School Leaders: Building Community*, New Directions in School Leadership (San Francisco: Jossey-Bass, forthcoming).

Finally, I would like to recognize my past graduate students in EPSF 712, "Social and Cultural Foundations of Education," who helped me to puzzle-out various themes in youth development; the staff of the Interlibrary Loan Office at Georgia State University, for their retrieval of hard-to-find source books; Fred Frank, chair of the Educational Policy Studies department, for giving me release time from teaching to complete the manuscript revisions; Priscilla Ross, senior editor at SUNY Press, who believed in the project from its inception; and Camille Cordak and Bill Kahnweiler, two wonderful friends who lent moral support to my personal life in Atlanta.

Introduction

Several summers ago I visited a well-known workplace literacy program operated by a large needle-trades union in New York
City.[1] The young adults there, mainly recent Asian and Hispanic
immigrants, organized three classes for English as a Second
Language (ESL), even though the program directors were unable to
hire a teacher at the time due to lack of funds. The small group of
peer leaders, regular participants in the union's student council,
administered the program that July, conducting enrollment management duties, gathering curriculum materials, supervising volunteer teachers, and monitoring student progress throughout the
term. When I asked one of the instructional facilitators what pedagogical theory was underlying this program, she said "Freirean-
like," meaning (I assumed) participatory practices in curriculum
and instruction grafted onto a democratic social movement for
workers' rights.

In my view the students were able to shape liberating experiences through a *critical education*. That is, in this literacy program
a community of learners was afforded an opportunity to practice
democracy through a pedagogy that allowed them the freedom to
fully articulate (without the coercive force of jingoism) shared perceptions of bilingual and bicultural discrimination in their newly
adopted America.

In order to further the acquisition of English vocabulary
skills, for instance, the students were asked to name personal and
social problems that troubled them in their daily lives. Affixed to
one of the classroom walls I noticed a series of index cards with
handwritten commentaries about their realities, including "can't
communicate," "low education," "undocumented," "changing role
for women," "racism," "left family behind," "want easy money," "difficult to adapt to customs," "U.S. wants cheap labor," "no governmental help," "drugs," and "crime." The teacher was able to elicit
from the class a list of generative words drawn from the actual

experiences of these students that helped them name the sources of injustice in their lives. By breaking silences first with the vocabulary of students' subjectivities, the adept teacher could then build a host of generative themes to advance reading and writing skills, furthering critical inquiry and understanding in this particular community of learners.

What I witnessed that day was Freirean-styled education that offered these young adults opportunities to vocalize personal and sociocultural oppressions, providing insights into their identities as first-generation immigrants in America. The point is that a critical education fashioned along these lines affords fresh glimpses into what it is like to live in a First World country where limited English-language skills and green-card status place them in semi-skilled labor markets in the city. The result of this predicament keeps them in lower-income occupations, residing in low-rent tenements, exposed to street crime and drug sales, and restricted in social mobility.[2]

But there is more to empowering education than simply naming (and blaming?) one's problems on structural conditions buttressed by class advantage, thus linking immigration and labor policies impacting students' lives to the powerful influences of corporate and social elites on Capitol Hill. One can build community through the promise of democratic action—from the bottom up. In fact, the literacy classes I visited encouraged activism through grassroots participation in their labor union (Samper and Lakes 1994). For instance, one summer the students recruited Mexican flower vendors on the city streets, enrolled them as Associate Members (since they didn't belong to the union), and signed them up for ESL classes. Additionally, they led a rank-and-file rally at city hall to publicize the deplorable laboring conditions of these immigrant vendors and forced the top labor leaders in their union to address the attendees.

Freirean-styled education as shown above is a social process linking participants, young and old alike, in consciousness-raising approaches to grassroots community economic development. While dismantling authoritarianism in critical classrooms certainly is important, empowering education works best when students in non-school settings are engaged in transformative-praxis-as-movement-activism (not dialogic teachings decoupled from local struggles) that asks stakeholders to actively overturn their oppressions.

Grassroots Development Abroad

Consider the literacy crusade in Nicaragua, modeled upon
Freire's theories of educating poor adults in Third World Christian
"base communities" (see Barreiro 1984; Kanpol 1996; and Van
Vugt 1991). Beginning in 1980, less than one year after the collapse of the Somoza dictatorship, a social experiment founded
upon the revolutionary ideology of the Sandinista National
Liberation Front (FSLN) linked youths and adults in a cultural
struggle for democracy. The rapid mobilization of secondary and
post-secondary school students (termed 'brigadistas') into remote
zones in order to teach peasants reading and writing in fact was
aimed at quickly rebuilding the war-torn nation—from the bottom
up (Hirshon 1983).

The crusade itself was billed as a political priority, that is, a
pedagogical project that assisted the FSLN by forging alliances
between students and peasants. Thousands of volunteer brigadistas, youths at least twelve years of age with a primary education,
were coupled with adult technical advisers into squadrons dis-
patched to the front, where this new army of guerrilla fighters
would take up their arms (pens, papers, and primers) against the
enemies of ignorance. The national literacy campaign, only a five-
month effort, was an attempt to keep a fragile coalition of anti-
Somoza supporters together in the tumultuous wake of revolutionary triumph. "The war had been traumatic," writes Sheryl Hirshon
(1983), a technical adviser in the crusade. "What better way for
young people to make the transition from the violent, nightmare
past than to plunge into a profound and positive activity, one hon-
oring the heroes and martyrs of the liberation struggle. The carrying out of such an ambitious mobilization would increase the people's respect both for themselves and for the capabilities of their
new government" (p. 8).

The designers of this particular short-term campaign, however, perhaps never fully anticipated how grassroots development
would emerge from base communities, that is, from the stakeholders themselves. The Sandinista leaders obviously desired to incul-
cate among illiterates an education that raised their awareness of
injustice and poverty, thereby leading to human dignity and self-
worth. Thus, the FSLN envisioned systematic lessons in political

themes. Brigadistas, placed directly in peasant villages or urban barrios, were to deliver weekly lessons in alphabetization with the aid of revolutionary primers. Yet the Sandinista government likely underestimated the psychological dimensions of creating a sustainable pedagogical project for social change involving "outsiders" (many from the privileged classes in Nicaragua) brought into indigenous communities. Each brigadista would have to gain the acceptance and trust of their hosts. In the countryside, these youths would reside with the villagers; eat and sleep in their homes; harvest their crops for food or gather firewood for their stoves; become acquainted with their extended families; learn from community elders; celebrate town customs and festivals; and on and on. When the teacher and the student are crossing a number of boundaries in efforts at building relationships from the ground up, critical education and grassroots development takes time—lots of time.

Sustainable development, then, is best orchestrated when grassroots groups welcome technical advisers and other outsiders to participate and collaborate in building up organizational infrastructures (Kleymeyer 1991). What this means is that indigenous groups desiring small-scale solutions to problems within their grasp will devise and implement projects or programs that make use of the human and material capital at hand. Resources external to the group, such as vocational expertise or financial services or governmental aide, can be utilized in the developmental process as well, but should not be controlled from the top down.

Grassroots groups, such as neighborhood associations, production cooperatives, and ethnic coalitions, will initiate development not merely to seek economic improvements; social and cultural empowerment is equally important here (see Annis and Hakim 1988; Ekins 1992; Mariz 1994; Rowbotham and Mitter 1994). For instance, a group of young indigenous men and women formed an Educational Fair in the 1970s to promote both cultural revitalization and self-help economic efforts among the Quechua Indians of highland Ecuador (Kleymeyer 1992). When invited by other local villagers, the group assists community members in identifying problems of poverty or illiteracy. Interestingly, the fair utilizes sociodramas and puppet shows in order to give audience members a vehicle for self-reflection and self-expression of their difficulties as well as the working out of possible solutions. The consequences of sustainable development through this initial consciousness-raising method has been impressive in that region, resulting in the establishment of local enterprises including community bakeries, artisanal workshops, and community centers.

According to development expert Charles Kleymeyer (1991, pp. 38–39), bottom-up strategies can be both *intangible* and *tangible*. In the former case, development programs can lead to (a) improved skills in communication, leadership or management; (b) a stronger sense of self; (c) establishment of civil rights and liberties; and (d) an increased ability to leverage services from the state. In the latter case, grassroots development can lead to (a) increases in production of agricultural or manufactured goods; (b) increases in family income; (c) a building to be used for organizational activities; and (d) a road or water system. Additionally, Kleymeyer advises that the continual support for development projects at the grassroots level (whether their objective is tangible or intangible), long after any one specific initiative has ended, requires strenthening local organizations to maintain supportive coalitions, networks, and federations. Each project must build effective and viable activism in a long-term, capacity-carrying mode so that further development efforts are possible.

In the next section, I provide a brief look at the potential for grassroots groups to create local development strategies in this country. Green activists, in particular, provide us with some insightful lessons on how critical education has informed their struggle for environmental justice in low-income communities of color.

Grassroots Activism at Home

Hazel Johnson and her daughter, Cheryl, are community leaders engaged in the eradication of discriminatory toxic dumping and neighborhood pollution practices. They are fighting environmental racism in their own housing project, Altgeld Gardens, on Chicago's South Side, near polluting industries such as steel mills and paint manufacturers (Ervin 1992; Sennett 1993). The housing project itself sits atop a landfill where nineteenth-century industrialist George Pullman dumped toxic materials from his railroad car works. Now the area is host to numerous landfills and trash incin-

erators. Residents have recently discovered that their neighborhood has become the target of "fly dumping," hit-and-run waste
disposal by small firms unable or unwilling to pay for legitimate
hazardous-materials removal. (Neighbors once found eight barrels
of chemical waste from a film company doing business on the
north side of town.)

Spurred by the knowledge that their neighbors suffer high
rates of respiratory problems likely associated with the toxic haz-
ards there, and that new-born babies in the area seem to have
many more birth defects, in 1982 the mother-daughter team
formed People for Community Recovery (PCR). This grassroots
activist group, operating out of a storefront in Altgeld, has lobbied
city government to halt new landfill permits, insisted that the
Chicago Housing Authority remove asbestos from Altgeld Gardens,
and obstructed the delivery of wastes at a local landfill by halting
dump trucks from entering the grounds. The latter environmental
action, organized by PCR with support from Greenpeace and other
"green" groups, resulted in a mass mobilization of 500 people at
the gates of the site; seventeen people were arrested that day,
including Hazel Johnson. Perhaps most significant about this particular organization are the strategies utilized to gain a critical
education. Community research activities are their foremost
means in gaining knowledge. Canvassing the housing project with
a survey asking about residents' chronic respiratory problems or
troubled pregnancies, for example, brings critical knowledge to
these activists in preparation for their political campaigns.

Grassroots organizations such as PCR create programs that
provide opportunities for residents of all ages to band together, col-
lect data, and share the knowledge they have of social, political,
educational, and economic inequities in their locale. As spokespersons for quality-of-life concerns, today's citizen-activists are drawn
into democratic actions because struggles for decent housing, adequate health care, quality schools, crime-free neighborhoods, and
sufficient jobs are multidimensional and interrelational.

Neighborhoods nowadays are collapsing for any number of
reasons, including social and environmental degradations as well
as patterns of deindustrialization and corporate flight. Community
economic development, moreover, needs an integrated approach,
according to grassroots activist Marcia Nozick (1993, p. 20), who

offers a framework of five principles or action areas which taken together can build sustainable communities: (a) gain economic self-reliance: reclaim ownership of our communities; (b) become ecologically sustainable: develop green, clean, and safe environments; (c) attain community control: empower members of a community to make decisions affecting their community, workplace, and daily lives; (d) meet the needs of individuals: look after our material and non-material needs; and (e) build a community culture: get to know who we are.

Community organizers recognize that discriminatory practices, such as facility siting issues, stem from injustices against low-income, impoverished neighborhoods of color. In fact, citizen-activists represent a new social movement of minority environmentalists (Bullard 1990).

Low-income communities are disproportionately affected by the poisonous wastes generated from factories nearby. Corporate practices that place toxic industrial production and poisonous dumping and landfills in locations where poor people of color live is "environmental racism"—a term that means minority communities suffer the most from industrial pollution. For example, the 1987 study "Toxic Waste and Race," by the United Church of Christ Commission for Racial Justice, found a strong association between race and hazardous-waste facilities locations (Bullard 1990). The commission highlighted that three out of the five largest commercial hazardous-waste landfills were located in black or Latino communities, and one-third of these landfills were situated in five Southern states. Three sites in mostly black ZIP code areas of Alabama, Louisiana, and South Carolina comprised 60 percent of the region's hazardous-waste landfill capacity.

What began as a local fight to close down a medical waste incinerator situated in the South Bronx, for instance, expanded into a broad-based grassroots movement for social justice concerns in greater New York City (Laboy 1994). The Bronx Clean Air Coalition, formed in the summer of 1991, includes more than sixty community-based organizations that publicize issues of environmental racism through a variety of action efforts, such as rallies, health fairs, voter registration drives, and marches. The air pollution created by this incinerator caused a noticeable rise in respiratory illness cases at the local emergency room. In their efforts to stop it, the citizen-activists, according to one coalition member, have had to become "environmental justice experts in what seems like a flash of lightening" (Laboy 1994, p. 4).

As a result, there are ongoing efforts of self-education around the ecological deterioration of their community. In this particular area of the borough, for instance, a sewage de-watering plant is next to a sludge treatment plant which is next to a new sludge pelletization plant near a floating prison barge adjacent to a meat and produce distribution center. The coalition members, filing numerous affidavits, demand that the New York State Department of Environmental Conservation conduct a full environmental impact study of the area. In partnership with other grassroots organizations, such as the Northeast/Puerto Rico Environmental Justice Network and the New York City Environmental Justice Alliance, issues of environmental racism are brought forth in numerous coalition efforts, including working for community stewardship of vacant lands, arguing for affordable housing, creating a local environmental justice library, planning a local conference on sustainable development, and starting a youth lead prevention project.

Grassroots activists attend to a critical education as they mobilize for political power nationally as well. At the First National People of Color Leadership Summit on the Environment, held in Washington D.C. in October, 1991, and attended by about six hundred leaders of grassroots organizations, participants in the four-day event shared first-hand knowledge about environmental racism while attempting to build alliances and coalitions of like-minded individuals. One speaker, from the Southwest Network for Environmental and Economic Justice, noting this historic first-time gathering of minority environmentalists, remarked:

> Communities of color have won many victories in the face of environmental racism and the EPA's inaction. When we are organized, we have tremendous power. And that is what we are about at this meeting—*powerizing* ourselves to go back to our communities. . . . We are about building a movement (quoted in Moore 1993, p. 4).

"Think globally, but act locally," grassroots activists remind us, beginning in one's backyard, through small-scale, decentralized, local control. In fact, social justice movements create opportunities for individuals to realize their interdependence in terms of "place." To know the land upon which one settles, the resources that are drawn for daily existence, and the folklore there requires an historical oral or written record of earlier peoples and their cultural ways (see Sale 1985). A sense of ownership overtakes us and drives our democratic actions. Once we know our place, we begin to make connections between our natural world and the potentialities we see in ourselves and our neighbors. The notion of ownership provides bounded spaces so we can carry out indigenous projects for human growth and development at the manageable level of city blocks, neighborhoods, and communities.

Community activists also instruct us to recapture the democratic impulse through making connections by way of small-scale human associations (Bookchin 1986). To celebrate town meetings, for example, allows localized libertarian practices to bring citizens into face-to-face contact for decision-making purposes. Use grassroots organizations for citizenship training and leadership development. Look to the local community of contested politics for winnable solutions. Promote the notion of taking responsibility for solving our own problems.

The Educational Impulse

Grassroots activism captures the flavor of what John Dewey perceived in 1927 as a movement "toward democratic forms" in his "search for the Great Community" (1927, pp. 146–47). The problem of democracy, he claimed, was that in order to "cure its ailments" one needed "more democracy," yet the public's interests were scattered, mobile, and undefined. Dewey preferred that individuals search for democracy through "associated living" as members of groups to which each belongs and then in coalitions that "interact flexibly and fully in connection with other groups" (1927, p. 147). For Dewey, humans engaged in enriching civic participation develop a "fullness of integrated personality" when members of varying groups are dedicated to the reinforcement of values in an organic whole.

This Deweyan ideal is now embodied in what is termed a "Living Democracy," in the words of Frances Lappé and Paul

DuBois (1994, p. 287), co-directors of the Center for Living Democracy in Vermont, which promotes and celebrates grassroots activism through social projects framed in an "emergence of the democratic self." They explain that personal alienation and political apathy result in blockages to civic duty and community participation, but are overcome by citizens of all ages engaged in real-life activities devoted to solving problems in the public arena. Social ennui, despair, cynicism, and powerlessness will be transformed, they charge, as individuals begin to rethink and reapply "hope-instilling, practical tools" that affirm their "relational self-interest and relational power" in democratic life (1994, p. 6).

Community building promotes a Living Democracy or a "renewal of the commonwealth tradition," according to Harry Boyte (1989), a noted theorist of citizen-activist movements. Citizens become "reenfranchised," Boyte writes, "through a process of education for public life that teaches new and more communal ways of looking at information about issues, that conveys a series of skills specific to a dynamic public arena, and that reembeds the objects of struggle and action once again in culture and a sense of human agency" (pp. 147–48).

The educational impulse just noted is firmly lodged in the history of social movement activism in this country. At the Highlander Folk School in Tennessee, for example, founder Myles Horton infused in students a hybridization of important ideas on democracy and education from a wide series of events and thinkers in his day. He drew upon pragmatism in the writings of John Dewey and William James, social reforms enacted at various big-city settlement houses, experiential teachings at the Danish Folk Schools, real-life problem-solving activities by his native Southern Appalachians, and social justice ministering from his Christian upbringing (Adams 1975). What is important for our purposes is understanding Horton's commitment to helping people by first asking them to examine their sociocultural oppressions. "He knew what he must do," Horton's biographer writes, in anticipation of "an educational program" guiding the founding of Highlander:

> Get behind the common judgments of the poor, help them learn to act and speak for themselves, help them gain control over decisions affecting their daily lives. . . . Rather than

learning to make decisions for the poor, as he sought to do in the beginning, he now knew that he should help people make their own decisions (Adams 1975, p. 24).

Highlander's residential workshops linked a broad spectrum of social movement actors across racial, ethnic, and gender lines and still informs the critical pedagogy offered for community leadership development. For instance, in her memoirs civil rights activist Rosa Parks (1992) writes with candor about her stay at the school in the summer of 1955. She recalls at length:

> I spent ten days at Highlander and went to different workshops, mostly on how to desegregate schools. Everything was very organized. We all had duties, and they were listed on a bulletin board each day. We shared the work and play. One of my greatest pleasures there was enjoying the smell of bacon frying and coffee brewing and knowing that white folks were doing the preparing instead of me. There was swimming in the man-made lake, volleyball, square dancing. It was quite enjoyable to be with the people at Highlander. We forgot what color anybody was. I was forty-two years old, and it was one of the few times in my life up to that point when I did not feel any hostility from white people. I experienced people of different races and backgrounds meeting together in workshops and living together in peace and harmony. I felt I could express myself honestly without any repercussions or antagonistic attitudes from other people (pp. 105–6).

From the labor conflicts of the 1930s to the civil rights movements in the 1950s through today's workshops on community organizing, environmental activism, and literacy work, among others, Highlander eschews any singular ideological mindset that could limit the spread of popular education to the struggling masses. The school is devoted to a cultivation of indigenous community leaders from a diversity of backgrounds and experiences.

Of course, Horton's is not the sole voice in articulating a pedagogy of empowerment and activism. Public actors elsewhere are encouraged to gain knowledge about their local struggles—and themselves—in order to partake of progressive social movements that build healthy communities at the grassroots (see Dyson and

Dyson 1989). Radical educators, such as Freire, have carefully described the pedagogical steps to a critical consciousness-raising,
requiring group analysis of problem-posing in creating, designing,
and implementing alternative strategies for development (see
McLaren and Leonard 1993). Like Horton and Freire, Chicago community activist Saul Alinsky desired a critical education for his organizers predicated upon their understandings of power analysis,
including studies of organizational problems, conflict tactics, communication methods, and leadership methodologies (see Alinsky
1971).

Successful community building depends upon new and
emerging leaders, young and old, who are schooled in a critical
education that brings them into coalitions with subaltern participants engaged in shaping democratic praxis from the bottom up.
Progressive social movements bring teachers, community leaders,
and activists together, Michael Apple (1993) charges, to formulate
a political project "enhancing democracy at the grass roots,
empowering individuals who had heretofore been largely silenced,
creating new ways of linking people outside and inside the schools
together so that schooling is not seen as an alien institution but
something that is integrally linked to the political, cultural, and
economic experiences of people in their daily lives" (pp. 40–41).

As integral members of coalitions working for justice and
equity, children and teens already participate in a wide range of
intergenerational activities for peace and justice, including the liberation struggles of women, gays, and lesbians, African Americans
and Latinos, among others (see Hoose 1993). Some youths are
integrated into alternative living arrangements that heighten their
critical consciousness at an early age. Shandin Rudesill (1994), for
example, age 20, recalls his experiences as a young child living in
the Twin Oaks commune, a 400-acre egalitarian, income-sharing
community in Louisa, Virginia. Children were raised by the entire
commune as siblings in an extended family, with all kids living
together in one building. Their caretakers, other than biological
parents, were adult "primaries" who were selected for their caregiv-
ing abilities in a division of domestic labor along the lines of the
Israeli kibbutzim. Children were encouraged to participate in
healthy group activities developing positive values of self along
with a moral and ethical vision of the good society.

When asking young people to join intergenerational alliances, democratic principles must be extended fully to them as members of that organization. This means youthful participants must not be disconfirmed or excluded from the decision-making aspects of small groups; they are allies and equal partners in activities leading to the promise of democratic action.

Community changes start with a critical education for justice through activism leading to workable solutions. Intergenerational coalitions are the best organizational design enabling individuals collectively to engage in allied struggles for neighborhood improvements. By enlisting teams, partnerships, and coalitions into the calculus of community change, citizen-activists of all ages participate effectively in manageable social organizations. Through connection to each other individuals become empowered and hopeful that genuine democracy is workable and possible.

Youth Policy

Young people are capable of participation in public life, as indicated by their spirited volunteerism in civic actions and community service (see Radest 1993). Youth development expert Karen Pittman (1991) suggests that participation is the best way for adolescents to engage in the "building and rebuilding of themselves, their families, their communities, and the larger institutions that shape the quality of American life" (p. 85). Still, school-aged youths often are overlooked as stakeholders in public affairs. They are summarily dismissed as key players in setting their own agenda for developmental efforts (Beilenson 1993). In fact, some critics contend that there is a widespread assault on youths today. Critical educator Henry Giroux (1996) charges that right-wing policymakers "demonize" adolescents for their perceived decadence and immorality, or simply dismiss them altogether. "American society at present," he writes, "exudes both a deep-rooted hostility and chilling indifference toward youth" (p. 31).

Few would question that funding for youth development programs receives heightened public attention in recessionary times.[3] "Given the current political reality," according to Dorothy Stoneman (1989), director of YouthBuild USA, the best way leaders in the youth field have found to increase the resources available to youth programs is to fashion programs which work, and then persuade the legislators that more such programs should be funded. We can't wait for the illusive national policy supporting comprehensive youth development. We have to take what we know works, and form coalitions which can sell it to the public right now. If we create a confusing geography of funding streams going this way and that, then so be it (p. 3).

In fact, congressional policymakers often deride the efficacy of recreational and educational programming in non-school settings for inner-city teens, such as Midnight Basketball, often claiming this form of social welfare spending is pork-barrel legislation. Such an oppositional stance among legislators often pits more liberal advocates of prevention programs against moderates or conservatives desiring a stronger criminal justice system. Liberals would argue new prison construction is just one more form of political patronage of a different stripe. Child welfare advocates contend that it is far costlier to incarcerate and house children in penal institutions during their lifetimes compared to expenditures for quality youth development efforts. Still, a number of recisionary bills in Congress at the time of this writing have placed several important youth programs on the chopping block, such as the Department of Labor's Summer Youth Employment and Training program.

AmeriCorps, President Clinton's favorite community service program, is slated for a reauthorization battle as well. (Partisan support from Capitol Hill—or a presidential veto—may keep this program afloat.) In 1993 when he called it the "Summer of Service," Clinton wanted an exemplary program of national service that paired youthful volunteers with civic projects benefitting the disadvantaged. He launched AmeriCorps, an eight-week national demonstration project for teenagers, as a trial balloon that year. It attracted 1,500 participants from around the country, of which 75 percent were minorities, who each earned minimum wage and, if they chose, $1,000 in educational credit to be applied to their tuition. AmeriCorps is administered by the Corporation for National and Community Service through funds from the

National and Community Service Trust Act of 1993 and now employs about twenty thousand young people, more than one-third of whom are from low-income families. In the first year of its operations AmeriCorps members at fifty-two local sites planted more than 200,000 trees; removed two thousand pounds of trash from an urban river; built, maintained, and restored 311 campsites, eighty-eight miles of park trails, and seventeen bridges; cleaned up sixty-one inner-city neighborhoods, including graffiti removal; tutored 7,638 preschool, elementary, and junior high schoolchildren; established after-school programs for 4,565 children; screened 1,100 low-income children for lead toxicity; and provided emergency medical service to more than 1,500 people (Waldman 1995).

Another federal delinquency-prevention program, the Youth Challenge Corps was piloted that same summer and received congressional authorization in the fall of 1993, under the U.S. Office of Juvenile Justice and Delinquency Prevention, of $44 million targeted for dropouts aged sixteen to eighteen (Battista 1993; Weaver 1993). Corp members numbering 173 (two-thirds were black or Hispanic; one-quarter were female), began a five-month residential program that operated along the lines of a military boot camp, including a strict regiment of physical training as well as academic learning toward a high school equivalency diploma. Once they completed the residential program (about one-third of the initial trainees dropped out of the Corps before completion), the youths were provided aftercare services, such as linkages to mentors in the community for help in receiving job training or additional schooling. Each youth was eligible to receive up to $2,200 for educational advancement as well. While boot camps have gained widespread bipartisan support, it seems that policymakers now want to convert federal funds for these experimental projects back to the states in the form of block grant apportionments.

The latest youth policy emerging from the U.S. Senate (sponsored by Nancy Kassebaum, a Republican from Kansas) is a block grant scheme which would distribute $2 billion to about two dozen federal youth programs. Critics charge there are a number of difficulties with this measure, including (a) identification of youth programs that are eligible for funding under this category, (b) distribution of monies to municipalities and cities, and (c) appointments to local governing boards from the community of youth workers (*Youth Today* 1995). The divestiture of youth development funds through governing boards suggests that county experts will be able to allocate resources fairly to their constituencies. Some policy critics voice a concern that by consolidating fiscal sources into community block grants, funding for national demonstration projects will be cut out. This would leave little room for experimentation, replication, and dissemination of exemplary models and organizational designs, program products, and research documentation of what works best with youths, especially projects residing in communities of color.

Ironically, with teen violence, runaways, pregnancy, drug abuse, and homelessness on the rise, one would think that prevention programs for delinquent youths or rehabilitation and treatment for incarcerated juveniles would be paramount in social policy circles. But that just is not the case. More states are adopting stricter measures that would try juveniles as adults for serious crimes, effectively locking-away young people in prisons for longer terms (Males and Docuyanan 1996). Often, these kids are sent to jail with minimal rehabilitation and subjected to draconian measures from a criminal justice system that has hardened its views about juvenile reform (Conniff 1996). The apparent increase in "warehousing" of juvenile offenders is accompanied by a vigorous prison-building program nationwide. Illicit gang activities and teen murders have captured the attention of adults desiring swift law-and-order justice for violent juveniles; few have patience for educational strategies and rehabilitative activities integrating youth into community.

Political trends out of Washington D.C. may be indicative of a national mood of intolerance toward the poor. Some policy critics suggest that plying disadvantaged youths with more short-term, stopgap federal aid leads to welfare dependency and passivity, perpetuating a negative self-image among the populace. Certainly the federal government is an employer of final consequence for inner-city kids, offering provisional assistance to those unlikely to find meaningful work in their own impoverished communities. When joblessness is coupled with limited recreational and educational options in communities of color, there are few attractive alternatives other than gang membership for adolescent youths (and pre-

adolescents as well). Who can blame impoverished kids for gravi-
tating to their neighborhood posse for the safety in numbers
offered by a small group alliance which then implicates them in a
variety of enterprising but illegal and very deadly street economies.

Conclusion

Rarely does the public view positive images of children and
teens engaged in educational reconstructions. We more commonly
believe that youths living in poverty are hopelessly damaged,
ruined at an early age, forever broken and dysfunctional in the
underclass of society. This viewpoint is consistent with the more
popular "at-risk" discourse that blames low-income children for
failed lives due to deficits embedded in their own impoverished
home and dysfunctional family settings (Swadener and Lubeck
1995).

The field of youth development has bought into a deficits paradigm as well, as demonstrated by Karen Pittman (1996). While
gaining legitimacy over the past decade for their expertise in adolescent prevention, youth workers still follow a public health model
that identifies, isolates, and then treats the subject in order to
restore him or her to good health, meaning adjustment into mainstream or dominant culture. Like medical doctors, youth workers
have looked for problems and symptoms as if the organism were
sustained in vitro, without consideration that human beings grow
to their fullest potential in a variety of interactive systems. Pittman
explains at length:

Development requires engagement. It is fostered through
relationships, influenced by environments and triggered by
participation. And it is both ongoing and resilient. We cannot
just intervene at one point and assume all will be fine; neither
can we with good conscience not intervene, assuming that it
is too late. This need for constancy in relationships, environments, and engagement means that those best positioned to
influence development are the "natural actors" in youths'
lives—family, peers, neighbors, and community institutions.
Relationships, environment, and participation are the
essence of what defines community. These key things can be

artificially structured—young people can be assigned mentors, bussed to safe and stimulating environments, and required to do service. But these key ingredients are primarily found in and generated by the community. Programs and organizations do have an impact on youths' lives, but this impact is either amplified or dampened by the quality and congruence of what else is going on in young people's families, peer groups, and neighborhoods. The impact of family and community life on youth development is unchallenged. There are, as always, young people who "beat the odds," but it is the differences in family and community that determine the odds (pp. 6–7).

Why target youth development and critical education in this book? First, I want to describe some of the intergenerational organizations presently at work trying to ameliorate the destructive consequences of poverty through a Freirean-styled approach to grassroots development. These nonprofit organizations mainly are small-scale, self-initiated, decentralized, and situated in homogeneous geographic entities responding to specific needs (see Comer 1993; Heath and McLaughlin 1993; McLaughlin, Irby, and Langman 1994). Second, I want to illuminate ways that youths are included as equal partners in the designing, planning, and executing of programs, and to highlight their investments of ownership with, connection to, and involvement in neighborhood renewal. And, third, I want to illustrate memberships in learning communities that provide youths a critical education, empowering them as citizen-activists to organize their neighborhoods for sustainable grassroots development promoting economic, social and cultural interests (see Jennings 1992b). In this sense, a politically active community coalition is able to achieve some measure of self-determination even "within constraints imposed by the larger political economy in which it is embedded" (Littrell and Hobbs 1989, p. 48).

Our precious youth are the next generation to inherit the legacy of economic deindustrializations and community disinvestments begun in the latter decades of the twentieth century. We must start to encourage and facilitate partnerships of young people in sustainable, capacity-building approaches to revitalization of our inner cities. We desperately need their youthful energy and tireless strength, their boundless assets and valuable skills, their special qualifications and talented gifts for the important work ahead.

In Chapter One, *Community Economics*, I profile a number of grassroots efforts at economic development and job creation involving teens and young adults. I highlight several financial efforts repositioning local capital and allied resources for minority communities. In Chapter Two, *Neighborhood Improvement*, I describe efforts by young people to reclaim their communities in novel ways leading to safer and greener rebuilt neighborhoods. One exemplary model combines vocational training and housing rehabilitations into a comprehesive design for youth and community development. In Chapter Three, *Health and Wellness*, I discuss how community violence obstructs healthy adolescent development, erecting barriers to productivity and functionality. I offer a sampling of peer projects in various venues that address the topics of conflict resolution, teen parenting, and self-esteem. In Chapter Four, *Street Arts*, I examine how community arts programs are introduced into neighborhood crime and substance abuse prevention efforts for inner-city youths. Projects such as murals capture the lived experiences of teens derived from their cultural struggles in the ghettos and barrios of America. In Chapter Five, *Youth Leadership*, I explain how teens enter grassroots social movements that provide trainings in leadership development. Young people can gain the skills and tools that present them as organizers and activists, bringing people together for democratic social change. In Chapter Six, *Beacons of Hope*, I describe community development efforts through intergenerational, faith-based organizations. I profile several individuals involved in an urban ministry that is helping to revitalize one low-income neighborhood in the South.

1

Community Economics

America's inner-cities often exhibit deterioration of infrastructure due to the loss of industrial jobs. Boarded-up factory sites and empty warehouses are the visible result of deindustrialization policies which have removed wage-earners from their jobs (see Bluestone and Harrison 1982). The subsequent decline of stability in cities dependent upon a local economy to sustain human welfare is abundantly evident; low-income communities have large numbers of abandoned buildings, higher percentages of absentee landlords, and declining housing stock. The social and psychological costs of deindustrialization and disinvestments are massive, eroding the human psyche and leading impoverished residents to feel abandoned, isolated, and alienated.

In a number of localities across the country, grassroots organizers in communities of color have made headway by bringing hope and agency to the poor through sustainable development (see Brandt 1995; Dyson and Dyson 1989; Perry 1987; Williams 1985). San Antonio, for instance, once ranked as one of the poorest cities in the nation, has benefitted from the capable leadership of community-based Latino activists trained in a critical education approach to learners' empowerment as practiced by the Industrial Areas Foundation (IAF) (see Rogers 1990). In Baltimore black community activists affiliated with IAF have taught lay citizens how to create a network of base communities that identify and solve pressing educational, economic, social, and political problems (see McDougall 1993).

State and local chapters affiliated with the IAF national office can claim a legacy from founder Saul Alinsky, a University of Chicago sociologist who began in the postwar years assisting low-income citizens in gaining political power, self-knowledge, and systematic affiliation with others in similar oppressed circumstances. Perhaps Alinsky's greatest claim to fame was organizing in his own south Chicago backyard (Brazier 1969; Fish 1973). Black church leaders in the local neighborhood of Woodlawn joined with Alinsky in the late 1950s in a fight with municipal elites over substandard housing and urban renewal. In the decade-long struggle there, IAF citizen-activists organized into a federation of over ninety associations in the area which forced the University of Chicago to re-evaluate its expansion plans south into the Woodlawn area. They obtained funding for a Head Start program, contracted with local industries for job training for the neighborhood unemployed, began an experimental schools project, and participated in Model Cities planning grant development for proposed social service agencies and low-income housing units.

Interestingly, this pioneer organizing effort considered youth development initiatives, such as education and employment, to be an important component in its overall agenda for economic development and community justice. Such is also the case with Project Quest in San Antonio, which was started in 1991 by Communities Organized for Public Service (COPS), the IAF/Texas affiliates who researched and studied a job training system to better serve those disadvantaged by existing human development services in the city (Garr 1995). In fact, their comprehensive plan was adopted unanimously by the city council, now serves as a training model, and is being considered for adoption in other municipalities as well. COPS citizen-activists found that the city had lost about fourteen thousand skilled production jobs during the 1980s, although they were replaced fourfold by new service sector jobs, about one-half of which were high-wage, high-tech positions. Project Quest was started to match eligible unemployed Latino residents with customized training earmarked for those high-end places in local corporations. The program is supported to the tune of $3.7 million annually, partly with help of state and local funds as well as with the assistance of the Private Industry Council, a quasi-governmental agency administering welfare-to-work programs through the Job Training Partnership Act (JTPA).

Dramatic social costs accompanying neighborhood disinvestments have prompted U.S. policymakers to formulate education and employment initiatives, like JTPA, designed to lessen the consequences of joblessness and underemployment, especially among the inner-city poor (Levitan and Shapiro 1987). The Job Training Partnership Act, in particular, funds vocational training for economically disadvantaged adults and adolescents (see Rist 1986). Yet, as noted above, some community-based organizations have used these federal entitlements in novel ways to spread the message of self-help neighborhood revitalizations and financial reinvestments.[1]

What follows is a description of one town's grassroots approach to sustainable economic development through an IAF-styled coalition of religious organizations and a Latino social service agency. We will see how teens were employed through JTPA summer employment monies to assume jobs which allowed them an opportunity to research and study the community's forgotten poor, many of whom were positioned at the margins due to plant closings and corporate disinvestments in the region.

Economic Development

The Puerto Rican Organization Program, Inc.(PROP), a community-based agency in Windham County, Connecticut, offers bilingual vocational education focusing upon aspects of community economic development.[2] PROP was established in 1974 as a non-profit corporation for people of Hispanic origin that advocates improvement of conditions and opportunities for all Latinos in their efforts to achieve self-sufficiency. The agency provides a wide range of bilingual social services, including referrals to health services, family planning, job training and placement, and legal, financial, and shelter assistance.

In a ten-week PROP program that was funded in 1994, JTPA summer youth training funds provided Latino teens with an opportunity to strengthen their English-language comprehension as well as help them to gain valuable job exploration skills through paid employment in one of the area's nonprofit agencies. Young adults ranging in ages from seventeen to nineteen received traditional academic instruction in math and English in a three-hour time slot from 9:00 a.m. to noon. In the afternoons the students went to their job placement sites, such as the town's cooperative food store, the local Northeast Action Council, American Cancer Society,

Windham Area Interfaith Ministry, or a nearby nursing home, where they worked twenty hours per week for minimum wage.

This program offered a healthy dose of personal and career development activities as well. For example, the students were provided with "personal conduct" seminars in their native language. At one session I observed, attended by six females and one male, a training on sexually-transmitted disease prevention by a member of the PROP staff (the AIDS case manager) seemed a relevant choice of topics given that four of the students were single mothers. As for the career exploration component of the program, aside from formal workbook lessons, students were offered several off-campus experiences, including visits to a bank for purposes of opening an account and learning how to deposit and withdraw money and to the local library in order to secure a borrower's card. The students were provided a town newspaper in English as well, offering them a resource by which to practice their reading comprehension, look for job offerings, and learn about current events in their own locale.

The community development component of this program provided these students with hands-on experiences that introduced them into the work cultures of nonprofit agencies in the town. Although they were employed mainly as clerical aides in several local agencies, PROP participants were afforded constructive experiences providing for the development of positive work habits and attitudes. The main feature of this program, however, and what makes this offering different from most traditional employment and training programs, is the commitment to grassroots development by asking youths (and paying them a weekly stipend) to be agents for community betterment.[3]

For example, one student, Celia, age 18, was placed as a research assistant with the Economic Development Committee of Windham Area Interfaith Ministry (WAIM), whose mission is to "discover and act upon unmet community needs" and to "fully utilize community resources to accomplish a variety of economic opportunities."[4] The organization is situated in a New England mill town that is faced with the growing social and economic problems resulting from a major plant closing due to corporate deindustrialization and disinvestment practices over a decade ago. WAIM's five-step economic development goals are as follows: (a) increase community cooperation that leads to empowerment and interdependence; (b) challenge economic institutions to work in partnership with the local community through reinvestment in the community; (c) develop economic resources such as credit unions, community development loan funds, viable worker-owned small businesses, and useful skills-building educational and training programs; (d) work toward a more equitable and inclusive sharing of resources among all people; and (e) examine and evaluate the values and life styles by which we live in this time of local, national, and international upheaval and change.

WAIM leaders adapted their model of sustainable community economic development from the well-known organizing efforts of the Naugatuck Valley Project (NVP) in Western Connecticut. The NVP is a grassroots response to the disinvestments that devastated the region's economic center in mill towns, mainly brass factories, along the Naugatuck River Valley in the 1960s and 1970s (Brecher 1990). With the formation of NVP, an Alinsky-styled reinvestment project in the mid-1980s, community leaders in the valley had clout; a broad-based coalition of about fifty religious, labor, community, and business groups mobilized support for economic redevelopment strategies that would preserve jobs or create new ones.

NVP is a citizen-activist organization targeted toward community control over corporate economic and industrial policy. NVP's earliest experiences were in negotiating workers' buyouts for firms contemplating plant closings. Plant officials at Seymour Speciality Wire, for instance, accepted an employee stock ownership plan, allowing 250 workers to keep their jobs. Similar plant buyouts with area industries were negotiated with corporate owners in varying degrees of success. But other economic actions have spun off from the coalition efforts to date. The project leadership created a small-scale, worker-owned health care business, for example, that employs over thirty home care aides, African American and Latina women residing in nearby low-income neighborhoods.[5]

NVP brought together diverse constituencies for the purpose of initiating local and statewide organizing campaigns. The project staff realized that the education and training functions of its citizen-activist campaigns are crucial. Individuals need leadership development, tools, and skills in order to gain access to information and create networks of power through which to challenge corporate elites and municipal leaders. NVP now conducts leadership workshops "to help member groups draw their own members more deeply into their own and project activities" (Brecher 1990, p. 103), and is thus a model of Freirean critical education.[6]

In Windham, summer youth employment with PROP-WAIM provided the research assistant, Celia, an opportunity to assess the job skills and training needs among low-income residents of the area.[7] She prepared interview questions for a preliminary community survey to find out how much individuals knew about the plans for corporate redevelopment of the former thirteen-building mill complex in town. (Local and regional economic development officials, using $3 million dollars in state funding, are negotiating a deal to convert a portion of the huge structure for light industry, small businesses, and some retail shops.) Her "snowball sample" of interviewees, culled from her own Latino neighborhood, were asked to answer an eleven-item questionnaire, prepared in English and in Spanish, about their employment status, job skills, training needs, and previous work history. Additionally, her research efforts led to monitoring regional economic development plans as reported in the daily newspaper as well as studying the sketches for mill redevelopment on file at the town hall.

Celia informed the forty low-income citizens she contacted in her residential neighborhood about potential economic benefits (or pitfalls) from the pending mill project. In turn, the knowledge she gathered from her research endeavors—a preliminary assessment of job skills and training needs of potential employees—was forwarded, along with survey results from other constituencies, to the PROP-WAIM community leadership.

What is most important about this model of youth development are the critical understandings that young people gain from associations with community coalitions and grassroots organizations. Celia, a single mother with two small children, used this particular employment opportunity to further her cognitive growth in bilingual education, which was at the ninth-grade level when the project began. She prepared the survey in both English and Spanish, kept a notebook of difficult vocabulary words, read English-only newspapers, and verbally communicated with diverse populations. Yet, direct participation with PROP-WAIM taught her that citizen-activist groups could utilize broad-based, interfaith, cross-class, area coalitions for the purposes of research and development into the economic affairs of a community.

Teens can become empowered to discover a sense of community in their own towns, perhaps helping to preserve a civic-mindedness sustained by face-to-face communication and the free-flowing exchange of information. Unfortunately, the PROP-WAIM coalition in 1994 failed to surface community initiatives beyond its initial investigatory stages. The next year, however, PROP principals were lobbying the town selectmen to seek data concerning lead abatements and absentee ownerships of deteriorating rental units occupied mainly by Puerto Rican tenants.[8] But to my knowledge, that effort has not led to significant enterprise development, say, of a minority construction business.

I surmise that community organizing in this town is much more difficult precisely because of bicultural and bilingual barriers. Some of the inhabitants have held misperceptions about each other, and tensions may have escalated between city officials and Latino residents, who constitute 15 percent of the population. One exciting victory to date in sustainable economic development that combats racism and ignorance, while building cultural pride and ethnic sensitivity, has been the printing of a monthly Spanish/English language newspaper, a joint venture (with shared after-profit revenues) between PROP and the publisher of the town daily.

Financial investments like the bilingual newspaper help residents to direct capital toward their own communities of color. This sustainable economic development engages low-income participants in revitalization efforts leading to self-sufficiency, particularly in smaller communities. According to economist Ron Shaffer (1989, p. 6), "Development involves structural change in the community," which includes (a) modification of factors of production; (b) better utilization of existing resources; (c) changes in the structure and function of existing institutions; and (d) changes in attitudes and values of the production. Grassroots economic development aids human interests, however, because personal betterment—not business efficiency—is the ultimate goal of the entire process. In other words, the concept of sustainable economic development from the bottom up is laden with fundamental values of social justice and equity. The entire process empowers local citizens into studying, designing, planning, and executing proactive strategies and decision-making approaches leading to improvements in the quality of their lives. Furthermore, voluntary associations of citizens working in decentralized settings can change the entire civic culture of our market-oriented economy from one of competition to one of cooperation (see Hirst 1994).

In the next section, I describe a project for sustainable development, an inner-city credit union, that builds an economic base for lending to low-income African-American residents. It details how local teens trained in banking and loan operations there create a learning community as well.

Community Lending

Community development lending and banking practices have the potential to politicize the uses of capital in business formation. Such programs challenge assumptions about how allocations of financial resources are determined in elite policymaking circles far removed from grassroots control. In Durham, North Carolina, for instance, the Self-Help Credit Union provides statewide financial services to "nontraditional" customers such as employee-owned businesses, nonprofit groups, small rural enterprises, and low-income home buyers (Sinzinger 1993). The model for this institution is derived from the cooperative bank in Mondragon, Spain, which sustains the economic feasibility of workers' cooperatives through members' resources that are earmarked for regional projects (Morrison 1991). At Self-Help, where the total loans and lines of credit have reached more than $40 million, almost one-half of all commercial loans are awarded to minority businesses and about one-third to female borrowers. Self-Help directors believe that the way to empower disenfranchised populations is through financial arrangements that stimulate enterprise growth and development in low-income communities. Ownership is the key to social change for communities. Thus, financial institutions like Self-Help Credit Union provide residential mortgages or business loans accommodating disadvantaged populations.

Community lending practices can reclaim resources for local control as well. For example, the South Shore Bank, established in 1973, is engaged in economic development activities in deteriorating neighborhoods on the south side of Chicago (Taub 1988). A subsidiary of the Illinois Neighborhood Development Corporation, the bank plays a major role in generating resources—both for-profit and not-for-profit—in investment strategies primarily aimed at housing improvements and structural modifications. The bank has lent over $51 million for rehabilitations to almost one-third of the entire housing stock in the area. Unlike traditional real estate development practices, however, which often benefit whites by turning run-down minority neighborhoods into gentrification projects, community development banks such as South Shore have managed to improve the social and economic conditions of low-income residents without accompanying out-migrations and displacements.[9]

Financial institutions can become chartered as local community development credit unions. Organized and managed as nonprofit cooperatives, they are owned and controlled by members who are affiliated in some common attachment through community organizations, such as a housing or civic group, a community coalition, or a church. These financial institutions not only provide low-cost loans to members, but they also "encourage savings, promote community reinvestment and neighborhood revitalization, and educate members about financial and community issues" (Parzen and Kieschnick 1992, p. 19).

Consider the fully operating Youth Credit Union in Springfield, Massachusetts, a subsidiary of the D.E. Wells Federal Credit Union (FCU), which serves low-income African-American residents in the nearby Hill Section of Springfield, Massachusetts.[10] Wells FCU, chartered in 1959 as the Mt. Calvary Baptist Brotherhood Federal Credit Union, sought a community-based alternative to discriminatory credit practices. Mainstream banking practices, such as redlining, reinforced racist practices by financial institutions in the city excluding minority residents from loans, mortgages, charge accounts, and other banking services. The credit union was originally staffed by volunteer members of the church congregation and offered small loans on household purchases, such as appliances and furniture. The credit union serves the African-American community, more importantly, with much needed technical knowledge about rudimentary financial skills, including how to obtain low-cost credit, which in 1959 was available to blacks only with a white co-signer. Thus, the early credit union was founded as a small scale, self-help effort to assist community members with their financial needs.

This community development credit union operates as a cooperative enterprise in that it draws heavily on volunteers for its operations. Therefore when an applicant seeks a loan at this institution, the credit rating is evaluated by administrators drawn from within the low-income neighborhood. Credit awards are extended to individuals based upon personal reputation and character—no procrustean banking regulations here. One long-time member of Wells FCU expressed his views on the two kinds of financial institutions this way: "The credit union is a place to come where people understand you, your problems. The credit union will give you a chance, while the bank won't" (quoted in Jerving 1993, p. 5).

Perhaps a reigning "folk theory" in the African-American community impels residents to purposely avoid dealing with commercial financial institutions large or small.[11] Carol Aranjo, Wells FCU executive director, evidently believes so. She explains that because of established racist practices in the banking industry, most blacks she comes into contact with would rather turn to alternative credit sources, such as liquor stores for check cashing and rental centers for appliance loans, than trust anyone else with their money. "Blacks have been exploited for so long by whites and slick blacks," she charges, that they "tend to be secretive about finances because they have been victimized" (quoted in Jerving 1993, p. 8).

The Youth Credit Union (YCU) was started by Aranjo in 1988 to counter the prevalent fear among minority adults of financial institutions. YCU was conceived as a place for children and youths to begin to save money and gain access to credit through a democratic, nonprofit cooperative devoted to stewardship of low-income residents' earnings. But over time these efforts have resulted in a youth organization where students are taught the skills of financial literacy.

In the spring of 1988, the young members at Wells, ages seven to seventeen, opened their doors for business at YCU, which was chartered as a legal youth credit union one year earlier. On opening day alone seventy-three children signed up for membership, depositing $1,200. The board of directors consisted of one representative from each of the four age groups: seven to nine, ten to twelve, thirteen to fifteen, and sixteen to seventeen. Although an adult advisor was assigned to each age group to assist the children in their decision-making duties, the youths ran their own operations. They set policies on lending practices such as loan limitations, age requirements, prepayment plans, and fee setting. Youth members were involved in all aspects of the financial institution as loan officers, clerks, managers, and on the credit committee.

The common goal that comprised a mission for these youths was their desire to learn all aspects of setting up and running a credit union. "We decided what we should be doing as youth for youth," one former YCU manager remarked. "We set up standards. . . . We set up workshops. We decided what we needed to accomplish as black youths, as a credit union working together." Another teen noted: "It's a lot of responsibility. Knowing that you have to make sure that the board and credit union run well. There is a benefit in the long run" (quoted in Jerving 1993, p. 18, 82).

YCU members attended Saturday workshops on money management and budgeting issues, how to purchase wisely, stock market investments, and, incidently, ways to fill out a job or college applications. They learned about their duties as board members, as well as more technical skills such as accounting and computer operations, business planning, and research and development. The youths attended annual meetings of the National Federation of Community Development Credit Unions and talked to interested adults at regional conferences and local venues about operating a low-income financial cooperative.

YCU offers financial services for youths in inner-city Springfield, but it also serves to channel youthful energies in creative and positive outlets. YCU is a place to "watch young people grow," Aranjo remarked to me. Youths there gain a good understanding of what people need to succeed in their community. Self-esteem and confidence building are outgrowths of the variety of credit union outreach activities, including speaking opportunities at schools and civic organizations, hosting Urban League and NAACP events, and assisting in neighborhood improvement efforts. YCU members view their credit union as a community-based organization, a youth center in their own neighborhood, and a safe place that sanctions their efforts at attaining responsible adulthood through leadership development. Here they learn the promise of democratic action: that a collective financial enterprise can provide low-income African-Americans with credit and lending opportunities for their economic advancement and social mobility.

The D.C. Wells Federal Credit Union *is* an alternative banking institution. But YCU is a second home for youths where they engage in peer relationships devoted to teamwork, communication, problem solving, and self-esteem building. They often become positive role models for others in the community, especially the younger ones, setting an example which tells their friends that membership in the credit union is a meaningful experience for black youths. And that self-confidence carries over into other social networks outside of their immediate "family." "On the street," Mark, age 17, a credit union board member notes,

> I'm representing the credit union. I'm keeping a good image. Even when I'm on the streets with my friends, I have to keep that representation up. I can't fall short. Never fall short. Always think positive. I'm proud of the little kids who are members. They look up to me (quoted in Jerving 1993, p. 46).

He adds, "When I tell the kids we run the whole thing, they don't believe me" (quoted in Jerving 1993, p. 68). And, at home, Mark's mother has even noticed how he has become more "business-minded" and "careful with his money." He doesn't spend his disposable income on frivolous items. Mark is saving his money, evidently for a college education and a future business career. The financial education gained at YCU opens possibilities for others like Mark to build a hopeful future.

These low-income teens might channel their newly acquired financial literacy toward economic revitalizations. They have been provided with the tools and skills for self-help development. Each business venture is a small step that holds the potential for empowering new indigenous leaders to come forward to recognize job creation and employment priorities within their own impoverished communities. The financial education gained at YCU opens up possibilities for a hopeful future, or, as one adult credit union adviser remarked, his son now was able to realize that "dreams can come true" (quoted in Jerving 1993, p. 20).

In the next section, I examine additional ways that financial knowledge is disseminated to youths for the purposes of starting small-scale business ventures. Enterprise education offers the tools and skills to stimulate economic development (see Stern et al. 1994). Each venture mobilizes a variety of resources toward solving employment and training problems in low-income communities.

Enterprise Education

In the Southeastern region of this country, youths can avail themselves of REAL Enterprises, a nonprofit agency which funds school-based community development corporations for loans to budding teen entrepreneurs.[12] REAL (Rural Entrepreneurship through Action Learning) Enterprises was created to assist rural communities with small business development; however, its program model is applicable to urban settings as well.[13]

REAL offers technical assistance from several chapter offices in the states of Georgia, North and South Carolina to educators for the development of entrepreneurship training leading to school-incubated enterprises. Teachers desiring the REAL program model enter a contractual agreement for membership, pay a yearly fee, and subscribe to a menu of products and services which includes staff-development workshops, on-site consultations, data collection, monitoring and evaluation processes, instructional resources, and promotional materials, among others.

REAL offers start-up capital for new businesses as well, a novel feature that distinguishes this program because it awards loans to youths with promising ventures. For instance, one successful REAL enterprise secured a market niche by offering New York-style delicatessen to weary travelers near an exit ramp off Interstate-95 in St. Pauls, North Carolina. The "Way Off Broadway" deli owners repaid their start-up loans within two years, showing the community and business establishment that indeed young adults could operate a profitable venture.[14]

The Georgia REAL loan guarantee program, termed "Start Up," encourages young entrepreneurs to invest in their home towns and, with the support of local lenders, builds a financial mechanism for economic development efforts there. The key to any student's success in securing a start-up loan is the drafting of a feasible business plan. Georgia REAL Enterprises suggests that a "community support team committee" consist of at least three advisors, such as a bank loan officer, a Chamber of Commerce representative, a successful entrepreneur, or a representative from the small business development center. This group of adults will help a student-applicant secure a 10 percent community guarantee on the bank loan from an organization or group of individuals in the town; or a student may offer a 10 percent equity contribution up front. A waiver of either community guarantee or equity contribution is possible, but strongly discouraged. The bank provides up to 90 percent of the total business cost. In the event a borrower defaults, Start Up repays 80 percent of the loan (up to $20,000) and the community group repays 10 percent. The bank risks 10 percent of the loan balance.

REAL Enterprises facilitates a partnership program between youths and adults and between schools and businesses in communities that realize they need to support their young people's creative ideas for employability through sustainable economic development. The REAL way is one important effort in helping communities spread the message (to rural and urban teens alike) that neighborly spirit and good will extend only so far. When groups of adults provide local financial backing, risking their hard-earned money toward support of a teenager's entrepreneurial dreams, hope and opportunity are rekindled in youth. REAL entrepreneurs now have a reason to stay in their communities and hometowns after high school graduation. The life skills they gain in the creation, organization, and enactment of a potential business venture are unparalleled, contributing to personal empowerment and success in organizational life. This entrepreneurial model, moreover, might be used for the creation of cooperative ventures that emerge within low-income communities, and are dedicated to socially responsible services or other local needs (Krimerman and Lindenfeld 1992). A nonprofit recycling center, for instance, may be organized as an employment vehicle for unemployed people in town. A worker-owned bakery may provide jobs for under-employed individuals in the neighborhood.

While enterprise educators have ready audiences in their business or marketing classes, youth workers in non-school settings have to devise different approaches when spreading the word of entrepreneurship to city teens. For example, in Camden, New Jersey, the Education, Training, and Enterprise Center (EDTEC) specializes in technical assistance services to community-based organizations serving minority teens, ages 14 to 18.[15] EDTEC is a minority-owned firm founded in 1985 and devoted to sustainable development through enterprise training in communities of color. Their "New Youth Entrepreneur" curriculum offers a twelve-module training program about the paths and pitfalls of economic development, including topics on entrepreneurship as a career option, using creativity and logic to solve problems, and the value of academic preparation in implementing business ideas. This program, requiring twenty hours of class instruction, focuses on low-cost business start-ups with financial investments arranged through peer partnerships or parental loans. The kids are expected to actually start a small business.

Inner-city teens throughout the country have participated in summer programs using EDTEC curricular materials and workbooks. For example, in 1991 the Omaha YWCA recruited twenty-five teens for an eight-week summer program. Students were assigned to five subgroups for the trainings, which also included lessons in career readiness. Each group created an inexpensive venture, developed a business plan, and marketed their products at an open-air sales fair. The summer enterprises, selling confections such as cookies, candy, and popcorn, for example, netted the kids five hundred at the end of the day. The next year YWCA program directors doubled the summer enrollments to fifty. In Ohio, the Youth Entrepreneurship Success Strategy, a summer youth employment program in Cuyahoga County, provided East Cleveland teens small start-up loans for enterprise development. One successful venture, a fruit salad business named "MJM Salads," repaid its loan and earned $150 in profits for its three female partners. The girls received $100 as winners of EDTEC's Young Entrepreneurship Award that year. Other small-scale ventures have included floral arrangements, silk screening T-shirts, janitorial services, car detailing, window washing, baby sitting, and novelty sales, among others.

EDTEC co-founders Aaron Bocage and George Waters (1990, p. 9) write, inner-city entrepreneurs are the "role models and new heroes we want for our kids." This program brings minority business owners (mentors) together with youths in order to help adolescents realize that legitimate enterprise developments are a positive alternative to drug dealing and other illegal street trades. As a resource for community development, EDTEC's entrepreneurship education trainings nationwide can bring poor people into positive strategies for revitalizing their own communities. "But there is no magic," Bocage and Waters warn. "We have to train people to be ready when the opportunities finally do come" (p. 10).

Research and Development

Any trainings for entrepreneurship start with a needs analysis, that is, a study of economic indicators in the local arena. Shaffer (1989) points out that the democratic nature of this inquiry, which he terms "community economic analysis," is dedicated to "improve economic opportunity and quality of life through group decisions and actions." "Community economic analysis," he continues, "is an action-oriented study of how a community is put together economically and how it responds to external stimuli. Specific problems, resources, and alternative actions must be identified" (pp. 10–11). This means undertaking a massive technical and structural analysis of one's environment, including a detailed understanding of relationships among sociopolitical, cultural, and economic institutions.

School-aged youths can be brought into the research and development process by surveying what needed goods and services already exist in the local economy or are unavailable for expansion due to restrictions upon and limitations of capital in low-income areas (see Stern et al. 1994). In Chicago, for instance, Bethel New Life, a community development corporation on the poverty-stricken west side of town, has assisted three local high schools with the establishment of enterprise "venture club" activities. Student members have begun analyzing economic and employment opportunities in anticipation of creating new businesses, including a school office supply store and a student operated credit union that will serve the community at large (*Newsnotes* 1991).

School leaders might begin to view partnerships with community-based organizations as advantageous for heightened youth development here (see Heath and McLaughlin 1994a). In New York City, for instance, the New Visions schools chartered a number of small high schools in various venues around the city's boroughs. In the Williamsburg section of Brooklyn, a community-based organization named El Puente and school administrators now jointly operate an academy for Latino youths. These local students benefit from direct access to a variety of neighborhood service agencies, health, arts, recreation, and social centers when engaged in economic research and development projects (Willen 1992). Recently, the kids have conducted a survey of neighborhood trees (Dillon 1994).

Consider the educational opportunities at the Rindge School of Technical Arts in Cambridge, Massachusetts, where ninth-grade inner-city students engage in an alternative vocational education program devoted to sustainable community economic development. The school-based program, CityWorks, offers studies in the architecture, public affairs, and city planning of Cambridge through hands-on technical training in the urban community. The goal of this one-year program, according to its founders, is "to help students understand their community and its needs, and ultimately to see themselves as people who can affect that community and create new opportunities for themselves and others who live and work there."[16]

Rindge students are grouped into small work crews with a vocational teacher who assists them in field-based projects, such as "walking around the block" (a three-week project in the beginning of the academic year), in order to compile an inventory of neighborhoods, residents, and industries surrounding the high school. On the streets students conduct interviews with pedestrians and storekeepers, gathering information about their relationships to the community's residential settings and workplace sites. The students take a closer look at important physical and natural features, such as the locations of buildings, park benches, mailboxes, street signs, trees and plantings, and noted social features, like local hang-outs and graffiti markings. They even note the common street sounds heard on the block. In the shops students apply their field experiences to the technical arts in order to showcase their talents through "studio presentation boards." The vocational shops are laboratories where the kids fabricate their boards using original artwork and lettering, computer graphics, and photos, while integrating scientific concepts and math principles as well as measurement exercises and communications skills into their designs.

Advanced curricular activities in this program require skills in map making, videography, blueprint preparation, and architectural drawing. In one year alone, for instance, the students designed and built scale models for a future museum, interviewed an NAACP chapter founder about his organizing efforts to create a nearby pocket park, and developed a pamphlet highlighting routes to eight of the city's best pastry shops.

In the last project of the academic year, "Community Development," students create businesses and services to be located in Cambridge based upon their needs assessments of the community. Project assignments have included opening a restaurant, creating an autobody shop, and designing a teen center. Each student team prepares a site plan for their community development project, paying special attention to local zoning and building codes, density factors, and parking regulations, among others. They complete a "report card" evaluating the site location for reasonable rents, closeness to public transportation, accessibility to parks, safety and convenience for customers, and availability of parking. They execute a business plan, create scale models of the facility, and produce working drawings of the building. Upon project completion, CityWorks students host an open house to give parents and community members a chance to view and to critique the projects.

At the Rindge School low-income students have an opportunity to realize the possibilities for employment right there—in their own neighborhoods and residences. By exploring "the strengths and weaknesses of the indigenous economy," Rindge School executive director Larry Rosenstock (1991, p. 436) contends, his students gain insight into "the unmet needs and underutilized resources" that drive community economic development. The transformation of vocational schools using CityWorks project methods offers low-income urban teens the knowledge base upon which they may begin to problematize ways to reclaim their own neighborhoods.

Conclusion

The schools can become an important platform for launching city youths into the community for purposes of studying, planning, and then implementing a variety of small-scale business enterprise and employment activities. Institutional linkages are the defining reality here, according to policy analyst Paul Weckstein (1989), who writes:

Once economic development is seen as a process whereby communities utilize their resources, human and otherwise, to define and solve their social and economic problems and gain greater control over their destinies, then it becomes easier to stake out a role for the schools in that process which is consistent with their broad educational role. As the community begins to better assess various needs which are not being met (e.g., health care, housing and transporation), to assess the resources available, and to develop strategies to begin to act on those needs, it becomes more natural for those in the community who are oriented toward this larger agenda to recognize the schools as a key community source (p. 76).

Citizen-activists can look to the schools—and to youths—for assistance in building local leadership within learning communities capable of initiating and carrying out sustainable development.

Good leaders recognize the educational impulse in community struggles for economic justice. Organizing, after all, offers a theory of critical education: authentic inquiry into the lived experiences of the powerless in society. It is in grassroots leadership, long-time civil rights and labor activist Si Kahn (1991) explains, that people "learn something new about themselves. They find dignity in place of mistreatment. They find self-respect instead of lack of self-confidence. They begin to use more fully the skills and abilities that they possess: to work with other people, to influence, to speak up, to fight back" (p. 10). Evidently Saul Alinsky knew all along that critical education is the foundation of sustainable development. "Real education," he notes, "is the means by which the membership will begin to make sense out of their relationship as individuals to the organization and to the world they live in, so that they can make informed and intelligent judgments. The stream of activities and programs of the organization provides a never-ending series of *specific* issues and situations that create a rich field for the learning process" (1971, p. 124).

2

Neighborhood Improvement

Social projects in nonprofit organizations bring kids together for community-building efforts in novel ways.[1] Young people can assume leadership roles, for instance, that combat urban crime and violence, substance abuse and alcohol dependency, gang-related activities, early school leaving and academic remediation, and teen pregnancy and suicide.

Consider one city-wide prevention approach to curbing neighborhood violence through reforms of a juvenile justice system in California (*New York Times* 1994). In Los Angeles County, a jury of their peers means just that for teens caught breaking the laws in misdemeanor cases. These courts comprise an adult judge along with a jury of six to twelve teens, high school students who volunteer for this after-school duty once a week or fortnightly. In Los Angeles, the six-member peer jury handles three or four cases at each session. First time nonviolent offenders between the ages of fourteen and eighteen are selected by the city's probation department for "teen court." Each defendent presents their own case; the probation officer acts as the prosecution. Jurors question the defendant and prescribe the types and lengths of sentencing, although the judge has final say. Typical sentencing in these cases usually involves lengthy community-service terms involving roadside and schoolyard cleanups, as well as essay assignments. Upon successful completion of the punishment, all charges are expunged from the juvenile's record.

Teen courts began in 1983 in Odessa, Texas, and there are now about 150 nationwide. It is reported that recidivism rates drop to single digits under this alternative system of jurisprudence (state juvenile courts in Texas, for instance, operate recidivism rates of 30 to 50 percent). Some critics charge that these courts deal only with youths who commit petty crimes, and nonviolent offenders generally would not repeat their crimes in most circumstances. Supporters say that the courts offer a window of opportunity to affect kids' negative behaviors before it is too late. Perhaps each defendant sees their jury of peers acting in a responsible manner and fulfilling the role of fair and impartial citizen in this volunteer activity.

Teen jurors often say that they learn more about the criminal justice system in America. Yet youthful involvement in this program seems to be limited by patriarchal and authoritarian adult designs. One might ask: Are adults merely showcasing so-called "model youths" for token appearance in front of their troubled peers? What initial and on-going trainings in leadership skills do the teen jurors receive? What policy-setting activities do the teens engage in during their tenure on the court? Who is responsible for continuous program improvements, managerial practices, and evaluations of the juries? Is peer involvement authentic here?

Certainly teens are valuable resources in a wide variety of peer prevention efforts. And youth workers can ask young people to join with them as partners in organizational leadership designs. Still, adults have to rethink how they view children as participants, and what roles they assign adolescents in the policy-setting and deliberative functions of a small group. An organization will be operating along democratic lines, researcher John Gastil (1993) cautions, "if it has equally distributed decision-making power, an inclusive membership committed to democracy, healthy relationships among its members, and a democratic method of deliberation. Group deliberation is democratic if group members have equal and adequate opportunities to speak, neither withhold information nor verbally manipulate one another, and are able and willing to listen" (p. 6).

For our purposes small groups cannot expect to be democratic unless youth workers perceive adolescents as equal contributors, not clients with an array of behavioral deficits. According to prevention expert William Lofquist[2] (1989, pp. 47–48), there is a continuum of three styles or approaches on this matter. His "The Spectrum of Adult Attitudes Toward Young People" suggests that, in Style #1, youths are treated as objects, because authority is vested in adults who supposedly know what is best for teens and can make decision on their behalf. In the adult-designed activity,

Lofquist charges, the young person is there merely to take advantage of the program; young people are not asked to assume leadership roles. In Style #2, where young people are viewed as recipients, adults will allow some exemplary youths limited participation in leadership roles, but only under close supervision and solely for the purposes of learning skills that can be used in the future. In Style #3, in believing young people are valuable resources, adult leaders will bring them into the planning process of the organization at its earliest point. Training programs for organizational effectiveness, Lofquist notes, are useful for teaching youth workers how to facilitate organizations that function in equitable and democratic ways.

Obviously, in an organizational setting that is operated along democratic lines, young people can become responsible partners in authentic programs that ensure that their real needs are being met at the same time that their community's needs are being satisfied (see Swinehart 1990).[3] The point is that social projects begin the long process of neighborhood revitalizations by involving youths and adults together in problem-solving and decision-making activities. Youth organizations practicing small group democracy increase the capacity of local communities to set their own future pathways for positive growth and development.

The youth programs highlighted in the next three sections of this chapter—Safe Neighborhoods, Green Neighborhoods, and Rebuilt Neighborhoods—support healthy adolescent development primarily because adults view young people in equitable partnerships. Young people are genuine community resources and essential stakeholders who assist in solving pressing social problems in their own neighborhoods.

Safe Neighborhoods

A grassroots community-based group in South Los Angeles was formed in the aftermath of the uprisings in April, 1992, and named Action for Grassroots Empowerment and Neighborhood Development Alternatives (AGENDA). It has organized a youth initiative that brings teens together for the purposes of investigating crime and public safety issues among peers in their own locales.[4] Neighborhood adolescents are viewed as a valuable but, at present, untapped resource, according to the project's chairman Anthony Thigpenn. Yet, with their active input into community affairs, AGENDA establishes an important model for teen empowerment that is both "youth-driven and youth-responsive" and leads to democratic action.[5]

In December, 1993, AGENDA's youth initiative, Agenda for Action Among Youth (AAAY), began taking its first steps in combatting gang violence and community crime by surveying about five hundred peers on a range of issues critical to the operations of safe and healthy neighborhoods. Twelve teen interns, hired to assist the AAAY team in their organizing efforts, administered a twenty-six question "Youth Issues Survey." Responses were gathered at area schools, churches, malls, and local hangouts. Area youth were asked, for instance, about the numbers of available jobs, recreation programs, educational opportunities, and teen programs in South L.A. Additionally, AAAY team members wanted to learn from their peers about perceptions toward inter-ethnic conflicts and public safety, specifically whether the Los Angeles Police Department was "helping" or "hurting" the community. After the survey team analyzed the data, they identified four key areas— substance abuse, gang violence, poor schools, and a lack of job opportunities—that would become rallying points for organizing area teens into devising an action plan or agenda-building campaign for finding solutions and strategizing ways to solve community problems.

With the infusion of grant monies for youth empowerment projects in the riot-torn areas, in the summer of 1994 AGENDA offered an AAAY Summer Internship Program that provided training for up to twenty youth leaders in public policy agenda development and community organizing. In the former activity, the interns learned how to research and analyze public policy problems and potential solutions, formulate agendas, and plan direct-action campaigns. In the latter activity, the interns learned how to recruit and mobilize constituencies, build grassroots organizations, select and develop leaders, coordinate and facilitate meetings, and acquire skills in public speaking.

In AGENDA, young people are empowering themselves to have a voice in the rebuilding of their own neighborhoods. AAAY teen leaders speak for themselves, act on their own behalf, and help other peers join together for a direct-action campaign to win positive changes in their own communities.

Another model of grassroots teen empowerment addressing health and public safety concerns for low-income youths operates on the East Coast, in the low-income Highbridge area of the South Bronx, New York City.[6] The Take Charge/Be Somebody! Youth Network (TC/BS) was funded in 1990 with a five-year demonstration grant from the U.S. Department of Health and Human Services' Center for Substance Abuse Prevention. TC/BS encourages community development through the active participation and involvement of teens in neighborhood programs devoted to adequate employment, educational, entrepreneurial, health, and recreational opportunities as alternatives to the destructive forces of drug dealing and gang-related problems.

Neighborhoods in the South Bronx were particularly hard hit by the white-flight phenomenon that began in the the 1960s when numerous moderate-income, blue-collar families fueled a movement of out-migration to suburban tract homes (Breslin 1995). They left in their wake established inner-city neighborhoods like Highbridge with large populations of low-income, impoverished tenants living in buildings owned by absentee landlords. Banks and insurance companies turned their back on the area, and drug dealers took over. Block after block of buildings fell to either the city's wrecking ball or arson fires. But the area, in the 1990s, is experiencing a revival through community redevelopment efforts, mostly funded by private foundations and government agencies.

Neighborhood improvements in the South Bronx are the legacy of a few bold citizen-activists, such as the Banana Kelly Community Improvement Association and the Mid-Bronx Desperadoes, who organized to stop the lawlessness, take back the streets, and seek grassroots solutions to a host of economic, social, and political problems. Over the past two decades they have brought public pressure to bear upon absentee landlords by organizing tenant associations and established community watch programs against crime in the neighborhoods; they have created block associations to seek redress from city officials for everything from irregular trash collection to inadequate police protection, and lobbied banks and insurance companies to reinvest in their neighborhoods again.

This is the context in which TC/BS was founded by two area activists as a demonstration project. It is composed of seven organizations in a partnership that gives local teens a voice to address urban issues impacting their lives and to develop youth-run programs for the betterment of all residents. TC/BS youth are considered a valuable resource in Highbridge and are important contributors to strengthening community-led organizations by mobilizing peers to advocate for social change. Of course, they are also role models to other youths who will see a cohort of proud and responsible leaders forming a task force to direct positive growth within their own community.

In order to gather a leadership cohort that is truly representative of the diversity in Highbridge, TC/BS founders created a Youth Council (later called the Youth Senate) as a policy-making board for teens in the area.[7] A Youth Network was created where teens could meet and discuss urban issues important to them, and an Adult Council was formed to bring residents together for community-led decision making and strategic planning activities. Some of the projects that evolved from the Youth Senate center upon health care, including an AIDS/HIV informational pamphlet. (See Figure 2.1) Some focus on youth employment, including peer interviewing and resume preparation trainings and an assessment of job prospects through a survey of area employers and employees. Some center on community arts, including peer-led video production projects that document the Highbridge community in a variety of safe neighborhood improvement efforts, and the "Highbridge Voice," a monthly newsletter about the TC/BS community partnership.

Finally, this project serves as an employment vehicle for some of the area's activist youth. For example, TC/BS founding member and Highbridge resident Omar Ortiz, age 23, joined the Network when he was eighteen years old and became employed as a youth program organizer. His leadership efforts at the local level have proven noteworthy. In the summer of 1994 he was selected to attend a national Hispanic/Latino Leadership Training Institute in Washington D.C. and now he is seeking a position on the local school board. A TC/BS success story, Ortiz teaches low-income youths in New York City to follow in his footsteps and, in his words, to "have a voice . . . use it . . . take ownership of it" (quoted in *Highbridge Voice* 1993, p. 8).

FIGURE 2.1

Take Charge/Be Somebody! An AIDS Presentation. Photograph by Omar
O. Ortiz. Left to Right: Tameika Terrel, Arlene Maldonaldo, Tino Caiafas,
Miranda Franklin, and David Baez.

Gang and substance abuse prevention efforts can provide
critical education targeted to low-income youths in smaller towns
as well. In Fitchburg, Massachusetts, for example, the U.S.
Department of Health and Human Services, Adminstration for
Children and Families, funded a three-year demonstration project
beginning in 1992 for training Latino youths.[8] The program is
titled *Pa'Lante*, which means "forward" in Spanish, and teaches
area young people to value their bilingualism and biculturalism as
positive attributes when seeking employment in the community.
The teens, ages 15 to 18, are provided internships at various
health care facilities where they served as medical interpreters for
patients.

Thirty youth trainees were recruited and interviewed by two
Hispanic social service agencies in the town. Participants were
offered counseling/support services, pre-employment training,
medical terminology and communications classes, substance
abuse and violence prevention activities, entrepreneurship educa-

tion, and leadership development seminars. In this latter activity, *Pa'Lante* youths were provided trainings led by Teen Empowerment of Boston, external consultant to the project.[9]

The Teen Empowerment model of youth development was created in 1974 in Somerville, Massachusetts, by founder Stanley Pollack. The program works with adolescents to enhance their abilities at organizing projects that solve actual community problems. The trainings bring diverse groups of what he terms "high risk" and "low risk" youths in contact through motivational exercises, skills building, and behavioral management and change processes, all leading to peer leadership development. Using a systematic curriculum of four modules, the teens learn how to design and execute media events, educational workshops, and social activities that are used as community outreach efforts in building a broad-based neighborhood youth organization. It is through the specific organizing endeavors, however, that teen activists meet other youths who are brought into the empowerment process. For instance, dozens of rival black and Latino gang members in South Boston came together through a day-long Youth Peace Conference held in May, 1993. This important anti-violence event was created and run by paid teenage organizers trained in Pollack's youth development model. At that specific conference the attendees went to workshops on topics related to getting jobs, stopping racism, and advancing better police/gang relationships. Teen Empowerment organizers have successfully staged rallies, vigils, and marches that memorialized slain neighborhood youths. They have hosted drug-free dances and parties to bring safe, fun, positive strategies to youths in their desire to build healthy communities.

At *Pa'Lante*, some of the trainees became organizers in citywide peer leadership efforts as well. In fact, several youth forums were organized with teens and community leaders that highlighted public safety and substance abuse problems in and around Fitchburg. By developing a visible presence as knowledgeable and vocal Latino youth leaders (an outgrowth of the education they received through Teen Empowerment), the teens are starting a citywide youth council for dealing with safe neighborhood issues relevant to their lives.

Pa'Lante is a youth employment training collaborative that seems to work. Evidently a culturally relevant service was established here which utilized the minority community of Latino youths in a gang prevention, job training, and youth leadership development strategy that not only affirmed the kids' linguistic gifts but also recognized that bicultural residents need quality health care. From this basic program philosophy a diverse membership formed the broad-based community coalition.

Perhaps most noteworthy is the network of community groups allied in fighting drug-related gang violence in the area. In fact, this project resulted from an initiative of the Fitchburg Safe and Healthy Neighborhood Coalition. This group of seven neighborhood associations fights poverty and crime through prevention strategies targeted to family stability, health, public safety, equal opportunity, education, and economic opportunity. The Carlisle Center for the Prevention of Substance Abuse, a nonprofit educational research and development organization, forges long-term partnerships "as a catalyst for change" with communities committed to the health and safety of youth, families, and neighborhoods. At the Carlisle Center, it should be emphasized, sustainable development is an approach that "honors Freire's advice that helping communities to change requires a deep understanding of the community's history, a strong sense of humility, and a profound respect for the wisdom of community members."[10]

Healthy neighborhood improvements require a concerted effort by stakeholders focusing upon a prevention system that is comprehensive, long-range, and sustainable. Yet coalition building is a complex organizational process lined with many paths and pitfalls; numerous barriers can derail seemingly good intentions among the citizenry devoted to community and personal empowerment (Wallerstein 1992; Wolff 1992).[11] Federal demonstration grants, nonetheless, can assist low-income communities in the systemic change process. What is needed are opportunities to develop and nurture "strategic alliances," or community partnerships in which organizations, agencies, and individuals together counter unemployment, drug abuse, and violence on the streets of their neighborhoods (Williams, DeMarco, and Barstow 1994).

In the next section, I profile two projects that approach neighborhood improvements from an ecological perspective. Local youths learn how food production, for instance, intersects with sustainable community development.

Green Neighborhoods

Headquartered in Lincoln, at the Massachusetts Audubon Society's Drumlin Farm Education Center and Wildlife Sanctuary, a three-year pilot program presents an exemplary model of neighborhood improvement: a food project.[12] On just four acres of land (the farm also has a twelve-acre garden), the Drumlin Farm's Food Project (DFFP) yields a wide variety of vegetables that are trucked to sites around Boston for sale or donation to food pantries, soup kitchens, homeless shelters, and farmer's markets. In the final year's season (1994),[13] for instance, over forty thousand pounds of produce, including beets, potatoes, beans, cabbage, tomatoes, squash, peppers, broccoli, and cauliflower, among others, were harvested and distributed to families in low-income neighborhoods via a coordinated network of more than six hundred people from schools, shelters, churches, social service agencies, and other volunteers. (See Figure 2.2)

This unique demonstration project is one of fifteen that the Youth Service Corps chose as recipient of a $10,000 grant from the federal agency's Commission on National and Community Service. The area's suburban kids as well as city teens participate in community service through a summer eight-week work program which continues after school for part-time volunteers during the fall and spring. The youths spend four days a week on the farm engaged in tilling, planting, composting, weeding, and harvesting their crops. Then they spend one day a week in Boston at one of the city's shelters preparing the food they have grown. Participants receive a daily stipend and are bound by a workers' contract at the rural and urban sites, on field trips, and on public transportation that identifies inappropriate workplace conduct. A range of offenses can result in warnings, several day's lost wages, or termination for infractions such as absence, tardiness, smoking, littering, vandalism, fighting, drinking, drug dealing, stealing, and weapons possession. The teens are placed into manageable crews, led by an older youth leader, and engage in a variety of manual labor activities related to the production functions of a working farm.

Here we have urban and suburban kids thrown together, many of whom have never tended a garden, placed in leadership positions, and asked to work cooperatively with peers and adults

FIGURE 2.2

The Food Project. Photograph by Todd Magliozzi. Left to upper right: Tom
Bonoma, Melissa Schatsby, and Amelia Ravin.

from a diversity of ages, cultural backgrounds, and geographic neighborhoods. What was it like for them in this setting?[14] Their comments touched on a variety of physical, technical, and personal aspects of the experience. The physical labor of gardening involved hard work hoeing in the field, how dirty one could get in a day, getting soaked in the rain and burned in the sun, bitten by bugs, and sweating from backbreaking work. The technical knowledge gained included how to harvest vegetables, several types of hoes and organic pesticides, and the shape of plants, vegetables, and weeds. Finally, the personal aspects of the job included waking up early every summer day, naming the many friends they've made, working at the city shelter, riding the commuter rails, listening to "real" Boston accents, and learning about rural/urban and racial/ethnic differences.

The DFFP's "Farm to Family Program" is noteworthy in that youths were brought into contact with low-income adult residents in the city. The Food Project sold shares in the harvest of 1993 and delivered the organically-grown produce weekly to residents in the Dudley Street neighborhood of Roxbury. Over eight thousand pounds of fresh vegetables were delivered, washed, weighed, and boxed by DFFP youth workers for two-dozen shareholders that season. Accompanying each grocery bag of produce was a weekly bulletin prepared by the Food Project crews that reported the latest news from Drumlin Farm, listed various recipes, and profiled youth workers, staff, and community participants. Shareholders were invited to the Farm to visit or work in the fields along with the teens on Fridays during the summer months. In fact, Friday was community lunch day at the Food Project; workers, staff, volunteers, guests, and shareholders joined together under a tent to taste a diversity of culinary treats, and each crew was responsible for choosing recipes and gathering fresh produce in the preparation of these dishes.

Interestingly, DFFP entered into coalitions with other community-based groups in Boston to advance the greening of neighborhoods. For instance, the Dudley Street Neighborhood Initiative (DSNI), a grassroots organization promoting community economic development in the Roxbury area, supported the Food Project as a bottom-up investment in its area youths (Medoff and Sklar 1994). According to DSNI human development committee leaders, the holistic growth of the neighborhood included the active participation and leadership of youths who are "among our richest resources. . . . we must assure them of the gifts they hold and of the gifts they are" (p. 171). Thus, neighborhood youths were engaged in a variety of street beautification projects as well.

Another youth development model linking community service to local greening efforts is The Natural Guard (TNG), a nonprofit organization headquartered in New Haven, Connecticut. TNG connects children and youths to neighborhood improvement through in-school, after-school, and weekend activities, such as vacant lot cleanups, recycling projects, litter and pollution patrols, community gardens, and tree inventories and planting programs.[15] TNG was founded in 1990 by folksinger and peace activist Richie Havens to provide multiple opportunities for youths in the movement for environmental justice.

Havens is most often remembered for his 1969 Woodstock performance of the Beatles tune "Here Comes the Sun," but he also understands youth development. If you give kids something positive to do with their lives, he says, the attraction of hanging out in a gang or selling drugs will lessen. In fact, his personal agenda is to offer youths some of the resources with which to begin to clean up their surroundings. The six major goals of TNG are as follows: (a) *to empower youth*, helping them to see themselves as a key force for creating change; (b) *to generate service projects* designed to protect and enhance the environment, provide nutritional and economic benefit, foster social integration and develop leadership skills; (c) *to integrate youth programs* and service activities with existing community-based programs in order to afford members maximum exposure to and appreciation of our country's rich and diverse cultural heritage; (d) *to present career opportunities* in environmentally-related fields by integration of daily school curriculum with field work and outdoor exploration through chapter travel exchange opportunities; (e) *to foster a spirit of advocacy* by teaching the skills necessary to achieve goals of environmental protection and enjoyment; and (f) *to create an entire generation of environmentally aware youth* armed with tools and knowledge necessary to address environmental concerns, empowered with an appreciation and respect for all life.

Through local chapter initiatives in California, Connecticut, Hawaii, Illinois, Maryland, New Jersey, New York, and Belize,

Central America, youths from kindergarten through high school are given the tools, information, and mentorship with which to stage hands-on environmental actions, particularly of concern to residents living in economically-deprived communities. A bilingual coloring book, for instance, was produced by the Natural Guard chapter in New Haven. Bolstered by a $40,000 foundation grant for lead poisoning prevention, the Guard's program coordinator joined with first graders in one of the poorest sections of the city to develop the eight-page English-Spanish coloring book that highlights awareness of human contact with toxic lead hazards in the home. In California, the Los Angeles chapter members adopted a ten-mile stretch of the Harbor Freeway in South-Central L.A. for beautification and provided a lesson in community stewardship as well. Their project entailed planting trees and maintaining their habitat as a litter-free zone. In New York, the Brooklyn chapter members have organized tree plantings and community lot cleanups, as well as highway beautification efforts to paint over graffiti-covered bridges. In the New Jersey chapter at Ocean County, teens have organized environmental clubs in twelve of the areas fifteen high schools. They have planned local Earth Day celebrations, sponsored environmental conferences with the general public, cleaned beaches, and started a battery recycling program.

The Natural Guard is on the front lines of the battle for environmental justice, capturing the attention of the public, policymakers, and government and business leaders at local, state, national and international levels. Guard members have prepared testimony on ecological issues for town commissioners and state legislatures and participated in international Earth Day summits for children at the United Nations in New York and at Nickelodeon Studios in Florida. They delivered their message of environmental justice on a television talk show hosted by Phil Donahue, visited the offices of two U.S. Senators active in the green movement, and went to the White House to meet with the Vice-President. TNG members have written numerous letters to elected officials and corporate executives to voice their concerns about the environment.

TNG founder Richie Havens believes that kids are already interested in ecological issues. "It is adults who need re-educating," he charges. This organization is trying to create a new generation of environmentally aware youth with a healthy respect for themselves and their surroundings based on an ecological ethic promising democratic action. A neighborhood trash clean-up of a vacant lot, for instance, may have as one short-term goal the elimination of rodent breeding grounds, which in turn curtail the spread of human disease and infection accompanying feces droppings and bitings in nearby dwellings. But in the long run the involvement of practical improvement efforts at the site offers a critical education through activism. This means environmental projects have the potential to empower youths; they, in turn, apply the learning experiences toward furthering connections with others about a range of community justice issues tied to sense of place.

The Natural Guard "Kid's Garden" in New Haven, for example, is a community undertaking that targeted a piece of abandoned property, termed an "orphan parcel" by the city, for development as a garden. The Guard petitioned the city for "adoption" of the lot, but after two years with little hope of winning a lease, the group turned to the owner of the property. The owner happened to be a grocery store merchant, he agreed to the garden venture, and he offered his store as a site for selling the produce grown there. When faced with removing debris from the lot strewn with broken bottles, condoms, hypodermic needles, used auto parts, and broken concrete slabs, the Guard entered into a coalition with another grassroots organization, the Sister City Project, for staffing a massive clean-up campaign at the site. The soil was prepared for planting by testing, rototilling and composting. The town's parks and recreation department provided wood chips and compost; the local police department offered horse manure from their equestrian stables; others donated fertilizer, seeds and bulbs. Over time, the grocer decided to donate his vacant lot to the New Haven Land Trust, a nonprofit organization that preserves land for public use in the metropolitan area. The garden is now a permanent green space for local residents.

What did these youths learn from their efforts at community development when actively engaged in a process of transforming a vacant lot into a neighborhood garden? TNG Director Diana Edmonds suggests that participants gained an understanding of "real food" like watermelon, corn, strawberries, cherries, apples, as well as ways to can and preserve it, bake and cook it.[16] If youths only know personal diets from their corner fast-food establishments, she offers, just imagine what they must be feeling and thinking about the "real food" they grow, taste, sell, or donate. Imagine, too, the sense of ownership of place among inner-city kids who never saw the potential of neighborhood improvements until they were willing to risk failure at trying something new: the garden project. These are the so-called "at-risk" kids everyone talks about, but to Edmonds they are "kids who take risks."

Greening neighborhoods must be sustainable as well. What good does it do to reclaim a trash-strewn city lot when the local street toughs will reclaim their territory in forty-eight hours? Street toughs need to get the message that they, too, are valuable members in local community-building activities, events, and programs. Who protected the Natural Guard Kid's Garden from vandalism and theft? The Guard's politics of community gardening in New Haven was built upon strategic alliance-building in coalitions, so that any group with a stake in the neighborhood was welcomed into the process. The supposed enmities of the cops toward the poor (or vice versa) were put aside to make way for a fragile partnership of community groups that monitored the garden's upkeep. Occasional acts of illegal dumping, for instance, were reported to the police. Word of the garden has spread throughout the local area, resulting in adult benevolence and tacit guardianship toward these youths practicing hands-on neighborhood revitalization.

In the next section I profile a nationally-known youth development project that gives inner-city, school-aged dropouts vocational training and a chance to earn a high school diploma. This project is best known for its peer leadership and community-building activities.

Rebuilt Neighborhoods

YouthBuild USA is an exemplary youth development program that battles undereducation and joblessness by involving young people in housing production activities through chapter offerings in major cities throughout the United States.[17] YouthBuild students are afforded opportunities to engage in urban renewal projects, learning actual trade skills in building construction while earning credit for their high school graduate equivalency degree or diploma.[18] Many of the trainees excel in this setting with peers who initially have similar barriers to overcome in order to succeed. About 65 percent are African American; 80 percent are male.

The YouthBuild program was started by Dorothy Stoneman in 1988 as an outgrowth of her prior ten years working with the Youth Action Program (YAP) in East Harlem, New York. YAP was a vehicle for neighborhood development and grassroots leadership which benefitted from sponsorship by the East Harlem Block Schools, which provided a number of educational programs serving residents of all ages in the community (Stoneman and Bell 1988). The YouthBuild organizational design, however, is quite unique; it is a sophisticated and comprehensive approach to youth and community development with seven distinct initiatives: (a) *a community service program* offering low-income people affordable housing; (b) *an alternative school* giving disadvantaged youths another path toward earning a diploma; (c) *a job training and pre-apprenticeship program* providing vocational education in construction-related trades; (d) *a leadership development program* helping young people to assume positions of responsibility in their program and in community affairs; (e) *a youth development program* helping them grow into healthy and productive members of society; (f) *a long-term mini-community* building young people's commitment to positive lifestyles through peer friendships; and (g) *a community development program* strengthening the capacity of community-based organizations to take ownership for their own neighborhoods.

Since its inception, program trainees have applied their skills and competencies to a variety of interesting and worthwhile construction projects that provide real-life, hands-on, practical experiences in building healthy communities. Past projects have included renovating an empty church basement and a vacant film studio to create two community centers, gutting and rehabilitating three abandoned city-owned buildings for housing homeless young people with children, establishing three transitional residences for homeless youths and two transitional residences for homeless single mothers and their children, building a neighborhood park on an empty lot, and starting a construction company using program graduates. Additionally, the youths organized two crime prevention youth patrols, as well as a coalition to create youth employment programs in New York City, as a tool for political action campaigns over a number of teen advocacy issues.

The original YAP program, moreover, offered peer governance and leadership activities directly to the young participants who were invested with the power to improve the quality of their lives. Their critical education, according to one of the original members, consisted of "the meetings, the discussions, the decisions we had to make" (1988, p. 5).

> We learned group dynamics, how to deal with people and problems. We were empowered, because the program was based on our ideas. We got a sense of pride, of importance, something teenagers in East Harlem don't get anywhere else (p. 5).

Another program graduate noted:

> Having the knowledge that it's possible to do things makes a difference to me as I look to my future. I want to have a YES, I WILL DO IT future, not a doubting one. Not having something to achieve would make my life not worth living (p. 12).

Stoneman believed that if youth workers instilled a deep sense of care and love for the young people in the progam, these youths could "recover from past invalidations" by participating in significant decision-making practices that act as "a powerful and immediate antidote to the feeling of being insignificant and dumb" (p. 15).

First pioneered in YAP youth development practices, authentic peer leadership extends into actual, ongoing, and meaningful administrative structures in YouthBuild. For example, memberships on the YouthBuild Policy Committee, the governing body of this organization, offers promising trainees an opportunity to develop as leaders through advocacy on behalf of their peers. The program director, one staff representative, and six to ten trainees (elected by secret ballot of their peers) meet as a group regularly. This committee, if operating along the lines of a small group democracy, can surface issues that are of importance to the young people. The policy committee is responsible for an array of duties, including the hiring and/or firing of staff, interviewing new trainees, consulting on program design, suggesting improvements to program management, reviewing the yearly budget, planning events, and overall decision making in the program.

Youth governance within the context of a unique organizational structure such as YouthBuild gives trainees a significant voice in policy-making matters. The design really does offer participants important learning opportunities about one's leadership roles and peer-group responsibilities. These young people become genuine stakeholders and role models in their programs, providing them with a chance (some might even say a "second chance") at rebuilding their lives and their communities. Thus, underlying the mission of this building rehabilitation and construction trade training program—and carried forth into the YouthBuild philosophy throughout its history—is leadership development: a belief that adolescent growth is motivated when young people are empowered to release the "love, hope, and positive energy" inside each of them (Stoneman and Bell 1988, p. 15).

Consider the oppressive conditions of young people of color residing in low-income neighborhoods (see, for example, Kotlowitz 1991). They have been told over and over again that they do not count. They are undereducated, under- or unemployed, and unlikely to succeed in life. Racist social and cultural practices toward minority communities continually disconfirm a resident's own intelligence, self-worth or self-esteem, and initiative (see King 1981). "Young people in oppressed communities have lived in relative poverty and powerlessness," Dorothy Stoneman (1989) charges, "in an affluent society which values wealth and power, and which has given them little respect, little opportunity, little of importance to do, and has not cared enough to protect them from the temptations of drugs, from the physical decay of their environment, from the breakdown of their families and overwork of their parents, and even from homelessness and hunger" (p. 3).

I have heard a number of YouthBuild participants, graduates, and national and local staff members on several occassions say that their program cohorts are "like a family."[19] Perhaps the young people, many of whom have led troubled lives, now realize that they have new friends—brothers and sisters—who really care about their well-being, training successes, and future aspirations. The notion of forging family-like settings in these programs offers a real challenge to youth workers.[20] They are dealing with trainees of diverse backgrounds, many of whom come from an impoverished life of continual street survival. Distrustful of adults in general, cynical young people are alienated and angered by a racist system that puts them at the margins of society. But YouthBuild does an exceptional job, in my view, by preparing staff who understand the program's goals and mission. They carry out supervising, facilitating, counseling, instructing, and managing duties as competent members of a balanced team. Youth workers nurture the young people, and help them to find a voice.

Conclusion

Youth workers who exhibit cultural awareness and sensitivity can begin to prepare individuals for democratic actions through an ethic of interconnectedness in partnerships in grassroots alliances and neighborhood coalitions. Young people and adults gain the skills and tools of leadership when given opportunities for a critical education and therein the power to confront the oppressions in their lives. Problematizing and strategizing for community justice offers the people practical applications leading to sustainable development.

One final example: Teens as Community Resources (TCR), a nonprofit agency in the city of Boston, serves as a kind of model for youth development by awarding small grant monies (under $5,000) to kids interested in initiating an organizing and/or community service project.[21] The proposals must focus upon peer leadership, be sensitive to issues of diversity among participants, and exhibit democratic operating procedures and organizational designs.

It should be noted that every program sponsored and funded by TCR is informed and guided by the knowledge and experience of teens. In other words, not only are the grant applications generated and executed by youths, but the staff, administration, and policymaking board of TCR involve active teen participation. Interestingly, TCR teens perform a wide variety of tasks in the grantmaking process, such as establishing funding criteria, conducting site visits, providing technical assistance, interviewing applicants, and evaluating proposals.

Projects like TCR empower adolescents to have a voice in the actual decisions that benefit them and their own communities. Teens are seen as important resources in neighborhood improvement efforts; they are citizen-activists for community empowerment.[22]

3

Health and Wellness

Duke Porter, age 20, and LaRie McGruder, age 18, are young adult leaders from New Haven, Connecticut, who have created a game called "Survivin'-N-Da-Hood," derived in part from their experiences with peer mediation among black adolescents (Weizel 1994). Ever since their mid-teens, the brother-sister team has been engaged in peer counseling activities, using conflict resolution techniques to disarm potentially violent disputes in the community. Yet the game was developed from personal experiences; both individuals have lost several friends to street violence and prison. The terrible tragedy of wasted lives in their own communities prompted Duke and LaRie to develop this activity, which enables high school participants to make realistic decisions about school, work, and socializing. The game's appeal is widespread. It is used in several peer tutoring programs in the city, and a club has been formed with about 75 teen-age members dedicated to helping peers make responsible life choices.

A park in southwest Detroit was the setting for a multimedia antiviolence program in the summer of 1993, co-sponsored by the Matrix Theatre and Latino Family Services Youth Center (Hopgood 1993). The event featured a morality play about gangs, drugs, and peer pressures, written by local youths at the Center who created large-scale puppets as a vehicle to disseminate their message about conflict resolution. The three puppets were "Fear" (ten feet tall and painted purple), "Pain," and "Faith," representing real-life concerns among the youths. Julius Matsey, age 16, one of the puppeteers, believes that this staged event will highlight the seriousness of teens' convictions about urban problems. These novice dramaturgists scripted the protagonist, Faith, to free the people from despair and eradicate Fear and Pain from their communities.

In the summer of 1993 in Atlanta, Lamar Harris spent his time assisting youths with a school play (Worrell 1993). Harris, 19, is an ex-football player who was shot in the back during an outburst of street violence involving a gang fight when in the tenth grade. He went on to finish high school and was planning to attend college. In responding to the call for community service that summer, Lamar vowed to tell the kids his experiences with gang membership.[1]

These are just three examples of youth leadership activities devoted to community service among many social projects that benefit adolescent health and safety. Duke and LaRie from New Haven, Julius from Detroit, and Lamar from Atlanta together are building better neighborhoods by engaging in democratic actions that draw upon their experiences to educate peers about an issue of real concern to teens: community violence.

Community Violence

Social and cultural progress is dependent upon quality peer interactions in which youths engage in learning opportunities with positive role models. Yet many children have great difficulty maintaining firm peer contacts. In home environments complicated by urban poverty, promising youths sometimes succumb to a social isolation that diminishes their chances for long-term positive social relationships. For example, children of public housing projects typically recoil from the violent life of their communities. "Isolated against an increasingly hostile world they hesitate to trust those in their immediate environment" (Schmitz 1992, p. 43). Children living in housing projects often feel doomed by dire poverty and related factors of crime, violence, fear, and isolation which subvert their chances at educational achievement and classroom success (see Kotlowitz 1991). When school settings themselves are sites of numerous criminal activities (Haas 1988), it would appear that children of poverty are increasingly victimized, doubly disadvantaged, and unable to escape the debilitating effects of campus and community violence.

Consider the dangerous world of today's youth. Teens experience a higher crime rate than any other age cohort. They are twice as likely as adults to be victims of theft and violence. In fact, in the twelve to nineteen age group (just 14 percent of the population age twelve or older), teens are likely to be victims on average of 1.9 million violent crimes and 3.3 million thefts annually (*Teenage Victims* 1991).

In a recent study by the National Center for Education Statistics (National Center 1993, Indicator 52), researchers found trend data suggesting that late teens, age sixteen to nineteen, are statistically the highest percentage victims of violent crime, including robbery, assault, and rape, among all youths (percentages are per thousand persons). Ninety-one percent of individuals in the 1991 cohort of teens were victims of crime. This is an increase of 19 percentage points over the same-age cohort of teens in 1988. If controlling for age and race, males in that same-age cohort exhibited an increase of 32 percentage points from 1988 to 1991. The highest percentages of crime victimization by race are blacks, age sixteen to nineteen. Evidently, in a time span of just three years, the data shows that youth's personal safety has eroded substantially.

What about the statistical indicators of youthful offenders? The data on the number of arrests per 1,000 persons revealed that late teens, age fourteen to seventeen, have the highest arrest ratios in the population (National Center 1993, Indicators 57 and 58). Their rate of 132 percent in 1990 outranks young adults, eighteen to twenty-four years, by about 6 percentage points, and middle-age adults, twenty-five to thirty-four years, by almost 50 percentage points. Of persons arrested in the fourteen to seventeen age group that same year, almost fifty out of a thousand persons were involved in some type of serious crime, larceny and theft being the most common type of criminal activity; vandalism and stolen property were leading minor offenses. Sadly, 13 percent of all youthful offenders under age eighteen in 1990 were arrested for murder or manslaughter. Arrest ratios for youthful offenders in the teenage cohort have remained relatively high, in triple-digit figures for the past twenty years.

Finally, we round out this compressed portrait of violent teenage life with a quick glimpse at youth indicators of death (National Center 1993, Indicator 51). The data suggests that the leading cause of mortality is homicide, with motor vehicle accidents second. Among non-white males in the fifteen to twenty-four age category, the death ratio by homicide is about ninety individuals out of every hundred thousand persons. The dramatic rise in violent deaths in America today is even more apparent when reviewing the data longitudinally. That is, in a time span of 30 years, from 1960 to 1990, the rate of deaths by homicide has doubled for non-white males. Non-white females have double-digit homicide rates as well (about 15 percent).

What possible impact could prevention projects have on educating youths in these violent times? Anti-violence trainings, such as conflict resolution, are noteworthy. Learning activities can engage teens in a comprehensive critical education that highlights positive alternatives in working together peaceably to deal with community problems. Public health expert Deborah Prothrow-Stith (1991, p. 28) argues that changing public behavior toward violence "requires a broad array of strategies; strategies that teach new ways of coping with anger and aggressive feelings." Powerful pedagogical messages can be delivered by peers (under the guidance of youth workers) who exert an important influence as mentors in the lives of socially isolated and disengaged youths (Swinehart 1990; Woyach 1993).

Teens often believe that their peers, who are similar to them in race and gender, also have allied values and attitudes. They may take gender and race into consideration, moreover, when viewing status groupings within classrooms and friendships at school (Hallinan and Williams 1990). Black adolescents, for instance, are more likely to seek out other students rather than adults when desiring to communicate their problems (Clark 1991). Age differences influence peer relationships as well. Teens may find that they are modeling the exact behaviors of their own adolescent reference groups, whereas, young adults may find that normative influences among peers may allow more individuality and freedom of expression (Bank, Slavings, and Biddle 1990).

Research on school-based peer tutoring (Maheady, Harper, and Mallette 1991), coaching (Hall and McKeen 1991), counseling (Diver-Stamnes 1991), and instruction (Farris 1991) suggests that there is a growing popularity in having youths turn to each other for information about the harsh realities they are faced with in daily settings. Peer education techniques are quite useful when dealing with teen health and welfare issues (Kim et al. 1992). Peer-led training has been offered in adolescent prevention education on smoking (Wiist and Snider 1991), runaway and homeless youth (Podschun 1993), alcohol abuse (Massey and Neidigh 1990), AIDS and HIV infection (Rickert, Jay, and Gottlieb 1991), adolescent pregnancy and parenting (Rubenstein, Panzarine, and Lanning 1990), and a variety of wellness topics, including weight control, nutrition, exercise, and worrying (Dittmar and Handwerk 1991).

The following anti-violence youth projects in Florida, Massachusetts, California, Georgia, and Connecticut offer examples of youth development through prevention education. We will see how inner-city youths are allied in coalitions and partnerships with adults (Hefner 1988; Nessel 1988).

Palm Beach County, Florida. In South Florida, eight African-American teens from Pleasant City organized a thirty-minute television talk show titled "Catch the 411," a one-time performance (funded in part by the MacArthur Foundation) featuring rap lyrics, street interviews, a panel discussion on "gangsta" rap with audience participation, and a marching band contest (James 1994). The theme of the show was gangster rap lyrics and their supposed violent effects on teenagers.[2] The teens chose gangster rap as a theme for the show, one of them voiced, because it "causes a lot of problems for adults. We're trying to listen to them, but they need to listen to our opinions, too." The youths are members of Center Stage players, a neighborhood arts group under the direction of an adult theatre professional. They rehearsed the show after school and on weekends over a three-month period.

Here are several highlights of the show.[3] In the street interview segment the group went to the county courthouse entrance and asked numerous individuals: How do you feel about gangster rap? Do you feel it affects teenagers? Do you feel so-called gangster rappers degrade women? Do you think gangster rap influences kids in joining gangs? Does it make our teenagers violent?

In the studio segment, the players organized a five-member panel of influential African-American members of the community. There was a director of outreach programs, an assistant middle school principal, two church pastors (one was president of the community's redevelopment corporation), and a gangster rapper named "Homicide" played by one of the Center Stage members. The adult panelists talked about the negative messages and profanity in rap. They saw no socially redeeming value in the music which, they remarked, cast a shadow over the community. Furthermore, they said the lyrics were degrading to women and detrimental to young people in general. The panelists fielded numerous questions from the studio audience.

In the next-to-last-segment, the players featured a challenge of the bands contest: video clips of high school and middle school marching band halftime football shows were featured with cash prizes of $200 and $300 raised from corporate sponsors going to the winners. The show concluded with the youths performing an anti-drugs rap song in front of their neighborhood community center.

"Catch the 411" might influence young viewers who are faced with pressures by some gangs to sell drugs and use guns, along with counter-pressures by their parents not to engage in illicit activities. Most teens do care about this double-bind that affects their daily lives, but few can clearly articulate their views to other peers in a "high concept" performing arts format.[4] Maybe rappers are most effective in communicating to teens in this regard. Thus, the Center Stage youths created a television show using rap songs to bolster their anti-violence messages. This show reached out to the television audience with an upbeat message that said teens do focus upon their own cultural struggles by engaging in problem-posing of issues concerning their community.

Boston, Massachusetts. An important street program named Gang Peace serves as a nonprofit violence prevention agency for local youth in the Roxbury section of Boston (Bowers 1992). Gang Peace, founded by Rodney Dailey in 1989, provides a safe place for adolescent clients who have been involved or hurt in gang activity or fear for their personal safety. They have a place to go after school with an understanding staff that involves teens in positive peer group support sessions and recreational, educational, and social activities.

Gang Peace is a primary advocate for the vocational development of clients as a way to stave-off the lure of gang membership. The organization, moreover, desires to free youths from the attraction of drugs and violence by raising the community's awareness of gang-related deaths. In fact, this program has been credited by the Boston Police Department with dramatically lowering the rate of homicides both city-wide and in the gang-ridden neighborhoods where Gang Peace clients reside.

Most youth workers know that they must first establish trust among the local gangs before they attempt to defuse potentially explosive situations. At Gang Peace, active gang members are given information about CPR techniques and first aid skills for victims of gunshot wounds, which could help save a member's life. In other instances, gang members receive job contacts or housing assistance or remedial education. Gang Peace staffers offer these youths a variety of nonviolent alternatives to resolving interpersonal conflicts.

Ongoing Gang Peace activities include: the street outreach program which works with active gang members to mediate and resolve disputes between various gangs or factions within gangs; violence prevention seminars (about 160 per year) for community organizations, schools, churches, and direct service providers; case management activities including counseling, guidance, support, court appearances, and youth services assistance serving more than 600 minority youths; a remedial tutoring program staffed by about forty-five young adult volunteer mentors from local colleges; and a job training program of career education, such as resume preparation, securing a job, and keeping or losing a job.

Additionally, Gang Peace helps clients with GED preparation and testing, offers entrepreneurship training in conjunction with Junior Achievement, gives assistance with school-assigned homework, and teaches workshops on health and wellness topics. Gang Peace operates a sound studio for neighborhood musical groups and a clothing and apparel business. The variety of social events includes rap competitions, talent shows, sober dances, cookouts, field trips, beauty pageants, and sports teams.

A monthly eight-page newsletter, titled "Peace Talk: The Stories Making Peace," is prepared by the youth clients with personal narratives as a vehicle for disseminating their voices into the community.[5] In Issue #2, for instance, the lead story tells of the death of May Flores, the twenty year-old receptionist of Gang Peace and mother of a three year-old girl. The article was written by her boyfriend's sister, Geneka, who recalls the love and energy radiating from May. Geneka, age 16, also contributed an article about growing up in the projects and the effects of death on the stability of her family life (an older brother is in prison for murder; an uncle was a victim of domestic violence). Geneka's brother and newsletter co-editor, Kayoss, offers a poem about his grief at losing his girlfriend May (pregnant with their child at the time of her death) and the feeling that he is alone now. The newsletter contains additional information such as telephone hotlines, announcements for meetings, a monthly calendar, and a puzzle game.

Gang Peace enjoys a good relationship with teens and gang members mostly because its director, Rodney Dailey, cares deeply about kids. Evidently, he is a "wizard," a term used by policy analysts Milbrey McLaughlin, Merita Irby, and Juliet Langman (1994) that refers to adults who lead youth organizations which succeed where many others have failed. Wizards create places where youths are welcomed, where they feel safe, where they are encouraged to be somebody, and where they can grow-up. Wizards develop "environments that draw adolescents, that demand and receive the commitment, energy, and hard work of youth. They reach, motivate, and promote young people, sometimes including gang members, whom many dismiss as unreachable, irredeemable, or hopeless" (p. xvii).

Dailey, a former gang member in his late 30s, is a role model for youths (Zoll 1994). He was into guns and drugs as a teen, and after entering a drug treatment program, he walked away from street violence forever. As a young adult, Dailey attended Roxbury Community College and later received his baccalaureate degree from the University of Massachusetts. But instead of leaving his own community after graduation, he stayed on in order to give back to his neighborhood something positive in the way of leadership development. Dailey converted the front part of his Roxbury apartment (the first floor of a former crack house) into a storefront street organization, and paid the monthly rent on the place through out-of-pocket expenses. Now, the nonprofit organization has four full-time staff, three hundred volunteers, and an annual budget of $300,000. They receive funding from public and private sources, including the United Way. Gang Peace is well recognized locally and nationally due to the efforts of Mr. Dailey.

Given the tremendous efforts of youth workers like Dailey to stem the tide of street violence in just a few neighborhoods, small-scale grassroots programs such as Gang Peace could be replicated throughout crime-ridden areas of Boston—and in most municipalities nationwide. Raising funds to support youth development specifically targeted to curb gang violence, however, is no easy task. As indicated in the next example, asking public officials to endorse a massive anti-violence prevention effort from the bottom up is fraught with political intricacies and fiscal entanglements.

Los Angeles, California. Consider the birthing pangs of "Hope in Youth," a city-wide violence prevention effort in Los Angeles County. In early 1992, a grassroots coalition of nine religious denominations and four community organizations proposed a comprehensive anti-gang program that calls for the creation of 160 family outreach teams of counselors, social workers, teachers, and parents to assist youths who are at-risk due to involvement in gangs. There are an estimated 100,000 gang members in the county. The teams would help the kids with their schooling, family problems, and job opportunities.

The coalition of interfaith pastors and community-based activists responded to the street violence that claimed 771 lives in L.A. County in 1991, and presented their projected budget in mid-March at a public rally drawing more than a thousand persons to a South Los Angeles church (Katz 1992a; Stammer and Rabin 1992). Hope in Youth would cost upwards of $20 million per year, coalition leaders estimated; the program operating for a five-year period would hire about five hundred paid street counselors. Most of the funds would be raised from churches and synagogues, private foundations, and among various quarters in city government.

Promises of municipal support for Hope in Youth surfaced later that year. In July the L.A. County Board of Supervisors pledged $2.9 million for the project (Katz 1992b), and in November the L.A. City Council voted to contribute $2.5 million dollars for the project (Rainey 1993). But the Mayor at that time, Tom Bradley, threatened to veto the project, saying the city could ill afford the costs. Interestingly, two opposing council members representing South-Central Los Angeles, the area hardest hit by the riots in April and May, feared that these funds would be diverted from the Community Redevelopment Agency's plans for building low-income housing in the fire-damaged community. Other critics charged that this new program was untested; its efficacy in curbing gang violence was being called into question. Some said that successful youth programs targeted to gang interventions already were in existence, and that Hope in Youth would be in competition for the scarce funds available. And a few opponents complained that not enough black churches were represented in the coalition.

Six months later, in July, 1993, the next mayor, Richard Riordan, officially released the funds for Hope in Youth (O'Neill 1993; Rainey 1993). Riordan backed the gang prevention program as a campaign pledge in his mayoral bid for office, and once elected he persuaded county officials to deliver on their earlier pledges. The church-led coalition, along with the four grassroots community organizations schooled in the activist politics of Saul Alinsky's Industrial Areas Foundation[6] (using highly visible public rallies and demonstrations with media presence) continually pressured their elected representatives to support the program. Then, in October, the County Supervisors finally relented and freed the $2.9 million promised a year earlier (Rivera 1993).

In preparing the budget for the next fiscal year, Riordan doubled the pot of money for Hope in Youth, but he ran into opposition by existing prevention agencies in the city that wanted the proposed financial support for their development efforts. After a series of amendments to the budget, mayoral vetoes, and a narrow vote in council chambers, a compromise measure was reached. The $5 million appropriation was split in half, with one-half of the money going to Hope in Youth and the other half to the remaining anti-gang agencies (Rainey and Corwin 1994).

What can we learn from this massive effort to combat community violence? The allocation of public monies for youth development programs often become subject to fickle political winds. For instance, $1.2 billion of federal funding for separate crime prevention programs, including Hope in Youth, were named in the Clinton Crime Bill of 1994 until bipartisan compromises in the House of Representatives cut these programs altogether and reduced funding down to $380 million for competitive block grant awards (Seelye 1994). With the politics of governmental devolution swiftly impacting the availability of funds, more nonprofit organizations these days are forced to seek alternative sources of support in the private sector.

Atlanta, Georgia. One community organizer in Atlanta told me that twenty dollars is all the money he needs in order to "make a healthy community."[7] A former county police officer and a prison guard, Tyrone, age forty, engaged African-American youths in small-group peer discussions at their community center. He holds group on Thursdays at 6:30 p.m. with boys aged eight to seventeen, and anywhere from three to twenty show up at any given time. His strategy is to get $20 in pizza to entice the boys into the center's lounge for a meal between recreational periods. Then, as Tyrone facilitates, the boys talk for about an hour on a variety of personal issues stemming from their lived experiences, such as sexuality, violence, and drug use. Tyrone concentrates upon conflict resolution strategies, sometimes using audio-visual and curricular resources he borrows from a local substance abuse prevention center.

One time he didn't have the money—twenty dollars is equivalent to his monthly power bill, he offered—to bring pizza, and one tough kid, a drug pusher, started to challenge him. The youth got the others to leave the session. Then, all of the boys started throwing rocks at Tyrone's truck and at Tyrone. They said something like "Don't be coming around here; but if you come, bring pizza." Tyrone suggested to me that this meant the boys *did* want him around, but they were testing him. They gave him an "out," so to speak: if he wasn't afraid of them, he'd be welcome back, and, as a show of good faith, he would remember to bring pizza.

Tyrone talked to me about the role model he projected for the boys; his purpose was to show them he was "willing to die" for something. Youth workers like Tyrone recognize the need for adults to help young men realize their responsibilities as future fathers. Too often boys just don't know what is involved in a positive male parenting relationship, particularly with regard to child raising.

Bridgeport, Connecticut. Some anti-violence projects offer parenting skills for males, providing fathers' support groups, home visits, and peer counseling sessions. One notable, long-standing teen father's program in Connecticut, for instance, located at the Bridgeport Y.M.C.A., was visited by First Lady Hillary Clinton during one of her husband's presidential campaign stops (Fitzpatrick 1994). Director Manuel (Manny) Cardona, connected with this particular program for over twelve years, offers that most of the boys don't know how to be a father because they are from single-parent

families. In order to recruit Latino boys into the program in its earliest days, he relates, posters were hung in the men's rooms of local
bars and boys' clubs. He also visited recreation areas, stopped at
street corners, and talked to young fathers in the East End, the
Hispanic community of Bridgeport. Nowadays the boys just walk
into his office; they know where they can find Manny.

When Mrs. Clinton visited the program in 1992, she met teen
father Alex Morales who talked about his proud commitment to
care for his infant son. The next year Alex was murdered in the
city, a victim of street violence. Alex was a symbol, Manny relates,
of the precarious future facing young fathers who are exposed
daily to street life with its drugs and guns, gangs and violence,
poverty and joblessness, despair and hopelessness.

Springfield, Massachusetts. At the Dunbar Community Center
in Springfield, Arthur Robinson builds African-American esteem
through self-empowerment activities for males, ages six to eighteen,
many of whom come from single-family households without a live-
in father.[8] Robinson, coordinator of "Project Access," explains that
this peer program gives youths the abilities to make educated decisions for themselves in an attempt to "recapture and reclaim the
developmental process" from the streets.

In an effort to curb youth violence, for instance, Robinson
teaches the boys what he terms "self-defense," that is, creative conflict resolution strategies that help them to recognize the warning
signs of potentially hazardous encounters and trouble spots. In
fact, several of the project participants showcased their knowledge
of conflict resolution skills in a role-playing exercise and discussion
group held at the third annual citywide "Make It Happen Youth
Conference." Peer-led workshops were offered on a variety of topics,
including racism, HIV/AIDS and STD prevention, peer pressures,
dating issues, communication and leadership skills, and dropping
out of school. Ten of the Dunbar youths helped to organize the teen
conference; another six facilitated the workshops.

Crime prevention is just one part of an extensive curriculum
at Project Access with the following eight program objectives: (a)
develop an understanding of African and African-American history
and culture; (b) understand the importance of wellness; (c) understand the importance of spirituality; (d) develop an understanding

of cooperative economic systems; (e) develop decision-making skills for self-awareness and personal planning; (f) understand the importance of leadership; (g) understand the concept of community service; and (h) develop an understanding of manhood and womanhood.

Adult male mentors play an integral part in the guidance of boys through the curricular objectives of this program. They are "the resources" that Robinson turns to for assistance with youth development. When they visited a computer manufacturing firm owned by African-Americans in town, for example, the boys got to see a model of black entrepreneurship for economic and enterprise development. Other mentorship opportunities give the boys opportunities to interact with adult males through community service, recreational, educational, and social activties.

These adult-youth relationships embody what youth policy expert Marc Freedman (1993, pp. 34–35) refers to as the three essential elements in the classical concept of mentorship: *achievement*, which gives the boys encouragement and succor from adults along the developmental path; *nurturance*, which provides the boys with a transitional figure as chaperone for their life lessons; and *generativity*, which propels the boys toward their own assumption of voluntary duties with the next generation.

Project Access's male mentors, moreover, being dedicated to helping boys become men, receive training in a formal ritual ceremony. Modeled along the lines of Afrocentrist's Jawanza Kunjufu's (1985) Simba program or Nathan and Julia Hare's (1985) passage plan, this ritual prepares them to assist with the socialization and development of Robinson's participants. These mentors offer their guidance so that the initiates can obtain the necessary skills for completion of the curriculum. The ritual ceremony is scheduled to be held in conjunction with yearly Kwanzaa festivities. The urgency of this process is accentuated by Kunjufu (1985):

> We must develop programs and organizations to protect and develop African-American boys because a conspiracy exists to destroy African-American boys. The motive of the conspiracy is racism, specifically European-American male supremacy. . . . The method is to eliminate positive male role models; discourage emotional and spiritual development; de-emphasize academics (p. 32).

Project Access is an Afrocentric youth development program that emphasizes cultural awareness and black pride.[9] It teaches young black men about their ancestral roots, offering them a clearer sense of self-identity and exposing them to a framework for planning their future life course.

Conclusion

The variety of prevention programs just profiled gives young people what writer and poet Luis Rodriguez (1993, p. 9) calls "complete literacy" by offering adolescents a variety of positive strategies to help facilitate their entry into adulthood. This form of literacy enables them "to participate competently and confidently in any level of society one chooses" by combining skills for self-preservation on the streets with conflict resolution and anti-violence trainings (see Prothrow-Stith 1991) and an undertanding of their own racial and ethnic identities, through workshops on racism and cultural oppressions (see Nieto 1992).

In the preface to *Always Running*, his autobiography of gang life in Los Angeles in the 1960s and 1970s, Rodriguez (1993) writes of the trepidation that he feels today for his teenage son, Ramiro, who may be lost to the violent streets as well. He tells of how Ramiro needs a critical education which illuminates "the systematic nature" of what is occurring to Chicano adolescents in their own impoverished neighborhoods (see Moore 1991).

Rodriguez relates two incidents in Ramiro's life that point out the potential for critical understanding. One time, the boy and a few of his friends were picked up by the police and dropped in a nearby barrio where they were forced to "tag" their insignias in the presence of rival gang members. Then they were left to find their own way home—a common police practice, we are told. Another time, aware of the shooting death of a Puerto Rican friend named Efrain by the Latin Kings, Ramiro drove through that gang's territory and saw their graffiti that celebrated the killing with "Efrain Rots" exhibited on one wall. These events made Ramiro think about the choices he must make, his father writes, "not just once, but every time they come up" (1993, p. 10).

How does Rodriguez know that Ramiro can puzzle-out the events of his daily experiences in order to set himself on a more righteous or moral path? There are no certainties here. Yet in his memoir, begun when he was sixteen but left unfinished until his teenage son joined a gang in Chicago, Rodriguez reveals those critical incidences where a young Luis came into contact with caring adults. For instance, Rodriguez recalls how neighborhood prevention programs had a major impact upon his growth, providing close personal contact with youth workers who cared about the positive development of Chicano teens. He fondly remembers Chente, director of the John Fabela Youth Center, who offered young Luis a job at the neighborhood Youth Corps, where teenagers were engaged in a variety of community service activities. Time and again Chente created possibilities for Rodriguez's healthy development. As project supervisor one summer, for instance, Luis led thirteen gang members in a mural program. Chente once saw the crude barrio images Luis had painted in his bedroom. Later, anticipating Rodriguez's interest in community art, he purchased for Luis a coffee-table edition of Mexican muralists. "There are lots of people involved in your life now," Chente once remarked to Rodriguez (1993, p. 159), reminding him that numerous caring adults will nurture his interests in positive ways. Chente cautioned Luis, however, that the struggles for growth and development are fraught with personal choices.

One time Chente invited Rodriguez to attend weekly consciousness-raising sessions comprised of activists and students. But one night Luis came to the study group high on drugs. When Chente realized Luis's state of mind, he remarked (1993, p. 159), "What we're doing is not something you decide to do when you feel like it. Whether you're ready or not, this struggle will go on. . . . Either the craziness and violence [of the streets]—or here, learning and preparing for a world in which none of this [escape through drugs] is necessary."

4

Street Arts

Street arts allow students opportunities to understand their world in meaningful ways; they realize a cultural identity and self-affirmation from the public who views their work. In this sense, there is a progressive civic impulse embedded in the activity of showcasing visual and performing arts, because anti-elitist connections between cultural production and viewing through public exhibition (in performance halls and gallery spaces) finds alternative channels.[1]

There is a recent tradition of train paintings on subway cars in places around New York City that emerged in the 1960s as "self-identifying messages" by inner-city teens (Castleman 1982). Ironically, works by major figures in this art underworld are coveted by gallery owners and museum curators today. For our understanding of youth development and critical education, however, we wonder how these teens, fearing arrest, developed the skills and social networks to create designs and execute graffiti writings in dangerous train yards and tunnels at night. What was the instructional process in this community of subaltern participants? Researcher Craig Castleman (1982) explains at length:

> Long before they attempt to paint on trains, young writers will develop their style through practice in sketch pads and often on walls around their neighborhoods. They also will frequently seek out more experienced writers to teach them the ropes. Young writers who do not have the skill or talent necessary to create designs of their own will often ask more skillful friends to "give" them styles. "Master" writers will frequently have one (perhaps a younger brother) or even a large group of young proteges whom they will bring along. Writers

seem to enjoy the role of teacher and take pride in the accomplishments of their students, as well as take pleasure in the admiration and respect they receive from them (p. 24).

Today some graffiti writers are provided a socially acceptable alternative in which to channel their creative energies (through sign painting, silkscreening, photography, sculpture, videography, and mural making). The Los Angeles Conservation Corps, for instance, employs teenage graffiti writers to work as muralists in a federally-funded program to curtail wanton vandalism in the city (Pool 1992). In Philadelphia, the Anti-Graffiti Network, a nonprofit, city-run program to stop spray-can vandalism, has been in operation since 1984 (Finnigan 1991). The participants work with spray cans, but their artistic images and designs are derived from positive themes (they even engage in library research for ideas). The quality of their graffiti is better than hastily tagged writings as well; other street artists tend to respect these large-scale, colorful wall murals. And the positive reinforcement for their art from passersby is a boon to these youths' self-esteem and moral development.

The designing and painting of contemporary wall murals is an appropriate vehicle for youth development that lends itself to the production of social images of inner-city life in affirming the lived experiences of low-income residents by drawing their attention, as a street audience, into grassroots communications. "Through the murals, the people have reappropriated art as visual expression," claim Eva Cockcroft, John Weber, and James Cockcroft (1977), three American experts on this particular public art form. They continue:

From the onset the murals have had an audience; community residents have celebrated, loved, and protected them because they have had a part in them. They have seen images of their humanity reflected in the murals. The murals have told the people's own story, their history and struggles, their dignity and hopes (p. xxii).

Community muralists work in the tradition of the famous Mexican artists Diego Rivera and José Orozco, whose visions of social realism told a story of the people's struggles under oppressive colonialism. But unlike these protest artists, contemporary muralists dedicate their art and their social activism to a ghetto or barrio realpolitik that brings them into grassroots organizing, specifically with area youth.

Outdoor mural-makings on the walls of city buildings are labor-intensive activities usually involving one or two professional artists and a handful of untrained individuals. Neighborhood teens are often employed on these projects (during the summer months and in non-school hours in the academic year) and are useful helpers, especially lending their physical prowess to the lifting and placing of scaffoldings and platforms for paintings that range in heights up to forty feet.

The street life during execution of mural paintings comes alive with passers-by eagerly asking questions about designs and the meanings of visual imagery. The worksite on the street becomes what mural expert Alan Barnett (1984, p. 17) terms "an ongoing town meeting" because community residents young and old alike are drawn into the process; merchants contribute art supplies, neighborhood children occassionally ask for a brush, street corner winos offer design criticism, and police officers comment on the progress.

At the site of one mural in the Uptown neighborhood on Chicago's near-Northside, artist Turbado Marabou recounted these aspects of a "town meeting" during the two weeks it took his crew of six local teens and one artist's assistant to complete their wall project, titled "Living Off the Waters of Creation":[2] Young kids came by and asked to paint (they were given a *very small* brush). People from nearby apartment buildings looked out their windows periodically to view the progress. An orange-robed Hindu swami who lived nearby was a colorful pedestrian, and his likeness was incorporated into the mural design. The prostitutes, alcoholics, and drug dealers who frequented that street corner where the mural was placed moved to the opposite side of the street during its execution. A spray-artist stopped by to assess the quality of workmanship, and Turbado let him "hang with the situation." An older street artist who frequented the worksite was named in the mural's credit box out of respect for his seniority among graffiti writers. Numerous people came by to speak to Turbado and ask questions of him and his helpers, monitoring the situation as it progressed, perhaps claiming they didn't understand the meaning of the mural, or simply thanking the artist for helping to beautify the community. Mr. Imagination (a.k.a. Gregory Warmack), a nationally known self-taught Chicago artist, was on the street viewing the completed mural as well.[3]

Another way to capture the lived experiences of urban youths in development projects is through the performing arts. Agitprop stagings have been a mainstay of radical political organizing in this country, especially within the twentieth-century trade union movement (see Taylor 1972). By combining activist politics and aesthetic images, some of the earliest imaginative theatrical pieces ushered forth a variety of thematic perspectives on the working-class struggles at hand.[4] For example, in response to a 10 percent wage cut in 1926, the textile workers in Passaic, New Jersey, went on strike. Their efforts were embodied in Michael Gold's *Strike!*, produced by the Workers' Drama League, an organization composed of American playwrights with leftist leanings. By the middle of the next decade, a host of full-length radical plays opened at professional theatres on Broadway in New York City; other productions were staged locally and in regional workers' or college theatres nationwide. In postwar America, radical playwrights went to the streets once again to gather material from rallies, demonstrations, and marches in the era of civil rights, Vietnam protests, the women's liberation movement, gay and lesbian rights, environmental justice, and other democratic exercises in the public sphere.

A lasting boost in community arts occurred during the Depression, when the U.S. government funded a number of innovative programs through the Works Progress Administration and the Farm Securities Administration. Among the most noted efforts in the 1930s were the documentary photographs taken of dust-bowl migrants, the post-office wall murals, the Federal Theatre project, and the folk recordings of Appalachian Mountain musicians.

Continuing in this vein is the Foxfire project, a community arts program begun in the late 1960s that affords youths the opportunity to explore the rich heritage of their Southern Appalachian communities (see Wiggington 1973). In the North Georgia mountain town of Rabun Gap, Foxfire founder Eliot Wigginton created an innovative program for high school youths to interview elderly residents and document their experiences in rural ways. The students captured the craft production techniques and homemaking skills of their elders in visual and written form and produced a series of popular trade books recording these efforts.

How are urban youths introduced to community arts? In Boston, for example, a nonprofit program called Artists for Humanity offers inner-city teenagers opportunities to explore their creative energies through a variety of visual projects (Ross 1992a). Their paintings on T-shirts, murals, and found objects such as furniture, ladders, and doors originate from the lived experiences of each participant. One door painting features a black male with a target painted on his chest; he is standing in flames in front of an American flag backdrop. The T-shirts display urban images, many of which depict gang violence.

The career development outcomes of programs like this comprise an important objective for securing funding in the community arts world (mainly through federal summer youth employment program funds) and help youths with entrepreneurship training for marketing their works, managing their studios, and operating student-run businesses. Many program participants have elevated their self-esteem and improved their communication skills through venues which require public speaking to diverse audiences in order to explain the art projects. Interestingly, the youth workers at Artists for Humanity contend that teens can overcome their fears of death and violence through the making of street art. A mural program for middle school students offers collaboration on designing and executing images of community life. In this sense, creative and therapeutic designs are "a perfect nonviolent expression. . . . without destroying public property or hurting someone else," the program director notes (Ross 1992a, p. 14).

The visual and performing arts for inner-city youths are democratizing influences reaching outward to new communities of individuals engaged in the creative process and to new venues for attracting audiences interested in these forms of cultural expression. Kids react positively when they realize that their works are legitimized in public spaces as mural designs on street corner buildings, as sculpture in transportation centers, or as theatrical performances in park district buildings (see Heath and McLaughlin 1994b). What follows is a profile of five street arts projects in the cities of Chicago and Atlanta.

Dance

"Moving in the Spirit" (MITS) is an urban arts project for youths at risk in inner-city Atlanta that uses dance as a vehicle to instill the workplace values of discipline, commitment, responsibility, and accountability.[5] (See Figure 4.1) This unique after-school program, over eight years old, empowers young people to become self-reliant by applying business procedures to the dance experience. This means students enter into an "incentive system" (negotiated with the directors of the nine community centers or shelters where this service is being offered) which rewards them with daily points for successful participation in program activities, including punctuality, calling in when sick, and staying the entire time. Bonus points are given as well for activities such as teaching class, performing at special events, and helping with office clerical duties. At the end of their term, depending upon the incentive system in place at that site, the students will have earned enough points or "MITS dollars" for, say, a pizza party, gift certificates to a local record shop, coupons for grocery store purchases, or transportation vouchers.

In the Apprentice Corporation, for instance, MITS's teen performance company, adolescents used the incentive system as a way for participants to earn 1,200 "dollars," the purchase cost for joining the summer road tour to performance bookings at various sites around the country. Any remaining "dollars" accrued by the students are used to "purchase" donated items of clothing, toys, jewelry, and electronics in the MITS Christmas Store. The teens are issued checking accounts for over-the-counter transactions, giving them a sense of realistic financing.

MITS co-founder and executive director Dana Marschalk described the faith-based origins of this project.[6] In the summer of 1986, after graduating from the University of Georgia with a degree in small business administration, she participated as a counselor in a summer Bible camp with children from a local housing project in urban Atlanta. There she realized that short-term "bootstrap" projects by well-meaning social reformers like herself could not really build genuine community with low-income people; the youth workers always leave the inner-city at the end of the summer. "There is not a basis for a real relationship here," she thought.

FIGURE 4.1

Moving in the Spirit. National Tour Explosion. Photograph by Louie
Favorite. Dancer: Chris McCord

Out on the streets one day after camp she noticed that the kids were dancing; a natural part of their lived cultural experiences, they were just making up steps. Dana had a background in dance at the University and so she started to do their movements—"very street, very beebop." Her dancing with them built the bridge for a real relationship. The most valuable thing she realized that summer, which she continues to relearn every day, is that "it's not about giving them all this wonderful information (by which to change their lifestyles); it's about working together, feeling that they are valuable, affirming who they are as individuals."

Moving in the Spirit offers four programs and services for critical education: Stepping Stones, The Apprentice Corporation, The Performance Company, and The Resource Network. Stepping Stones is an entry-level program using dance as a means to reinforce school curriculum. More than three hundred children, ranging in age from primary grades to high school, participate in the program in weekly after-school classes in nine community-based sites. Each dance teacher in this program is required to keep a notebook in order to track the progress of their kids, monitor the incentive system for point accrual, record a daily journal entry of reflection upon their students and classes, update or revise their lesson plans, and maintain a file of parental permission/release forms.

The Apprentice Corporation is an advanced program for teen dancers (many of whom participated in Stepping Stones). Membership is by yearly audition, and classes emphasize problem solving and creativity. There are twelve dancers in the company, a multiracial, multiethnic, and gendered mix of inner-city kids who perform in public spaces in the city as well as in summer venues throughout the U.S. Multiple cultural struggles are reified in the making of dances within this urban ensemble. For instance, in the 1994 tour season, choreographic titles and themes included: "Force" addressing the absurdity of violence, "Pressure" dealing with the stark statistics of teenage pregnancy, "Behind Dark Glasses" addressing the issue of self-esteem and the painful road to healing, "Freedom" promoting racial reconciliation, "Preconceptions" encouraging teenagers to postpone sexual involvement, and "Pregnant Pause" illustrating the possible consequences of fly-by-night relationships.

The Performance Company is a multicultural and intergenerational professional modern dance ensemble that addresses issues of urban culture and social justice. They produce two major productions each year and are featured at local cultural events in the city of Atlanta. These dancers also serve as role models for younger dancers in MITS programs. The Resource Network coordinates volunteers, instructors, mentors, and workshop leaders as resource support for youth participants in MITS programs. The Network's mission is accomplished through counseling and training in the areas of career opportunities, public speaking, alcohol and drug abuse, AIDS education, and teen pregnancy prevention.

Moving in the Spirit is located at the FCS Urban Ministries, a faith-based organization that sponsors a wide variety of programs for low-income residents in three Southeast Atlanta neighborhoods.[7] FCS Urban Ministries provide affordable housing, affordable goods and services, family health care, neighborhood land acquisition, low-income rental property management, sports leagues, tutorial services, mentoring programs, and youth development activities, among others.

Photography

The Youth Photography Education Project offers community photographing sessions as well as classroom and darkroom study for inner-city teens.[8] This six-week program, first held in the summer of 1991, reached out to housing project youths through coalition-building activities that drew a neighborhood social service agency, a tenant association, and an area church into partnership with a nonprofit organization of photographers and artists, as well as two academic departments at a historically black university in Atlanta. A number of volunteer-mentors, including several professional photojournalists (two from the local newspaper), worked with the teens that summer as well. In-kind and technical support was provided by area camera shops and photo businesses.

The purpose of this photo project was to provide twelve low-income youths, ages ten to fifteen, a chance to study and view their own community in novel and unique ways. The students were taught how to use the camera, encouraged to document their community, and asked to improve their observational and writing skills.

One day a week was devoted to community photographing sessions; they took pictures of whatever caught their fancy—building structures, people on the streets, gardens and trees, motor vehicles, friends, family members, etc. The second day each week was taken up with classroom writing and darkroom activities. Students learned the rudiments of photography, such as naming camera parts, loading and unloading film, identifying darkroom chemicals, and developing and printing photos. Participants were also given literacy techniques for naming their art through text. In this activity, students learned to write brief descriptions of their photographs, drawing out their ideas and feelings about the content of their work in narrative form. They were asked to describe the composition of their pictures as well. For this activity students kept a journal in which to record the details of their community photo sessions.

In the three months of autumn after the project ended, two exhibitions of the students' work were held, one at the housing project's community center and the other at a local art gallery. The show, titled "My Neighborhood: Through a Camera," featured the youths' black-and-white photos from their summer session. It should be noted that each image in the gallery exhibition was available to the public for a purchase price of sixty dollars, 60 percent of which went directly to the artists and 30 percent went into funding the next year's Youth Photography Education Program.

Interestingly, the next year a "Kids Eye View" program was co-sponsored by the local newspaper and the regional offices of Eastman Kodak Company. This was another collaborative venture involving local youths from the Atlanta Housing Authority communities as apprentice photojournalists. Eight teenagers were hired in the summer of 1992 to document the fifty-nine events at the National Black Arts Festival in Atlanta. The kids' photos and accompanying text were published in a festival catalogue, highlighting the photographers' feelings and thoughts about this special celebration of black heritage through the arts.

Fine Arts

A successful community arts program in Chicago named Gallery 37 makes it possible for urban youths to receive arts instruction along with summer employment.[9] This eight-week pro-

gram brings talented teens from a variety of neighborhoods, operating under large tents on a three-acre site in the downtown area.
Begun in 1991 by the Chicago Department of Cultural Affairs and
funded in part by the federal Job Training Partnership Act/
Summer Youth Employment Program, Gallery 37 has employed
more than 1,200 youths as apprentice artists at the gallery space
in the first three years of operation. Due to its highly visible location in "the Loop," Gallery 37 brings community arts directly to the
public. Passers-by are allowed access to the site in order to view
the works-in-progress, participate in outreach events during the
week and free art classes on Saturdays, purchase original artwork
at a retail tent, or attend a live performance. Each tent houses
temporary studios where teens learn the skills of jewelry and
adornment, architecture and design, ceramics, mosaics, print-
making, weaving, furniture painting, textile arts, creative writing,
journalism and photography, videoarts, and percussion work. (See
Figure 4.2)

Apprentice artists are chosen for this program through a competitive juried selection and/or interview process. Each youth's
visual or literary artistic talent is evaluated through portfolio sub-
missions of samples of their work, including a letter of recommen-
dation from their teacher or community leader. All applicants are
required to take a basic skills math and reading test prior to
employment (a post-test is administered upon program completion
as well). Apprentices are hired in the downtown gallery and at
eleven neighborhood sites. The teens work twenty hours per week
at minimum wage. About three-fourths of the apprentices are
minorities: In the summer of 1994, for instance, with more than
nine hundred youth artists downtown and at neighborhood sites,
43 percent were African-American and 21 percent were Latino, with
8 percent Asian/Pacific Islander and 1 percent Native American. In
addition, 60 percent of the teens are economically disadvantaged.[10]

Gallery 37 provides summer employment to professional
artists as instructors and teaching assistants. Their presence
offers numerous opportunities for mentoring relationships and
leadership roles between youths and established artists. Over con-
secutive summers, if selected, the more advanced apprentices rise
in the ranks to become senior crew leaders and, if possible, teaching assistants to the instructors.

FIGURE 4.2

Gallery 37. A mural project led by local artist Ivan Watkins and Mexican artist Alejandro Romero who worked with the apprentice artists to create this colorful piece of public art. Photograph by Dawn Martinez.

Neighborhood kids can benefit from the outreach efforts of Gallery 37 as well. The satellite sites attempt to capture the interests of youths through creative activities that affirm the cultural identities of each residential area. Satellite artists in several Latino communities, for instance, concentrated their efforts on creating crafts and multimedia projects with Mexican, Puerto Rican, and Afro-Caribbean influences. Additionally, with co-sponsorship by the Chicago Public Art Group (profiled in the next section), project teens assisted in the painting of several wall murals. At a southside Chicago site named Gallery 50, apprentice artists painted a mural in Ma Houston Park (named after a noted local female civil rights activist) that reflected African-American themes in the traditions of arts, athletics, community empowerment, education and family.[11]

At another satellite on the north side of town, named Gallery Uptown, apprentice artists painted a mural on the outside wall of the Prologue School, an alternative high school for at-risk teens.[12] The images portrayed the vivid street life of this dangerous, gang-infested neighborhood. Out of respect for two African-American educators at the school, their portraits were embodied in the foreground of the mural with both figures pointing to a symbolic schoolbuilding in the upper-right-hand-corner with a graffiti slogan written on its walls, "Education is not a privilege; it is a right!" Perhaps this was done as a totemic reminder to pedestrians that there is indeed hope and promise for youths in this abject community.

Gallery 37 was named for the vacant downtown site, Block 37, that remains undeveloped due to a depressed real estate market. In tranforming an empty lot into lively gallery space in the heart of the city, however, critical educators now gain a valuable lesson in how to recast job training programs.[13] Rather than establish another "make work" project for unemployed urban teens, Gallery 37 became a prototype for youth development that combines arts instruction with meaningful work experiences. An exemplary program model to be copied by other communities, Gallery 37 is visibly on the streets, hiring professional artists, providing public gallery spaces throughout the city, and offering quality art supplies and state-of-the-art equipment to local youths simply so that they might celebrate, affirm, cherish, identify, share, and enjoy the cultural diversity of their own experiences.

Murals

The Chicago Public Art Group (CPAG) is a long-standing collective of talented visual artists who assist communities in the creation of public art works, specifically wall murals, sculptures, and mosaics.[14] CPAG principals have been responsible for ushering forth a contemporary mural renaissance in Chicago. Through community partnerships with social service agencies, labor organizations, schools, neighborhood associations, and business groups, their efforts have led to the development, design, and execution of over 150 works of public art.

First organized in 1970 as the Chicago Mural Group (CMG) by John Weber and William Walker, this multiracial and multiethnic collective of twelve muralists joined in a grassroots organizing effort with neighborhood groups for purposes of awakening cultural awareness through public art (Cockcroft, Weber, and Cockcroft 1977). From its inception, co-founder Weber sought the participation of local teenagers "from economically deprived and culturally excluded communities" to work alongside professional muralists in neighborhood-based projects (1977, p. 150). The hiring of youths as assistants was considered integral to the achievement of genuine community-building practices; otherwise, it might be misconstrued that the mural projects were just another format for commissioned works by artists isolated from their public audiences. In other words, CMG actively sought the inclusion of youths in mural-making efforts, desiring to utilize the talents of promising young artists for purposes of teaching them "the trade."

CPAG has continued the tradition of youth apprenticeships as artist assistants in neighborhood public arts projects. In its best sense, this training model becomes what youth policy analysts Shirley Brice Heath and Milbrey McLaughlin (1994b, p. 487) term "an institution of curricular authenticity." The point here is that individuals are not one-dimensional recipients of learning. In apprenticeships and peer education settings, youths become actively engaged in complex levels of meaning-making through the execution of real-life tasks. Their social participation is interdependent with a sense of belonging and working together "in ongoing communities of practice." "Learners in groups," these two analysts note, "have access to the social distribution of knowledge and

FIGURE 4.3

Chicago Public Art Group (1). Students painting the collaboratively designed mural *By All Means Necessary*. Photograph by Olivia Gude.

skills through personal, interpersonal, and community working together" (1994b, p. 473).

Consider the sociocultural context of a mural design process in its formative stages. In the summer of 1992, a collaborative mural project joined CPAG, Gallery 37, and the Neighborhood Institute (a grassroots economic development agency in the South Shore area of Chicago) and led to employment for thirteen teen apprentices, ages fourteen to nineteen, and three professional artists. Together they created a two-thousand square foot outside wall mural titled "By All Means Necessary" that invokes African motifs and images of American popular culture in a black and white palette.[15] (See Figures 4.3, 4.4, & 4.5) Their input into this project was truly participatory. "Our conversations were far-reaching and sophisticated," the CPAG artists Olivia Gude and Dorian Sylvain noted. "Several students commented on the complexity of

FIGURE 4.4

Chicago Public Art Group (2). Students painting the collaboratively designed mural *By All Means Necessary*. Photograph by Olivia Gude.

FIGURE 4.5

Chicago Public Art Group (3). Students painting the collaboratively designed mural *By All Means Necessary.* Photograph by Olivia Gude.

the issues, the many angles from which a problem could be viewed." "We focused on interlocking visually and thematically the many issues facing young people in the community." After several weeks of group discussions and design proposals, the mural theme and "organizing principle" were chosen by consensus: "By All Means Necessary," one youth's misquote of Malcolm X's noted saying "By Any Means Necessary." Then, the team commenced work on the mural plan. CPAG artists reported at length:

> We used various art exercises to develop the mural plan. We explored abstract relationships of black and white, made thumbnail sketches, drew various ideas and images, and did visual research.

Students were assigned to generate images for various sub-themes. Typically, an inititial sketch would be developed and re-developed by other students and artists, working back and forth with the original creator. Though some students made "specialities" of such areas as initial visualization or abstract designs, we challenged all students to develop skills in refining artwork. Though all ages of youth artists participated in this work, it was clear that regardless of other talent, the older students had more patience for learning how to carefully develop early sketches through several stages.

The final drawing was put together as a collage. We made extensive use of the xerox machine to adjust the sizes of various components. On the last days of design, the artists and students clustered around the final drawing carefully inking areas and refining the junctures between areas.

At the end of the design process, we held a critique in which the students evaluated their work by the standards they had developed during the first week. We feel this is a particularly important part of the process because in an age of multiculturalism, it is vital that young artists understand the multiplicity of ways that a work of art can be viewed.

Certainly one could argue that this group of youths came together in an apprenticeship setting for pecuniary advantages alone—guaranteed employment for six weeks of the summer. By actively including their participation in all stages of the mural production, however, CPAG artists expected more out of their charges than just hired help. The lengthy description just presented of the design process confirms that indeed these youths were valued and dedicated members of that indigenous community, with imaginative ideas and creative thoughts put to good use in a collaborative venture. Even their individual talents, such as graffiti lettering, were affirmed by the professional muralists who "respected and incorporated" their writings into the mural; the youths were "challenged to develop and expand their artistic range." CPAG's artists valued the youths' self-expressions and openly taught them first-hand technical skills and aesthetic sensibilities in a public arts project devoted to objectifying their cultural identities. And, as testament to the success of an authentic apprenticeship experience using groups of inner-city teens, CPAG artists could report that: "The students formed a cohesive, disciplined and loving team."

Theatre

The vocational and career development aspects of a critical education extend into the performing arts as well.[16] For instance, on the day I visited "TeenStreet," a grassroots performance project of Chicago's Free Street Theatre (FST), that afternoon's activities included a "jobs forum" on career opportunities led by five guest speakers.[17] At the start of the session, each of the presenters shared their educational achievements, occupational trainings, and performance credits with the kids. There was a stage manager, a theatre critic and dramatist, a dancer and arts administrator, an actor and FST board member, and an assistant to a casting director. Then, each guest speaker led a discussion section for purposes of explaining in greater detail the various nuances of their professions. In one section, for instance, the kids were shown a sample resume and asked to think about the importance of gathering references. In another section, the presenter talked about theatrical "cattle calls" and the way dancers are chosen for performances by audition. One speaker showed a series of composite photographs, or "head shots," and told the kids about the importance of starting their own portfolios. After about an hour, when all of the teens had attended each session, the participants reconvened for a panel discussion on career issues. A few questions were fielded by the panelists from among the twenty-two teens in attendance, participants in the FST employment program for low-income youths.

TeenStreet participants were exposed to a number of career exploration activities in that six-week summer program. A "tech forum" was held which featured a different set of guest speakers: a theatrical producer, a stage manager, a technical director, and a set designer. The kids also toured performance spaces in the city, which rounded out their exposure to the arts and entertainment industry. This model of critical education, most importantly, offers underemployed and underprivileged inner-city youths theatrical training while earning wages in an employment setting as "performer trainees." Program participants create and develop original theatre works, and then present them at city park settings and neighborhood festivals.

TeenStreet prepares youths in the performance arts with a heavy emphasis upon the development of job skills such as self-discipline, self-esteem, punctuality, taking direction, focus, and team work, leading to career successes. Each applicant's creativity is tapped in the writing of twenty-minute ensemble pieces during the summer program, an authentic learning outcome that advances their literacy and communication levels as well.

At the beginning of the school year, talented participants in the summer program are invited to audition for a place in the professional youth troupe. This performance company engaged in shows that resonate with the lived experiences—and raw emotions—of urban kids exposed to violence, drugs, unemployment, and poverty in their gang-infested residential and housing project communities throughout the city. In 1992, the company created "Standing Out in a Drive-by World," an hour-long show about teenage identities that won praise from audiences and critics alike. Their next production, "Learning to Breathe in a Box," is a piece about how teens keep faith in themselves—against all odds. Their latest show, "Mad Joy," written and performed by the teen company, displays an eclectic mix of classical music, hip-hop jazz, and bebop poetry to their performance art. (See Figure 4.6)

TeenStreet productions reveal what FST artistic director David Schein names the "poetics of kids lives";[18] their dramatic productions underscore the pain as well as the pleasure—and a wide range of human emotions in between—of the harsh and inhospitable world they inhabit. TeenStreet director Ron Bieganski has called these works "a kind of guerrilla theatre," yet the shows succeed in turning agitprop theatre into performance art by "marrying plaintive tales of life in the ghetto and an avant-garde formal structure" (Krasnow 1993, p. 38).

Conclusion

The visual and performing arts outlined in this chapter offer anti-elitist messages derived from the positionality of youths on the margins of society. Their creative displays of ancestral origins,

FIGURE 4.6

Free Street Theatre. TeenStreet company. Performance of a piece titled "Mad Joy." Photo by Kristine Wolff. Left to right: Brian Vines, Tameka Flowers, Joshua Mitchell, Kim Johnson, Meka Hayes, and Keli Stewart. Center: Valerie Hilderbrand.

identity politics, and subcultural alliances describe both literal and figurative meanings of street life in urban America.

A teenager's social imagination and utopian vision can be developed through individual artistic presentation. When provided apprenticeship settings with connections to professional artists, impoverished kids will learn that their cultural struggles can be shaped into aesthetic expressions. For instance, African-American teens at the Prologue School made art projects from recycled materials. Their instructor was Mr. Imagination, a lifelong Chicagoan who taught the students how to comb the community for discarded items and refuse, such as bottle caps, paintbrushes, and other materials lying on the streets or alleyways, that could be turned into imagined figures with African imagery.[19] Scavenging for "junk" now takes on new definition for these youths who daily are exposed to litter-strewn neighborhoods. Hopefully, they are stimulated by an ecological consciousness-raising through improvisations with found objects as well.

Professional artists and performers in social projects with youths have ample opportunities to share their technical expertise as well as their political orientations through movement activism and organizing. Public art muralists, for instance, aid community activists in representations depicting themes of solidarity and unity, oppression and repression, confrontation and contestation, and affirmation and celebration.[20] Teen apprentices are taught how to design and execute pictorial images and accompanying wall writings that reify cultural struggles as present-day reminders of important aspects in the life of the neighborhood. They learn that cultural understandings inform the reading of community murals. Hopefully, they bring soulful expressions to their own handiwork in these collective efforts at street restoration and civic beautification in sustainable community development.

The street arts may provide a variety of complex psychosocial meanings depicting anomie in a teenager's life. On the other hand, their visual displays and theatrical stagings simply may illuminate optimistic messages that justice and equity are forthcoming. The educational role of community murals resides in the articulation of shared values, bringing together individuals who privilege their images of identity and solidarity (Conrad 1995). Such positive affirmations of social change further democratic principles in a praxis that is accessible to artist and viewer alike.

5

Youth Leadership

Leadership is a "relationship among people," says Robert Woyach (1993, p. 5). An expert on the topic, he offers eight tasks for preparing youths by (a) shaping visions and goals (envisioning), (b) helping groups make decisions (consensus-seeking), (c) resolving conflicts (negotiation), (d) motivating members (creating rewards), (e) getting recognition for the group (creating an image), (f) getting respect for the group (gaining legitimacy), (g) attracting support and defending the group (advocacy), and (h) cooperating with other groups (coalition-building). Each skill group forms part of the foundation for effective leadership. Yet youths engaged in the activities of leadership, Woyach cautions, also must be aware that their exercise of power requires a judicious balance of personal goals, group interests, and community needs. This triadic balance of personal, group, and community marks the *authenticity* of genuine leadership in a democatic society. For example, Martin Luther King, Jr., Woyach writes, was able to assume an authentic role as leader because:

> He did not see the civil rights movement as a way to force his will on other people. He did not put his personal interests ahead of the interests of the movement. At the same time, Martin Luther King, Jr., had strong ideas of what civil rights meant and how they could be won. He would not abandon those values simply to forge agreement within the group (1993, p. 11).

King managed to balance the interests of activist African-Americans with oppositional forces in society by reaffirming to the public that this cultural struggle upheld the highest of democratic principles through nonviolent social protest.

Youths can learn leadership skills through contact with influential adults in ways that prepare them for democratic actions as well. For example, one of the more successful efforts nationwide is the Hugh O'Brian Youth Foundation (HOBY), a nonprofit organization devoted to "motivating tomorrow's leaders today."[1] A television celebrity, O'Brian established this program upon returning from an inspiring visit with Albert Schweitzer in Africa in 1958. Its purpose is to bring high school sophomores in contact with recognized adult leaders through yearly workshop and seminar activities. Early efforts were limited to youth development activities in California. But over the years as the program grew, HOBY directors invited selected tenth-grade students from across the nation who were nominated by their school principals to a three-day seminar held in their home states in the spring. Then two representatives, male and female, from each state were chosen to attend the annual International Leadership Seminar, held in late summer and attended by youths from two-dozen countries around the globe. More than 13,800 students were involved in HOBY activities in 1993. At the 1993 seminar, for instance, held at Ohio State University in Columbus, HOBY participants (also known as "ambassadors") attended seminar presentations, question-and-answer sessions, and small-group discussion sections on a variety of topics, such as "Toward a Cleaner Earth: Pollution Prevention," "Entrepreneurship: Does the American Dream Still Live," "Thinking Globally," "The Civic Responsibility of a Leader," "Health Care Issues of Today & Tomorrow," and "Public Support for the Arts."

This program offers teens the chance to realize that their individual goals may someday, somehow contribute to solutions to problems posed by membership in the human community. If an opportunity to understand their own personal ambition leads to social and civic consciousness in adulthood, then the efforts of HOBY adult volunteers to nourish young ambassadors have not been wasted. In a recent poll of alumni, for instance, over 80 percent of the 2,349 respondents reported that they were positively influenced to assume leadership positions in civic or volunteer organizations. Whether they joined progressive organizations with social justice agendas is unknown.

Another youth organization, Student Pugwash USA, is geared to leadership primarily among college-age students.[2] Founded in

1979, it was named after the Pugwash Conferences on Science and World Affairs, which began in 1957 in Pugwash, Nova Scotia, as a response to the development of the hydrogen bomb. This group is dedicated to building commitment among young people to comprehend the responsible uses of science and technology in the resolution of critical global issues and future sustainability. Students examine a variety of science and technology issues, such as peace and security, environment, energy, health and medicine, biotechnology, population and development, information technologies, industrial competitiveness, and access and equity. There are Student Pugwash USA chapters at over forty college campuses as well as some high schools across the nation. Each year chapter organizers offer lectures, forums, and seminars on topics related to the social and ethical dilemmas posed by the responsible use of science and technology. At their Eighth International Conference, for instance, in June, 1994, at Johns Hopkins University, both students and adult professionals in related fields joined in a week-long discussion on topics such as "Resource Stewardship for Environmental Sustainability," "Designing the Future—From Corporations to Communities," and "Preventive Diplomacy and Conflict Resolution for a Secure Future." "By exploring alternative perspectives and imaginative solutions to pressing domestic and international concerns," the organization's mission statement reads, "our programs change lives by empowering young people to confront problems of global and local relevance and to affect positive change within their communities."

Leadership skills can be enhanced through seminars, conferences, and workshops in order to acquaint young people with a variety of social, economic, and political issues in preparation for their civic calling as adults. Yet young peoples' understanding of justice and equity is heightened through their actual participation in grassroots community building when integrated into local organizations or coalitions that are furthering youth initiatives. This means community service activities can be viewed as a way to enhance leadership development by positioning teens and young adults for the enactment of their own civic ideals. But youths have to be brought into small-group democracies where their voices are legitimized and their presence is validated. Several organizations do just that, making it possible for activist youths to design and implement grassroots projects while furthering their real-life knowledge about democratic social change.

YouthAction's Community Youth Initiative (CYI), a nonprofit organization devoted to developing activist leaders, provides a variety of internship opportunities in "community struggles for social, economic and environmental justice"[3] to young adults between the ages of eighteen and twenty-five. According to the project director, CYI's goals are three-fold: (a) to develop young leaders in local, state or regional public service organizations; (b) to develop permanent youth programs which support the continued development of new, young leaders year after year; and (c) to develop up to fifty new young leaders for community action.

CYI internships take young adults from a variety of cultural backgrounds and provide them with a year-long stipend and health benefits. Interns are trained in leadership tasks and organizing skills and placed in organizations associated with the initiative in order to stimulate a youth component and sustain the project after they leave. These young adults, in local coalitions with teens, have been instrumental in expanding the body of knowledge, tools, and skills that are needed for youthful participants to understand the underlying causes of social problems, to participate in the creation and implementation of grassroots solutions, and to lead community struggles in the years to come. Former interns throughout the country have involved young people from inner-city neighborhoods in voter registration drives, helped students in community service programs tie their participation to political actions, assisted youths in learning about local and state environmental justice activities, interested teens in reforms of the school-based tracking system, organized youth affiliates for tenant associations in city housing projects, and created area-wide youth advocacy councils.

Another nonprofit project devoted to grassroots leadership development, Southern Community Partners in North Carolina, operates an internship model similar to YouthAction's CYI in combining service with social change, but is limited in geographic scope to about a dozen states in the South.[4] The college-age fellows (or "Partners" as they are termed) are selected in a competitive grants application process which requires that each young adult, age twenty to twenty-six, propose a fundable community development project with a youth leadership initiative. "Successful applicants will exemplify qualities of idealism and practical effectiveness," the program brochure notes, "which will be a model and an inspiration for others to become active in their communities."

Each finalist receives a two-year stipend, annual program expenses, health insurance, and technical support from the home offices (for about $56,000 per fellow). Former Partners have established model programs across the country for young people, linking students and young adults with disabilities in meaningful volunteer work in nonprofit agencies, for example, training peer educators to educate adolescents in preventive health issues, offering community arts to area youths, and developing initiatives to combat environmental racism through several community- and campus-based organizations.

This latter program is affiliated with the Campus Outreach Opportunity League (COOL), which is devoted to student involvement in community service and dedicated to educating and empowering college students so as to strengthen the practice of citizenship through national service.[5] Prompted by the Los Angeles riot in April, 1992, a six-week summer institute held by COOL and funded by the Ford Foundation provided sixteen young people of color opportunities to study urban poverty. They worked in an academic setting, but also visited community-based organizations in four cities and sought strategies and proposals for social change (Cashman 1992).

The National Student Campaign Against Hunger & Homelessness is another COOL affiliate tapping the energy of young adult activists. It seeks to sustain a coalition of student-community partners who understand poverty and to engage in social practices that attempt to ameliorate hunger and homelessness.[6] This program is guided by four objectives: (a) to train students in strategies to improve or create service programs which meet the needs of the hungry and homeless in their communities; (b) to promote collaborative efforts between students, educators, communities, and issue groups to share ideas and implement effective programs; (c) to educate and expand the anti-poverty movement through conferences, on-campus workshops, and community/citywide training sessions; and (d) to implement programs to fight poverty, based on firsthand experience of the hungry and the homeless.

National or local service for college-age students and young people, as we have seen, can be directed toward the cultivation of indigenous community leaders who use their skills and tools to build alliances with youths in self-help neighborhood organizations. It can even create spin-off projects that may eventually become permanent service providers in the local arena (see Brager, Specht, and Torczyner 1987). Contemporary social critics are beginning to recognize the benefits of these community development efforts, which are now viewed as the *new* civic education. Voluntaristic practices capture the democratic ideal of citizenship through service learning, which Barber (1992), Butts (1989), Coles (1993), Gorham (1992), Janowitz (1983), Moskos (1988), Radest (1993), and others have suggested will revitalize the values of social responsibility and community commitment that have been disrupted by an ethic of rugged individualism in modern American life.

In the next section, I present several development projects involving teen activists where youth leaders gain the tools and skills needed in order to direct their peers in political campaigns linked to environmental justice, gay rights, and anti-poverty issues.

Teen Activism

Young activists can stimulate their own peers to think about environmental actions in their local community. From its home offices in Santa Cruz, California, environmental justice group Youth for Environmental Sanity (YES!) offers speaking tours and workshops with school-aged students. What is unique about this group is that YES! is entirely organized and administered by young adults.[7]

In 1990 two high schoolers, Ocean Robbins and Ryan Eliason, developed the idea of a national tour of teens speaking about environmental degradation and conservation issues. Their project receives financial support from several socially responsible corporate sponsors and Earthsave, a nonprofit environmental, health, and educational group. YES! is dedicated to empowering and inspiring others to take positive action for the future of life on Earth. The tour facilitates youth speaking to other youth about environmental justice issues. (See Figure 5.1)

FIGURE 5.1

Youth for Environmental Sanity. The YES! Tour. Photograph by Adam Patton. Left to right: Rachel Cherry, Karen Thompson, Sol Soloman, and Ocean Robbins.

Their national speaking engagements (termed "the YES! Tour") have reached over 450,000 students in seventy-two cities nationwide. They offer junior and senior high school students an opportunity to view a lecture and slide presentation on ecological problems and solutions, attend a Saturday empowerment workshop, learn about summer camps, and read eco-newsletters and training manuals for gathering ideas on local environmental actions. In just one academic year, 1992–93, twenty-seven cities in sixteen states were visited by the YES! Tour, with more than 130,000 students receiving the messages of democratic social change.

The YES! Tour showcases its four-member troupe in a forty-five-minute presentation that covers a wide range of issues, such as global warming, deforestation, toxic waste, environmental racism, and overpopulation. In their opening act, the teens present their version of a popular game show, "We're in Jeopardy." The show speaks to the variety of environmental disasters, but is presented to the audience in a light-hearted way using parodies of the school nerd, "Dennis Dweeb," the surfer-party boy, "Jammin' Jimmy," and the Valley girl, "Hyper Heather." After the mock game show, participants offer a two-minute reflection of their own concerns about the global situation and what motivates them to change it. Then they present a fifteen-minute multimedia slide show accompanied by recorded music and live narrative. Next in their highly interactive routine, the troupe offers a number of ecological solutions, such as recycling, consuming less, eating organic foods, reducing population growth, educating yourself, caring for the bioregion, etc. In the closing minutes of the show, the actors ask the students to do their part toward saving the environment by rallying the audience's voices in unison to say "yes!" to practical measures that they will put into action.

Youth for Environmental Sanity facilitates several summer camp programs nationally (in the states of Massachusetts, Montana, and Oregon) and internationally (in Singapore and Taiwan) for the purpose of offering young people organizing activities in week-long rustic, residential settings. Each camp invites thirty to forty participants ranging in ages from fourteen to twenty-five for a variety of exciting group experiences leading to heightened ecological sensitivities, including oppression studies to overcome prejudices, and community organizing to begin local coalition building. Additionally, leadership development skills are presented through exercises in team-building, communications, drama, media coverage, and conflict resolution. A folksinger-activist assists in the efforts in building an esprit de corps among campers at each site as well. In late July, an "audition camp" is offered to recruit potential YES! volunteers who have expressed a desire to organize a regional tour or to assist in the local operations.

YES! engages youths in a critical education and grassroots coalition-building project for the purpose of teaching peers about environmental degradation, as well as politicizing them to organize for social change. The group has published two manuals, an Earth Action Guide (EAG) and a Tour Action Guide (TAG), to assist local participants with their community activism. The EAG presents tips in building school-based eco-clubs, including facts and figures on various forms of ecocide and "how-to-do-it" action ideas on recycling, saving trees, conserving water and energy, eating organic foods, boycotting polluting industries, and writing letters to state and national representatives. The TAG offers a step-by-step manual for starting a regional speaking tour, including subtopics on suggestions for running meetings, tips on financial management and fund raising, and advice on scheduling the engagements and gaining media attention.

Community-building efforts inspired by YES! national speaking tours and their follow-ups have resulted in the formation of several regional organizations. In Houston, Texas, for example, a group of teens organized the Student Action Network for the Earth (SANE), a regional coalition of environmentally active youths who sponsor conferences and publish their own newsletter. And, in Portland, Oregon, a group of pre-teens formed Youth for Environmental Awareness (YEA!) for the purpose of delivering presentations to area schools, community groups, and government agencies.

In YES! we witness an environmental movement involving so-called "green teens," young adults who adopt the activist strategies of their once-countercultural, college-aged parents (Better 1992). These socially aware youths firmly believe that environmental justice is necessary today to ensure the future of humanity. Green teens believe they can make a difference by showing others that their generation is concerned, involved, and engaged in a grass-roots social movement with both educational and political dividends. Creative leadership development activities inspired by YES! "demonstrate the abilities, dedication, and motivation of young people" (Thompson 1992, p. 19) participating in service activities among teen activists.

Publicizing the effects of global degradation has awakened political consciousness, enabling young citizen-activists to engage in democratic actions through progressive social movements. For example, in northeastern Connecticut, the staff of Equity Trust, Inc., a nonprofit corporation concerned with the principles of community economics, offers a summer training program entitled "Community Builders." The program exposes up to twenty teens, ages fifteen to eighteen, to experiences in leadership development, community organizing, and democratic action.[8] The camp is operated by long-time advocates and national leaders in the community land trust movement and gives youths the skills and tools they need to begin planning for anti-poverty projects in their own neighborhoods. In 1993, their first year of operation, sixteen youths from throughout the U.S., many recruited by local land trust agencies in their communities, attended the summer camp. After a one-day orientation session, the teens boarded a bus for a twenty-day tour of community development projects in the region. The tour included housing rehabilitations and youth programs in New York City, a food bank and community credit union in western Massachusetts, a community land trust and a housing cooperative in Maine, and ecology sessions (along with hiking and camping) in the White Mountains of New Hampshire.

Community Builders is a critical education project for activist teens; they learn that poverty is a structural condition created by inequities in an economic system that blames the victim for lack of capacity and failed upward mobility. Linking theory to praxis in the shaping of critical consciousness among participants, this summer camp offers youths an opportunity to experience first-hand the possibilities for community development. They speak to organizers of land trust neighborhood revitalization projects and engage in hands-on experiences at each site, primarily in construction or farm and gardening activities.

Camp director Chuck Matthai hopes that each participant gains a sense of the possibilities for creating genuine community through their travels. It is the memories of the people, places, and programs they see that give these youths a sense of project co-creation back home, perhaps, at first, just as stories about what really works. "Stories are absolutely essential," he offers, because they "engage people's imagination." And, more importantly, stories lend credibility to the storyteller. As a result, these youth activists gain access to personal narratives of social change, affirming their own voices as authentic community leaders.[9]

Gay teens in western Massachusetts who are affiliated with the Pioneer Valley Gay, Lesbian, and Bisexual (GLB) Youth Project, begun in 1991, can participate in a youth organization that sustains their grassroots activism as well.[10] The primary mission of this project is to help gay teens break down the isolation that they experience in their day-to-day lives and to facilitate a healthy coming-out-of-the-closet process, the most psychologically vulnerable period in their adolescence. This subgroup has about a 30 percent higher suicide rate than teens in general. In fact, the peer support activities, such as skiing trips, roller skating parties, movies, and picnics, provide important social contacts in supportive networks under the guidance of caring and happy adult mentors. Furthermore, the teens can be assured that confidential discussions of, say, sexuality or homophobia will be monitored by the gay mentors in a trusting and safe environment. Here kids learn self-esteem building skills through adult role models in one-on-one discussions as well as peer group rap sessions.

Educating students in area schools about homosexuality is one of many community-based activities ushering forth from the GLB Youth Project. The kids have contacted guidance counselors for information about referrals and led peer trainings at regional prevention centers. Outreach efforts have included the creation of public service announcements about gay issues for the local radio station, the campaign for public library books of interest to gay youth and their families, and the production of a chapbook by the GLB Youth Project participants.

Activists in this project also appeared in December, 1992, before the Governor's Commission on Gay and Lesbian Youth in a public hearing about discimination against gay teens. The sixteen-member commission includes congressional representatives, teachers, high school students, and others from the gay community. Several months later, in April, 1993, six of the youths received citations by the state commissioner of the Department of Public Health at a special ceremony to honor their courage in voicing the stories of their lives. The following October gay youths from the GLB Youth Project asked area legislators to support the bill prohibiting discimination against homosexuals in public education. Due to their efforts, in December, 1993, the governor signed into law the nation's first ban on discrimination against gay youths who daily face identity crises in Massachussett's public schools.

It is apparent that the GLB Youth Project allows gay teens opportunities to expand self-development efforts through leadership activities targeted to expanding civil rights. What this means is that youthful activism can shape an identity politics surrounding the homophobic oppressions against adolescent gays. They *personalize* the cultural struggles against homosexuals, moreover, and give faces and names to their publicized pain. Some of the stories of their sexual "coming-out," for instance, are published in the Pioneer Valley GLB Youth Project (1993) chapbook, titled *Chapter One*, revealing to other teen readers the complexities of liminal responses at that time.[11] Kim writes:

> I came out to someone I knew was gay. It was the most beautiful and relieving experience of my life. Maybe this is why I fell for her so hard and so quickly. I felt as if she were the one with whom I would spend my life, sharing my hopes, my dreams, and myself.
>
> I know now that I should not have expected so much so soon, no matter how strongly I felt. I also know that coming out was the best thing I could have done for myself. I have gained so much since that day—self-esteem, self-respect, and happiness (1993, p. 5).

Justin speaks about coming-out at fourteen, a high school freshman at the time of his first sexual encounter, and of telling his best friend as well as his mother about his sexual orientation. About this latter event, he says:

> My mother's response was typical, "What did I do wrong?" I reassured her that it was nothing she had done. These feelings were natural and I'd pretty much always had them. We discussed this for about forty-five minutes and laid some ground rules, which I thought were very reasonable.
>
> My mom is very supportive but she doesn't say much about it so neither do I. I am one of the lucky ones. She never told me to get out of the house and has never said anything derogatory to me about the gay lifestyle (1993, p. 20).

Pioneer Valley GLB Youth Project politicized the youths; their participation before the Governor's Commission on Gay and Lesbian Youth led to formulation of a new policy for civil liberties in public education in the state of Massachussetts. Peer harassment of gay students was carried on in school buildings which failed to establish an atmosphere of personal safety. Principals prohibited gay student organizations and functions, and were intolerant of differing sexual orientations. With hopes of combatting the ugly consequences of homophobia and rescuing other teens from the alienation, rejection, and isolation they suffer being on the margins of adolescence social life, activist youths in this project were encouraged to speak out and let their voices be heard.

Youth Workers

In Pioneer Valley GLB Youth Project we see how teens engage in democratic actions to advance justice and equity. They learn from caring adult leaders, that is, the youth workers who guide them in the projects and show them that cultural struggles require teaching and knowledge both personally, pedagogically, and politically connected to emancipatory practices.[12] This means that gay teen participants, for instance, arrive at an understanding of their homosexuality or bisexuality, an awareness of oppressions against their sexual orientations, and a social praxis of gay activism. This is achieved in part through their peers but also with the guidance and nurturance of project youth workers, such as outreach coordinator Phil Gauthier and about ten gay mentors.

Phil, age twenty-five, became involved in youth issues in the Pioneer Valley through membership in ACT-UP which, at the time, was involved in distributing condoms at area high schools to help prevent the spread of sexually transmitted diseases, especially AIDS. He learned from students about confidentiality when counseling gay teens, empowerment through peer support groups, creation of safe havens for meetings, and community support through mentorship activities. The GLB Youth Project received a $1,400 grant for start-up costs from a private, grassroots community fund that helped to advertise the peer support groups and train adult mentors. The gay mentors, in particular, are important to the success of this project because they help integrate and acculturate youths into the diverse gay, lesbian, and bisexual communities in the region. Several mentors are former GLB Youth Project participants as well who now attend colleges in the area.

Youth workers who happen to be alumni and in their 20s can bring special vitality to a development project. Often their expertise is rooted in historical praxis that led to self-discovery and liberation during adolescence, but they are close enough in age to the teen participants so as not to create serious intergenerational misunderstandings. In other words, project alumni may very well have been the teen activists in their cohorts who assumed leadership positions, placing them in the vanguard of organizing for democratic action.

Consider the personal story of youth worker Tony Melton, age twenty-two, an intern at the Atlanta chapter of YouthBuild USA, who exhibits leadership skills as a role model among African-American trainees.[13] Tony skipped a lot of school, got into trouble with the law, missed too many days to graduate, and eventually dropped out (with just one semester left) only to experience the frustrations of a tight labor market in his hometown of Tallahassee, Florida. Employers had little use for a man of his talents, and they "gave me the run-around," he said. After filling out applications and returning for positions that were nonexistent or already taken, and discouraged by the failure to land a job quickly, Tony "laid around for a few months" until he learned of a vocational training program through YouthBuild Tallahassee.[14] After attending an orientation meeting and hearing about the alternative high school certification aspects of this program (the GED), he reevaluated his options for earning a diploma. The construction component of YouthBuild, however, did not readily appeal to him, but neither did returning to the regular high school where teachers "didn't reach out to me." So Tony signed on as a YouthBuild trainee.

At YouthBuild Tallahassee, Tony assumed important peer leadership duties, such as chair of the policy committee which helped to facilitate an understanding of program management and governance issues. For instance, when his committee petitioned the program director for a change in the lunch policy requiring students to stay on-site for safety reasons, the trainees felt that a closed campus was unfair. They were young adults raised in the surrounding neighborhoods who were "street smart" and knew how to conduct themselves in public. But the director vetoed the committee's proposal, even after several options were presented. Still, Tony learned valuable lessons in how to serve as a liaison between his peers and the staff of youth workers.

Tony was also a member of the local chapter's youth caucus, a public relations committee that required participation in numerous civic activities, such as a voter registration drive, a canned food drive, and many public speaking engagements and mentorship opportunities in local elementary and middle schools. These events heightened an awareness of community service and values clarification. Leadership in the local chapter provided opportunities to represent trainees at national meetings. Tony attended the first YouthBuild USA conference in Washington D.C. and lobbied congressional representatives for their fiscal support of the program; he was elected to the National Steering Committee in Boston for a two-year term.

After graduating from the program in 1992, Tony volunteered his services at the local chapter for over one year until he was hired as a staff intern. His job was to organize the recent graduates into an alumni organization that was "more like a family," he said, to "keep you in, tied with the YouthBuild concept. When you come through YouthBuild, you're with YouthBuild for life." His graduate cohort participated in social events and in construction-related activities, including housing renovations and emergency building repairs through the city's redevelopment agencies.

In 1994, Tony was selected as a national service participant in AmeriCorps and placed as an administrative intern in the Atlanta chapter of YouthBuild. There he is learning about the technical and educational aspects of program start-up and assisting with operations and management. Tony gets to interact with a new crop of trainees each year which is like "sailing across the sea to the new land . . . where I can help (maybe) a youth five years down the road."

YouthBuild leadership development activities have provided Tony with new insights and understanding about how to give back to the program. He has learned the foundations of effective role modeling and gained the skills of authentic leadership, where youth workers allow young people numerous opportunities to voice their opinions in organizational designs. Leadership development, Tony claims, is "taking responsibility for making things go right: your life and your community and your program and your household." It is a self-help philosophy that teaches empowerment, that is, to get beyond your oppressions and victimizations and begin to actualize yourself in ways that make a difference in the world. Tony learned that he could "take charge" of his life. "Hey, I want to do something with it!" he says. Now *he* is a youth worker, helping the next generation of teens grow and develop as loving and caring human beings.

Conclusion

Abdi Soltani (1996, p. 8) is an activist with Youth for Justice and a participant in an intergenerational demonstration with Californians for Justice against efforts to rescind affirmative action in the state. He reflected that he felt compelled "to take a closer look at the way organizers and activists perceive youth organizing, youth leadership, and young people's roles in social-change movements." "It seems to me," he continues, "that while many organizations say they support the political work of students and youth, most have not really examined the best way to move this work forward." Youths are needed intergenerational partners in mobilization efforts for justice. Still, many older activists may discount and marginalize them, unsure how to bring youths into grassroots campaigns without treating them as naive and idealistic or hard to manage and out of control. They may be treated shabbily as volunteers for grunt labor or as office adornments and ignored entirely in the leadership development process. "An organization that avoids working with young people," Soltani concludes, "is probably avoiding deeper questions about its mission and its methods" (p. 8). The real problem, in my view, is adultism.

My awareness of adultism was heightened one summer by participation in a three-day leadership development workshop led by YouthBuild USA.[15] I recall several activities that clarified for me a number of issues surrounding the oppression of young people. In one instance, a six-member panel of teens was asked to respond to a variety of questions about their youth. The moderator queried: "What is great about being young?" "What is hard about being young?" "Can you think of a time when you were disrespected or mistreated because you were young?" I was touched by one young African-American male in particular, age fifteen, who revealed that he was angry because his mother cashed his weekly paycheck without his consent. In another exercise, we were asked to articulate our negative perceptions of youths. Numerous pejoratives surfaced: including "troublemakers," "violent," "bad attitude," "disrespectful," "immoral," "irresponsible," "apathetic," "abusive," "sneaky," and "illiterate," among others. When asked to list the positive qualities of youths, however, the group was rather dumbfounded to learn that few adjectives from our list (such as "creative," "energetic," "good-hearted," "helpful," "adventurous," "innocent," and "spontaneous,") rarely if ever entered the popular culture of media representations of teens. Adult-dominated society, it seems to me, invalidates adolescence as an affirmative stage of human development, silencing the ideas of young people and reinforcing their helplessness and powerlessness in the world.

Adultism is derived from years of experiences in social relationships where kids are undervalued and underappreciated. Rather than infantilize and warehouse our youths in custodial institutions until they are "of age," we can begin to realize the potential contributions young people offer toward societal reconstructions. Youths are important and valuable resources; they may be viewed as "new sprouts," nascent and inchoate members of intergenerational partnerships, allied in cultural struggles and critical pedagogies that challenge oppressions and remake communities at the grassroots.

The projects profiled in this chapter show that the barriers of adultism can be identified by young leaders, and then peeled away. Just listen to what some of the teens are telling us (*Community Catalyst* 1994, p. 2):[16]

Betty: Adults think we don't care what they say. We do want to listen to what they say, if they have something good to say.

Keisha: Adults that don't understand youth, and try to make decisions for youth, that's what I don't like. How can they say, "This what youth want?" Hello, people. Youth should be part of the decision-making process.

Eric: Let youth speak out on issues more. Pull one over to the side. Say "How you doin'? How you feelin'?" If you ask how they are feeling, that will help.

Betty: The youths can't make everything happen by themselves. We need adults too. We want to work with them to make a better society.

We need to hear more voices of youths tell us of their hopes and dreams. They can become equal partners in a covenant of service devoted to possibilities and promises for justice, for community, and for democracy.

6

Beacons of Hope

When reshaping and empowering the lives of individuals who are under the yoke of oppressive conditions and impoverished settings that are destructive to genuine community, sustainable development offers inner-city residents hope, not despair. In fact, an array of intergenerational grassroots efforts become what scholar and activist Cornel West (1993) terms "beacons of hope," because they "affirm the humanity of black people, accent their capacities and potentialities, and foster character and excellence requisite for productive citizenship" (p. 88).

Yet community leaders continually must counteract widespread feelings of moral decay spreading throughout their low-income, impoverished neighborhoods. Perhaps the underlying driving force behind grassroots leadership in this country, for organizers and activists alike, is an understanding that it takes more than bricks and mortar to build sustainable communities. The despair in communities of color, West (1993) offers, is

> not overcome by arguments or analyses; it is tamed by love and care. Any disease of the soul must be conquered by a turning of one's soul. This turning is done through one's own affirmation of one's worth—an affirmation fueled by the concern of others. A love ethic must be at the center of a politics of conversion (p. 29).

The spiritual call-to-arms of West's "love ethic" is echoed by others with their ears close to the ground (see Furfey 1978). "Our love for the poor," theologian James Cone (1993) charges, "demands that we participate in their liberation struggle, fighting against the forces of oppression" (pp. 77–78). "*Love*," says Michael Christensen

(1988), pastor of an urban ministry in San Francisco, means "go to the people, live among them, work with them, take it to the streets. Journey with them and understand their needs" (p. 92).

Community activists Mel King and Samantha George (1987) recognize that grassroots development, moreover, has the potential to transform the material conditions of inner cities in "a fresh dynamic" that ushers forth "decent and affordable housing, employment, clean streets and parks, thriving businesses, security, comfort, and yes, even luxury" (p. 218). Yet, in their caveat to fellow community leaders, they, too, caution that sustainable development goes beyond mere physical improvements. "Create structures that stimulate the development of consciousness," King and George charge, "so that . . . people grow into a spiritual community. Community development should provide empowerment on the multiple dimensions of material, rational, and spiritual life through practical activity aimed at liberation" (p. 219). In other words, self-determination for people of color through grassroots initiatives can liberate the soul from the racist conditioning in which oppressed individuals "identify with the chains of their own bondage" (p. 225).

The spiritual devotion to hope that John Perkins, chair of the Foundation for Reconciliation and Development in California, offers for leaders of faith-based communities is instructive here.[1] Neighborhood development, in his view, is informed by three key principles: reconciliation, relocation, and redistribution. *Reconciliation* means that we love our neighbors as human beings united in our love for God. Thus, we are reconciled to each other across all racial, social, or economic boundaries. *Relocation* means that we minister to the poor by living and working within their own geographic entity. We join with them in a covenant that solves the problems of our community. *Redistribution* means that we mobilize our spiritual and physical resources to enable people to reach their fullest potential. Our lives are devoted to building community from the bottom up, in self-determined ways, through inspired grassroots leadership that extends outward from the local church in a practical ministry with the poor. Reconciled blacks and whites can join together in partnerships through democratic actions that sustain an urban spirituality driven by love and informed by faith.[2]

The notion of a ministry dedicated to the spiritual development of the urban underclasses provides special challenges to community leaders residing in inner-city neighborhoods (Bird 1990; Cone 1992; Heim and Roehlkepartain 1986; Linthicum 1991; Meyers 1992; Pierce 1984; Roberts 1994). Urban congregations have turned their attention to ministering through direct charity services, such as soup kitchens, homeless shelters, free clothing and furniture stores, and others. Church leaders are attempting broad-based interfaith partnerships, however, by building grassroots organizations relying solely upon membership funds whereby pastors can set their own social justice agendas that reflect the common values and attitudes of their parishoners.

Effective political organizers and community activists have emerged from faith-based institutions, especially among individuals who are trained in Alinsky-styled political action campaigns (see Greider 1992, chapter 10; Hinsdale, Lewis, and Waller 1995). For example, the Industrial Areas Foundation offers training programs on power analysis as a critical tool "that allows people to act for themselves, to transform themselves from passive participants who are content to have things done for them into actors who initiate change in their inner as well as outer lives" (Rogers 1990, p. 50).

At an IAF workshop in Los Angeles in 1986, researcher Mary Rogers (1990) observed incidences of an empowering education involving two pastors who were asked to lead a role-playing session that would recruit church people into the organization. After five minutes of rather banal conversation about their frustrations with the ministry, as church leaders unable to translate the gospel of Jesus Christ into a praxis of hope (rooted in the quotidian acts of solving people's problems in effective ways), one minister voiced his powerlessness in a way that peeled away his persona. Rogers described this critical event as follows:

> The conversation suddenly becomes personal, and the pastor's hurt shows in his eyes and softens his voice. People in the classroom are quiet, struggling to understand the emotions unleashed as the pastor moves from theological generalities to the specifics of his feelings. He has provided an opening to himself—a vulnerability—that allows us to feel what he feels and perhaps to understand something of his nature. And sitting there in the classroom, we realize that this kind of opening could allow a connection with him to develop, perhaps the beginnings of a relationship (p. 52).

By revealing the inner depths of self, the pastor is providing other trainees with glimpses of the self-revelatory and self-transformative nature of this exercise (see Vella 1989). One student's emotional catharsis, however, conveys an important lesson for all engaged in leadership trainings for community economic development: democratic actions are sustained by a praxis of love among participants young and old alike, in personal relationships of trust, through face-to-face communications, in conversations at people's homes, at their churches and synagogues, at neighborhood associations, and at civic organizations.

Grassroots activism in faith-based organizations purposely begins with the spiritual dimensions of human connections through leaders gently networking with others, all the while demonstrating God's love. At an IAF organizing drive in Atlanta, for instance, a Sunday service in early 1993 titled "Building the City of God: Moving toward Justice" signified a defining public moment in the growth of a broad-based, multi-issue, multi-racial, and metro-wide coalition of community building.[3] At the end of that night, thirty churches pledged to send more than three hundred parishoners to follow-up training sessions on power analysis and political activism in house meetings—attended by no more than twenty people and led by leaders from local congregations. These folks will benefit from a critical education that prepares them to become researchers in their own neighborhoods, first by naming personal oppressions, and then by gathering data about inequities in education, employment, crime/safety, housing/homelessness, and health through small-scale "action teams."[4] This faith-based organization will be successful, according to spokespersons of the interdenominational alliance sponsoring the IAF effort, "if we build from the bottom up, and if the church is willing to not only engage in the good works of charity, but also the oftentimes more difficult challenge of collectively struggling for justice and reform."[5]

Mindful that any struggle of people's liberation requires transcending oppressions, urban ministries in communities of color can empower residents for the exodus: "moving out of Egypt—not allowing victimization to control the mind or behavioral patterns any longer. To fight against despair is to see life as a journey, a journey that will be full of ambiguity and vulnerability but also of grace and hope and humor and joy" (Russell 1992, p. 195; also, see Walzer 1985). By accepting the prevailing social, economic, and political order, a minority community's spirit will be crushed and doomed to be forever victimized and powerless (see King 1981). Yet residents can be mobilized in concrete ways to improve their material and spiritual conditions (see Stoecker 1994). What follows are brief descriptions of four journeys in which community leaders of several urban ministries are rebuilding a poor neighborhood near downtown Atlanta.

An Urban Ministry

Jon Abercrombie is a community leader operating an urban ministry in Atlanta.[6] He is executive director of FCS Urban Ministries (FCSUM), a faith-based, parachurch organization serving the inner-city neighborhoods of Atlanta, specifically low-income residents in the Summerhill area. Summerhill, a vital community up to the 1950s, was virtually destroyed by urban renewal in the 1960s, displacing residents through construction of an extensive interstate highway system and the building of Atlanta Fulton County Stadium (home of the Braves) and adjacent parking lots.[7] At one time there were 22,000 residents; that figure is now about 2,500. Approximately 70 percent of the residents are unemployed or welfare-dependent.[8]

Founded in 1978 by Bob Lupton, FCSUM serves as a bridge by bringing suburban and urban churchgoers into partnerships with the city's poor, building community alliances through an umbrella of faith-based ministries.[9] Some of the most successful development projects "reweaving the tapestry of neighborhood" are: Moving in the Spirit,[10] offering dance education, tutorial, and mentorship programs for school-aged children; Charis Community Housing, a nonprofit developer and property manager for multiple- and single-family dwellings, transitional housing, and apartment rentals; and FCS Community Economic Development, Inc., delivering an array of enterprises attending to health and dental care, child care, affordable goods, job training, and recycling services.

Jon has an extensive background of training and experiences in counseling indigent families and children at risk. More importantly, as a lay minister, he is able to articulate the visions of a urban ministry faced with the practical day-to-day complexities of solving human problems through an organizational leadership driven by the Christian obligation to charity. "Ministry in the city," Jon offers, "is the reconciling of those who have been separated. It is a process that allows for the healing of past sins and transgressions—the church, if it operates in these terms, focuses not on division but on uniting." "The role of the church," he continues, "is to encourage the reconciliation of individuals with their God and then with each other."

Faith-based leaders by and large are faced with individuals alienated by the system of poverty in America. Perhaps social welfare programs have created a level of dependency among the underclasses, in part stifling their dreams and hopes for self-improvement, family security, and neighborhood growth (Pope 1992). On the other hand, urban communities have been exploited for a very long time by governmental and corporate interests in a profit-driven colonizing of minority residents (Jennings 1992a, 1992b; King 1981). Whatever the reasons, poor people nonetheless see "programs come and programs go," Jon acknowledges, which makes his job all the more difficult. A ministry must "engender hope," he charges, because "urban communities have often become very cynical about the possibility of real change." Thus, like other grassroots activists, Jon realizes that many neighborhood people are faced with "overwhelming odds" to fail miserably. How does he rekindle feelings of hope and possibility there?

FCS Urban Ministries provides *sustainability* in the face of despair and hopelessness. "Giving voice to the buried dreams and visions of people in the community" rebuilds trust and connection among the residents, but that alone is not enough. Establishing lines of communication and information is important as well, so that people gain the tools and skills, the "know-how to produce their own newsletter and the hardware to do it." Yet of greatest importance in building community, Jon recognizes, is "creating models of hope," such as when Charis Community Housing renovated an old stockade (GlenCastle, which was formerly Atlanta's debtor's prison) and turned it into a sixty-nine-unit apartment complex for transitional or long-term housing for the working poor (Spring 1989). In the spring of every school year, school-aged children in the Stepping Stones Program of Moving in the Spirit enact their lived experiences through words, pictures, and movement "before adoring crowds" of family members, neighbors, and friends. The FCSUM Adopt-A-Grandparent Program matches volunteers with senior citizens who reach out to one another through relationships based upon love and caring.

Finally, according to Jon, an urban ministry is sustainable in the people's eyes due to a boundless faith in justice: "the notion that God cares about what we are doing even if it appears that we are losing." Democratic actions nourish the soul. How else does one explain why "so many of the neighborhood people have learned the ability to keep on in the face of overwhelming odds." The struggle is never-ending, however "we will one day scale the walls that imprison us."

Doris Perryman, age thirty-five, works for community economic development in Summerhill.[11] As director of the Summerhill Real Estate Company, a subsidiary of Summerhill Neighborhood, Inc., and in concert with Charis Community Housing, a division of FCS Urban Ministries, she helps local residents find affordable housing in the neighborhood. Using funds and volunteers from faith-based institutions, Charis has built more than 117 homes and ninety apartments, with about two-thirds of the properties located in the Summerhill community. They are the low-income housing provider in the area.

Interestingly, Doris was a recipient of quality affordable housing over a decade ago in the same neighborhood. She was granted an apartment in a twenty-unit complex that Charis had recently acquired. Since the apartments were self-managed, the tenants were active participants in the care and upkeep of the buildings. She served as repairs coordinator, attended monthly meetings, and helped out in light maintenance duties. This was her entree into an urban ministry devoted to community development, but she left the Summerhill neighborhood after five years. Then, one day while at a bus stop, Jon Abercrombie noticed her standing at the curb and stopped his car to offer her a lift downtown. Later, over lunch, he explained that Charis was developing a real estate department, and there was part-time employment for her there. "This presented me an opportunity to do something career-related," she said, "something to make a positive impact or positive difference in somebody's life." Her return to Summerhill "felt so right," she related. "Some things we just know, and I just knew that."

Doris arranges bank loans and mortgage lending services to individuals interested in resettling in the area. New homes are available at the Orchards, for example, a planned subdivision for mixed-income residents that represents an innovative approach to rebuilding a neighborhood. Summerhill Neighborhood, Inc., a community development corporation, purchased seventeen vacant lots in this particular subdivision targeted for residential usage, with one-third apportioned for low-income residents.[12] The purpose is to build about twelve market homes with price ranges that would attract middle-income families, some born and raised in Summerhill, who desire a return to this neighborhood because they believe in the notion of "relocation" or "reneighboring" (as advocated by John Perkins and Robert Lupton). Charis constructs the rest of the lots for low-income families by utilizing volunteer labor among faith-based congregations who use the house as their mission project (similar to Habitat for Humanity) and by gathering building materials donated by local businesses.

Doris sits on the Homeowner Selection Team that interviews prospective residents who are awarded a new home if they qualify. Selection requires sponsorship from a local church or faith-based organization, performing seventy-five hours of voluntary labor on the house, and the ability to meet a monthly obligation of the $250 no-interest mortgage payment. "I've seen people cry," she related, when turning over the house keys to new grantees. She recalls:

> I can remember a lady one time: divorced, five little girls. I stopped by her house; she called it "little Vietnam." She had a very, very tiny house, but neat and clean. She was afraid to let the little girls go out and play. I recommended her to Charis for a house. . . . It affected the mother, her whole view of live. She [had] survived from day to day, not making any real progress. [Now] she acquired a new sense of stability.

Doris has seen how property ownership changes the individual spirit, leading to character development of an entire neighborhood, as older houses are getting repaired, yards are being mowed, gardens are being planted.

The residents are taking an interest in their community, moreover, by getting to know their neighbors and organizing block meetings to talk about social issues of importance to them. For instance, a new partnership of residents is in its embryonic stages in Summerhill. Neighbors United Coalition represents the birth of a grassroots citizen-activist group "with a new attitude" that is willing and able to tackle problems in the community (Rhenwrick 1995). The coalition is characterized by an equitable partnership in all aspects of information sharing, interpretation, and response. More importantly, the group has begun to "formulate visions, leaders, and activities" around a variety of neighborhood issues. These include vacant lot clean-ups, abandoned buildings and automobiles, zoning violations, trash on the streets and sidewalks, traffic sign and signal repairs, park improvements, leaking water hydrants, sewer and drainage problems, and many others.

"Charis homeowners," Doris notes, "are really pioneers; they're willing to take a chance and be the forerunners" in resettling the area. They are building community, however, by sharing problems and seeking solutions; this is the key to resettlement in the neighborhood. It "is where a large percentage of residents understand interdependency—you've got to look at the big picture in order to make it better for one."

Andre Turnipseed, age thirty-one, believes in the notion of faith-based community development.[13] A recipient of a Charis home in 1984, Andre then began his long association with FCS Urban Ministries. First he worked in warehouse operations at the Home Resource and Furniture Center, a community economic development division of FCS that recycles used or donated items, home furnishing and building materials, while helping young adults with jobs and training. Then he worked as construction trainee at Charis Community Housing. Now Andre is director of construction for Charis, and he coordinates all aspects of this FCS division. On a typical day he may have to contact the subcontractors, facilitate the volunteers, manage a carpentry crew on-site, and schedule material deliveries. This is a tough job, both physically and mentally taxing. Yet Andre is motivated by his longstanding commitment to an urban ministry. "I made a choice," he says, "a conscious decision to come down here [to the Summerhill neighborhood]—I didn't have to do that!" He remarks:

I feel like from step one I was actually brought down here by God's divine wisdom. My receiving the house, getting involved [in Charis], that total process. As I look back on it, that's the reason I'm here right now: to be a role model; [we] need more black role models in a lower-income area. You need that!

Andre is a role model for others, particularly younger trainees on the Charis construction crews. Certainly he teaches them the technical skills required to put a house together, but he carefully attends to their spiritual needs as well. He wants his trainees to grow and develop into responsible, caring adults. Andre is an urban missionary, he claims, taking troubled souls and victims of impoverished circumstances, abusers of drugs and alcohol who have been beaten down by a low-income mentality that says, "I don't see anything any better. My daddy was here, my mother was here, and so I'm going to be here—no ambition, no hope, no dreams," and turning them around.

Finally, Andre recognizes that his development work at Charis provides quality housing stock in a mixed-income neighborhood where low-income families will have an opportunity to own a home. For example, a recent Summerhill resident speaks about her joy in receiving an affordable house, "helping to make my dream a reality" (Leach 1995). She writes:

On December 16th, I moved into a Charis House. I call it the house that God built, owns, and is the head of. Words could never describe what I felt. . . . joy filled my heart and praises went up. I always dreamed of being a homeowner. You know when God's in charge, all things are possible.

An earlier recipient, Susan Edwards, is a former Summerhill native who moved away when the community began to deteriorate in the 1970s and now lives with her daughter in a house built by Charis (*The Neighborhood Voice* 1992). "I know that the neighborhood is just starting to work on turning itself around," she says, "but in the end it will be worth it" (p. 3). "To have a sense of ownership," Andre remarks, is what his urban ministry is all about, helping people "to become more stable, to build community—I think about empowerment."

Fronita King, age 24, provides an ethic of love and care to youth in Summerhill.[14] From an early age she realized that working with underprivileged children was her calling. "This was always

something that was in me, always a 'gut thing' to do," she says.
And due to her strong religious upbringing in the Pentecostal
"Holiness" reformation movement, especially her summer church
camp experiences among a group of young people devoted to spiritual devotion and personal development, Fronita has emerged as a
youth worker in the Summerhill community of Atlanta through
the Martin Street Church of God.[15] Her work in this ministry's outreach efforts, for instance, involves weekly counseling sessions for
adolescent female detainees at the nearby Fulton County Detention
Center. "It gives me [an] opportunity to share with them about the
love of Jesus," she says, "and to help them to understand that
there is a better way of life as opposed to skipping school, or getting in fights, or gang banging." At her own church, as youth
leader Fronita assists with the Wednesday night "prime-time" service for young people, participates in a youth choir that travels to
other Atlanta neighborhoods, and tends to the mentorship and
tutoring needs of participants in the fellowship. She is active in
state-level Christian leadership development as well.

"Let kids know . . . there is another side of life that maybe you
haven't been exposed to," Fronita noted, when I asked about her
philosophy for youth and community development. The Martin
Street Church will "welcome you to be a part of that [ministry]," she
offered, "and participate with us because we are about making each
other strong." But what happens when you take street kids from the
neighborhood and attempt to bring them into the church family?
Fronita volunteered that there is a socializing process at work here,
whereby, the "unchurched," as she calls them, actually see their
peers in positive roles "excited about what they're doing." For example, six teenage girls from the neighborhood have been attending
Wednesday night youth services for several months, thanks to
Fronita's generous offer to chauffeur them weekly. But their conduct
in church is "totally different than our children," she notes, who
have embodied the ethics of formal religion: "they have the behavior,
they have the language, they know how to dress." Yet Fronita has
begun to see a change in attitude among the girls, particularly since
she has taken a caring, loving approach to their development. She
told me:

When we have prime-time services, our kids may mumble
something to each other, but they're not going to carry on a

conversation, or they're not going to play with any toys that they brought. But the young ladies from the community will do those things. . . . They haven't been exposed or maybe never been in a situation where they have to act a certain way. So, what I have found is, since I've been bringing them, I've seen a change in their character. They don't talk as much [in services] as they used to when they first came. When I would pick them up they'd have food (chips, drinks, and candy) to eat during prime-time. I've had to say things like: "You can't keep talking." "You can't eat that during service." That kind of thing has really helped them to better themselves.

Hopefully, the youth ministry at Martin Street Church, with Fronita's help, will bring more low-income children and teens into a faith-based congregation dedicated to building sustainable community in Summerhill.

Jon, Doris, Andre, and Fronita are just four community leaders actively seeking partnerships with families in transformative journeys leading to development of an urban neighborhood. Their ministries offer love and hope for children and teens; young people gain the knowledge in faith-based projects that these four adults desire and actively encourage healthy growth and adolescent development.

Conclusion

Faith-based organizations devoted to adolescent and community development in poor urban neighborhoods are few in numbers (Mincy 1994). Since the 1940s, the Catholic Church has launched several initiatives targeted to curtailing Latino youth gang memberships, aside from its recreational offerings through Catholic Youth Organization sports leagues. The most successful of these efforts combine moral training with a social justice agenda for teenagers at weekend retreats (Stevens-Arroyo and Diaz-Stevens 1993). The nondenominational Youth for Christ (YFC), begun in 1944, is very active in African-American and Latino gang interventions through some of its 235 local chapters (Maxwell 1994). At the YFC chapter in Chicago, for example, Gordon McLean runs a Juvenile Justice Ministry that initially reaches incarcerated gang members through Bible studies in local detention centers and prisons, and after their release through monthly gang summits in neutral territory (Bird 1990; Tapia 1994).

Imaginative congregations desiring to reach "unchurched" kids often fund local initiatives when the violence accompanying gang activity threatens their own personal safety. A citywide coalition of black clergy in Philadelphia, for instance, began in the spring of 1994 to send church volunteers into the streets one night a week to talk to alienated youths (*Christian Century* 1994b). Dubbed "Operation Dialogue," this program was established to heighten adult presence in unsafe neighborhoods and protect schoolchildren from potentially deadly crossfire among rival gangs. Anti-violence programming is offered by faith-based organizations in a handful of cities across the country.

Several prominent national organizations of black clergy recently have renewed their dedication to an activist ministry by reaching the growing numbers of unchurched males involved in gang activity. Two-hundred and fifty pastors in the minister's caucus of the National Rainbow Coalition vowed to "steer 100,000 at-risk youth away from unnecessary incarceration" in grassroots educational and political efforts across the country (*Jet* 1995, p. 40). The Congress of National Black Churches similarly supports a "practical Christianity" of urban ministries leading black males back to the church (*Christian Century* 1994a, p. 440).

Research has shown that religious affiliation and participation among children and youths tends to have a positive effect upon adolescent behaviors, minimizing high-risk practices associated with substance abuse, sexual activity, and delinquency (see Mincy 1994). Yet the massive developmental problems facing low-income youths do not seem to be adequately addressed by faith-based institutions to date. Black churches, for example, may provide numerous sports activities but give short shrift to prevention programs (Rubin, Billingsley, and Caldwell 1994).

Faith-based organizing has the potential to attract the interests and abilities of young people. By directing their energies into healthy adolescent development, participants can gain spiritual renewal *through* a critical education. For instance, after researching the dance ministry of Moving in the Spirit, a division of FCS Urban Ministries, an opportunity was afforded for me to assume a leadership role in that (parachurch) faith-based organization. I was invited to join the community board that oversees the operations, budget, long-range planning, and program goals and policy-setting objectives. (Additionally, all board members are expected to demonstrate their commitment by providing personal financial support for the organization.)

This dance ministry for community justice helps urban youths become empowered through performance art that gives voice to their lived experiences. Ironically, participation in this project offers me critical insights as well. That is, I learn about the positionalities of young people through their conversations about race, class, and gender oppressions and struggles; they also tell me about their dreams, visions, and hopes. These kids inform my understanding of what critical educator Henry Giroux (1992) claims are the "specificity of contexts in which power is operationalized, domination expresses itself, and resistance works in multiple and productive ways" (p. 79). Consequently, this dance ministry, in a localized setting, helps deepen my cultural analysis as a critical educator (see Kanpol and Yeo 1995).

One time I accompanied the Apprentice Corporation in an after-school show at the Macon Youth Development Center (YDC), a juvenile justice facility for incarcerated girls in a remote area outside of the city of Macon, Georgia.[16] At the YDC we entertained more than one hundred inmates, supervised by a handful of youth workers, about 90 percent of whom were African-American, gathered together from six or seven residential cottages on the property. The performance lasted forty-five minutes with a five-minute question-and-answer session afterwards. I do not remember all of the choreographed pieces (this being the first time I had seen the entire production), but several ensembles were memorable: a dance about the civil rights movement, one on teenage pregnancy, another symbolic of AIDS activism.

The most popular piece was "One Night Stand," a duet featuring a male and a female member of the troupe performed in a romantic interlude accompanied by a recording of Frank Sinatra's "Strangers in the Night." The audience loved this number! After their initial whistling and hooting at Steven, age sixteen, a black male dancer in the performance company that night,[17] every time some sexual innuendo arose throughout the concert members of the audience would shout aloud or talk among themselves about an image provoked by the dancers. Usually the youth workers would give stern looks to the kids to quiet them down. Afterwards, several girls in the audience asked a number of questions to the teen dance troupe, including if Steven was dating anyone. I gathered that his affirmation signified to them that he was heterosexual and, in their minds, available for dating, or, more likely, merely a sex object for their female gazes. Interestingly, one of the youth workers sitting nearby whispered to me, "Uh, oh, he shouldn't have said that." I wondered: did he mean that these "reform school girls" fit the cinematic stereotypes as sexpots, obsessed with male bodies? As the students filed out of the assembly hall in groups based upon cottage assignments, one inmate remarked to me: "These kids are going to be somebody someday!" I responded reflexively, "You can be somebody too!" She smiled back in my direction.

On the return drive to Atlanta, two dancers accompanied me: Steven and Angie, age sixteen, a white female. They seemed comfortable around me, and maybe they let down their guard somewhat, evidently tired-out physically since the event was after a full day of school. Both kids knew that I really supported the dance troupe; I had praised them after the show and told them how much the YDC girls liked their work. While it seemed that Steven and Angie were flirting with each other at times, they, too, could have adult conversations one-on-one with me—an interesting juxtaposition or layering of cross-gender peer and intergenerational discourses. Sexuality was the dominant theme that night. For instance, Steven talked about how one time at an all-boys YDC he was called a "fag" by several audience members; he recalls how they challenged his sexual orientation. Then he talked about a recent track team incident when one of the opposing boys got wind of Steven's dance involvement and said to fellow teammates within earshot of Steven, "There's a bitch on their team." Steven took this homophobic episode rather harshly, he told me, and said he had threatened to hit the kid with his spikes. I replied, "You really need an adult male to talk to about your feelings." I told Steven how fortunate he was in being an accomplished dancer at his age, and what a great vocational opportunity this art form offered him. Yet I did mention the problem of homophobia accompanying a dance career. My sister, a modern dance choreographer, once told me many female dancers assumed male dancers are gay. Hearing this, Angie said, "Don't tell him that!" Instead of shutting down in my presence, however, Steven seemed to be receptive to our conversations about sexual identity and public performance. He opened up to to me about a number of homophobic slurs received since dancing, and he told me what it was like to be working with a group of female teen dancers.

Perhaps because I showed great interest in listening to both kids that night, they were able to share with me some of their lived experiences. Angie told me, "Men are scum!" I found this proto-feminist remark interesting. Apparently, she was in the process of ending one relationship and starting a new liaison with another boy. I didn't probe. She and Steven continued talking about their dating experiences in high school. Mostly I just listened to them, trying not to interrupt their dialogues. Once, Steven asked Angie, "Does he touch you?" about her latest boyfriend's sexual advances. I laughed, but elbowing Steven, charged, "You crossed the line on that one." "I like hugs," responded Angie. Another time Angie told me about her favorite rock group, "Nine Inch Nails," and the fans who wear all-black outfits to their concerts. She called them "goth-ic." Steven quipped: "I guess that I'm gothic then." We laughed at his pun on skin color. Then Steven told me about his initial concerns associating with female peers, especially in such close physical contact through lifting and holding them in dance performances. Angie offered, "Yea, he's learning about [female] hygiene." We laughed. Obviously, I offered a safe place for these two teens to speak frankly and openly to one another and to me—with humor.

We can initiate democratic actions and critical learnings simply by sending a message to youths that gracefully acknowledges: "I respect you and think that what you have to say is important. I'm listening." Once trust, honesty, and openness are mutually established, the symbiotic process of cultural analysis begins.

Conclusion

This book celebrates human agency and citizens' power to act upon our convictions and make a difference in the world. The projects for youth development gathered in these pages are grounded in a pedagogy of possibility and hope. Individuals can design and create activities by engaging in meaning-making events in their search for workable solutions. In fact, there is a "quiet revolution" occurring right now of everyday people joined together in a "commonsense, roll-up-your-sleeves approach to local problems" (Garr 1995, p. 5). But hardly anybody knows about it, and very few people are talking about its concrete ramifications.

I have argued that seeking answers to our more vicious social problems is possible when citizens of all ages come together in a common struggle—a grassroots, voluntary activism that recognizes the educational process within political empowerment. Young people are integral to learning communities where pedagogy informs development, through memberships in associations devoted to improvements in their quality of life. Children and youths can be linked into mobilizations that challenge privileged myths, hegemonic narratives, and monocultural practices derived from a social totality devoted to technocratic-capitalist domination over nature and authoritarian-patriarchal control over people.

Emancipatory praxis prompts critical inquiry and reflection as well as collective action in progressive, democratic organizations where people are authenticated and affirmed (see Welton 1993). That is, a variety of themes in critical education offer young people mutuality, cooperation, commitment, and solidarity so that together they may (a) explore self-identities in positive, healthy, affirmative ways; (b) develop a spiritual ethic of love and care for others; (c) practice racial and ethnic reconciliations, gender affirmations, and interfaith harmonies; (d) accept diversity, respect cultural differences, and learn toleration; (e) examine structural barriers that limit human empowerment; and (f) create coalitions and partnerships that are proactive, countering racism, sexism, adultism, and classism in social life (see Kanpol 1994). Authentic learning communities allow participants opportunities to share human needs, identify values, deepen their connections to one's inner self, to peers, to family, to church, to neighborhood, and to the global community.

At sites of production dedicated to cultural struggles for social justice, as profiled in this book, youth workers offer children and teens a viable way to solve real-life problems in critical practices which "embody a pedagogical project aimed at enabling ways of thinking and structures of feeling that open and sustain actions that express an ethically informed expansion of human possibility" (Simon 1992, p. 46). The pedagogical project becomes a vehicle for transformative learning; students are engaged in understandings which challenge comfortable taken-for-granted assumptions about self and society. Youth workers facilitate the learning process by helping kids to reframe ethical and moral commitments through "questions, analyses, visions, and practical options that people can pursue in their attempts to participate in the determination of various aspects of their lives" (Simon 1992, p. 47).

Certainly teachers themselves may serve as critical educators in aiding and abetting school-aged children through projects that recast the terms upon which youths recognize their connection to self and society (see Purpel 1989). "Engaged pedagogy does not seek simply to empower students," writes critical pedagogue bell hooks (1994, p. 21). "Any classroom that employs a holistic model of learning will also be a place where teachers grow, and are empowered by the process." Youths can engage in community building with teachers as caring and loving mentors.[1]

Yet youth development practices, in my view, work best when kids and adults engage in participatory decision makings and practical democratic actions away from schools. Nonprofit organizations are best suited to attracting students *voluntarily, willingly, and noncoercively* in projects that construct economic enterprises and community associations from the ground up. Remember, too, that young people's commitments to their neighborhoods strengthen when the democratic foundations of citizenship are doable and realizable, as a praxis rooted in problem-solving for community change (see Zeller 1993).

"The vitality of democratic citizenship," scholar Morris Janowitz (1983) rightly points out, "cannot be maintained by the existing range of political forms, such as voting and political participation." He continues: "Historically, citizenship and patriotism have included various forms of local self-help currently associated with the idea of community or national service. Participation in these activities gives the idea of obligation concrete meaning" (p. 203). A political education derived from service to disadvantaged neighborhoods, moreover, gives rise to a civic culture where people enter dialogues about the conditions of poverty. "Community service can strengthen a democracy," claims Eric Gorham (1992) in an important new book on civic education. "Community conversations foster associational life," he continues, "and adhere individuals to each other and to the republic by allowing citizens with different interests, self-understandings, and commitments to attend to problems together. In short, they establish places where contestation and cooperation among citizens can occur simultaneously; and these places may also permit individuals to work out their own understandings of 'good citizenship' by listening to others do the same" (p. 181). Citizen-activists who understand the crisis of Americans in need recognize that genuine democracy is equated with the strength of their reconstructions.

"Communities would be wise to recognize and make use of the vital resources available in their young citizens," charged a national panel of policy experts studying youth development over two decades ago (National Commission on Resources for Youth 1974). Their message, still timely two decades later, is worth repeating at length:

> Young people are impatient. When they see a problem, and they get an idea about how to cope with it, they want action. Often their enthusiasm can carry them over obstacles that would discourage adults. And their optimism seems to accelerate their ability to develop skills necessary for dealing with problems. Added to enthusiasm and optimism are physical and mental energy and a remarkable capacity for single-minded dedication to something they feel is truly important. With support from the school and community, young people can develop and learn to use the problem-solving skills so

desperately needed for coping with current and future social
problems (p. 134).

In dozens of youth development programs I reviewed during field
research for this book, few young people struck me as lazy or, for
that matter, anomic and dispirited. A boundless energy is chan-
nelled by youths into projects requiring self-discipline, positive attitudes, and an ethic of industry from beginning to end. Yes, several of
the young participants I met readily articulated their fears living in
environments where neighborhoods are crumbling, but, as self-
identified youth-at-risk, they spoke to me as well about "beating
the odds" and realizing their dreams and visions. Perhaps what
many of the kids involved in development projects are experiencing
together are (a) youth-community initiatives from the grassroots,
(b) sites serving as safe havens, (c) positive peer leadership activities, (d) youth workers and program graduates as role models, (e) a
voice in policy-setting and decision-making matters, (f) vocational
skills and job creation strategies, (g) enterprise planning and
entrepreneurial designs, (h) partnerships and coalitions with community activists and organizers, (i) citywide youth alliances, and
(j) communication and dialogue about adultism, among other
themes in their critical education (see Curtis 1996).

Generating positive alternatives for sustainable development,
however, means changing the reality of our inner cities. Community
economic development should be driven by long-range, capacity-
building practices bubbling up from the bottom, among the very
people who reside there (McKnight and Kretzmann 1984; McKnight
1987; McKnight 1995; Weckstein 1989). When assessing needs and
directing practices toward building neighborhoods, community leaders might start by charting the gifts of residents, including young
people, in shared partnerships for planned growth and development.

For example, sustainable community development begins on a
block-by-block basis, according to black activist Mel King (1987), in
citizens' associations for each street. Residents are interviewed and
vital family information is surfaced of "talents and skills present."
Then the data is published in a directory to "ensure that people will
have a forum to make contact and share services; that sufficient
technical and material back-up from financial and educational institutions in the area is secured; and that the collective imagination of

the people there is stimulated to deal with problems in the most creative and humanizing manner" (p. 105). Any number of creative problem-solving activities in its wake will have been fueled by the power and love of citizen-activists generating sustainable and self-sufficient solutions in economies of scale for a slum-free society.

The democratic actions most cherished by youths are in neighborhood organizations eliciting possibility and promise, assurance and success (see Morris and Hess 1975; Williams 1985). Through (re)building one's communities, via various leadership activities, inner-city children and youth may realize a sense of ownership and belonging that at present is available in the mean streets. The young people of our cities are awaiting adult guidance in their quest for education and empowerment, agency and liberation.

Appendix A:
Resource Directory

Action for Grassroots Empowerment
and Neighborhood Development Alternatives
2826 South Vermont Ave., Suite 11
Los Angeles, CA 90007

Atlanta Photography Group
75 Bennett Street, NW, Suite H-2
Atlanta, GA 30309

Campus Outreach Opportunity League
1511 K Street, NW, Suite 307
Washington, DC 20005

Carlisle Education Center
Education Development Center, Inc.
875 Westford Rd.
Carlisle, MA 07141

Chicago Public Art Group
1255 S. Wabash Ave.
Chicago, IL 60605

Christian Community Development Association
P.O. Box 32
Jackson, MS 39205

City Year
11 Stillings St.
Boston, MA 02210

Community Builders
Equity Trust Inc.
539 Beach Pond Rd.
Voluntown, CT 06384

Community Fellows Program
Department of Urban Studies and Planning
Room 7-341
Massachusetts Institute of Technology
Cambridge, MA 02139

Community Partners
24 South Prospect St.
Amherst, MA 01002

Credit Union for Teens
D.E. Wells Federal Credit Union
864 State St.
Springfield, MA 01109

Development Associates
P.O. Box 36748
Tucson, AZ 85740

DO Something
423 West 55th St., 8th Floor
New York, NY 10019

Drumlin Farm's Food Project
P.O. Box 705
Lincoln, MA 01773

Dunbar Community Center
33 Oak St.
Springfield, MA 01109

Education, Training & Enterprise Center
313 Market St.
Camden, NJ 08102

Educators for Social Responsibility
23 Garden St.
Cambridge, MA 02138

FCS Urban Ministries
P.O. Box 17628
750 Glenwood Ave., SE
Atlanta, GA 30316

Federation for Industrial Retention and Renewal
3411 W. Diversey, #10
Chicago, IL 60647

Free Street Theatre
1419 W. Blackhawk
Chicago, IL 60622

Gallery 37
Department of Cultural Affairs
Chicago Cultural Center
78 E. Washington St.
Chicago, IL 60602

Gang Peace
318A Bluehill Ave.
Roxbury, MA 02121

Industrial Areas Foundation
36 New Hyde Park
Franklin Square, NY 11011

Institute for Community Economics
57 School St.
Springfield, MA 01105

National Coalition of Education Activists
P.O. Box 679
Rhinebeck, NY 12572

The Natural Guard
142 Howard Ave.
New Haven, CT 06519

Organizing and Leadership Training Center
25 West St., Third Floor
Boston, MA 02111

Pioneer Valley GLB Youth Project
P.O. Box 202
Hadley, MA 01035

The Prevention Center
4730 Walnut St., Suite 105
Boulder, CO 80301

Prologue Alternative High School
1105 W. Lawrence
Chicago, IL 60640

Puerto Rican Organization Program
738 Main St.
Willimantic, CT 06226

REAL Enterprises
295 E. Dougherty St., Suite 202
Athens, GA 30603

Rindge School
459 Broadway
Cambridge, MA 02138

The SIMBA Project
P.O. Box 42481
Atlanta, GA 30311

Social and Public Art Resource Center
685 Venice Blvd.
Venice, CA 90291

Southern Community Partners
P.O. Box 19745
North Carolina Central University
Durham, NC 27707

Student Pugwash USA
1638 R Street, NW, Suite 32
Washington, DC 20009

Take Charge/Be Somebody!
1375 Nelson Avenue
Bronx, NY 10452

Teen Empowerment
48 Rutland St.
Boston, MA 02118

Teens as Community Resources
100 Massachusetts Ave., 4th Floor
Boston, MA 02215

Video/Action Fund
3034 Q Street, NW
Washington, DC 20007

YouthAction
1830 Connecticut Ave., NW
Washington, DC 20009

YouthBuild USA
58 Day St.
P.O. Box 440322
Somerville, MA 02144

Youth for Environmental Sanity
706 Frederick St.
Santa Cruz, CA 95062

Periodicals

Build
P.O. Box 2409 JAF
New York, NY 10116

Community Catalyst
c/o Community Partners
24 South Prospect St.
Amherst, MA 01002

Grassroots Economic Organizing (GEO) Newsletter
P.O. Box 5056
New Haven, CT 06525

The Neighborhood Works
2125 W. North Ave.
Chicago, IL 60647

New Designs for Youth Development
c/o National Network for Youth
1319 F St., NW, Suite 401
Washington, DC 20004

Rethinking Schools
1001 E. Keefe Ave.
Milwaukee, WI 53212

Third Force
1218 East 21st St.
Oakland, CA 94606

Who Cares (a Journal of Service and Action)
1511 K St., NW, Suite 1042
Washington, DC 20005

YO! (Youth Outlook)
Pacific News Service
450 Mission St., Suite 506
San Francisco, CA 94105

Youth Today
1200 17th St., NW, 4th Floor
Washington, DC 20036

Notes

Introduction

1. Field notes from interviews with International Ladies Garment Workers Union educators Kitty Krupat and Maureen LaMar on July 29, 1993, in New York City. I visited a labor education class that afternoon in the Chelsea section of Manhattan.

2. Their union memberships evidently mitigated the more pernicious effects of poverty by protecting them with a decent wage structure and other rank-and-file benefits; the students were neither homeless or destitute.

3. To keep abreast of contemporary policy changes in Congress, see *Youth Today*, the bimonthly newspaper on youth work—the subscription address is listed in the *Resource Directory*.

1. Community Economics

1. JTPA funds have been used by several of the youth development organizations profiled in this book under Title II-B: Summer Youth Employment and Training. In both the House and the Senate, for fiscal year 1996, recisionary bills are proposed to eliminate this particular program.

2. This section is prepared from field notes with Rose Reyes at PROP in Willimantic, Connecticut, on July 18, 1994.

3. A variety of publications and audio-visuals about grassroots economic justice and community development actions in local venues nationwide are available from the Institute for Community Economics— see the *Resource Directory* for their address.

4. Personal communication with Cliff Glasberg, member of the WAIM Research and Development Committee in Storrs, Connecticut, on August 3, 1993.

5. I visited the Valley Care Cooperative in Waterbury, Connecticut, on August 12, 1993. Information about the NVP is gathered from field notes with Susan Wefold, NVP director, and from several employees at the Valley Care Cooperative.

6. Ms. Wefold identified one training manual that she recommends for community organizers and activists—see Vella (1989).

7. This section is prepared from field notes of WAIM Research and Development Committee meetings at the First Congregational Church in Willimantic, Connecticut, on August 3 and August 17, 1994.

8. Personal correspondence and newspaper clippings of tenant/landlord maintenance issues on Vermont Drive Apartments provided to me by Gil de Lamadrid, PROP executive director, on February 3 and November 14, 1995.

9. Sometimes it seems as if the McDonalds Corporation or other notable fast-food franchises spring forth overnight in low-income communities, often supported by the reigning myth that the local economy will be energized by this much needed boost in commerce. Yet, as some economists have shown, much of the profit is extracted from the local establishment in the form of surplus capital flowing out to private investors or shareholders, with continued disinvestments and deterioration of these neighborhoods. The franchise firms are problematic in other ways as well: they create mounds of nonbiodegradable trash; they hire youth workers for low-skilled and dead-end labor; their patrons consume dietary products of questionable nutritious value; and they heighten competition to locally-owned "mom and pop" stores. See Gunn and Gunn (1991).

10. This section is prepared from field notes with Carol Aranjo, chief executive officer of D.E. Wells Federal Credit Union in Springfield, Massachusetts, on August 26, 1993, and from a case study of the Wells Youth Credit Union (Jerving 1993).

11. On African-American "folk theory" and minority education, see Ogbu (1986).

12. This section is prepared from field notes with Paul DeLargy, founding director of Georgia REAL Enterprises in Athens, Georgia, on October 1, 1993. Program descriptions also are drawn from curricular materials, newsletters, and a videotape supplied to me.

13. For example, an urban REAL program at the Rindge School of Technical Arts in Cambridge, Massachusetts, is available for advanced

secondary-level students who are interested in starting their own businesses.

14. The delicatessen closed its doors after three years of operations and more than a half million dollars in sales. Apparently the profitable months were not enough to counter the seasonal slowdowns, as many customers were interstate travelers heading to and from Florida (*The REAL Story* 1990).

15. This section is prepared from personal correspondence and publicity materials with EDTEC of Camden, New Jersey, on September 9, 1993, and from personal correspondence with George Waters, vice president of EDTEC on May 9, 1995.

16. This section is prepared from personal correspondence with Maria Ferri, curriculum disseminator and staff trainer at the Hands and Minds Collaborative in Cambridge, Massachusetts, on October 18, 1993. Also, see Wirth (1992, pp. 173–75).

2. Neighborhood Improvement

1. Depending upon the mission of each project, operating funds are obtained (through donations, grants, and benefits) from private individuals, corporations and businesses, philanthropic and educational foundations, and governmental agencies, or any combination of the above.

2. Publications and training resources by William Lofquist are available from Development Associations of Tucson, Arizona,—their address is listed in the *Resource Directory*.

3. The booklet on youth leadership, *Youth Involvement*, is written by Bruce Swinehart (1990) and available from the Prevention Center of Boulder, Colorado,—their address is listed in the *Resource Directory*.

4. This section is prepared from personal correspondence and project materials supplied by Anthony Thigpenn, chairman of the board of AGENDA in Los Angeles, California, on May 9 and August 19, 1994.

5. Quoted from personal correspondence with Anthony Thigpenn on May 9, 1994.

6. This section is prepared from personal correspondence and project materials supplied by Omar Ortiz, youth coordinator of Take Charge/Be Somebody! in Bronx, New York, on March 29, 1995. This pro-

gram is directed by Linda Nessel of the Cornell University Cooperative Extension in New York City.

7. Interestingly, the Bronx Board of Elections helped out in the senate elections by opening their polling sites and voting machines to area youth.

8. This section is prepared from program materials, reports, and press releases supplied by Michael Gilbreath, project director at Carlisle Education Center in Carlisle, Massachusetts, on December 27, 1994.

9. The Teen Empowerment model of leadership development is protected by copyright. For further information, contact Stanley Pollack, executive director at Teen Empowerment, Inc.—his address is listed in the *Resource Directory*. This section is prepared from resource materials provided by Doug Ackley, program supervisor of Teen Empowerment, by personal correspondence on February 22, 1994.

10. Promotional brochure of the Center, "Preventing Alcohol, Tobacco, and Other Drug Problems," quoted at page 4. Additional partners brought into the grant-funded activity were: area hospitals, serving as internship sites; community-based organizations, which recruited and evaluated the teens; the regional Private Industry Council, which offered training policy; and several external consultants, who provided curriculum modules for bilingual instruction and leadership development.

11. Coalition building resources and community development materials, including articles by Thomas J. Wolff (1992), are available from Community Partners of Amherst, Massachusetts,—their address is listed in the *Resource Directory*.

12. Prepared from project reports and press releases supplied by Greg Gale, coordinator of the Food Project (a partnership with the Massachusetts Audubon Society) at the Drumlin Farm Education Center and Wildlife Sanctuary in Lincoln, Massachusetts, on September 30, 1994.

13. The Food Project has now incorporated as a nonprofit organization under Internal Revenue Service Code 501(c)3.

14. Derived from the 1994 end-of-year summary report.

15. Prepared from personal correspondence with TNG director Diana Edmonds in New Haven, Connecticut, on August 26, 1993.

16. Prepared from field notes with TNG director Diana Edmonds in New Haven, Connecticut, on August 23, 1993.

17. This section is prepared from publicity materials, monthly newsletters, and curricular resources (program handbooks, leadership development modules, and policy committee manuals were purchased by me) received from YouthBuild USA in Somerville, Massachusetts, through personal correspondence on September 8 and 21, 1993, and on April 15, 1994. Additionally, I have a number of press highlights in my possession, including Freeman (1993) and Ross (1992b). Furthermore, I gained a greater understanding of the program by attending the Youth Leadership Development Workshop sponsored by YouthBuild USA on June 22–24, 1994, in Cambridge, Massachusetts, at the Massachusetts Institute of Technology.

18. Additionally, YouthBuild programs offer students (a) classroom instruction in construction terminology and building theories/concepts, (b) driver's education in order to obtain a license and increase their employability, (c) counseling and referral services for problems in health, housing, child care, family and legal issues, (d) participation in cultural and recreation events, (e) preemployment training for resume preparation and interviewing skills, (f) peer counseling and support groups, and (g) career services in job placements and/or post-graduate education.

19. I have heard this remark often from program panelists and workshop leaders at the YouthBuild summer workshop at MIT. Additional evidence is provided by YouthBuild graduate Tony Melton, see my interview with him in Chapter Five, *Youth Leadership.*

20. In 1991 the program staff developed the concept of Mental Toughness, a ten-day "rite of passage" for the new recruits that helps to build family through a series of interpersonal experiences which bring the staff and young people into close and caring relationships.

21. Prepared from materials received on March 14, 1994, and as described in the eighty-four-page manual prepared by Deborah G. Langstaff (1991).

22. A model of teen community service, City Year, is described by participant/observer Suzanne Goldsmith (1993)—their address is listed in the *Resource Directory.*

3. Health and Wellness

1. Young adult leaders there participated in Summer of Service, a pilot project for President Clinton's national service plan. Community

service programs, scattered in three-dozen cities nationwide, paired youthful volunteers with civic projects benefitting the disadvantaged. Harris joined the nine-week national demonstration programs for college-bound teens.

2. For information on the origins of gangster rap, see the biography of its originator, rapper Ice-T (*Current Biography* 1994). Interestingly, the article suggests that Ice-T participates in anti-violence youth projects by lecturing on the subject at high schools, is a funder and board chairman of Hands Across Watts (working to end gang violence), and is a volunteer mentor in a youth project in South Central Los Angeles.

3. I viewed the show when it aired on public television in the West Palm Beach, Florida, viewing area on May 8, 1994.

4. The nonprofit Video/Action Fund (in Washington D.C.) helps grassroots organizations by enabling young people to tell their stories and voice their opinions on inner-city life—their address is listed in the *Resource Directory*.

5. Personal correspondence with Kelly K. Lindquist and Lisa Gladden of Gang Peace in Boston, Massachusetts, on July 22, 1994, and October 28, 1994. They graciously supplied me with program materials on both occassions.

6. The Organizing and Leadership Training Center in Boston, Massachusetts, continues the Alinsky/IAF tradition by helping grassroots organizations win broad-based political actions through citywide, interfaith, and multicultural coalitions—see the *Resource Directory* for their address.

7. I interviewed Tyrone Terrell at the offices of Dekalb Responds in Decatur, Georgia, on April 29, 1994.

8. This section is prepared from field notes of an interview with Arthur Robinson at the Dunbar Community Center in Springfield, Massachusetts, on August 3, 1994. He graciously supplied me with curriculum materials for "Project Access."

9. A similar type of youth development program for black males, named SIMBA (Saturday Institute for Manhood, Brotherhood & Actualization), serves incarcerated juveniles at a detention center in Atlanta, Georgia,—see the *Resource Directory* for their address. Also, for a policy perspective on black male youth development, see Mincy (1994).

4. Street Arts

1. For an explanation of the critical dimensions of anti-elitist cultural studies, see Trend (1992). Also, on political art, see Kahn and Neumaier (1985).

2. From field notes in an interview conducted with artist Turbado Marabou outside of the Prologue School Building at the southeast corner of Lawrence and Winthrop Streets in the Uptown neighborhood of Chicago, Illinois, on August 11, 1994. The completed mural, titled "Living off the Waters of Creation," is visible on the east side of the school building.

3. I spoke with Warmack that same day on the street in front of the mural as well as inside the Prologue School. He showed me the arts projects that his kids had produced from found objects in the neighborhood. For a biographical sketch of Warmack, see the essays by Patterson (1994). I viewed several of Warmack's pieces on display at the McIntosh Gallery in Atlanta, Georgia, on November 22, 1994.

4. Information for this section is drawn from Taylor (1972). For further treatises on people's theatre, see Boal (1979) and Klein (1978).

5. Information for this section is drawn from personal correspondence of October 19 and 26, 1994, and from field notes of an interview with Dana Marschalk, executive director of "Moving in the Spirit," in Atlanta, Georgia, on November 9, 1994.

6. MITS artistic director, Leah Mann, a choreography graduate of the University of Georgia, is founder and originator of this project as well.

7. FCS Urban Ministries is profiled in Chapter Six.

8. Information for this section is drawn in part from field notes of an interview with Robert W. Ginn, executive director of the Atlanta Photography Group on April 16, 1994. He graciously provided me with a catalogue of the photographic exhibition "My Neighborhood: Through a Camera: The University-John Hope Community," a catalogue of the National Black Arts Festival photo project "Kids Eye View," and a copy of the summary report of the Youth Photography Education Project (summer, 1991; prepared by coordinator Victoria Durant-Gonzalez).

9. This section is prepared from Gallery 37 publicity materials and from a field-site interview with program director Cheryl R. Hughes of the Chicago Department of Cultural Affairs, in Chicago, Illinois, on August 9, 1994. I toured the artists tents on the grounds of Gallery 37, talked to several instructors about the summer program, and chatted with some of the students while viewing their projects in various stages of completion.

10. In order to maintain the widest diversity of participants (based on family socio-economic status), salaries for those not JTPA-eligible were funded by the private sector.

11. I visited this site while it was in its earliest stages of painting production. I spoke with the professional artist, viewed the mural design and final drawings, and photographed the kids who were working on scaffoldings that day, August 11, 1994.

12. I visited this project site on August 11, 1994. See note 2.

13. For another innovation in JTPA-funded summer youth projects, see my profile on the Puerto Rican Organization Program (PROP) in Chapter One.

14. This section is prepared from materials provided and a site visit with Jon Pounds, director of the Chicago Public Art Group, in Chicago, Illinois, on August 11, 1994. He graciously hosted a half-day auto tour of mural and mosaic viewings in several Chicago neighborhoods.

15. Information and quoted matter comes from the final report of the mural project, "By All Means Necessary," prepared by CPAG artists Olivia Gude, Dorian Sylvain, and Turbado Marabou in 1992.

16. "Moving in the Spirit," profiled in this chapter, is another example of a performing arts program embodying the curricular objectives of vocational development and career exploration for urban at-risk youths.

17. I visited the program in Chicago, Illinois, on August 8, 1994. Interviews, publicity materials, press releases, and theatrical scripts were graciously supplied by David Schein and Ron Bieganski of Free Street Theatre.

18. The quote is from field notes of an interview with Schein on August 8, 1994.

19. See note 3.

20. One of the best-known mural and public arts programs employing inner-city youth is the Social and Public Art Resource Center (SPARC) in Los Angeles, founded in 1976 by muralist Judy Baca—see the *Resource Directory* for their address.

5. Youth Leadership

1. Information on this program is derived from publicity materials and personal correspondence on October 4, 1993.

2. This section is prepared from personal correspondence on October 20, 1993.

3. This section is prepared from personal correspondence and YouthAction publicity materials provided by director Karen Stults on February 2, 1994.

4. This section is prepared from publicity materials received on January 21, July 14, and November 2, 1994.

5. COOL mission statement derived from personal correspondence with Kimberly Lovelace of the Boston-based national meetings on January 31, 1994.

6. This section is prepared from personal correspondence on November 4, 1993.

7. This section is prepared from personal correspondence and YES! publicity materials provided by Ryan Eliason on October 11, 1993, and Ocean Robbins on April 26, 1994 (co-founders of YES!).

8. This section is prepared from field notes of an interview with Chuck Matthai, director of Equity Trust, Inc., in Voluntown, Connecticut, on August 5, 1993.

9. For a collection of fourteen personal narratives about youth activism, see Hoose (1993).

10. This section is prepared from field notes of an interview with Phil Gauthier, Outreach Coordinator of the Pioneer Valley Gay, Lesbian and Bisexual Youth Project in Hadley, Massachusetts, personal correspondence, and publicity materials on August 17 and 26, 1994.

11. Their stories are published in a copyrighted chapbook, *Chapter One* (Northhampton, MA: Pioneer Valley Gay Lesbian and Bisexual Youth Project, 1993). All writers (except one) knowingly listed their given names in the table of contents and were credited with a contributor's byline.

12. A noteworthy leadership training program for community activists in youth development operates out of the Massachusetts Institute of Technology, Department of Urban Studies and Planning. The Community Fellows Program, directed by Boston activist and politician Mel King, provides participants a year of critical study and reflection on youth issues and projects of concern for communities of color. I visited the MIT offices on June 23, 1994, received program information, met with the director, and was afforded access to their resource bank—their address is listed in the *Resource Directory*. For King's views on community-based education, see King (1989).

13. I interviewed Tony Melton at YouthBuild DeKalb in Atlanta on January 6, 1995.

14. For further information about YouthBuild program activities, see Chapter Two.

15. The workshop was held in Boston on the campus of the Massachusetts Institute of Technology June 22–24, 1994. There were about thirty participants and four leadership advisors from the YouthBuild national offices. Most of the participants were youth workers from nonprofit, community-based development agencies in the New England region, serving a diversity of teens through efforts at gang preventions, national service learning, environmental justice, African-American and Latino family services, and women's health issues, among others.

16. Teen Empowerment of Boston is profiled in Chapter Two.

6. Beacons of Hope

1. Material for this section was obtained from personal correspondence with Wayne Gordon, president of the Christian Community Development Association in Chicago, Illinois, on June 9, 1995.

2. The faith I refer to here is a "liberation theology" that informs poor people of Christian faith that the Bible and scriptural interpretations—and related symbols and values—have meaning for them in daily life as a starting point for their development perspectives, political awakenings, and cultural struggles—see, for example, Berryman (1987), Mahan and Richesin (1981), and Roberts (1994).

3. This section is prepared in part from IAF-Atlanta materials and press clippings supplied to me by Shirley Thomas on October 21, 1993, and additional information supplied by Lewis Finfer, director of the Organizing and Leadership Training Center in Boston, on IAF activities in Atlanta.

4. Described to me by Gerald Taylor, IAF organizer, in my office at Georgia State University on January 17, 1995.

5. "Statement of Atlanta Interfaith Sponsoring Committee," (n.d.; p. 3) in my possession.

6. I spoke with Jon Abercrombie at his home in Decatur, Georgia, on May 25, 1995. He provided me with published materials on FCS

Urban Ministries, press clippings, personal anecdotes, and a number of published essays on community economic development in correspondence on June 2, 1995.

7. In 1990 Atlanta was chosen to host the 1996 Summer Olympic Games. A new stadium is being built in Summerhill adjacent to the existing baseball facility, which will be razed after the Olympics are over. The community should benefit in the short run from economic development plans targeted at cosmetic improvements, such as new wall murals, for spectators at the games.

8. Researcher Amy Glass (1994) reports:

A study done by Summerhill Neighborhood, Inc., shows that in 1990 the population was 2,746; average household income was $7,670; unemployment was 66 percent; and average home value was $16,841. With 22 percent of the population over age sixty-five, Summerhill was aging faster than the rest of Atlanta; and with over one-third of the lots standing vacant—strewn with discarded sofas and abandoned houses, or paved over for Braves parking—the neighborhood was showing signs of dying out (p. 2).

9. FCSUM founder Robert Lupton's views on Christian community economic development and inner-city resettlement are explained in his published works—see Lupton (1989, 1993).

10. Dana Marschalk's dance ministry, Moving in the Spirit, is profiled in Chapter Four.

11. I interviewed Doris Perryman at the Summerhill Real Estate Company in Atlanta, Georgia, on January 30, 1995. She provided me with printed articles and newspaper clippings about the Summerhill community through personal correspondence on December 16, 1994.

12. The Summerhill Neighborhood, Inc., redevelopment plan is fully reported in a publication by the Capital Research Center out of Washington D.C.—see Glass (1994) and Olansky (1992).

13. I interviewed Andre Turnipseed of Charis Homes at my office of Georgia State University on January 17, 1995.

14. I interviewed Fronita King at the Martin Street Church of God in the Summerhill neighborhood of Atlanta, Georgia, on April 6, 1995. According to Fronita, the church has a membership of about 300 parishoners, mostly middle-class blacks who reside in the greater Atlanta area. Only about 2 percent of the congregation are Summerhill residents.

15. Fronita received an internship at AmeriCorps, and is working as a teaching assistant at an elementary school in Summerhill. She will use her educational stipend to complete an undergraduate degree program in Urban Studies at Georgia State University.

16. From field notes on April 26, 1995. I knew something about these lock-ups for juveniles, having toured the Lorenzo Benn YDC in Southwest Atlanta, a boys-only residential facility, as guest of a former student in one of my graduate classes.

17. Their names have been changed to protect the identity of teens reported in this section.

Conclusion

1. Teachers may begin to promote social justice and equity in their classrooms by offering students the skills and exercises which assist them in shaping a new civic culture (see Berman and LaFarge 1993). And, there is a variety of resources and curricula for school-based critical educators to assist those desiring grassroots activism for social change. For example, start a training workshop on non-violent social change (see Coover et al. 1977). Join the nonprofit organization Educators for Social Responsibility, and receive a mailing on their publications, programs, workshops, seminars, and summer institutes. Subscribe to the independent newspaper *Rethinking Schools*, and purchase their resource books. Their mailing addresses are listed in the *Resource Directory*.

References

Adams, F. 1975. *Unearthing seeds of fire: The idea of Highlander.* Winston-Salem: John F. Blair.

Alinsky, S. D. 1971. *Rules for radicals: A pragmatic primer for realistic radicals.* New York: Vintage.

Annis, S. and Hakim, P., eds. 1988. *Direct to the poor: Grassroots development in Latin America.* Boulder, CO: Lynne Rienner.

Apple, M. W. 1993. *Official knowledge: Democratic education in a conservative age.* New York: Routledge.

Bank, B. J., Slavings, R. L., and Biddle, B. J. 1990. Effects of peer, faculty, and parental influences on students' persistence. *Sociology of Education* 63(3): 208–25.

Barber, B. 1992. *An aristocracy of everyone: The politics of education and the future of America.* New York: Ballantine.

Barnett, A. W. 1984. *Community murals: The people's art.* Philadelphia: The Art Alliance Press.

Barreiro, A. 1984. *Basic ecclesial communities: The evangelization of the poor.* Maryknoll, NY: Orbis Books.

Battista, C. 1993. Boot camp for dropouts. *Boston Globe,* August 22, p. A73.

Beilenson, J. 1993. Looking for young people, listening for youth voice. *Social Policy* 24(1): 8–13.

Berman, S. and LaFarge, P. 1993. *Promising practices in teaching social responsibility.* Albany: State University of New York Press.

Berryman, P. 1987. *Liberation theology: Essential facts about the revolutional movement in Latin American—and beyond.* Philadelphia: Temple University Press.

Better, N. M. 1992. Green teens. *New York Times Magazine* (March 8), 44: 66–67.

Bird, B. 1990. Reclaiming the urban war zones. *Christianity Today* (January 15), 34, pp. 16–20.

Bluestone, B. and Harrison, B. 1982. *The deindustrialization of America: Plant closings, community abandonment, and the dismantling of basic industry.* New York: Basic Books.

Boal, A. 1979. *Theatre of the oppressed.* New York: Urizen Books.

Bocage, A. A. and Waters, G. E. 1990. Enterprise training for youth. *Commentary* 14(1): 4–10.

Bookchin, M. 1986. *The modern crisis.* Philadelphia: New Society Publishers.

Bowers, F. 1992. "Gang Peace" meets youths where they are. *Christian Science Monitor* 84(135): 10.

Boyte, H. C. 1989. *Commonwealth: A return to citizen politics.* New York: Free Press.

Brager, G., Specht, H., and Torczyner, J. L. 1987. *Community organizing.* New York: Columbia University Press.

Brandt, B. 1995. *Whole life economics: Revaluing daily life.* Philadelphia: New Society Publishers.

Brazier, A. M. 1969. *Black self-determination: The story of the Woodlawn Organization.* Grand Rapids, MI: William B. Eerdmans.

Brecher, J. 1990. "If all the people are banded together": The Naugatuck Valley Project. In *Building bridges: The emerging grassroots coalition of labor and community* (pp. 93–105), eds. J. Brecher and T. Costello. New York: Monthly Review Press.

Breslin, P. 1995. On these sidewalks of New York, the sun is shining again. *Smithsonian* 26(1): 100–11.

Bullard, R. D. 1990. *Dumping in Dixie: Race, class, and environmental quality.* Boulder, CO: Westview Press.

Butts, R. F. 1989. *The civic mission in educational reform: Perspectives for the public and the profession.* Stanford: Hoover Institution Press.

Cashman, S. D., ed. 1992. *Healing the heart of the cities: Young voices speak out.* Durham, NC: Campus Outreach Opportunity League.

Castleman, C. 1992. *Getting up: Subway graffiti in New York.* Cambridge, MA: MIT Press.

Christensen, M. J. 1988. *City streets, city people: A call for compassion.* Nashville: Abingdon Press.

Christian Century. 1994a. Young black men and church. April 27, 111: 439–40.

———. 1994b. Churches in the streets. September 7–14, 111: 807–8.

Clark, M. L. 1991. Social identity, peer relations, and academic competence of African-American adolescents. *Education and Urban Society* 24: 41-52.

Cockcroft, E., Weber, J., and Cockcroft, J. 1977. *Toward a people's art: The contemporary mural movement.* New York: E.P. Dutton.

Coles, R. 1993. *The call of service: A witness to idealism.* Boston: Houghton Mifflin.

Comer, J. P. 1993. The potential effects of community organizations on the future of our youth. *Teachers College Record* 94(3): 658–61.

Community Catalyst. 1994. Teen empowerment. November/December, pp. 1–2. [Community Partners, Amherst, MA]

Cone, J. H. 1992. *For my people: Black theology and the black church.* Maryknoll, NY: Orbis Books.

———. 1993. *My soul looks back.* Maryknoll, NY: Orbis Books.

Conniff, R. 1996. Crackdown on kids: Meet the teens in lockup. *The Progressive* 60(2): 27–29.

Conrad, D. R. 1995. A democratic art: Community murals as educator. *Teachers College Record* 97(1): 116–31.

Coover, V., Deacon, E., Esser, C., and Moore, C. 1977. *Resource manual for a living revolution.* Philadelphia: New Society Publishers.

Current Biography. 1994. [Biography of Ice-T.] September, pp. 19–22.

Curtis, L. A. 1996. Investing in what works. *The Nation* 262(2): 18.

Dewey, J. 1927. *The public and its problems.* New York: Henry Holt.

Dillon, S. 1994. 30 New High Schools Report First-Year Success. *New York Times,* May 15, p. B2.

Dittmar, C. A. and Handwerk, J. 1991. The health advocates: A peer education program. *Wellness Perspectives: Research, Theory and Practice* 7: 43–51.

Diver-Stamnes, A. C. 1991. Assessing the effectiveness of an inner-city high school peer counseling program. *Urban Education* 26: 269–84.

Dyson, B. and Dyson, E. 1989. *Neighborhood caretakers: Stories, strategies and tools for healing urban community.* Indianapolis: Knowledge Systems, Inc.

Ekins, P. 1992. *A new world order: Grassroots movements for global change.* London: Routledge.

Ervin, M. 1992. The toxic doughnut. *The Progressive* 56(1): 15.

Farris, R. A. 1991. Micro-peer teaching: Organization and benefits. *Education* 111: 559–62.

Finnigan, D. 1991. Graffiti vandals brush up on good citizenship. *Los Angeles Times*, November 18, p. A5.

Fish, J. H. 1973. *Black power/White control: The struggle of the Woodlawn Organization in Chicago.* Princeton, NJ: Princeton University Press.

Fitzpatrick, J. 1994. Shouldering fatherhood as a teen-ager, with pride. *New York Times*, July 17, sec. 13, p. 1.

Freedman, M. 1993. *The kindness of strangers: Adult mentors, urban youth, and the new voluntarism.* San Francisco: Jossey-Bass.

Freeman, A. 1993. "We need love, We need support, We need skills." *Historic Preservation* 45(3): 26–31.

Furfey, P. H. 1978. *Love and the urban ghetto.* Maryknoll, NY: Orbis Books.

Garbarino, J., Dubrow, N., Kostelny, K., and Pardo, C. 1992. *Children in danger: Coping with the consequences of community violence.* San Francisco: Jossey-Bass.

Garr, R. 1995. *Reinvesting in America: The grassroots movements that are feeding the hungry, housing the homeless, and putting Americans back to work.* Reading, MA: Addison-Wesley.

Gastil, J. 1993. *Democracy in small groups: Participation, decision making, and communication.* Philadelphia: New Society Publishers.

Giroux, H. A. 1992. *Border crossings: Cultural workers and the politics of education.* New York: Routledge.

References 161

———. 1996. Hollywood, race, and the demonization of youth: The "kids" are not "alright." [Review of C. Woods and L. Clark (Director), 1995, *Kids* (Film) Shining Excalibur] *Educational Researcher* 25(2): 31–35.

Glass, A. 1994. Fishing in bureaucratic waters: A midterm review of the Summerhill revitalization. *Philanthropy, Culture & Society* (February), pp. 1–8.

Goldsmith, S. 1993. *A City Year: On the streets and in the neighborhoods with twelve young community service volunteers.* New York: The New Press.

Gorham, E. B. 1992. *National service, citizenship, and political education.* Albany: State University of New York Press.

Greider, W. 1992. *Who will tell the people: The betrayal of American democracy.* New York: Simon & Schuster.

Gunn, C. and Gunn, H. D. 1991. *Reclaiming capital: Democratic initiatives and community development.* Ithaca: Cornell University Press.

Haas, M. 1988. Violent schools—unsafe schools. *Journal of Conflict Resolution* 32(4): 727–58.

Hall, L. and McKeen, R. L. 1991. Peer coaching as an organization development intervention in the public schools. *Education* 111: 553–58.

Hallinan, M. T. and Williams, R. A. 1990. Students' characteristics and the peer-influence process. *Sociology of Education* 63(2): 122–32.

Hare, N. and Hare, J. 1985. *Bringing the black boy to manhood.* San Francisco: Black Think Tank.

Heath, S. B. and McLaughlin, M. W. 1994a. The best of both worlds: Connecting schools and community youth organizations for all-day, all-year learning. *Educational Administration Quarterly* 30(3): 278–300.

———. 1994b. Learning for anything everyday. *Journal of Curriculum Studies* 26(5): 471–89.

Heath, S. B. and McLaughlin, M. W., eds. 1993. *Identity & inner-city youth: Beyond ethnicity and gender.* New York: Teachers College Press.

Hefner, K. 1988. The evolution of youth empowerment at a youth newspaper. *Social Policy* 19(1): 21–24.

Heim, D. and Roehlkepartain, E. C. 1986. Urban ministry: Strategy and faith for the city. *The Christian Century* (May 14), 103: 491–95.

Highbridge Voice. 1993. [Profile of Omar Oliver Ortiz.] (Bronx, NY), July, 1(1), p. 8.

Hinsdale, M. A., Lewis, H. M., and Waller, S. M. 1995. *It comes from the people: Community development and local theology.* Philadelphia: Temple University Press.

Hirshon, S. L. 1983. *And also teach them to read.* Westport, CT: Lawrence Hill & Co.

Hirst, P. 1994. *Associative democracy: New forms of economic and social governance.* Amherst: University of Massachusetts Press.

hooks, b. 1994. *Teaching to transgress: Education as the practice of freedom.* New York: Routledge.

Hoose, P. 1993. *It's our world, too!: Stories of young people who are making a difference.* Boston: Little, Brown.

Hopgood, M. 1993. Youngsters anchor antiviolence event. *Detroit Free Press,* August 6, p. B1.

James, M. 1994. Teens target gangsta rap in "Catch the 411." *Palm Beach Post,* May 6, p. 4D.

Janowitz, M. 1983. *The reconstruction of patriotism: Education for civic consciousness.* Chicago: University of Chicago Press.

Jennings, J., ed. 1992a. *Race, politics, and economic development: Community perspectives.* London: Verso.

———. 1992b. *The politics of black empowerment: The transformation of black activism in urban America.* Detroit: Wayne State University Press.

Jerving, J. 1993. *Changing youth: Starting a youth credit union and learning center.* Dubuque, IA: Kendall/Hunt.

Jet 1995. National Rainbow Coalition's new public policy institute brings ministers together to rekindle social activism. (February 27), 87: 38–40.

Kahn, S. 1991. *Organizing: A guide for grassroots leaders.* Silver Spring, MD: National Association of Social Workers.

Kahn, D. and Neumaier, D., eds. 1985. *Cultures in contention.* Seattle, WA: The Real Comet Press.

Kanpol, B. 1994. *Critical pedagogy: An introduction.* Westport, CT: Bergin & Garvey.

———. 1996. Critical pedagogy and liberation theology: Borders for a transformative agenda. *Educational Theory* 46(1): 105–17.

Kanpol, B. and Yeo, F. 1995. Inner-city realities: Democracy within difference, theory, and practice. *The Urban Review* 27(1): 77–91.

Katz, J. 1992a. No help for "Hope in Youth." *Los Angeles Times*, March 18, p. B1, B4.

———. 1992b. County gives $2.9 million to gang program. *Los Angeles Times*, July 22, p. B1, B3.

Kim, S., McLeod, J. H., Rader, D., and Johnston, G. 1992. An evaluation of prototype school-based peer counseling program. *Journal of Drug Education* 22: 37–53.

King, M. 1981. *Chain of change: Struggles for black community development.* Boston: South End Press.

———. 1987. Work that must be done so that there is a future. In *The future of work* (pp. 99–108), eds. D. G. Gil and E. A. Gil. Cambridge, MA: Schenkman Books.

———. 1989. On transformation: From a conversation with Mel King. *Harvard Educational Review* 59(4): 504–19.

King, M. and George, S. 1987. The future of community: From local to global. In *Beyond the market and the state: New directions in community development* (pp. 217–29), eds. S. T. Bruyn and J. Meehan. Philadelphia: Temple University Press.

Klein, M. 1978. *Theatre for the 98%.* Boston: South End Press.

Kleymeyer, C. D. 1991. What is "grassroots development"? *Grassroots Development* 15(1): 38–39.

———. 1992. Cultural energy & grassroots development. *Grassroots Development* 16(1): 22–31.

Kotlowitz, A. 1991. *There are no children here.* New York: Anchor Books.

Krasnow, D. 1993. TeenStreet. *High Performance*, Fall, pp. 38–39.

Krimerman, L. and Lindenfeld, F., eds. 1992. *When workers decide: Workplace democracy takes root in North America.* Philadelphia: New Society Publishers.

Kunjufu, J. 1985. *Countering the conspiracy to destroy black boys.* Chicago: African American Images.

Laboy, N. 1994. Struggle for survival in the South Bronx. *Everyone's Backyard* (Citizen's Clearinghouse for Hazardous Wastes, Falls Church, VA), 12(2): 4–5.

Langstaff, D. G. 1991. *Teens as community resources: A model of youth empowerment.* New York: Plan for Social Excellence.

Lappé, F. W. and Dubois, P. M. 1994. *The quickening of America: Rebuilding our nation, remaking our lives.* San Francisco: Jossey-Bass.

Leach, T. 1995. A dream come true. *Neighbor News* (FCS Urban Ministries, Atlanta, GA), 3: 1.

Levitan, S. A. and Shapiro, I. 1987. *Working but poor: America's contradiction.* Baltimore: Johns Hopkins University Press.

Linthicum, R. C. 1991. *Empowering the poor.* Monrovia, CA: MARC.

Littrell, D. W. and Hobbs, D. 1989. The self-help approach. In *Community development in perspective* (pp. 48–68), J. A. Christenson and J. W. Robinson, Jr. Ames: Iowa State University Press.

Lofquist, W. A. 1989. *The technology of prevention workbook.* Tucson, AZ: AYD Publications.

Lupton, R. D. 1989. *Theirs is the kingdom: Celebrating the gospel in urban America.* New York: HarperSanFrancisco.

———. 1993. *Return flight: Community development through reneighboring our cities.* Atlanta: FCS Urban Ministries.

Mahan, B. and Richesin, L. D., eds. 1981. *The challenge of liberation theology: A first world response.* Maryknoll, NY: Orbis Books.

Maheady, L., Harper, G. F., and Mallette, B. 1991. Training and implementation requirements associated with the use of a classwide peer tutoring system. *Education and Treatment of Children* 14: 177–98.

Males, M. and Docuyanan, F. 1996. Crackdown on kids: Giving up on the young. *The Progressive* 60(2): 24–26.

Mariz, C. L. 1994. *Coping with poverty: Pentecostals and Christian base communities in Brazil.* Philadelphia: Temple University Press.

Massey, R. F. and Neidigh, L. W. 1990. Evaluating and improving the functioning of a peer-based alcohol abuse prevention organization. *Journal of Alcohol and Drug Education* 35: 24–35.

Maxwell, J. 1994. YFC celebrates golden year. *Christianity Today* 38(11): 72–73.

McDougall, H. A. 1993. *Black Baltimore: A new theory of community.* Philadelphia: Temple University Press.

McKnight, J. 1987. Regenerating community. *Social Policy* 17: 54–58.

———. 1995. *The careless society: Community and its counterfeits.* New York: Basic Books.

McKnight, J. and Kretzmann, J. 1984. Community organization in the 80s: Toward a post-Alinsky agenda. *Social Policy* 14: 15–17.

McLaren, P. and Leonard, P., eds. 1993. *Paulo Freire: A critical encounter.* London: Routledge.

McLaughlin, M. W., Irby, M. A., and Langman, J. 1994. *Urban sanctuaries: Neighborhood organizations in the lives and futures of inner-city youth.* San Francisco: Jossey-Bass.

Medoff, P. and Sklar, H. 1994. *Streets of hope: The fall and rise of an urban neighborhood.* Boston: South End Press.

Meyers, E. S., ed. 1992. *Envisioning the new city: A reader on urban ministry.* Louisville: Westminster/John Knox Press.

Mincy, R. B., ed. 1994. *Nurturing young black males: Challenges to agencies, programs, and social policy.* Washington, D.C.: The Urban Institute Press, 1994.

Moore, J. W. 1991. *Going down to the barrio: Homeboys and homegirls in change.* Philadelphia: Temple University Press.

Moore, R. 1993. Environmental racism: What it is and how we can fight it. *FIRR News* (Federation for Industrial Retention and Renewal, Chicago, IL), 5(1): 3–5.

Morris, D. and Hess, K. 1975. *Neighborhood power: The new localism.* Boston: Beacon Press.

Morrison, R. 1991. *We build the road as we travel.* Philadelphia: New Society Publishers.

Moskos, C. C. 1988. *A call to civic service: National service for country and community.* New York: Free Press.

National Center for Education Statistics. 1993. *Youth indicators.* Washington, D.C.: Author.

National Commission on Resources for Youth. 1974. *New roles for youth—in the school and the community.* New York: Citation Press.

The Neighborhood Voice. 1992. Welcome home. May 1, 1(1), p. 3. [Summerhill Neighborhood, Inc., Atlanta, GA]

Nessel, L. 1988. A coalition approach to enhancing youth empowerment. *Social Policy* 19: 25–27.

New York Times. 1994. "Teen court" gets tough about crime. December 18, p. 33A.

Newsnotes (Center for Law and Education, Inc., Cambridge, MA). 1991. Two communities pursue new approaches to vocational education. (December), no. 43:7–10.

Nieto, S. 1992. *Affirming diversity: The sociopolitical context of multicultural education.* New York: Longman.

Nozick, M. 1993. Five principles of sustainable community development. In *Community economic development: In search of empowerment and alternatives* (pp. 18–43), ed. E. Shragge. Montreal: Black Rose Books.

Ogbu, J. U. 1986. Stockton, California, revisited: Joining the labor force. In *Becoming a worker* (pp. 29–65), eds. K. Borman and J. Reisman. Norwood, NJ: Ablex Publishing Corp.

Olasky, M. 1992. Downstairs philanthropy in Atlanta. *Philanthropy, Culture & Society,* (Capital Research Center, Washington, D.C.) February, pp. 1–8.

O'Neill, A. W. 1993. Riordan frees up funds for Hope in Youth. *Los Angeles Times,* July 19, p. B1, B8.

Parks, R. 1992. *My story.* New York: Dial Books.

Parzen, J. A. and Kieschnick, M. H. 1992. *Credit where it's due: Development banking for communities.* Philadelphia: Temple University Press.

Patterson, T. 1994. *Reclamation and transformation: Three self-taught Chicago artists.* Chicago: Terra Museum of American Art.

Perry, S. E. 1987. *Communities on the way: Rebuilding local economies in the United States and Canada.* Albany: State University of New York Press.

Pierce, G. F. 1984. *Activism that makes sense: Congregations and community organization.* Ramsey, NJ: Paulist Press.

Pioneer Valley GLB Youth Project. 1993. *Chapter one.* Northhampton, MA: Author.

Pittman, K. J. 1991. A framework for defining and promoting youth participation. *Future Choices* 3(2): 85–90.

————. 1996. Community, youth, development: Three goals in search of connection. *New Designs for Youth Development* 12(1): 4–8.

Podschun, G. D. 1993. Teen Peer Outreach-Street Work project: HIV prevention education for runaway and homeless youth. *Public Health Reports* 108: 150–55.

Pool, B. 1991. Youths wielding spray-paint cans learn difference between vandalism and art. *Los Angeles Times,* August 13, p. B1.

Pope, J. 1992. The colonizing impact of public service bureaucracies in black communities. In *Race, politics, and economic development: Community perspectives* (pp. 141–49), ed. J. Jennings. London: Verso.

Prothrow-Stith, D. 1991. *Deadly consequences: How violence is destroying our teenage population and a plan to begin solving the problem.* New York: HarperCollins.

Purpel, D. E. 1989. *The moral & spiritual crisis in education: A curriculum for justice and compassion in education.* Granby, MA: Bergin & Garvey.

Radest, H. B. 1993. *Community service: Encounter with strangers.* Westport, CT: Praeger.

Rainey, J. 1992. L.A. votes $2.5 million for Hope in Youth project. *Los Angeles Times,* November 25, p. B1, B8.

————. 1993. Mayor's pledge of anti-gang funds in limbo. *Los Angeles Times,* July 20, p. B1, B4.

Rainey, J. and Corwin, M. 1994. Anti-gang agency given $2.5 million. *Los Angeles Times,* June 8, p. B1, B8.

The REAL Story. 1990. Final curtain for the Way Off Broadway Deli. (REAL Enterprises, Athens, GA), Fall/Winter, II(3), p. 10.

Rhenwrick, G. 1995. Neighbors United Coalition of Summerhill. *Neighbor News* (FCS Urban Ministries, Atlanta, GA), March, 3: 1.

Rickert, V. I., Jay, S. M., and Gottlieb, A. 1991. Effects of a peer-coun-seled AIDS education program on knowledge, attitudes, and satisfac-tion of adolescents. *Journal of Adolescent Health* 12: 38–43.

Rist, R. C., ed. 1986. *Finding work: Cross-national perspectives on employment and training.* Philadelphia: Falmer Press.

Rivera, C. 1993. County frees funding for Hope in Youth program. *Los Angeles Times,* October 13, p. B1, B4.

Roberts, J. D. 1994. *Liberation and reconciliation: A black theology.* Maryknoll, NY: Orbis Books.

Rodriguez, L. J. 1993. *Always running: La vida loca, gang days in L.A.* Willimantic, CT: Curbstone Press.

Rogers, M. 1990. *Cold anger: A story of faith and power politics.* Denton, TX: University of North Texas Press.

Rosenstock, L. 1991. The walls come down: The overdue reunification of vocational and academic education. *Phi Delta Kappan,* 72(6): 434–36.

Ross, E. 1992a. Art program offers life lessons. *Christian Science Monitor* 84(181): 14.

———. 1992b. YouthBuild: A new start for young adults, *Christian Science Monitor,* December 22, pp. 7–8.

Rowbotham, S. and Mitter, S., eds. 1994. *Dignity and daily bread: New forms of economic organizing among poor women in the Third World and the First.* London: Routledge.

Rubenstein, E., Panzarine, S., and Lanning, P. 1990. Peer counseling with adolescent mothers: A pilot program. *Families in Society* 71: 136–41.

Rubin, R. H., Billingsley, A., and Caldwell, C. H. 1994. The role of the black church in working with black adolescents. *Adolescence* 29(114): 251–66.

Rudesill, S. 1994. Rediscovering my roots in community. *Communities: Journal of Cooperative Living* (Fort Collins, CO), 84(2): 54.

Russell, V. E. 1992. A lesson on urban spirituality. In *Envisioning the new city: A reader on urban ministry* (pp. 190–202), ed. E. S. Meyers. Louisville: Westminster/John Knox Press.

Sale, K. 1985. *Dwellers in the land: The bioregional vision.* San Francisco: Sierra Club Books.

Samper, M. D. and Lakes, R. D. 1994. Work education for the next century: Beyond skills training. In *Critical education for work: Multidisciplinary Approaches* (pp. 95–107), ed. R. Lakes. Norwood, NJ: Ablex Publishing Corp.

Schmitz, S. 1992. Three strikes and you're out: Academic failure and the children of public housing. *Journal of Education* 174: 41–54.

Seelye, K. Q. 1994. House approves crime bill after days of bargaining, giving victory to Clinton. *New York Times,* August 22, p. A1, B6.

Sennett, F. 1993. An urban refusal. *The Neighborhood Works* (Chicago, IL), 16(5): 9–13.

Shaffer, R. 1989. *Community economics: Economic structure and change in smaller communities.* Ames: Iowa State University Press.

Simon, R. I. 1992. *Teaching against the grain: Texts for a pedagogy of possibility.* New York: Bergin & Garvey.

Sinzinger, K. 1993. N. Carolina's Self-Help Credit Union seeks to be a "resource for change." *Washington Post,* April 25, p. A3.

Soltani, A. 1996. Getting on the bus with youth organizing. *Third Force* 3(6): 8.

Spring, B. 1989. An Atlanta prison gets converted. *Christianity Today* (April 7), 33: 53–54.

Stammer, L. B. and Rabin, J. L. 1992. Hope in Youth coalition flexes political muscle. *Los Angeles Times,* November 29, p. A1, A38–39.

Stern, D., Stone, J., Hopkins, C., McMillon, M., and Crain, R. 1994. *School-based enterprise: Productive learning in American high schools.* San Francisco: Jossey-Bass.

Stevens-Arroyo, A. M. and Diaz-Stevens, A. M. 1993. Latino churches and schools as urban battlegrounds. In *Handbook of schooling in urban America* (pp. 245–70), ed. S. W. Rothstein. Westport, CT: Greenwood Press.

Stoecker, R. 1994. *Defending community: The struggle for alternative redevelopment in Cedar-Riverside.* Philadelphia: Temple University Press.

Stoneman, D. 1989. *Notes towards a national youth policy.* Somerville, MA: Youthbuild USA.

Stoneman, D. and Bell, J. 1988. *Leadership development: A handbook from the Youth Action Program of the East Harlem Block Schools.* New York: Youth Action Program, Inc.

Swadener, B. B. and Lubeck, S., eds. 1995. *Children and families "at promise": Deconstructing the discourse of risk.* Albany: State University of New York Press.

Swinehart, B. 1990. *Youth involvement: Developing leaders and strengthening communities.* Boulder, CO: Partners for Youth Leadership.

Tapia, A. 1994. Healing our mean streets. *Christianity Today,* July 18, 38: 46–48.

Taub, R. P. 1988. *Community capitalism: The South Shore Bank's strategy for neighborhood revitalization.* Boston: Harvard Business School Press.

Taylor, K. M. 1972. *People's theatre in amerika.* New York: Drama Book Specialists/Publishers.

Teenage Victims. 1991. Bureau of Justice Statistics. Washington, D.C.: U.S. Department of Justice.

Thompson, K. 1992. YES!—Youth for Environmental Sanity. *Cultural Survival Quarterly* 16(2): 19–23.

Trend, D. 1992. *Cultural pedagogy: Art/education/politics.* New York: Bergin & Garvey.

Van Vugt, J. P. 1991. *Democratic organization for social change: Latin American Christian base communities and literacy campaigns.* New York: Bergin & Garvey.

Vella, J. 1989. *Learning to teach: Training of trainers for community development.* Westport, CT: Save the Children Federation.

Waldman, S. 1995. AmeriCorps: A fight to the finish. *Who Cares* 2(4): 44–45.

Wallerstein, N. 1992. Powerless, empowerment and health: Implications for health promotion programs. *American Journal of Health Promotion* 6(3): 197–201.

Walzer, M. 1985. *Exodus and revolution.* New York: Basic Books.

Weaver, J. 1993. Marching toward a high school diploma. *New York Times,* August 29, Sec. 13, p. 1.

Weckstein, P. 1989. Youth, employment and education. *Future Choices* 1(1):71–76.

Weizel, R. 1994. Real-life choices in a roll of the dice. *New York Times*, March 20, Sec. CN, p. 23.

Welton, M. 1993. Social revolutionary learning: The new social movements as learning sites. *Adult Education Quarterly* 43(3): 152–64.

West, C. 1993. *Race Matters*. New York: Vintage.

Wigginton, E., ed. 1973. *Foxfire*. New York: Anchor Books.

Wiist, W. H. and Snider, G. 1991. Peer education in friendship cliques: Prevention of adolescent smoking. *Health Education Research* 6: 101–8.

Willen, L. 1992. From vision to reality. *New York Newsday*, October 20, p. I13.

Williams, C. E., DeMarco, M., and Barstow, M. K. 1994. Community partnerships: A national prevention initiative. *New Designs for Youth Development* 11(3): 4–7.

Williams, M. R. 1985. *Neighborhood organizations: Seeds of a new urban life*. Westport, CT: Greenwood Press.

Wirth, A. 1992. *Education and work for the year 2000*. San Francisco, Jossey-Bass.

Wolff, T. J. 1992. *Coalition building: One path to empowered communities*. Amherst, MA: AHEC/Community Partners.

Worrell, K. 1993. Some teens spend summer serving others. *Atlanta Journal*, August 4, Sec. B, p. 1.

Woyach, R. B. 1993. *Preparing for leadership: A young adult's guide to leadership skills in a global age*. Westport, CT: Greenwood Press.

Youth Today. 1995. YDC block grant bill moves ahead in Senate. July/August, 4(4), p. 16.

Zeller, L. H. 1993. Youth community service: An overview. *National Civic Review* 82(1): 36–43.

Zoll, A. 1994. Gimme shelter. *Boston Sunday Herald*, June 19, pp. 8–11.

Index